Certificate Stage

Module C

Information Analysis

Revision Series

9191/F99

British Library Cataloguing-in-Publication Data

A catalogue record for this book is available from the British Library.

Published by AT Foulks Lynch Ltd
Number 4
The Griffin Centre
Staines Road
Feltham
Middlesex
TW14 0HS

ISBN 0 7483 3919 1

© AT Foulks Lynch Ltd, 1999

Acknowledgements

The past ACCA examination questions are the copyright of the Association of Chartered Certified Accountants. The answers to the questions from June 1994 onwards are the answers produced by the examiners themselves and are the copyright of the Association of Chartered Certified Accountants. The answers to the questions prior to June 1994 have been produced by AT Foulks Lynch Ltd.

We are grateful to the Chartered Institute of Management Accountants and the Institute of Chartered Accountants in England and Wales for permission to reproduce past examination questions. The answers have been prepared by AT Foulks Lynch Ltd.

CONTENTS

PREFACE

The new edition of the ACCA Revision Series, published for the June and December 1999 examinations, contains a wealth of features to make your prospects of passing the exams even brighter.

Examiner Plus

This book contains all the new syllabus examinations from June 1994 up to and including December 1998 plus the examiner's official answers. All the exams are set out in chronological order at the back of the book.

We have cross referenced all these questions to their topic headings in the contents pages so you can see at a glance what questions have been set on each syllabus area to date, topic by topic.

The inclusion of these questions and answers really does give students an unparalleled view of the way the new syllabus examinations are set and, even more importantly, a tremendous insight into the mind of the Examiner. The Examiner's answers are in some cases fairly lengthy and whilst the Examiner would not necessarily expect you to include all the points that his answers include, they do nevertheless give you an excellent insight into the sorts of things that the Examiner is looking for and will help you produce answers in line with the Examiner's thinking.

Features

Step by Step Answer Plans and *'Did you answer the question?' checkpoints* will be fully explained on the following two pages.

Tutorial Notes

In some situations the examiner's official answers benefit from a little extra explanation when they are to be used as a learning aid. Where appropriate, we have incorporated extra workings or explanatory notes, so that you derive the maximum benefit from these answers in preparation for your own exam.

Topic Index

The topics covered in all the answers have been indexed. This means that you can easily access an answer relating to any topic which you want to consider by use of the index as well as by reference to the contents page at the front of the book.

The Revision Series also contains the following features:

- Practice questions and answers - a total bank of around 80 questions and answers

- An analysis of the new syllabus exams from June 1994 to December 1998

- Update notes to bring you up to date for new examinable documents and any changes to legislation as at 1st December 1998.

- The syllabus and format of the examination

- General Revision Guidance

- Examination Technique - an essential guide to ensure that you approach the examinations correctly

- Key Revision Topics

- Formulae and tables where appropriate

HOW TO USE THE ANSWER PLANS AND 'DID YOU ANSWER THE QUESTION?' CHECKPOINTS

STEP BY STEP ANSWER PLANS

A key feature in this year's Revision Series is the Step by Step Answer Plans, produced for all new syllabus exam questions from June 1995 to June 1998.

Students are always being told to plan their answers and this feature gives you positive assistance by showing you how you should plan your answer and the type of plan that you should produce before you attempt the question.

Of course, in the exam, your answer Plan can be less fully written than ours because you are writing it for yourself. We are producing an answer plan which communicates the details to you the student and therefore is of necessity much fuller. However, all the detail is there, written in a way which shows you the lines along which you should be thinking in order to produce the answer plan.

You will notice that the Answer Plans start and finish with the exhortation that you must make sure that you have read the question and that you are answering it correctly. Each time you write down the next step in the Answer Plan, you must ask yourself - 'Why am I including this step?' 'Is it relevant?' 'Is this what the Examiner has asked me to do and expected me to do?'

Help with the answer

In addition, if you really do get stuck with the question and cannot see how to approach it, you may find it helpful to turn to the answer page, **cover up the answer itself!,** and start to read the Answer Plan. This may trigger your memory such that you can then return to the question itself and gain all the benefit of doing the question properly without reference to the answer itself.

Practice makes perfect

Like all elements of examination technique the time to learn how to plan your answers is not in the examination itself. You have to practise them now - every time you produce an answer - so that when you come to the examination itself these answer plans will be second nature.

It is probably a good idea to sketch out your answer plans in the way we have produced them here (but remember they can be briefer) and then compare them swiftly to our Answer Plan at the back of the book (don't look at the answer itself at this stage!).

This may indicate that you have completely missed the point of the question or it might indicate one or two other areas that you might wish to explore.

Then, without having yet looked at the answer itself, start writing your answer proper and then compare that with the examiner's own answer.

'DID YOU ANSWER THE QUESTION?' CHECKPOINTS

This is another feature included in this year's edition of the Revision Series. They are included in the new syllabus exam answers from June 1995 to June 1998.

At various points of the answers, you will come across a box headed **'Did you answer the question',** followed by a brief note which shows you how the printed answer is answering the question and encourages you to make sure that your own answer has not wandered off the point or missed the point of the question completely.

This is an invaluable feature and it is a discipline you must develop as you practise answering questions. It is an area of examination technique that you must practise and practise again and again until it becomes second nature. How often do we read in an Examiner's report that candidates did not answer the question the Examiner had set but had simply answered the question that they wanted him to set or simply wandered off the point altogether? You must make sure that your answers do not fall into that particular trap and that they do rigorously follow the questions set.

A good way of practising this aspect of examination technique is to imagine an empty box headed up 'Did you answer the question?' at the end of the paragraph or paragraphs you are about to write on a particular topic. Try and imagine what you are going to write in that box; what are you going to say in that box which justifies the two or three paragraphs that you are about to write. If you can't imagine what you are going to put in that box, or when you imagine it you find that you are struggling to relate the next few paragraphs to the question, then think very hard before you start writing those paragraphs. Are they completely relevant? Why are you writing them? How are they relevant to the question?

You will find this 'imagining the box' a very useful way of focusing your mind on what you are writing and its relevance to the question.

SUMMARY

Use the two techniques together. They will help you to produce planned answers and they will help you make sure that your answers are focused very fully and carefully on the question the Examiner has actually set.

1 SYLLABUS AND EXAMINATION FORMAT

FORMAT OF THE EXAMINATION

	Number of marks
Section A: compulsory questions based on a case study	55
Section B: 3 (out of 5) questions of 15 marks each	45
	——
	100
	——

Time allowed: 3 hours

Introduction

This paper introduces the different types of information systems and how they can contribute to the management decision making process. It includes coverage of the development, introduction and use of computer-based information systems and the advice that might be given regarding the control, privacy and security procedures. Students' appreciation of the role of IT in the organisation will be reinforced in Paper 12, where the strategic implications of IT are examined. Students are assumed to be familiar with the basic components of computer systems - hardware and software - and the ability to relate to business the basic structure of a computer, computer peripherals and communications devices.

(1) SYSTEMS TO HANDLE AND PROCESS INFORMATION

(a) Systems theory, classification of systems and the nature of feedback and control. The emphasis here will be on the use of these concepts in a business context and in relation to financial information systems

　　(i) an outline of general systems theory
　　(ii) definition of a system
　　(iii) types of system
　　(iv) basic elements of systems control
　　(v) positive and negative feedback
　　(vi) delays in systems.

(b) The nature of systems needed for transaction processing

　　(i) data capture
　　(ii) batch systems
　　(iii) on line systems
　　(iv) data storage.

(2) FORMS OF FINANCIAL AND RELATED INFORMATION SYSTEMS

This section covers the different types of organisational structures and the different types of information systems

(a) Organisational structures.

(b)   Structures of information systems and their appropriateness to different organisational structures

>   (i)   development of different types of system
>   (ii)   independence of data structures from the organisational structure
>   (iii)   formal and informal information systems.

(c)   Types and nature of information systems for operational, tactical and strategic planning and control

>   (i)   management information systems
>   (ii)   internal reporting systems
>   (iii)   decision support systems
>   (iv)   executive information systems
>   (v)   strategic information systems
>   (vi)   expert systems.

3)   SYSTEMS ANALYSIS AND DESIGN

This section covers the design and use of human computer interfaces and the legal requirements of data protection legislation.

(a)   Basics of human computer interface design

>   (i)   means of interacting with a computer
>   (ii)   prototyping
>   (iii)   implications of poor design
>   (iv)   preferences for type of interface from novice and experienced users
>   (v)   validation and verification of data
>   (vi)   security measures depending on the type of system.

(b)   The requirements of data protection legislation

>   (i)   principles of the Data Protection Act 1984
>
>   (ii)   privacy of information
>
>   (iii)   accuracy of information
>
>   (iv)   accessibility of information
>
>   (v)   purpose for which the data is to be used
>
>   (vi)   ability of individuals to correct data held about them
>
>   (vii)   organisations distributing information should ensure the reliability of the information
>
>   (viii) effect of EC legislation.

(c)   Use of feasibility studies

>   (i)   assessment of the feasibility/desirability of potential computer projects from the viewpoints of technical, social, operational and economic feasibility including the use of cost benefit analysis
>
>   (ii)   the production of a feasibility report and project plan.

(d)   Requirement analysis

Use of appropriate fact-finding techniques in order to establish client's system requirements in terms of

- processes to be carried out
- outputs to be produced
- functional areas to be covered.

(e)   Determination of systems design criteria

To consider aspects such as

- client requirements
- need for internal controls
- client competence
- cost, budget and timescale constraints
- compatibility.

(f)   Systems analysis and design tools

Identification and application of appropriate systems analysis and design tools and techniques such as

- data analysis
- database management systems
- structured methodology
- prototyping
- CASE tools

to enable production of programme specifications, database structures, network specifications, document/screen layouts, dialogue design etc.

(4)   SYSTEMS EVALUATION

This section provides the criteria for evaluating potential and actual systems against performance criteria.

(a)   Identifying, agreeing and documenting criteria for evaluating potential suitable systems

(i)   systems proposals
(ii)   software design and documentation tools
(iii)   bench marking
(iv)   conversion plans.

(b)   Evaluating potential suitable systems and packages against agreed criteria

(i)   needs analysis
(ii)   systems development life cycle
(iii)   upgrade paths for hardware and software
(iv)   switching costs and costs of locking into manufacturers.

(c)   Designing and implementing procedures for systems operation and control

(i)   the application of administrative controls to the acquisition, development, use and maintenance of data processing resources

(ii)   the application of operational controls built into individual computer applications

(iii)   the issues raised by the concepts of privacy, data protection and computer misuse

(iv)   the use by internal or external auditors of computer-based audit techniques.

(d)   Drawing conclusions from the evaluation and proposing an optimal system

(i)   the possibility of creating an optimum system
(ii)   judging whether an optimum system has been achieved
(iii)   costing of different systems options
(iv)   prioritising needs
(v)   political considerations
(vi)   trade-off between strategic needs and impact on IT strategy
(vii)   cost of information and cost of lack of information.

(e)   Explaining, negotiating, agreeing and documenting systems modifications.

5)   IMPLEMENTATION OF SYSTEMS

This section covers the life cycle of a system and the backup systems needed for a system and also considers the role of the system developer in giving and seeking advice.

(a)   Negotiating and agreeing procedures and plans for the implementation, monitoring and maintenance of a new system

(i)   need for project management
(ii)   the tools of project management
(iii)   project team concepts
(iv)   monitoring criteria
(v)   organisation control
(vi)   systems changeover.

(b)   Informing and advising on relevant aspects of the nature/purpose/functions/ operation of the system to appropriate personnel

(i)   software upgrades

(ii)   role of database administrator

(iii)   system/network manager

(iv)   external impacts on IT system

(v)   advise on the appropriateness and completeness of user, administrator, software and hardware documentation.

(c)   Minimising the possibility of system failures

(i)   backup systems
(ii)   log file systems.

(d)   Obtaining and analysing information on the operation of the system

(i)   the need for measures of performance
(ii)   error detection and correction
(iii)   meeting new user requirements
(iv)   flexibility and adaptability
(v)   integrity
(vi)   effect of increasing volumes of transactions and users.

(e)   Systems modifications

(i)   create criteria for the changing and upgrading of systems
(ii)   effort expended in relation to the upgrading and improvement of systems

       (iii)   fault rectification
       (iv)   systems records
       (v)   alignment with manufacturers upgrades
       (vi)   training and retraining
       (vii)   help lines
       (viii)   user groups
       (ix)   advantages and disadvantages of experts/contractors.

Topics	J94	D94	J95	D95	J96	D96	J97	D97	J98	D98
Systems development strategies	1 O				1 O / 7 ●			6 O		1 □ / 4 □
Types of information systems	2 O	1 O								
Systems evaluation	3 O	4 O		2 O / 1 O		3 ● / 1 ●			1 □	
Systems design	4 O	6 O / 1 ●	7 O / 5 O	9 O / 5 O	3 O / 5 O	1 ●	7 O		3 □ / 9 O	2 □ / 3 □ / 9 O
Systems maintenance	5 O						9 O			
The feasibility study	6 O	7 O	6 O	3 O	2 O / 4 O		8 O		2 □	
The nature of information systems	7 O			1 O			5 O		8 O	
Security and data integrity	7 ●		4 O		9 O			9 O	7 O	7 O
The nature of decision-making		2 O	8 O			5 O		5 O		
Systems theory		3 O		7 ●		4 O		7 O		
Acquisition of hardware and software		7 O	10 O			6 O	3 O			
Systems implementation		5 O	10 ●	8 O			1 O / 2 O	1 □ / 3 □		
Office automation			2 O			2 O				6 O
Design of computer systems			3 O		1 ● / 8 O	3 ●	6 O		6 O	5 O
Project management			9 O		6 O	1 ●	4 O	4 □	4 □ / 5 O	
Systems development methodology				4 O						
DBMS				6 O		1 ●		8 O		
Computer software				7 O	6 ● / 7 ●			2 □		8 O

Key

The number refers to the number of the question where this topic was examined in the exam.

Topics forming the whole or a substantial part of a question:

□ Compulsory   O   Optional

Topics forming a non-substantial part of a question

■ Compulsory   ●   Optional

3 GENERAL REVISION GUIDANCE

PLANNING YOUR REVISION

What is revision?

Revision is the process by which you remind yourself of the material you have studied during your course, clarify any problem areas and bring your knowledge to a state where you can retrieve it and present it in a way that will satisfy the Examiners.

Revision is not a substitute for hard work earlier in the course. The syllabus for this paper is too large to be hastily 'crammed' a week or so before the examination. You should think of your revision as the final stage in your study of any topic. It can only be effective if you have already completed earlier stages.

Ideally, you should begin your revision shortly after you begin an examination course. At the end of every week and at the end of every month, you should review the topics you have covered. If you constantly consolidate your work and integrate revision into your normal pattern of study, you should find that the final period of revision - and the examination itself - are much less daunting.

If you are reading this revision text while you are still working through your course, we strongly suggest that you begin now to review the earlier work you did for this paper. Remember, the more times you return to a topic, the more confident you will become with it.

The main purpose of this book, however, is to help you to make the best use of the last few weeks before the examination. In this section we offer some suggestions for effective planning of your final revision and discuss some revision techniques which you may find helpful.

Planning your time

Most candidates find themselves in the position where they have less time than they would like to revise, particularly if they are taking several papers at one diet. The majority of people must balance their study with conflicting demands from work, family or other commitments.

It is impossible to give hard and fast rules about the amount of revision you should do. You should aim to start your final revision at least four weeks before your examination. If you finish your course work earlier than this, you would be well advised to take full advantage of the extra time available to you. The number of hours you spend revising each week will depend on many factors, including the number of papers you are sitting. You should probably aim to do a minimum of about six to eight hours a week for each paper.

In order to make best use of the revision time that you have, it is worth spending a little of it at the planning stage. We suggest that you begin by asking yourself two questions:

- How much time do I have available for revision?
- What do I need to cover during my revision?

Once you have answered these questions, you should be able to draw up a detailed timetable. We will now consider these questions in more detail.

How much time do I have available for revision?

Many people find it helpful to work out a regular weekly pattern for their revision. We suggest you use the time planning chart provided to do this. Your aim should be to construct a timetable that is sustainable over a period of several weeks.

Time planning chart

	Monday	Tuesday	Wednesday	Thursday	Friday	Saturday	Sunday
00.00							
01.00							
02.00							
03.00							
04.00							
05.00							
06.00							
07.00							
08.00							
09.00							
10.00							
11.00							
12.00							
13.00							
14.00							
15.00							
16.00							
17.00							
18.00							
19.00							
20.00							
21.00							
22.00							
23.00							

1   First, block out all the time that is **definitely unavailable** for revision. This will include the hours when you normally sleep, the time you are at work and any other regular and clear commitments.

2   Think about **other people's claims on your time**. If you have a family, or friends whom you see regularly, you may want to discuss your plans with them. People are likely to be flexible in the demands they make on you in the run-up to your examinations, especially if they are aware that you have considered their needs as well as your own. If you consult the individuals who are affected by your plans, you may find that they are surprisingly supportive, instead of being resentful of the extra time you are spending studying.

3   Next, give some thought to the times of day when you **work most effectively**. This differs very much from individual to individual. Some people can concentrate first thing in the morning. Others work best in the early evening, or last thing at night. Some people find their day-to-day work so demanding that they are unable to do anything extra during the week, but must concentrate their study time at weekends. Mark the times when you feel you could do your best work on the

timetable. It is extremely important to acknowledge your personal preferences here. If you ignore them, you may devise a timetable that is completely unrealistic and which you will not be able to adhere to.

4   Consider your **other commitments**. Everybody has certain tasks, from doing the washing to walking the dog, that must be performed on a regular basis. These tasks may not have to be done at a particular time, but you should take them into consideration when planning your schedule. You may be able to find more convenient times to get these jobs done, or be able to persuade other people to help you with them.

5   Now mark some time for **relaxation**. If your timetable is to be sustainable, it must include some time for you to build up your reserves. If your normal week does not include any regular physical activity, make sure that you include some in your revision timetable. A couple of hours spent in a sports centre or swimming pool each week will probably enhance your ability to concentrate.

6   Your timetable should now be taking shape. You can probably see obvious study sessions emerging. It is not advisable to work for too long at any one session. Most people find that they can only really concentrate for one or two hours at a time. If your study sessions are longer than this, you should split them up.

What do I need to cover during my revision?

Most candidates are more confident about some parts of the syllabus than others. Before you begin your revision, it is important to have an overview of where your strengths and weaknesses lie.

One way to do this is to take a sheet of paper and divide it into three columns. Mark the columns:

OK   Marginal   Not OK

or use similar headings to indicate how confident you are with a topic. Then go through the syllabus (reprinted in Section 1) and list the topics under the appropriate headings. Alternatively, you could use the list of key topics in Section 5 of this book to compile your overview. You might also find it useful to skim through the introductions or summaries to the textbook or workbooks you have used in your course. These should remind you of parts of the course that you found particularly easy or difficult at the time. you could also use some of the exercises and questions in the workbooks or textbooks, or some of the questions in this book, as a diagnostic aid to discover the areas where you need to work hardest.

It is also important to be aware which areas of the syllabus are so central to the subject that they are likely to be examined in every diet, and which are more obscure, and not likely to come up so frequently. Your textbooks, workbooks and lecture notes will help you here. (You may also find it useful to read the analysis of past papers provided in Section 2.) Remember, the Examiner will be looking for broad coverage of the syllabus. There is no point in knowing one or two topics in exhaustive detail if you do so at the expense of the rest of the course.

Writing your revision timetable

You now have the information you need to write your timetable. You know how many weeks you have available, and the approximate amount of time that is available in each week.

You should stop all serious revision 48 hours before your examination. After this point, you may want to look back at your notes to refresh your memory, but you should not attempt to revise any new topics. A clear and rested brain is worth more than any extra facts you could memorise in this period.

Make one copy of this chart for each week you have available for revision.

Using your time planning chart, write in the times of your various study sessions during the week.

In the lower part of the chart, write in the topics that you will cover in each of these sessions.

Example of a revision timetable

Revision timetable Week beginning:							
	Monday	Tuesday	Wednesday	Thursday	Friday	Saturday	Sunday
Study sessions							
Topics							

Some revision techniques

There should be two elements in your revision. You must **look back** to the work you have covered in the course and **look forward** to the examination. The techniques you use should reflect these two aspects of revision.

Revision should not be boring. It is useful to try a variety of techniques. You probably already have some revision techniques of your own and you may also like to try some of the techniques suggested here, if they are new to you. However, don't waste time with methods of revision which are not effective for you.

- Go through your lecture notes, textbook or workbooks and use a highlighter pen to mark important points.

- Produce a new set of summarised notes. This can be a useful way of re-absorbing information, but you must be careful to keep your notes concise, or you may find that you are simply reproducing work you have done before. It is helpful to use a different format for your notes.

- Make a collection of key words which remind you of the essential concepts of a topic.

- Reduce your notes to a set of key facts and definitions which you must memorise. Write them on cards which you can keep with you all the time.

- When you come across areas which you were unsure about first time around, rework relevant questions in your course materials, then study the answers in great detail.

- If there are isolated topics which you feel are completely beyond you, identify exactly what it is that you cannot understand and find someone (such as a lecturer or recent graduate) who can explain these points to you.

- Practise as many exam standard questions as you can. The best way to do this is to work to time, under exam conditions. You should always resist looking at the answer until you have finished.

- If you have come to rely on a word processor in your day-to-day work, you may have got out of the habit of writing at speed. It is well worth reviving this skill before you sit down in the examination hall: it is something you will need.

- If you have a plentiful supply of relevant questions, you could use them to practise planning answers, and then compare your notes with the answers provided. This is not a substitute for writing full answers, but can be helpful additional practice.

- Go back to questions you have already worked on during the course. This time, complete them under exam conditions, paying special attention to the layout and organisation of your answers. Then compare them in detail with the suggested answers and think about the ways in which your answer differs. This is a useful way of 'fine tuning' your technique.

- During your revision period, do make a conscious effort to identify situations which illustrate concepts and ideas that may arise in the examination. These situations could come from your own work, or from reading the business pages of the quality press. This technique will give you a new perspective on your studies and could also provide material which you can use in the examination.

4 EXAMINATION TECHNIQUES

THE EXAMINATION

This section is divided into two parts. The first part considers the practicalities of sitting the examination. If you have taken other ACCA examinations recently, you may find that everything here is familiar to you. The second part discusses some examination techniques which you may find useful.

The practicalities

What to take with you

You should make sure that you have:

- your ACCA registration card
- your ACCA registration docket.

You may also take to your desk:

- pens and pencils
- a ruler and slide rule
- a calculator
- charting template and geometrical instruments
- eraser and correction fluid.

You are not allowed to take rough paper into the examination.

If you take any last-minute notes with you to the examination hall, make sure these are not on your person. You should keep notes or books in your bag or briefcase, which you will be asked to leave at the side of the examination hall.

Although most examination halls will have a clock, it is advisable to wear a watch, just in case your view is obscured.

If your calculator is solar-powered, make sure it works in artificial light. Some examination halls are not particularly well-lit. If you use a battery-powered calculator, take some spare batteries with you. For obvious reasons, you may not use a calculator which has a graphic/word display memory. Calculators with printout facilities are not allowed because they could disturb other candidates

Getting there

You should arrange to arrive at the examination hall at least half an hour before the examination is due to start. If the hall is a large one, the invigilator will start filling the hall half an hour before the starting time.

Make absolutely sure that you know how to get to the examination hall and how long it will take you. Check on parking or public transport. Leave yourself enough time so that you will not be anxious if the journey takes a little longer than you anticipated. Many people like to make a practice trip the day before their first examination.

At the examination hall

Examination halls differ greatly in size. Some only hold about ten candidates. Others can sit many hundreds of people. You may find that more than one examination is being taken at the hall at the same time, so don't panic if you hear people discussing a completely different subject from the one you have revised.

While you are waiting to go in, don't be put off by other people talking about how well, or badly, they have prepared for the examination.

You will be told when to come in to the examination hall. The desks are numbered. (Your number will be on your examination docket.) You will be asked to leave any bags at the side of the hall.

Inside the hall, the atmosphere will be extremely formal. The invigilator has certain things which he or she must tell candidates, often using a particular form of words. Listen carefully, in case there are any unexpected changes to the arrangements.

On your desk you will see a question paper and an answer booklet in which to write your answers. You will be told when to turn over the paper.

During the examination

You will have to leave your examination paper and answer booklet in the hall at the end of the examination. It is quite acceptable to write on your examination paper if it helps you to think about the questions. However, all workings should be in your answers. You may write any plans and notes in your answer booklet, as long as you cross them out afterwards.

If you require a new answer booklet, put your hand up and a supervisor will come and bring you one.

At various times during the examination, you will be told how much time you have left.

You should not need to leave the examination hall until the examination is finished. Put up your hand if you need to go to the toilet, and a supervisor will accompany you. If you feel unwell, put up your hand, and someone will come to your assistance. If you simply get up and walk out of the hall, you will not be allowed to reenter.

Before you finish, you must fill in the required information on the front of your answer booklet.

Examination techniques

Tackling Paper 5

The paper consists of two sections. Section A contains a case study, followed by questions referring to it. All questions in Section A *must* be answered. The number of questions may vary from year to year but you can expect about four or five. The number of marks obtainable will also vary from question to question, but the total number of marks obtainable from Section A will always be 55. Study the case study carefully before attempting the questions. You will be expected to demonstrate that you can apply your knowledge to the situation portrayed in the case study, not simply to repeat everything you know about a particular topic.

Section B consists of five questions. Each is worth 15 marks. You are required to answer any *three* questions from this section. Again, where appropriate, you should apply your knowledge to a given situation.

In both sections, questions may take the form of essays or problems, and many will contain more than one part.

Your general strategy

You should spend the first ten minutes of the examination reading the paper. If you have a choice of question, decide which questions you will do. You must divide the time you spend on questions in proportion to the marks on offer. Don't be tempted to spend more time on a question you know a lot about, or one which you find particularly difficult. If a question has more than one part, you must complete each part.

On every question, the first marks are the easiest to gain. Even if things go wrong with your timing and you don't have time to complete a question properly, you will probably gain some marks by making a start.

Spend the last five minutes reading through your answers and making any additions or corrections.

You may answer written questions in any order you like. Some people start with their best question, to help them relax. Another strategy is to begin with your second best question, so that you are working even more effectively when you reach the question you are most confident about.

Once you have embarked on a question, you should try to stay with it, and not let your mind stray to other questions on the paper. You can only concentrate on one thing at once. However, if you get completely stuck with a question, leave space in your answer book and return to it later.

Answering the question

All Examiners say that the most frequent reason for failure in examinations, apart from basic lack of knowledge, is candidates' unwillingness to answer the question that the Examiner has asked. A great many people include every scrap of knowledge they have on a topic, just in case it is relevant. Stick to the question and tailor your answer to what you are asked. Pay particular attention to the verbs in the question.

You should be particularly wary if you come across a question which appears to be almost identical to one which you have practised during your revision. It probably isn't! Wishful thinking makes many people see the question they would like to see on the paper, not the one that is actually there. Read a question at least twice before you begin your answer. Underline key words on the question paper, if it helps focus your mind on what is required.

If you don't understand what a question is asking, state your assumptions. Even if you do not answer in precisely the way the Examiner hoped, you may be given some credit, if your assumptions are reasonable.

Presentation

You should do everything you can to make things easy for the marker. Although you will not be marked on your handwriting, the marker will find it easier to identify the points you have made if your answers are legible. The same applies to spelling and grammar. Use blue or black ink. The marker will be using red or green.

Use the margin to clearly identify which question, or part of a question, you are answering.

Start each answer on a new page. The order in which you answer the questions does not matter, but if a question has several parts, these parts should appear in the correct order in your answer book.

If there is the slightest doubt when an answer continues on another page, indicate to the marker that he or she must turn over. It is irritating for a marker to think he or she has reached the end of an answer, only to turn the page and find that the answer continues.

Use columnar layouts for computations. This will help you to avoid mistakes, and is easier to follow.

Use headings and numbered sentences if they help to show the structure of your answer. However, don't write your answers in one-word note form.

If your answers include diagrams, don't waste time making them great works of art. Keep them clear, neat and simple. Use your rule and any templates or geometric instruments you have with you. Remember to label the axes of graphs properly. Make reference to any diagrams in the body of your text so that they form an integral part of your answer.

It is a good idea to make a rough plan of an answer before you begin to write. Do this in your answer booklet, but make sure you cross it out neatly afterwards. The marker needs to be clear whether he or she is looking at your rough notes, or the answer itself.

Computations

Before you begin a computation, you may find it helpful to jot down the stages you will go through. Cross out these notes afterwards.

It is essential to include all your workings and to indicate where they fit in to your answer. It is important that the marker can see where you got the figures in your answer from. Even if you make mistakes in your computations, you will be given credit for using a principle correctly, if it is clear from your workings and the structure of your answer.

If you spot an arithmetical error which has implications for figures later in your answer, it may not be worth spending a lot of time reworking your computation.

If you are asked to comment or make recommendations on a computation, you must do so. There are important marks to be gained here. Even if your computation contains mistakes, you may still gain marks if your reasoning is correct.

Use the layouts which you see in the answers given in this booklet and in model answers. A clear layout will help you avoid errors and will impress the marker.

Essay questions

You must plan an essay before you start writing. One technique is to quickly jot down any ideas which you think are relevant. Re-read the question and cross out any points in your notes which are not relevant. Then number your points. Remember to cross out your plan afterwards.

Your essay should have a clear structure. It should contain a brief introduction, a main section and a conclusion. Don't waste time by restating the question at the start of your essay.

Break your essay up into paragraphs. Use sub-headings and numbered sentences if they help show the structure of your answer.

Be concise. It is better to write a little about a lot of different points than a great deal about one or two points.

The Examiner will be looking for evidence that you have understood the syllabus and can apply your knowledge in new situations. You will also be expected to give opinions and make judgements. These should be based on reasoned and logical arguments.

Case studies

A case study asks you to apply your knowledge in a particular situation. It is useful to spend up to a third of the time available for the question in planning your answer.

Start by reading the questions based on the case study. Then read the case study, trying to grasp the main points. Read the case study through again and make notes of the key points. Then analyse the case and identify the relevant issues and concepts. Before you start your answer, read the questions again along with relevant parts of the case study.

If alternative answers present themselves, mention them. you may sometimes find it helpful to consider short and long term recommendations separately.

Reports, memos and other documents

Some questions ask you to present your answer in the form of a report or a memo or other document. It is important that you use the correct format - there are easy marks to be gained here. Adopt the format used in sample questions, or use the format you are familiar with in your day-to-day work, as long as it contains all the essential elements.

You should also consider the audience for any document you are writing. How much do they know about the subject? What kind of information and recommendations are required? The Examiner will be looking for evidence that you can present your ideas in an appropriate form.

5 KEY REVISION TOPICS

The aim of this section is to provide you with a checklist of key information relating to this Paper. You should use it as a reminder of topics to be revised rather than as a summary of all you need to know. Aim to revise as many topics as possible because many of the questions in the exam draw on material from more than one section of the syllabus. You will get more out of this section if you read through Section 3, *General Revision Guidance* first.

1   Systems to handle and process information

The key topics to revise in this area are as follows.

- The relationship between data and information
- Elements of general system theory (GST)
- Control systems
- Decision support systems

See Lynchpin chapters 1–4.

2   Forms of financial and related information systems

The key topics to revise in this area are as follows.

- The electronic office
- Spreadsheet, word processing and database applications
- The decision making process
- Different types of information system: transaction processing systems, management information systems, office automation systems, executive information systems

See Lynchpin chapters 4 and 5.

3   Systems analysis and design

The key topics to revise in this area are as follows.
- Analysis of information systems
- Development of information systems
- Techniques for gathering information
- Dataflow diagrams
- Computer-assisted techniques and the auditor
- End-user computing: pros and cons of centralisation and decentralisation
- CASE tools
- Batch processing and on-line processing

See Lynchpin chapters 6–13.

4   **Systems implementation and evaluation**

The key topics to revise in this area are as follows.

-   Changeover procedures
-   Feasibility studies
-   Project planning techniques
-   Human resource issues
-   Cost-benefit analysis and risk analysis
-   The Data Protection Act 1984
-   Security issues

See Lynchpin chapters 14–16.

6 UPDATES

INTRODUCTION

Examinable documents

Every six months (as at 1 June and 1 December) the ACCA publish a list of 'examinable documents' which form the basis of the legislation and accounting regulations that will be examinable at the following diet.

The ACCA official Textbooks published in July 98 were fully up-to-date for these examinable documents published by the Association as at 1 June 1998.

The ACCA does not publish a list of examinable documents as such for Paper 5, but you should read your Students' Newsletter carefully to learn of developments that the Examiner might identify as being examinable.

In particular, you should be aware of the Data Protection Act 1998, which was given Royal Assent in August 1998, although its provisions will need further subordinate legislation before they become mandatory. The principles of the 1998 Act refer to all filing systems (including manual systems), so they go further than the 1984 Act which only applied to computerised systems.

7 PRACTICE QUESTIONS

1 FUNCTIONAL ELEMENTS IN A BUSINESS SYSTEM

Using general systems theory as the basis of your approach, identify and describe the main functional elements which must be identified within a business system, together with their related information requirements.

(20 marks)
(ACCA June 90)

2 DECISION SUPPORT SYSTEMS

(a) What do you understand by the term 'decision support system'?

(4 marks)

(b) The fundamental components of a decision support system are:

    (i)   dialogue management;
    (ii)   data management;
    (iii)   model management.

Briefly describe the functions of each.

(6 marks)

(c) Give an example of the use of a decision support system.

(5 marks)
(Total: 15 marks)
(ACCA Dec 93)

3 SYSTEM THEORY

You are required:

(a)   (i)   to define the key concepts of system theory.

(5 marks)

    (ii)   to explain the relevance of those concepts to the design of financial and management accounting systems within an organisation.

(5 marks)

(b)   (i)   to briefly explain the difference between open and closed loop control.

(5 marks)

    (ii)   to discuss whether an open or closed loop model would be appropriate for a manufacturing company.

(5 marks)
(Total: 20 marks)
(Pilot Paper)

4   ELECTRONIC OFFICE SYSTEM

Describe the ways in which each of the following basic elements of an integrated office system might be supported by an electronic office system:

(a)   document preparation;
(b)   message distribution;
(c)   personal information management;
(d)   information retrieval; and
(e)   analytic/decision support.

(20 marks)
(ACCA June 91)

5   ADOPTING A DATABASE

(a)   What reasons would you put forward for adopting a database as a basis for an information system?

(6 marks)

(b)   (i)   Describe the responsibilities and role in the organisation of the database administrator.

      (ii)   Explain, with the aid of appropriate diagrams, hierarchical, network and relational database structures.

(8 marks)

(c)   What are the essential functions and facilities of the data dictionary system which supports a database?

(6 marks)
(Total: 20 marks)
(ACCA June 92)

6   SYSTEM STRUCTURES

(a)   (i)   Define the term 'system' and explain the structure of a system.

(4 marks)

      (ii)   Define and distinguish between closed and open systems, with the aid of examples.

(4 marks)

(b)   Management support systems are aids to the decision-making process.

Describe the phases which, according to Simon, constitute that process.

(6 marks)

(c)   A decision support system is a type of management support system.

Produce a definition of a decision support system, suggest what facilities it might offer, and what its essential components might consist of.

(6 marks)
(Total: 20 marks)
(ACCA June 92)

7	AIRLINES, HOTELS, CAR SALES

(a)   For EACH of the following computer application areas:

     (i)   airline reservations;
     (ii)   hotel management;
     (iii)   car sales and repairs.

Describe:

     (i)   the main functions performed by the application;

     (ii)   the most likely features of a computer system used to support the application.

(10 marks)

(b)   List five benefits which should stem from the use of computing in such application areas.

(5 marks)
(Total: 15 marks)

8	COMPUTER-ASSISTED TECHNIQUES

Briefly discuss:

(a)   the computer-assisted techniques available to an auditor and the situations where they might be used;

(5 marks)

(b)   the use of structured walk throughs as a method of project control;

(5 marks)

(c)   the reasons for the popularity of spreadsheets;

(5 marks)

(d)   the various components which together constitute office automation.

(5 marks)
(Total: 20 marks)
(ACCA Dec 92)

9	END USER COMPUTING

The senior management of an organisation wish to encourage end-user computing in an attempt to reduce the backlog of computer applications awaiting implementation, and to make information more freely and speedily available to management.

(a)   What contribution might each of the following make towards reducing the applications backlog and encouraging the spread of end-user computing?

     (i)   Fourth Generation Languages;
     (ii)   Prototyping;
     (iii)   Information centres.

(12 marks)

(b)   What problems would you envisage arising as a result of the widespread introduction of small computer systems and end-user computing, and how might such problems be avoided?

(8 marks)
(Total: 20 marks)
(ACCA Dec 92)

10   DISTRIBUTED DATA PROCESSING

The trends towards distributed data processing and end-user computing can have a significant effect on the structure of information technology in an organisation.

(a)   (i)   Analyse the advantages and disadvantages of centralisation and decentralisation of information technology to a large organisation.

(5 marks)

      (ii)   Suggest some information technology activities which, despite the trend towards decentralisation, might best be carried out centrally.

(5 marks)

(b)   (i)   Explain why end-user computing is increasing and suggest examples of activities which end-users might be responsible for.

(5 marks)

      (ii)   What impact might end-user computing have on the organisation of the information technology function?

(5 marks)
(Total: 20 marks)
(ACCA June 93)

11   CASE TOOLS

The information systems department of your organisation currently makes use of a structured analysis and design approach for the development of computer systems. It is now contemplating the acquisition and use of a CASE tool, to be used in conjunction with the existing structured approach.

(a)   What tools and techniques would you expect the department to be currently using for systems development?

(12 marks)

(b)   As the project leader appointed to investigate this possibility, your first task is to explain to senior management outside the department what a CASE tool is and why such a tool is needed.

      Outline the content of your presentation to management.

(8 marks)
(Total: 20 marks)
(ACCA June 93)

12   SYSTEMS MODELLING TOOLS

(a)   Examine the use of three important systems modelling tools commonly used in structured analysis ie, the dataflow diagram, the entity-relationship diagram, and the state transition (or entity life history) diagram.

(9 marks)

(b)   Draw up a state transition (or entity life history) diagram, for the following procedure:

'An institute of higher education receives applications which are either rejected, accepted subject to specified 'A' level grades being achieved, or accepted unconditionally. Applications in the latter two categories can withdraw their applications at any time. Conditional acceptances are eventually either acepted or withdrawn. Once applicants commence their courses they become registered, but may suspend their registration at anytime, and either return as registered, but may suspend their registration at anytime, and either return as registered, or terminate as non-graduated. Applicants may either progress from year to year and graduate, or fail during or at the end of the course.'

(6 marks)
(Total: 15 marks)
(ACCA Dec 93)

---

13   COMPUTERS

Computers have been used as tools to support managerial decision making for a number of years. The various tools/aids can be grouped into the following categories:

- transaction processing systems
- management information systems
- decision support systems
- expert systems.

(a)   Define and distinguish between these categories ensuring that each is considered from the following aspects:

- applications served
- database facilities
- decision capabilities
- type of information available
- level served within the organisation

(14 marks)

(b)   In the context of information systems in a production control department, identify tasks which might be carried out for each of the categories of information system listed above.

(6 marks)
(Total: 20 marks)
(Pilot Paper)

---

14   BATCH PROCESSING

A batch processing sales accounting system has been operating successfully for a number of years. However, records rejected by the validation programs within the system have increased from 4% to 15% over the past six months, and computer operations staff it increasingly difficult to run the system within its established operating schedule.

(a)   Write a report to the chief accountant analysing the likely reason for the deterioration in performance.

(8 marks)

Following a review of current performance and future requirements, a decision has been taken to replace the existing system, and a statement of requirements for the proposed new system sent to selected suppliers, inviting them to submit a proposal for provision of the necessary hardware and software facilities for the application.

(b)   Itemise:

    (i)   The likely contents of the statement of requirements.

(6 marks)

    (ii)   The information that potential suppliers should include in their proposal.

(6 marks)
(Total: 20 marks)
(Pilot Paper)

15   SUCCESSFUL CONVERSION

(a)   Describe the important activities that should take place during systems implementation to ensure a successful conversion from the existing system to a new system.

(12 marks)

(b)   You have been asked to make a presentation to senior management on the case for introducing the prototyping approach to systems development into your organisation as an alternative to the conventional structured approach.

What are the major points you would cover in your presentation?

(8 marks)
(Total: 20 marks)
(Pilot Paper)

16   FEASIBILITY AND PROJECT PLANNING

Describe the activities encompassed within:

(a)   The feasibility study.

(b)   Project planning for systems implementation.

(15 marks)
(ACCA Dec 93)

17   FINANCE FUNCTION

You are the finance function representative on a project team charged with carrying out a cost benefit analysis on a proposed on-line order entry system. It is envisaged that the system will involve field sales staff using portable computers and communications links to enter data into a central computer system.

(a)   What factors would you expect to take into account under each of the following headings?

    (i)   The cost of developing, installing and operating the system;

    (ii)   The benefits which might result from the introduction of the new computer application.

(10 marks)

(b)   What techniques would you make use of to establish the potential profitability (or otherwise) of your proposed new system?

(10 marks)
(Total: 20 marks)
(Pilot Paper)

18   HUMAN RESOURCES

(a)   Drucker has suggested that the belief that computers reduce human resource costs has been prove wrong. Discuss.

(6 marks)

(b)   Analyse the problems faced by information system managers in the management of the human resources within the information systems department.

(8 marks)

(c)   Suggest programmes for personnel development, performance management and manpower planning which an information systems manager might implement in an effort to create a stable and effective environment for personnel within the information systems department.

(6 marks)
(Total: 20 marks)
(ACCA June 93)

19   MEASURING COSTS AND BENEFITS

The systems analyst must be prepared to carry out both cost-benefit calculations and risk analysis as part of the proposal for a new computer system.

(a)   (i)   Describe two methods for demonstrating the costs and benefits of such a system over a period of time.

(6 marks)

(ii)   What are the specific problems associated with the measurement of information systems costs and benefits?

(6 marks)

(b)   What aspects would you take into account when undertaking a risk analysis of the costs and benefits of a proposed computer project?

(8 marks)
(Total: 20 marks)
(ACCA June 93)

20   INVESTMENT OPPORTUNITY

Discuss the following propositions:

(a)   Information technology in an organisation should be regarded as an investment opportunity rather than an expense.

(8 marks)

(b)   Information technology services should be run as a business within a business and managed as a profit centre, using an appropriate chargeout technique.

(12 marks)
(Total: 20 marks)
(ACCA June 93)

21   PRODUCTIVITY, RELIABILITY, MAINTAINABILITY

Examine why productivity, reliability and maintainability are seen as major issues in the efficient and effective design of computer systems.

(15 marks)
(ACCA Dec 93)

22   COMPUTER SECURITY

(a)   You are an outside consultant specialising in computer security brought in by an organisation to advise on the security aspects to a new computer centre.

(i)   What potential physical threats would you make your client aware of, what precautionary measures would you suggest, and what techniques would you propose be implemented to control access to the computer centre?

(6 marks)

(ii)   You also feel that a contingency plan is an essential aspect of the new computing facility.

Explain to the client the purpose of such a plan, how it might be developed, and the standby options which are available.

(8 marks)

(b)   The Computer Misuse Act came into force in August 1990.

What are the three offences which the Act defines and the penalties permitted for each?

(6 marks)
(Total: 20 marks)
(ACCA June 92)

23   CONTROL EVALUATION

An internal audit control evaluation of a computer installation should cover each of the following important procedures:

(a)   disaster recovery;
(b)   environment controls and physical security;
(c)   input, output and file controls;
(d)   operations.

Describe the main objective of each procedure and suggest areas which should be the subject of particular scrutiny.

(20 marks)
(ACCA Dec 92)

24 DATA PROCESSING

(a) Describe SIX possible ways of validating data, both before it is entered into a computer system, and by use of a data validation program. **(6 marks)**

(b) Although computer systems should be designed to ensure accurate data processing, an auditor is likely to make use of one or more computer-based techniques, in order to check that accuracy.

Describe any THREE such techniques. **(9 marks)**
(Total: 15 marks)
(ACCA Dec 93)

25 FOOD WHOLESALER

(a) You have been appointed as head of a newly created internal audit section within the computer department of a large food wholesaler. The department has a number of operational systems, some on line and some batch processing, and a central corporate database. A significant effort is currently being devoted to new systems developments.

Your first task is to review the various types of controls which exist in the department and its computer systems.

Describe what you are looking for in your review.

(12 marks)

(b) In order to effectively perform an audit of a computer department as described above, you may well have to make use of computer assisted auditing techniques.

What computer assisted techniques are available, and where might you use them?

(8 marks)
(Total: 20 marks)
(Pilot Paper)

26 INTERNATIONAL INVESTMENT SERVICES LTD (IIS)

International Investment Services Ltd (IIS) employ a total of 600 staff, including 300 at their headquarters in London and the rest at 12 offices around the world. IIS specialises in providing advice and management of funds for investors, either individuals or organisations, who wish to take advantage of special conditions within the financial markets, such as areas which have beneficial tax laws, and occasions when there are major fluctuations in the currency markets.

Since its establishment in the 1970s, the management of IIS have always viewed information technology as a vital element in gaining competitive advantage in an area of business where success is dependent upon up-to-date information and fast, reliable communication. At the London headquarters there are about 140 specialist information systems staff, of whom about two-thirds are involved in systems development and the remainder maintain and operate the existing systems and provide technical support for users.

A large mainframe computer at the London headquarters provides a centralised database, which includes a real-time processing system that is fed with data directly from the major financial institutions around the world, such as the London Stock Exchange. High-speed telecommunications networks are designed to allow all IIS's personnel to access the information on the central mainframe and there is intensive use of these networks for electronic mail (e-mail) and other forms of electronic data interchange (EDI).

Dan Bates is the chief executive of IIS. Dan has become increasingly concerned that some of the organisations who are competing with IIS seem to be able to take better advantage of the changing conditions within the world's financial markets than IIS. Dan has discussed this issue with John Kline, the Information Systems Director. John assures Dan that IIS's hardware and communications systems are at least as well advanced as any of their competitors. The software performs well as a transaction processing system to handle clients' accounts and it processes the basic financial information that the investment staff require.

Dan discusses his concerns with Marie Sims, the Personnel Director, who has overall responsibility for staff and recruitment around the world. Marie assures Dan that IIS's investment appraisal staff are the best available in terms of both qualifications and experience and their salaries and conditions are considered generous within the industry. Dan next speaks to Frank Heinman, the Senior Investment Exective deputising for the Investments Director, who has taken a period of extended leave due to illness. Frank is relatively new to IIS and he mentions that one of his previous employers had been developing a sophisticated computerised investments analysis system. In 95% of instances this system is able to provide investment advice which is proving to be at least as effective as top-class human consultants, but it provides the advice much more quickly than a person could. The company concerned is naturally keen to take maximum advantage of its system and is therefore unlikely to make it available to the competition. When Frank left that employer, he had only seen a prototype of the system which produced printed reports, but he understood that the aim was to use a graphical user interface to the system.

Dan asks John Kline to discuss the situation with Frank Heinman and then report back to Dan in two days with some ideas on how IIS should react.

For the past several years IIS have developed their own software. When John Kline joined the company, IIS had standardised on the use of SSADM (Structured Systems Analysis and Development Methodology) in all development projects. John is aware that the Information Systems Department and its staff are regarded as elitist by other staff and that recent surveys of the users of the information systems have shown a decline in user satisfaction with the systems and the support they get from the Information Systems staff. John is considering whether IIS can usefully adopt a 'soft systems' approach to the new systems development projects.

Marie Sims has asked John Kline about the use of data flow diagrams (DFDs) in systems analysis and design. Marie has identified the following files within the personnel department which may be used during recruitment procedures:

- a job specification file holding a job descriptionof every job type in IIS

- an establishment file, holding, for each department, the maximum number of staff permitted for each job type

- a personnel file, holding details of each employee, one record per employee

- a vacancy file, holding details of unfilled vacancies

- an applicants file, holding details of all job applicants

- an interview file, holding a diary of all forthcoming interviews.

You are required:

(a)   to explain the features of a real-time system and why IIS has chosen one to handle the basic data fed from the financial institutions.

(10 marks)

(b)   to explain what an expert system is and describe some of the features of an expert system which could help IIS with its investment analysis and appraisal.

(10 marks)

(c)   to describe the main features of Structured Systems Analysis and Design Methodology (SSADM) and discuss features of soft systems methodologies which could be adopted by IIS.

(15 marks)

(d)   to use as many of the files mentioned in the case study as you consider necessary to draw a data flow diagram of likely recruitment procedures at IIS.

(10 marks)

(e)   to describe the use of prototypes and graphical user interfaces and discuss their appropriateness for applications such as the investment analysis application that IIS is considering.

(10 marks)
(Total: 55 marks)

27	BETTER BLOCKS LTD

Read the information about Better Blocks Ltd and then answer *all* the questions in this section.

Better Blocks Ltd produces and sells building materials such as bricks, blocks and cement. The company was established in the north of England in the 1960s by George Carlton. George was a bricklayer by trade who had inherited enough money to buy a local quarry and brick works which he called Better Blocks. He had identified various small quarries in the locality which were all independently owned and either competing for the same business or selling different products to the same customers. Over the next ten years, George's company systematically bought these quarries and effectively monopolised the local market. George Carlton believed that central control and administration was the most efficient and cost-effective way of running this sort of business that operated several sites. Under George's control in the 1970s Better Blocks continued to expand by taking over more quarries and in the 1980s George decided to take the opportunity to broaden Better Blocks' activities by buying out small independent builders' merchants.

In 1994, the company now owns 14 quarries with associated processing plants, and 27 builders' merchants. The builders' merchants all retail to the public and use manual sales systems. They all hold high stock levels, which is considered necessary because all purchase orders have to be processed by central office before being sent to the suppliers. There is no central warehouse or stores; each builders' merchant keeps its own stock. In addition, there are six local sales offices, each run by an area sales manager and staffed by a total of 18 sales representatives who try to sell Better Blocks products to construction companies. Better Blocks' growth was mainly due to George Carlton's direction and he insisted that as many of the business activities as possible were carried out from the company's central building in Leeds; this led to the establishment of centralised services such typing, administration and information systems.

From the early 1990s Better Blocks profits started to fall. George Carlton, now in his late 60s, has expressed the view that the company could no longer continue the policy of buying out smaller businesses as suitable businesses were now almost all owned by larger organisations such as Better Blocks and its competitors. Imported materials were also taking a larger share of the market. George advocated a period of consolidation. A customer survey at Better Blocks builders' merchants showed that the public viewed them as having a limited range of goods and slow service.

Janet Carlton, George's daughter, had studied economics and computer science at university and had worked her way up the Information Systems Department at Better Blocks. In 1983, in preparation for increased retailing activity, Better Blocks had purchased a mainframe computer to help process all payroll and accounting information. This was upgraded in 1989 to cope with increased activity. Janet Carlton was appointed Information Systems Director in 1991. Most processes carried out on the mainframe, such as processing delivery notes and issuing invoices, are operated as batch processes. All computerised data processing is carried out within the Information Systems Department so all the original data such as sales orders, purchase orders, delivery notes and reports from the builders' merchants are sent by post or delivered by hand on paper for input by the data entry staff. None of the builders' merchants, quarries or local sales offices have electronic communication facilities.

Bill Keane has recently joined Better Blocks as Financial Director. Bill has carried out an investigation and discovered that when deliveries are made to building sites the delivery notes have to be sent to head office in Leeds to be entered onto the mainframe by the data preparation staff. As a consequence, invoicing is very slow; the company has a poor record for collection of payments and an excessive level of bad debtors. The company's 18 sales representatives travel to Leeds to attend a weekly sales meeting. At one meeting Bill told them that they would have to tighten up on credit customers but the sales representatives complain that this is not possible unless they have up-to-date information about customers' credit position.

Bill Keane is also concerned about the high cost of salaries paid to the information systems specialists in the Information Systems Department. Looking at the activities of the department's staff, he is puzzled by the amount of time that is allocated either to adapting the mainframe software or visiting local sales offices to sort out individual problems. In line with George Carlton's views on centralised services and control, Better Blocks have a policy that managers' requests for information technology should be co-ordinated by the Information Systems Department and all tasks requiring computer services should be handled by them too. On visiting each of the six local sales offices, Bill Keane is puzzled by the amount of computer equipment they have and discovers that managers have been purchasing personal computers and printers but disguising the nature of the equipment under the heading 'Office equipment' on requisition forms.

Bill Keane arranges a meeting with Janet Carlton to discuss the situation. On hearing Bill's concerns, Janet says that she is aware of some of the difficulties but is surprised at the scale of the problems. Janet has tried to influence George Carlton to change the policy on centralised control and operation of the information systems but George is not inclined to support anything which involves additional direct costs or disruption to current operations. Bill and Janet agree to try to get some ideas together for a radical review of Better Blocks' information systems, and to put forward their suggestions to the board of directors as a matter of urgency.

Janet is particularly interested in the decentralissation of some aspects of the information systems, such as data entry of delivery notes and also in introducing a policy of end-user computing into Better Blocks' local sales offices. Bill wants to consider how to introduce information technology into the builders' merchants.

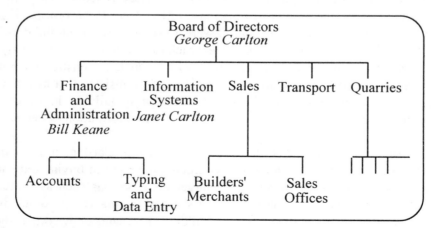

Better Blocks Ltd - organisation structure

You are required:

(a)   to explain what is meant by end-user computing and why there is a trend towards end-user computing. Discuss the advantages and disadvantages if Better Blocks adopt end-user computing in their local sales offices.

(10 marks)

(b)   to discuss the benefits and disadvantages of decentralisation of some of Better Blocks' activities, such as the data entry of delivery notes, compared with George Carlton's preferred policy of centralisation.

(10 marks)

(c)   to discuss the present organisation structure at Better Blocks and how it could be adapted to facilitate decentralisation and end-user computing.

(10 marks)

(d)   to outline how information technology could be used to improve the efficiency of Better Blocks' builders' merchants.

(15 marks)

(e)   to discuss the need to involve the users of Better Blocks' information systems in the development of new systems and how that involvement could be achieved.

(10 marks)
(Total: 55 marks)

28   JOHNSONS SPECIALIST BOOKS LTD

Read the information about Johnsons Specialist Books and then answer *all* the questions in this section.

Johnsons Specialist Books Ltd have a large bookshop with offices and warehouse in a university city. Johnsons have gained a good reputation for locating old and obscure publications and some of their clients pay Johnsons to research into the life history of particular titles and for other research services. The business was established in the early 1900s by George Johnson and has been owned and run by members of the Johnson family ever since. The business is organised in three sections:

- Shop and warehouse employing 7 warehouse staff and 12 shop assistants.
- Accounts and Administration employing five accounts clerks and ten typists/adminstrators.
- Research employing 15 researchers whose work includes travel to book shops libraries, etc.

In addition, each of these three sections has a manager and a deputy manager. The three managers and the Managing Director form the board of directors.

In 1993, James Johnson stated that he would be retiring from his position as Managing Director at the end of the year and he recommended that he be replaced by his niece, Mary Johnson, who was at that time the Research Director. For several years Mary has been encouraging the other directors to carry out a review of Johnsons' use of information technology. Currently there are a few stand-alone personal computers in use at Johnsons for tasks like accounts, word-processing and for accessing booklists and catalogues stored on CD-ROM.

Soon after her appointment as Managing Director, Mary Johnson contracted a computer consultant to lead a feasibility study on options for a comprehensive computerisation of Johnsons' information systems. The feasibility study report identifies three options. The following system (Option A) is chosen on the basis of lowest costs, and the report includes an outline of the quantified costs and benefits.

The new system - Option A

A centralised multi-user system is based upon a small, powerful mini-computer that has recently come onto the market. Johnsons' researchers will have portable computers and when out of the office they will be able to communicate with the mini-computer via the telephone system. The supplier of the system is keen to get it established in the market and has offered to make small modifications to its standard software to suit Johnsons' requirements.

Initial cost in year 1: £93,000

On-going maintenance and other costs in year 2 onwards: £37,000 per annum

Benefits:	Year 1	£23,000
	Year 2	£89,000
	Year 3	£64,000
	Year 4	£52,000
	Year 5	£42,000

Note: all figures are based on present-day prices, although costs and benefits are considered as occurring at the year end.

The option recommends the appointment of a computer systems manager who will be responsible for the implementation and ongoing administration of the system. Alan Baker is appointed to the post and one of his initial tasks is to act as project manager responsible for the new system.

During the feasibility study the major activities involved in the project have been identified and listed with their estimated durations and the order of tasks. The information is shown in this table:

Activity		Duration (days)	Preceding activities
A	Draw up detailed specifications	15	Start of project
B	Modify software	10	A
C	Wiring and cabling offices	4	A
D	Install new office furniture	3	C
E	Install and test hardware	5	D
F	Install and test software	4	B, E
G	Training	5	F
H	Data conversion	3	F
I	Changeover using parallel running	20	G, H
J	Acceptance testing	2	I

Alan Baker was not able to start his employment as soon as the board of directors at Johnsons would have liked. Alan is naturally very keen to make a good impression by getting the project completed smoothly and quickly. However, he is particularly concerned that activity B (modify software) is not directly under his control since it will be carried out by the system's suppliers. He is also concerned that there may not be sufficient slack time to cope with any problems that may arise.

Alan has noticed that the feasibility study has not considered any legislation relating to data protection or the need to register computerised processing of information. When asked about the existing arrangements, the administration section have replied that, as far as they know, the current payroll and accounts system is exempt.

Alan is considering how vulnerable the new system and its communications facility might be to access and use for unauthorised purposes or by unauthorised users. He has noticed that one of the benefits claimed for the new system is that it will reduce staff costs, since some of Johnsons' junior researchers and administration clerks will eventually be made redundant; the system will carry out the tasks that they currently do. Alan is considering whether this may raise security issues.

You are required:

(a)   to use investment appraisal techniques to assess the economic feasibility of the new system over five years - use the figures from the feasibility study report, given that Johnsons' cost of capital is 12%. Comment on the appropriateness of the various techniques available and of using a five-year time scale when dealing with information technology-based systems.

(15 marks)

(b)   to draw a network chart of the project's activities as listed in the feasibility study report and identify the critical path. Comment on Alan Baker's concerns about completing the project smoothly and on time.

(15 marks)

(c)   to briefly explain the purpose of data protection legislation, such as the UK Data Protection Act 1984, and outline its contents. In relation to Johnsons' likely uses of data and information, give examples of one use which would be exempt under the legislation and one that would require registration.

(10 marks)

(d)   to describe the risk of unauthorised access to the new system and discuss the measures that can be taken to combat them.

(15 marks)
(Total: 55 marks)

8 ANSWERS TO PRACTICE QUESTIONS

1	FUNCTIONAL ELEMENTS IN A BUSINESS SYSTEM

(Tutorial note: this is still a valid topic under the new syllabus but unlikely to appear in this format.*)*

A system can be defined as:

> A collection of men, machines and methods organised to accomplish a set of specific functions.

The modern business - or any other organisation - is one large system which is inevitably divided into sub-systems.

To identify a system we need to determine:

(a)   where its boundaries are;
(b)   why it exists at all; and
(c)   what the parts are and how they interrelate.

General systems theory (GST) tries to define generally the idea of the 'organised system', and also to categorise such systems.

GST:

(a)   highlights the existence of sub-systems, each one of which could well have objectives which conflict with others (this certainly applies in the establishment of cost centres, budgets and standards);

(b)   assists in the identification of the external environment's impact upon the system (many influences exert pressures which lead to change and conflict, ranging from governmental activities and industrial relations to shareholder expectations and competitor tactics);

(c)   clarifies problems arising in the design and the implementation of information systems which are intended to orientate decisions to the advantage of the organisation as a whole; and

(d)   emphasises the fact that the organisation must be dynamic, not static, and that all sub-systems within it are necessarily influenced in some way by various constraining aspects.

The GST approach allows dynamic, complex and sophisticated situations to be understood in broad terms. This approach is in itself a conceptual tool, often aided by operational research, and it is equally valid for all systems - a business organisation, an educational system, a central heating system, or whatever system is being examined.

As far as management is concerned, the systems approach is concerned with the system's stability and its growth under a range of probable circumstances, changes and policies. As a rule, some form of systems model is used as simulation.

A special form of modelling is system dynamics, which does not make use of existing knowledge, but which creates a large structure to demonstrate how policies, decisions and delayed responses are linked together to influence growth and stability. This makes scientists and other specialists aware of interactions which have hitherto been disregarded.

GST distinguishes between closed and open systems:

Closed system - This is independent of its environment. The system is neither influenced by, nor influences, its environment.

Open system - Open systems are concerned and interact with the outside world and are distinguished in that they have inputs and outputs, thereby exchanging information, energy or material with the environment.

There are seven major systems elements within a business system:

(a)   **Input**

This takes the form of money, materials, energy, decisions, information, etc. Physical input to information systems may be in the form of punched cards or manuscript documents while non-physical input might, for example, be telephone messages.

(b)   **Process**

This actually transforms the input into output. For example, in the case of an information system, raw (primary) data consisting of facts and figures is processed to become information.

(c)   **Output**

Output may take the same form as input. It is the system's reason for existence. The system's function or purpose must be accomplished through the output(s). If we take the payroll system as an example, the fundamental purpose of this is to calculate individual employee earnings (the output). Similarly, an accounts receivable system collects amounts due from customers and provides an 'outstanding debt analysis' (two outputs here).

(d)   **Feedback**

Through this the system continually receives information from its environment, which permits it to make adjustments to survive and maintain dynamic equilibrium.

It is worthwhile pointing out that in a business system the condition of entropy is avoided by receiving inputs and transforming them into a form of output. The term 'entropy' refers to the tendency for a closed system to become more and more disorganised over a period of time. The open system overcomes this condition and, indeed, can become even more organised: thus it may be said to be capable of 'negative entropy'.

(e)   **Standard**

This allows control to be exercised. In a budgetary control system the set targets allow budget variances to be assessed and action to be taken where necessary.

(f)   **Comparator**

This is the means by which comparison is made between the standard and the actual performance or results. A clerk in a manual system may compare actual stock-levels with book stock-levels to discover variances or deviations.

(g)   **Effector**

A vital part of the system: the effector takes any action to correct any variance or deviation discovered by the comparator.

It is also important in the study of systems to realise the importance of control sub-systems. These sub-systems are necessary so that the 'parent' system remains steady or is able to change without endangering its components.

A control system must, for example, make certain that a business organisation can survive unpredicted events by coping with them as and when required to do so. Such events could include non-delivery of raw materials, industrial unrest, competitor's activities, etc.

Systems can also be defined as either hard or soft:

Hard system features:

- Clear objectives;

- Easily-defined measures of performance;

- Easily-defined measures of control;
  eg, industrial production plants.

Soft system features:

- Objectives difficult to define;

- Decision making sometimes uncertain;

- Human behaviour affects performance;

- Control measures difficult to establish;
  eg, business management system, where human factors are difficult to control and predict.

It can be seen, therefore, that there are a considerable number of varying elements to a system.

2   DECISION SUPPORT SYSTEMS

(a)   A decision support system (DSS) is a computer-based information system that brings together sophisticated software, a high-level language interface, and the disciplines of operational research (linear programming, game theory, queuing theory, Monte Carlo simulation and network analysis) to help resolve the problems of planning and control.

Unlike transaction processing information systems, which are designed to solve structured problems, a DSS helps managers to solve problems that are ill-instructured, or unstructured - problems that do not lend themselves to automated decision-making because human judgement and subjective analysis are essential to their solution. The contribution of the DSS is to collect, organise, summarise, analyse and model data in a variety of ways. The manager then reaches a decision based on the processed data. This decision results from interaction between the manager and the information provided by the DSS.

Another way to define DSS is that they foster human learning, creativity and analysis, unlike a management information system (MIS), which is much more limited. Although the MIS helps to quantify a problem and then solve it, it is not designed to enable decision-makers to look inside a problem, to isolate parameters of the problem, and then ask what-if questions with regard to those parameters.

The type of support a DSS provides depends upon the nature of the problem for which the DSS is designed. Most DSSs present corporate management with a picture of the consequences of various plans of action should specified variable change.

(b)   Basic functional components of a DSS:

Dialogue management and model management are the components that make a DSS unique, distinguishing them from other information systems for management; without these the DSS would only be able to produce traditional reports and information.

Dialogue management enables a DSS to handle user interaction with the computer system; the precise manner in which a DSS handles communication between user and computer is a design decision made during system development, but every DSS requires:

(i)   a user interface by which the user and computer communicate;

(ii)   a method for controlling the dialogue, either by the system or the user;

(iii)   a request transformer, which translates the user request into code understandable by the DSS software.

Data management provides the DSS with the essential ability to store, retrieve and manipulate data. This requires:

(i)   a database;

(ii)   a database management system, to control the creation, maintenance and utilisation of the database;

(iii)   a data dictionary, to maintain data definitions and descriptions;

(iv)   a query facility to interpret requests for data and determine how these requests will be met.

There may also be the facility to access and retrieve data from external databases.

Model management; a model is an abstraction of something that is of interest to the person who constructs or uses it. Models may be narrative, graphic, or in the form of mathematical formulas. Those aspects of a business environment that can be measured and represented mathematically are the models used by DSSs. They include financial models, game theory, inventory control, planning models, resource allocation and scheduling.

Model management software will be required to enable a DSS to invoke models, retrieve and update model parameters, restructure models and link them together, so allowing the user to identify optimal decisions in crucial areas. Several cycles of programming and testing may be required before the model is ready to be used.

Also required are:

(i)   a modelling command processor, to accept and interpret model requests;
(ii)   a model execution function to run models;
(iii)   an interface to enable use of information from the database for modelling purposes.

(c)   *DSS application* - an example

An order is received for a product. A conventional MIS reports that it cannot be delivered in the timescale specified. The production manager uses a DSS to evaluate the consequences of refusing the order. A query language with a DBMS is used to check the customer's record; does the product have a generous mark-up? does the customer regularly place high value orders?

If the answers supplied by the DSS indicate that the customer is such that the order is worth pursuing, then the manager may consider options other than rejection. The DSS may be used to generate a scheduling model to analyse the possibility of other less important orders being delayed; a production spreadsheet model might be used to examine the implications of using sub-contractors, overtime or substitute components to fill the order. A cost-benefit model might be used to determine the effect of a lower profit margin or loss of goodwill. The final decision on whether to accept or reject the order will be reached by the production manager, but the information provided by the DSS will contribute significantly to this decision.

---

3   SYSTEM THEORY

Answer Plan

(a)   (i)   Examples of systems; definition; sub-systems; inputs; processes; outputs; environments; feedback mechanisms.

        (ii)   Analytical approach; helps define relationships between subsystems; ensures congruence of goals; helps define information requirements; redefinition of organisation structures.

(a)   (i)   Systems are found in science (the solar system), human biology (the digestive system), in business and in many others areas. Systems theory is the study of how systems are likely to behave and how they may be controlled, and has as many applications as there are different kinds of system. The definition of a system is complex, but in the areas that are of most interest to accountants -

organisations, financial systems, business systems and computer systems - the following definition can be used:

A system is a group of related elements or activities which are organised in order to achieve a specific set of objectives.

From this definition we can see that an organisation itself forms a system, as does the accounts department within the company, as does the computer system which produces the month end reports. The department is a sub-system of the company, and the computer programs and people running them form a sub-system of the department.

The key parts of the definition mentioned above are that the system has inter-related parts, and that the whole system is designed to achieve a specific objective or series of objectives. Systems theory attempts to describe the common properties of systems, to categorise types of system, to describe how they respond to their environment, and to show ways in which they may be controlled. The following description of how a system works will illustrate some of the common terminology used in systems theory. A system receives **inputs** from its **environment** (everything outside of the system which may affect its operation), carries out **processes** on the inputs, and produces **outputs**. The system will have a **feedback mechanism** which produces analysis of how it is performing, and enables a decision maker to modify the system as appropriate.

(ii)   The analytical approach of systems theory can be very beneficial to an organisation. There are several significant advantages:

- Systems theory provides a framework which will help the management of a company to examine how it is organised. It forces them to adopt an analytical approach to running the company, allowing them to step back from the day to day work of controlling the business and encouraging them to fundamentally redefine how it should be organised.

- It helps management to understand and modify how the different parts of the organisation interrelate. A company is a very complex entity. By breaking the company down into different subsystems, management can examine in detail how a specific department operates without losing sight of the overall organisational perspective. The way that other parts of the organisation relate to the department being examined are expressed as inputs to or outputs from the departmental subsystem. This helps break down the complex task of analysing the organisation into more manageable chunks.

- Systems theory can help ensure that the goals and objectives of different parts of the company are congruent. In many companies, the objectives of different departments are contradictory. In order for the sales office to achieve an objective of immediately supplying all customers with goods that they have ordered, stock levels must be high. The warehouse will need to keep stocks as low as possible in order to reduce its costs. These two objectives are incompatible. How they are reconciled should be defined by the overall management of the company. In the example described above, the compromise could be that the warehouse would keep sufficient stocks to supply a certain percentage (say 95%) of orders from stock, and that they will minimise their costs subject to that restriction.

- Systems theory can be used to help define the company's information requirements. Two different types of information are identified by systems theory. One type is necessary to monitor whether individual subsystems are operating correctly. The second type of information is required as output from one subsystem in order to be input to another subsystem. In a sales force, for example, information about how many calls each sales person is making is needed so that the sales manager can identify problems. Details about individual sales are required so that the payroll system can calculate how much commission is due to each individual.

- Systems theory can help in defining how a company should be organised. The structure of many companies evolves as they become larger and more successful. This can lead to inefficiencies which can be eradicated by a fundamental restructuring. The design of the new structure is made easier by adopting the systems theory approach to analysing the company.

(b) **Control Systems**

(i) An **open loop control system** is one which records and responds to its system's external environment as well as to its internal results. An example of this is the maintenance of a departmental budget. It must measure whether expenditure is being kept within the forecast limits, but it must also be able to respond to external influences. An economic recession may lead to a reduction in the amount of money that the department has to spend.

How an open loop control system works can be seen in the diagram below:

Figure 1: An Open Loop Control System

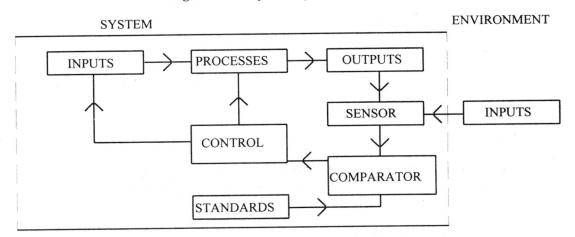

The system receives inputs, processes them, and produces outputs. The sensor is a device built in to the system that collects necessary information. The comparator is the means by which the actual results are compared with the pre-determined systems objectives. The control mechanism (also known as the activator or the effector), will take action when the system fails to meet its targets. There may also need to be action taken if the system's environment changes. In the budget example above, actual expenditure would be measured (by the sensor), compared with the forecast (by the comparator) and action taken by the departmental manager (the activator) to reduce costs if actual costs exceed forecast. The departmental manager may also need to take action by reducing expenditure if company sales are not as high as expected.

A **closed loop control system** is one where there is no direct link with the environment. Most closed loop systems are mechanistic in nature, and their only reactions to the outside world are indirect. An example of a closed loop control system is a water heating system. This sort of control system is illustrated by the diagram below:

Figure 2: A Closed Loop Control System

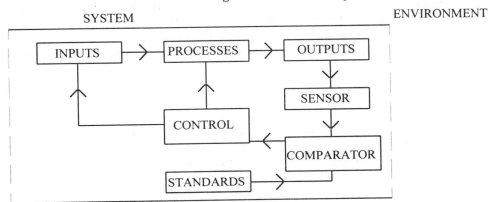

A heating system can continue to operate without any reference to its external environment, with the thermostat containing both the comparator and the activator. The only way that the heating system responds to the environment is when it is set up by a human setting the required temperature.

(ii)   The total company must be operated according to an open loop system. A manufacturing company (or any other organisation) exists to satisfy the needs of its customers, and so there must be mechanisms to ensure that customers are satisfied and that the company is meeting its sales and other targets. The company must also be sufficiently flexible to be able to respond to the actions of its competitors, suppliers and distributors. It must be capable of assessing the changing needs of its market by using research and by listening to its customers. It must also react to government action and to advances in technology.

4   ELECTRONIC OFFICE SYSTEM

An electronic office system can be used to support all the basic elements of an integrated office system.

(a)   **Document Preparation**

This involves such things as dictation, typing, document updating, copying, printing and storing of material.

To assist with the above the following could be used:

(i)   **Word processor**

Now used in most offices, and is either a dedicated machine or a personal computer running a variety of application packages. Word processors provide the following facilities:

(1)   mail merge, tying in with a database file;
(2)   dictionary, to check spellings;
(3)   thesaurus, to check word usage;
(4)   text copying and moving;
(5)   text editing and deletion;
(6)   text storage and retrieval.

A word processor allows the easy production and update of letters and documents. Standard letters can be personalised.

(ii)   **Microfilm Service**

Generally referred to as COM (computer output on microfilm). This allows for vast amounts of material to be copied and stored onto a strip of microfilm thereby producing savings in paper and storage space. Microfilm requires special redress, however, and cannot be retrieved back into the computer. This form of storage is, therefore, useful for historic or reference information only.

(iii)   **Voice recognition**

Although still in its infancy in terms of being used in an office environment, rapid technological developments could soon allow this to render the dictaphone extinct. The difficulties being encountered mainly arise in programming the computer to recognise accents and voice variances, but once these difficulties have been overcome then it is anticipated that voice recognition systems will play a major role in the total office system.

(iv)   **Desk Top Publishing**

This has now become very popular in the office environment. DTP enables documents to be produced to the same high quality as those produced by a professional printing firm. DTP packages incorporate a high quality graphics facility, which, together with low cost laser printers enables the economic production of eg:

(1)   advertisements;
(2)   newsletters;
(3)   documents;
(4)   circulars.

When assessing the equipment used in document preparation the photocopier should not be overlooked.

(b)   **Message Distribution**

Examples of equipment used are:

(i)   telephone;
(ii)   post;
(iii)   facsimile; and
(iv)   electronic mail.

Modern telephone systems allow for teleconferencing to take place, number storage, logging of numbers dialled including time spent, automatic re-dial etc. Most offices today make use of this type of system.

Although there has been and continues to be rapid growth in facsimile and electronic mail usage it is highly unlikely that the conventional mail service will be fully replaced. Electronic equipment used for mailing includes weighing equipment and franking equipment.

Facsimile machines are widely used and copies of a document can be quickly reconstructed at a distant location. This means that documents requiring urgent attention or alteration can be 'faxed' to the desired location and amended and returned within minutes. In addition facsimile machines are also able to reproduce maps and pictures.

Electronic mail is now becoming widely used - it is a practical alternative to the conventional mail and telephone services. With the continued increase in the numbers of managers who have their own work-stations, the use of communication by electronic mail will continue to grow. The advantages of electronic mail include:

(i)   the elimination of paper use;
(ii)   instant despatch and receipt of messages;
(iii)   avoidance of input duplication.

(c)   **Personal Information Management**

This involves the use of: diaries, filing trays, filing cabinets, wall charts etc,

Use of a personal computer - holds data and files frequently used. The PC computer could have its own backing storage and many different types of application packages can be installed on the machine.

Use of electronic diary - frequent appointments can be pre-set. Diaries are usually of a 200 year duration. Nagging facilities are provided to act as prompts for important appointments.

Use of psion organisers - of particular use to such individuals as sales representatives. Psions can be carried in a brief case or pocket and the data input through the psion can be directly input into the computer system at a later stage. Diaries, lists, addresses etc, can be held as reference data on the psion.

(d)   **Information Retrieval**

This involves reference to directories, timetables, catalogues, bibliographies and accessing internal and external databases.

The electronic office can provide fast and easy access to data via a local area network or via a wide area network. Data can either be transmitted via the telephone or directly onto a visual display unit. There are basically two types of data viewing: viewdata, provides an interactive service to the user whilst teletext provides the user with selected data but without the ability to interact with the database.

(e)   **Analytic/decision support**

This facility has been quite limited in the past but with the use of the microcomputer and packages such as spreadsheets, managers now have the opportunity to construct decision making models in order to conduct a series of what-if analyses. Decision making can then be performed on a more informed basis.

Many organisations are now making use of Decision Support Systems which incorporate tools such as:

(i)   the spreadsheet;
(ii)   graphics;
(iii)   statistical packages;
(iv)   4GLs; and
(v)   databases,

in order that they may achieve a better standard of decision making.

---

5   ADOPTING A DATABASE

Answer Plan

(a)   decreases duplication of data; data integrity; faster system development; data independence; information for management; improvement in standards

(b)   (i)   direct the co-ordinating, analysing and recording of data; maintenance of database; design & structure; planning; evaluation of changes; procedures; operating instructions; training

        (ii)   hierarchical - tree-like structure; network 'child' linked to any number of 'parent' data items; relational - more complex data links

(c)   functions: sets out details of each data item in the organisation

(*Tutorial Note:* Part (a) can best be answered by clearly identifying the reasons, followed by brief explanation of each. You are not required to identify the drawbacks. As in part (a), part (c) requires easily identifiable points.)

(a)   **Reasons for adopting a database as a basis for an information system**

Decreases duplication of data

As organisations have developed, they have adopted means of processing (collecting, validating, storing and accessing) data, and in recent years this has been stored electronically. However, often these systems have developed independently of each other, resulting in the same data being processed several times; this is referred to as 'data redundancy', and is costly. The introduction of a database management system (DBMS) can dramatically reduce these costs, and maintain an acceptable level of data redundancy.

Data integrity

In a file-based system data may be stored in different locations, so an amendment to a file in one system may be made at a different time to a file in another system. As data is shared in a database system, consistency of data is attainable. Procedures and standards can more easily be imposed when using a database system than when several concurrent projects are using their own files.

Faster system development

Once a large organisation has a sizeable database, analysts will often find that much of the data they need for a new system is already in existence; this enables their efforts to be directed towards the processing elements. The ability to manipulate data and to query the database will enable them to access that data more easily.

Data independence

Advancement from one technology to another is facilitated when using a database, as the database is application-independent. This mitigates the requirement to undertake major re-analyses and reprogramming following changes in hardware or the operating system.

Information for management

Senior management increasingly require an overall view of the organisation. This is facilitated by using management information systems, decision support systems etc.; these are dependent on the existence of a database.

Improvement in standards

To install and maintain a central database, standards need to be introduced and adhered to. Prior to this, standards may have varied from project to project; the result will often be an overall improvement in standards.

(b)   (i)   **Responsibilities and role of the database administrator (DBA)**

The individual selected for the post needs to be familiar with both the DBMS and the organisation. The DBA will direct the co-ordinating, analysing and recording of all items of data. This will involve analysing the data required by each application; designing a data model; preparing and maintaining a data dictionary and issuing instructions for its use.

The DBA will be involved with the maintenance of the database itself. The areas of responsibility of the DBS will include the design and structure of the database; the planning of any changes required in the database or any hardware changes; evaluating proposals to revise the database; formulating and implementing database procedures to ensure data integrity; production of operating instructions and provision of regular training for users and constantly appraising the performance of the database.

(ii)   **Hierarchical Database Structure**

The hierarchical database model is the simplest one. The data is arranged in a tree-like structure. In this model, any data item can be linked to any number of subsidiary data items, but to only one data item above it in the hierarchy. This method of linking data is referred to as the parent-child relationship.

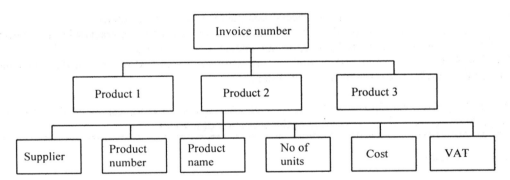

Network Database Structure

Unlike the hierarchical model, the 'child' data item can be linked to any number of 'parent' data items.

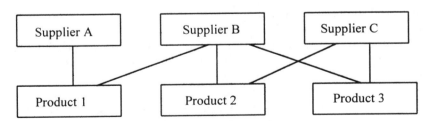

Relational Database Structure

This model also permits more complex data links than the hierarchical model. Using this model related data is stored in separate tables; appropriate links are created by defining the relationships between the tables.

(c)   **Essential functions of data dictionary system (DDS)**

A DDS sets out details of each data item in the organisation, avoiding the generation of incomplete data or inconsistent data definitions. It is usually a software tool, which records and processes data about the data used and processed by the organisation.

A DDS is essential to the management of data as a corporate resource, and the development of information systems, containing definitions and usage of the data within the database. A DDS facilitates control, uniformity, minimises redundancy of data and promotes improved documentation.

Essential facilities of DDS

This will usually include:

(i)   entity, relationship and attribute descriptions [with cross references to functions (re-word)];
(ii)   process descriptions;
(iii)   ownership (security/privacy);
(iv)   data structure, format and length;
(v)   facilitating access by providing cross-referencing and indexing features;
(vi)   facilitating documentation of information collected during the development of a system;
(vii)   providing information about application and data usage post-implementation;
(viii)   promote the adoption of systems development standards
(ix)   source code generation;
(x)   providing security features;
(xi)   providing a DBMS interface.

6   SYSTEM STRUCTURES

Answer Plan

(a)   (i)   elements of a system:inputs;processes;outputs;environment; feedback
         (ii)   closed system - independent of its environment; open system - interacts with its environment
(b)   Phases of decision-making: intelligence; design; choice; implementation
(c)   Decision Support System (DSS): definition; characteristics; - provided through data management module, management model or communication subsystem.

(*Tutorial Note:* As always, careful reading of what is required to answer this question satisfactorily is necessary (eg, define/distinguish between etc.). Also, be aware of the allocation of marks.)

(a)   (i)   **Systems**

A system is a group of related elements organised for a purpose. The essential characteristics of a system are that it has connected parts, and the arrangement is planned and organised with an objective in sight.

The four main elements of a system are:

Inputs: resources which might enter the system, in the form of people, finance, energy or information. Processes: the activities which convert the inputs into outputs. These may include recording, storing, calculating, transmitting etc.

Outputs: after completion of the process, the transformed resources will be issued into the organisational environment. The resource may be returned to its origin, or may be transmitted to a different system or a subsystem. Generally the system will have enhanced the value of the resource.

Environment: this constitutes the elements which impact on the system, and yet are located outside it. The system will receive inputs from the environment, and will respond to these.

Feedback: a flow of information also exists from the output element to the decision-maker (who serves as a control), based on the output or performance of the system; this flow is referred to as feedback. The decision-maker may then choose to adjust the inputs, the processes, or both.

(ii)   **Closed and Open systems**

A closed system is independent of its environment; no environmental influences impact on the system, nor does the system influence its environment. The behaviour of the system takes place because of internal interaction. There is no exchange of energy, information or material. In the business world, closed systems do not exist; a test tube experiment may be an example. Some scientific systems may be described as closed systems, though in reality there are few examples.

An open system is connected to, and interacts with, its environment. This type of system has inputs and outputs and therefore experiences an exchange of information, energy and material with its environment. An open system, therefore, needs to be capable of modifying its performance to maintain its existence in a mutating environment; it may do this by obtaining information about its environment and then responding appropriately. An information system is an example of an open system, as there is a requirement for it to adjust to the altering demands for information.

As its environment changes, a system may make short-term, operational changes, or it may make long-term, strategic changes. This may be illustrated by a tobacco company being affected by increased health awareness. A short-term response may be to produce a low-tar brand of cigarette; a long-term response may be to diversify.

(b)   **Phases of decision-making**

The three main steps in the decision-making process are characterised by Herbert Simon as intelligence, design and choice.

The intelligence stage involves examining actuality, and identifying and refining the problem. The environment is scanned to discover problems or opportunities which require a decision to be made. The phase commences with identifying the goals and objectives of the organisation; problem classification (e.g. programmed or non-programmed) is also included in this phase. If the problem is complicated, it may be necessary to separate it into secondary problems, to facilitate its comprehension. It is also important to ascertain the ownership of a problem. This phase is concluded with a problem statement.

The next stage, the design stage, entails devising, evolving and investigating potential solutions. The problem must be understood, solutions produced, and their feasibility ascertained. It will be necessary to establish evaluation criteria.

The choice phase involves selecting a particular course of action from those previously. The principles adopted for making the choice will first need to be established:-is the best outcome pursued, or will an adequate solution be sufficient?

Implementation is the final stage, though included in Simon's third stage. Implementation has been carried out successfully when the original problem has been solved; if this fails, the process is resumed. Although the typical route through this process is as described (intelligence, design and choice), at any stage a return to a previous stage can be made.

(c)   **Decision Support System (DSS)**

   A computer based system that helps decision-makers to confront ill-structured problems through direct interaction with data and analysis models.

DSS, unlike other information systems such as MIS, applies complex mathematical models to simulate the course of action of an organisational constituent in unstable circumstances. In a dynamic organisation, where expeditious responses are sought, every potential solution to a complex problem cannot be investigated.

The DSS should have the following characteristics:

(i)   provide support for decision-making and, in particular, support for semi-structured or unstructured decision-making;

(ii)   provide support for decision-making at all management levels, and provide systems to integrate between levels;

(iii)   provide support for decisions which are interdependent as well as those which are independent;

(iv)   provide support for all stages of the decision-making process (intelligence, design, choice and implementation);

(v)   support a variety of decision-making processes;

(vi)   be capable of adapting to diverse circumstances;

(vii)   be user-friendly;

(viii)   aim to enhance the effectiveness, as opposed to the efficiency, of decision-making;

(ix)   endeavour to assist, rather than replace, the decision-maker

(x)   be easy to create;

The above may be attainable due to three main components:

(i)   data management module - necessary to extract the required data from the company's database, or from external data sources;

(ii)   a management model - software facilitating the construction of models and permitting the modification thereof to depict individual scenarios;

(iii)   a communication subsystem (user interface) to enable the decision-maker to manipulate the model and extract data.

The decision-maker may also be considered as an essential component, as the interaction between the decision-maker and the DSS will provide original contributions.

7   AIRLINES, HOTELS, CAR SALES

(a)   **Airline reservation system**

(i)   Functions include:

- provision of information to potential customers on flight times, fares and availability, etc.
- making cargo reservations;
- maintaining passenger inventory and availability lists;
- maintaining passenger waiting lists, confirmation, cancellations, and no-show lists;
- keeping track of special requirements for diets, pets, wheelchairs etc;
- passenger check-in;
- ticket generation;
- preparing boarding manifests;
- cargo and passenger trim calculations;
- calculating optimum passenger routes;
- crew and maintenance scheduling;
- creation/maintenance of passenger profiles.

(ii)   Nature of the computer system:

- online real time;
- uses teleprocessing;
- applications largely at operational level;
- accesses own database;
- high capital costs;
- large computer configuration;
- backup essential.

Hotel management system

(i)   Functions include:

- reservation of rooms;
- guest reservation and check-out;
- rooms status;
- production of itemised customer invoices;
- maintenance of room inventory;
- food and drink stock inventory;
- day and night auditing;
- energy consumption regulation;
- videotext and electronic service provision;
- automated wake-up service;
- creation/maintenance of guest profiles;
- repair scheduling;
- rooms utilisation analyses;
- hotel facility bookings eg, tennis courts.

(ii)   Nature of the computer system:

- onsite office minicomputer with terminals for business applications;
- software package based;
- online realtime;
- links to national hotel reservation systems;
- applications mainly operational and control local database;
- low capital costs.

Car sale and repairs

(i)   Functions include:

- sales reports by salesperson;
- accounting reports;
- workshop repair and maintenance schedules;
- inventory control - vehicles;
- inventory control - parts;
- vehicle hire reports;
- sales analyses;
- customer preference analyses;
- preparation of loan agreements;
- warranty claim processing;
- vehicle leasing processing.

(ii)   Nature of the computer system:

- either bureau or onsite;
- online/batch input;
- small number of terminals;
- extensive package use;
- applications operational and control;
- local database;
- low capital costs;
- links to external database.

(b)   Benefits of these applications include:

(i)   customer service has improved and expanded;

(ii)   the level of efficiency has been raised; sales and office staff save both time and effort recording information necessary for operations and control;

(iii)   load and capacity potential has increased;

(iv)   information accuracy has increased, enhancing the firm's image and reducing losses due to errors;

(v)   query and interactive facilities provide the right information to the right person at the right time;

(vi)   management receives important information for planning, control and decision-making;

(vii)   business profits increase;

(vii)   information previously unavailable can now be generated within the required performance parameters.

8   COMPUTER-ASSISTED TECHNIQUES

Answer Plan

(a)   test data; parallel simulation; embedded audit module; data retrieval software; programme review or code anaylysis; programme comparison
(b)   early identification of flaws in coding, design or logic
(c)   ability to manipulate data, recalculate for 'what if?' questions; 3-D models; accessibility of model by users;
(d)   word processing; electronic mail; facsimile; teleconferencing; networking

Tutorial Note: Part (b) is looking for the use of structured walk throughs, not just a description of what one is. Note in Part (c) that you are required to cite reasons for the popularity of spreadsheets - therefore the question is looking for the advantages of using spreadsheets, not just a description of what one is.

(a)   **Computer-assisted techniques available to an auditor**

(i)   Test data: fictitious data is used to test the processing system; typically the ability of one or more application programmes to process data correctly, and to detect errors or irregularities will be tested.

(ii)   Parallel simulation: also known as the audit simulation model technique, simulates the processes which are performed by the organisation being audited. The simulation is accomplished by utilising the organisation's data and the auditor's own programme to produce a model of one or more of the application programmes used regularly. A comparison of these results against the results produced by the system being audited can then be made.

(iii)   Embedded audit module: this involves a programme segment or module being inserted into the typical processing cycle. It permits the monitoring and collection of data for auditing purposes; transactions entering the system are processed normally and at the same time are checked by the audit module.

(iv)   Data retrieval software: using generalised audit software (GAS) to extract or retrieve files from the organisation being audited.

(v)   Programme review or code analysis: this involves systematically examining the programme's source code to establish how the programme is executed.

(vi)   Programme comparison: this entails comparing two separate versions of the same programme, with the aim of identifying any changes in the programme and to ensure that control checks have functioned properly.

Other packages which auditors may utilise in specific situations are: flowcharting software; modelling packages; statistical analysis packages and those capable of generating random numbers.

(b)   **Structured walk throughs as a method of project control**

A structured walk through is a formalised review procedure adopted by some organisations. Their purpose is to identify errors or weaknesses at various stages of the system development, to ensure an accurate and comprehensive system. The walk through involves a review of the work of the developer by members of the project group or other appropriate individuals.

The developer arranges the walk through by selecting members and distributing pertinent review material in advance. The member should be apprised of their role, the objective of the walk through and have access to comparative specifications.

The review begins with the developer taking the group through the product in detail. Reviewers come prepared with comprehensive questions, and these are asked at this stage; this session is intended to identify errors, a list of which is collated and distributed to participants. The developer corrects the errors/weaknesses, and the participants are informed of the solution.

The review should be a non-threatening experience, where criticism is positively received; managers are typically not included at this stage.

Walk throughs should be conducted at various stages of the development cycle: a review of the computer system's functional requirements as stated in the specification can be conducted by a specification walk through. Design walk throughs, code walk throughs and test walk throughs should also be conducted.

The timing of walk throughs is important: they should be held sufficiently early in the cycle to avoid escalating problems, but far enough into the project to be worthwhile.

The completion of a successful walk through is often used as a condition of entry into the next development phase. Walk throughs also aid in the early identification of flaws in design, coding or logic; they are beneficial to the reviewers who learn about other aspects of the system and possibly acquire further technical knowledge; and they enhance communication among members of the review group.

(c)   **Spreadsheets**

Spreadsheets enable the user to create a model by means of a matrix of a large number of rows and columns, providing blank cells. The spreadsheet is typically used to manipulate numeric data, although the incorporation of text is possible, and simulate manual processes.

The application of a spreadsheet may be appropriate where repetitive calculations are being performed on different data sets; where the process involves a sequence of calculations such that the output from one calculation provides the input for the next; for the preparation of forecasts, and performing sensitivity analysis ('what if' scenarios).

The merit of the spreadsheet lies in the accessibility to the user of their spreadsheet model, their simplicity of format, and their ability to automatically perform recalculations.

The cells in the spreadsheet can be used to manipulate data. A cell can contain, for example, a fixed value, or a formula, linked to a variable. In the latter case a row of cells may, as an example, compute the sales revenue for a company over a five year period, using a formula based on a certain rate of growth of sales, a specific sales price etc. By altering any one of these variables (the contents of one cell) the figures contained on the spreadsheet can be recalculated automatically. Spreadsheets can also perform basic statistical analysis, though for complex analyses an application designed for this purpose is recommended.

The more recent spreadsheets enable three-dimensional models to be created, as well as graphical representation of the data. The most common spreadsheet packages are Lotus 1-2-3, Quattro Pro, Supercalc and Excel.

(d)   **Components of Office Automation**

Office automation encompasses the mechanisation of most information processing tasks carried out in an organisation.

The main components of an office automation system are:

(i)   Word processing: this is perhaps the most fundamental component. As more members of the organisation gain access to word processing, presentation of letters, reports etc can be improved. By introducing further elements, such as networking, shared access to files and printers becomes available.

(ii)   Electronic mail: enables the transfer of information electronically. This facility can be used in place of memos, to access other users within the organisation or dispersed worldwide, allows files to be sent as 'attachments', and permits this to be done in 'real time'. It is also possible to send the same message to many people while dispensing with the need for photocopying. It is quicker than producing memos/letters/sending files by internal mail etc, yet less intrusive than a telephone call, as messages can be accessed at the individual's convenience.

(iii)   Facsimile: this facility allows the transmission of exact copies of documents, and can be useful in sending documents and diagrams quickly, and for the verification of signatures.

(iv)   Teleconferencing: to facilitate presentations, meetings, discussions etc being conducted without the time element and inconvenience of travel.

(v)   Other pertinent advances in OAS are voice mail systems, image-processing systems and collaborative writing systems.

The increase in office automation has been brought about largely due to falling hardware prices, standard software and the interconnection of computers. Access to corporate databases is thus facilitated, as well as access to shared files, access to a variety of applications etc.

---

9   END USER COMPUTING

Answer Plan

(a)   (i)   FGL: do not require specialists; encourage users to develop applications themselves - avoids communication problems, less demands on programmers and analysts; system maintenance;
        (ii)   programmers productivity lagging behind advances in technology; user taking active role, analyst an advisory role; creating working model.
        (iii)   to deal with backlog of requests for new applications: user writes own applications, with IC providing assistance and support

(b)   inconsistent development resulting in unrelated technologies; potential problem areas: analyst's function; specification of requirements; stability and quality assurance; unrelated systems; access to corporate database

Tutorial Note: Note that the answer to Part (a) should focus on how each of the three components would achieve the two objectives specified. Avoid simply defining what they each mean. Also, note the two issues which are addressed in part (b).

(a)   (i)   **Fourth Generation Languages (4GLs)**

                Fourth generation systems, for example ORACLE, MANTIS, SQL, are based on the principle that development work may be better carried out by users rather than by programmers, and are often designed by users themselves, the more sophisticated ones in conjunction with programmers. By providing these tools which do not require specialists, development work can be accelerated, therefore reducing any applications backlog which typically exists. They also promote the efficient maintenance of existing systems, and encourage users to become involved in developing applications of their own. Fourth generation languages, sustaining the tendency of previous languages, ensure ease of system development takes precedence over the efficiency of machine performance.

                Designed to enable non-computing people to develop their own systems, 4GL - compared to third generation languages eg, COBOL - need fewer lines of code, are quick to write and maintaining them is easier. As they are designed to provide interaction between the user and the software, errors can be corrected as development of the application takes place.

There are several advantages to users of being in a position to develop their own systems: firstly, any communication problems between the developer and the user is avoided; also, as development is likely to be expeditious, the possibility that the requirements of the user may alter during the development period is reduced; finally, utilising this facility reduces the demand on the time of programmers and systems analysts which, in most organisations, is a scarce resource.

A 4GL should be easy to learn and use, have good written documentation as well as online help facilities, offer interactive use, be robust and be self-documenting.

(ii) **Prototyping**

Advances in computer technology have been very much focused on hardware developments and improving the efficiency of programmes. The productivity of programmers has not increased at a corresponding rate, which has aggravated the applications backlog. The situation has been exacerbated even more by the requirement to spend time on the maintenance of existing systems, much of which is due to inadequate systems analysis.

This route taken to remedy this situation has been to encourage user participation. Prototyping utilises the expertise of the user and the analyst to undertake the threefold task of analysis, design and implementation, with the user playing an active role in the design of the computer system, and the analyst taking an advisory role.

Prototyping involves the construction of a model of the proposed system using a 4GL. A working model is built by the analyst, which is used as a basis for discussion between the analyst and the user, with the aim of identifing improvements or changes that could be made. At this stage there is constant consultation, and ample opportunity to ensure the user and analyst are both aware of each other's comprehension of the problem. The outcome may be the decision to create a new prototype or to refine the current one.

The prototyping approach is useful in that it encourages the involvement of users and exposes them to useful computer experience as well as promoting the cooperation between user and analyst. It also enhances the fact-finding process, promotes improved analysis, and discovers flaws in the system.

This approach can however prove to be costly in terms of time and money. It may be unattractive to the controller of project funds, as the model may need creating several times, and may eventually be abandoned.

(iii) **Information Centres**

Information centres were first established to deal with the pressure from end-users requesting new applications, creating a backlog for information systems departments. The function of the information centre, first thought of by IBM, is to assist users to write their own applications. The IC provides the end-user with help on computing and technical problems, as well as general support.

The theory is that by making use of ICs, the information systems department are in a position to allocate their time to larger projects. Unfortunately, the IS department may be opposed to the concept, and management may not be inclined to establish an IC as it would be a project with cost-benefit difficulties. An IC also needs the support of senior management, which may be lacking; other problems which a potential IC project may typically encounter are the dilemma of who should control the IC, as well as the potential duplication of effort, unless the IC function is centralised.

(b) Computer hardware and software has, of recent years, become relatively less expensive, and the user has become more computer literate. To some extent this has resulted in computer systems being acquired by users without necessarily involving the information systems department, and without following standard IS procedures. The outcome in some organisations has been that the IS department remains central, and unrelated technologies exist peripherally.

There are distinct advantages to the growth of end-user computing, but several factors need consideration:

(i) the analyst's function: there is the risk that this function may be considered redundant. However, it should be borne in mind that while users may be in a position to develop their own systems, they will be less vigilant about exercising control procedures such as structured walk throughs. Also, implementing standards and policies to any level of consistency will be problematic.

(ii)   specification of requirements: lacking the experience of the analyst, end-users have difficulty preparing complete and accurate system requirement specifications.

(iii)   stability and quality assurance of the system: these may be compromised in the case of an end-user system.

(iv)   unrelated systems: with no development strategy, end-users may inadvertently duplicate an existing system; also many different types of hardware and software will be acquired.

(v)   access to corporate database: this could potentially be problematic, coping with requests from end-users for new information to be entered into the database, with a variety of end-users having different computer systems, and having disparate requirements of the system.

Recommended procedures for the organisation to follow would be:

(i)   establishing what is the total expenditure on information systems

(ii)   involving senior management in the identification of benefits afforded by proposed computer systems

(iii)   supporting isolated systems that have been successful

(iv)   advertising the systems which have not been successful, so that mistakes are not repeated

(v)   encouraging consistency and co-ordination

(vi)   where systems are outwith the main area of business activities, offering only minimal support

(v)   prioritising alternative IT investments

(vi)   establishing procedures which involve end-user departments in the planning process.

10   DISTRIBUTED DATA PROCESSING

Answer Plan

(a)   (i)   Centralisation: one set of files;economies of scale;staff shortages/turnover;ease of control. Decentralisation: local knowledge; speed of response; profit and costs awareness

        (ii)   IT strategy; standards; hardware/software; communications ; HRM; technical & auditing support

(b)   (i)   Increase due to technical progress, increased awareness; user-friendly; increased access to computers;
        (ii)   Emphasis on marketing of the IT dept; dispersal of IT personnel; information centre

Tutorial Note: In part (b) (i) you are being asked to identify reasons why end-user computing is increasing, not provide evidence that it is.Note that in part (b) (ii) you are required to focus on the organisation of the IT function.

(a)   (i)   Of late there has been a propensity to fragment large organisations into devolved business units. This autonomy has resulted in the decentralisation of information technology operations.

                 The justification for a decision to centralise or decentralise information technology may be as follows:

                 Centralisation:

                 •   there is a requirement for only one set of files: everyone in the organisation uses the same data, which is readily accessible in a standard format.

                 •   economies of scale: it may be advantageous to acquire one large computer, with greater processing capabilities, rather than several small computers. Centralisation of personnel may also remove unnecessary duplication of activity, and allow for regulation and control of analysis and programming functions. It is necessary, however, to balance the cost element against the benefits derived by users (which may be greater with decentralisation).

- staff shortages/turnover: centralisation mitigates the effect of both, so that individuals are less indispensable, and also they can be provided with greater scope in their working experience.

- ease of control: senior management is better placed to control operating functions, particularly when a standard reporting system is being utilised.

Decentralisation:

- local knowledge: computer personnel are favourably placed when they are close to the problem, and it is more likely that their solution will be fitting; when centralised staff are involved, local considerations may be overlooked, or their importance misjudged.

- speed of response: operational decisions can be made more expeditiously; line managers can respond more quickly to change as they are better placed to understand the local conditions and relevant factors.

- heightened awareness of profit and loss: with decentralisation of equipment and staff there may also be decentralisation of costs. senior managers and users will be more attentive to the costs associated with computing activities, as this will have a direct effect on the budgets and profitability of their department.

While centralisation promotes increased efficiency and control, decentralisation permits greater flexibility. Inherently, attempting to attain these two objectives creates a conflict.

In practice, new and improved technologies have diluted the merits of either structure; it may be most effective to have some aspects of the information system centralised, and others decentralised.

(ii)   Despite the trend towards decentralisation, experience indicates that some IT activities can be more easily accomplished centrally. These may include:

- devising an IT strategy for the group;
- initiating IT standards;
- procuring hardware and software;
- monitoring standards;
- supply of communications needs;
- human resource management;
- technical support;
- support for computer auditing.

(b)   (i)   The increase in end-user computing has occurred largely because of technological progress and a greater appreciation by the end-user of the application of computers.

Personal computers are customarily provided for managers, and workstations are often found in offices. When considering software, it has been determined that a userfriendly interface enhances the probability of the system meeting the approval of the user or management. Dissatisfaction has been caused due to the delay between making a request and the provision of information from the computer system; as a consequence, computer-based query languages have been developed which the user can use, and also applications which can be run from the user's personal computer or workstation (e.g. spreadsheets/databases).

Increasingly end-users are becoming responsible for the development of non-technical IT strategy, and are becoming ever more competent at utilising the computing facilities. This may be, for example, to obtain information from a corporate database.

(ii)   It is now necessary for the information technology function to adopt a marketing philosophy rather than a production mode of thinking. Significance is placed on perceiving the user as a customer, and of establishing the needs of the customer; on collaborating with the customer; emphasising customer service and marketing computer systems and services.

It is beneficial to foster a partnership between the IT practitioner and the user.

Increasingly more of the IT specialist's time will be spent with users, which produces a requirement for their attitude to be amended to a more user-friendly one. A large IT department may perceive a requirement for nonspecialist personnel.

End-user computing may also instigate the dispersal of IT personnel among other departments; in this event, control and communication should be maintained.

The IT function may respond to the increase in end-user computing by creating an information centre, which would, in essence, be a function within the IT department. Its purpose would be to encourage, train and support endusers.

11   CASE TOOLS

Answer Plan

(a)   organisations rarely use a specific methodology in practice , but adapt to suit. Aspects modelled: the functions; data relationships; timing characteristics; structure of the program

(b)   What a CASE tool is, and why it is needed

Tutorial Note: In part (a) the question requires you to indentify only those tools and techniques which are appropriate to a structured analysis and design approach for systems development. In part (b) be careful to explain both what a CASE tool is and why it is needed.

(a)   The structured systems analysis and design approach includes methodologies associated with the Yourdon consultancy. Included are methodologies published by DeMarco (1978) and Constantine (1978), and another termed STRADIS by Gane and Sarsen (1979) etc.. In practice, organisations rarely select a specific methodology and then comply verbatim with all the techniques and tools described therein.

Invariably, the adopted methodology will be adjusted to satisfy the requirements of the individual organisation, regarding both the tools used, and the methods adopted for using those tools.

When adopting the structured approach, four aspects of the system are modeled:

(i)   the functions: these are modelled by means of dataflow diagrams
(ii)   data relationships: these are modelled using entity relationship models
(iii)   timing characteristics: these are modelled by state transition diagrams
(iv)   the structure of the program(s): this is modelled by means of structure charts

To augment the detail available about the functional components of the system, two further tools should be used. They are the tools used for process specification (decision tables, decision trees and structured English) and the data dictionary, the latter providing details of each data item relevant to the system.

Techniques to ensure that the models of the system are accurate, complete and consistent, which might currently be in use by the department are:

(i)   ensuring that a clear distinction between logical and physical system views is made

(ii)   using various levels of data flow diagrams (DFDs): top-level DFDs illustrating the system in broad terms, with little detail, and low-level DFDs depicting each sub-system in greater detail and in isolation from the rest of the system

(iii)   normalisation, involving the structuring of data into ordered groups, and thus refining the entity relationship model

(iv)   coupling and cohesion, thus ensuring efficient models as depicted in structure charts

(v)   balancing, to confirm consistency across all models of the system

(vi)   structured walk throughs to identify flaws at an early stage

(b)   **What is a CASE tool?**

A CASE tool is a computer-aided software engineering development tool.

With the widespread adoption of structured analysis and design techniques has come the requirement to introduce different working routines; for example, the generation of paperwork; the requirement to keep specifications updated; the creation of monotonous tasks requiring thoroughness.

The introduction of software tools can enhance the efficiency and effectiveness of analysis and design activities, and moderate the effects of the different working practices described earlier.

The analysis and design stages of systems development lend themselves to computerization either by general purpose tools or by tools designed to relate to specific methodologies (e.g. Yourdon or SSADM).

One of the primary functions of the CASE tools is to effect the accurate, complete and consistent development of the various models upon which efficient systems analysis relies. It is important that the analyst has graphical representations to assist in explaining to the end-user the functions available with the new system.

Depending on the sophistication of the CASE tools adopted, the entire programming process can be entirely automated, to the point where the tools can at least partially translate the model into a working program.

Why is a CASE tool needed?

Typically the introduction of CASE tools into the information systems department can assist in new systems being development and maintained with greater efficiency. A CASE tool to support structured methods should:

(i)   be capable of supporting the particular method of systems development being used by the department

(ii)   be capable of producing good diagrams, by using a mouse

(iii)   have a central data dictionary, listing all the data elements relevant to the system

(iv)   be capable of assessing where changes would be beneficial, what those changes should be, and what would be the effect of such changes

(v)   facilitate access control, to prevent unauthorised access

(vi)   be capable of customisation, to meet the requirements specific to a department

(vii)   ensure completeness, consistency and that rules are adhered to

(viii)   be capable of producing prototypes so that the user can more easily ascertain what the new system will be like

(ix)   provide support for project teams.

12   SYSTEMS MODELLING TOOLS

(a)   The systems analyst makes use of modelling tools to:

(i)   focus on important system features;

(ii)   discuss changes and make corrections with minimum risk;

(iii)   check that the analyst has correctly interpreted user requirements and translated them in such a way that a new system can be designed and programmed.

Dataflow diagrams (DFD)

The most commonly used modelling tool.

It is concerned with identifying:

(i)   the functions the system is to perform, and the interaction between functions;

(ii)   the transformations that must be carried out on inputs to produce the required outputs;

(iii)   the processing the system must do, the source of its information and the recipient of its results.

Dataflow diagrams consist essentially of:

(i)   processes - shown by circles or bubbles, which represent the individual functions carried out by the system;

(ii)   flows - shown by curved, directed arrows, which connect the processes, and represent the information the processes requires or produces;

(iii)   data stores - shown by two parallel lines, which represent collections of data ie, files or databases;

(iv)   terminators, which show the external entities with which the system communicates.

The DFD is easy to understand, fits on to one page, and may be drawn by a computer.

For complex systems, the DFD will be structured into a series of levels, each progressively showing more detail of the system.

Because the dataflow diagram does not provide details about the major functional components of the system, two supporting tools are required, the data dictionary and the process specification.

Entity-relationship diagrams (ERD)

The dataflow diagram emphasises the funtions of a system, but provides little detail about data. The relationship between data stores may be so complex that it is necessary to portray them independently of the processing that will take place.

This is portrayed by the ERD, which has two major components:

(i)   entity types, shown as a rectangular box in the diagram, which represents a collection, or set, of objects;

(ii)   relationships, shown as diamond-shaped boxes, which represent the connections or associations between entities.

State transitions diagram (STD), or entity life history

A third aspect of systems is their time-dependent behaviour ie, the sequence in which data will be accessed, and functions will be performed. This may not be significant for many business systems, but may be crucial to online and realtime systems.

The STD has two components:

(i)   rectangles, which represent states that the system can be in:

(ii)   arrows, connecting states, which show the changes between one state and another; associated with each state change will be one or more conditions and actions.

(b) **A possible solution**

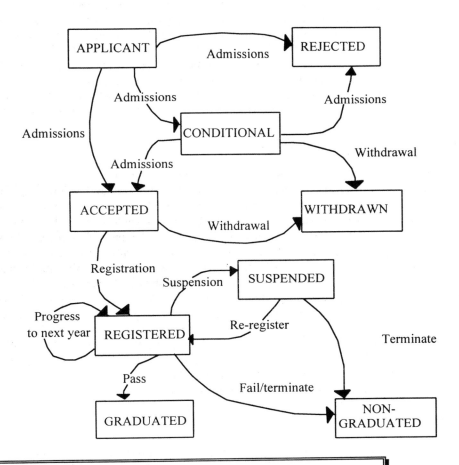

---

13   COMPUTERS

Answer Plan

(a)   **Transaction processing systems** - routine processing; for mechanisation of routine tasks; often involves the update of master file from transaction files unique to a particular application; only makes decisions based on pre-programmed rules; information available includes operational data, summaries and measures which monitor the system; serves operational management.

Management information systems - collects information used for management planning and control; used in any application requiring human management decision; can indicate decisions to manager; creates routine reports and exception reports, but can provide more detailed reports if requested; serve all levels of management, especially middle managements.

Decision support systems - used for semi-structured problems, enabling choices to be defined and evaluated; used when planning; requires interactive access to data; produces recommendations and evaluations of different courses of action; serve mainly senior management, but also anyone making strategic decisions.

Expert systems - used to provide specialist knowledge to decision makers; used when decisions requiring scarce expertise must be made; use a knowledge base and decision rules; information produced include decisions, recommendations and justifications; capable of making non-subjective decisions; used by senior management, specialists and non expert decision makers.

(a)   **Categories of Computer System**

The categories of computer system described below are not mutually exclusive, the edges between them are blurred and indistinct. Some specific applications may integrate two or more of the categories. Each type of system supports some aspects of managerial decision making. The most basic kind of system is the transaction processing system (TPS). This mechanises basic processes and is capable of simple choices. An example is an order processing system, where a discount might be given if the order satisfies the right criteria. A management information system (MIS) enables information (which may be output from a TPS) to be supplied to its users in a structured form. The format and timing of the information supplied must be appropriate to the person or persons receiving it. A decision support system (DSS) provides the ability to help managers to make *ad hoc* decisions from the information supplied to it. A DSS must be able to be changed as more is learned about the problem to be solved, whereas an MIS is more difficult to modify. This means that more initial effort and expertise must be put into the development of an MIS. An expert system enables a body of knowledge to be put into the computer, and can be consulted by non-experts when they need to access it.

(1)   **Transaction Processing Systems (TPS)**

Transaction processing systems involve the routine processing of everyday data and the mechanisation of routine tasks. These systems form the majority of applications. Although data and information are produced, the basic reason for these systems being produced is to save time and money by mechanising a particular process. Examples of such systems are order processing systems, payroll and inventory control. Different TPS may be linked together where appropriate (eg a sales order processing system, sales accounting, inventory control). The data requirements of a TPS are specific to the application, although the results of the system may be used to update a more general database. A traditional TPS would produce a transaction file which is used to update a master file, whereas an on-line TPS may update the master files as the transaction occurs. Only simple decisions which can be automated can be made via a TPS. The information produced by a TPS is mainly operational data used by the system itself, although summary reports are available for managers, and control statistics are needed to ensure that the system is operating according to plan. The organisational level served by a TPS is the level of management responsible for carrying out the operations that have been mechanised.

(2)   **Management Information Systems (MIS)**

Management information systems collect information that is used for management planning and control. They are used whenever there is a need for regular structured information, and are useful in any application that requires human management decisions. An examples of an MIS is a system that reports sales figures. The basic data would be an offshoot of a transaction processing system. The reports produced from the system are tailored to fit the needs of the recipients. Sales personnel would receive detailed sales figures for their territory by customer and by product, whereas sales managers receive information that is less detailed but would cover a wider geographical area, possibly including extra information (such as profit levels). Senior managers receive a basic summary of sales for all parts of the company. An MIS is not usually expected to make decisions itself, but can indicate where action needs to be taken. In the sales reporting system above, a special report can be produced showing all sales people that are not achieving their sales targets. Because this sort of report is only produced when it is relevant, it is known as an exception report. The databases that management information systems use can be accessed interactively by programmers, and some MIS include the facility for users to access the database via user-friendly fourth generation languages. The standard information produced by an MIS includes routine reports and exception reports, but more detailed special reports can be produced when required. An MIS will provide information to any decision-maker in the organisation, but are used most extensively by middle management.

(3)   **Decision Support Systems (DSS)**

Decision support systems are used to help solve semi-structured problems, enabling different courses of action to be evaluated and choices made. A DSS may well incorporate a series of operational research models, and use specialist sorts of software such as spreadsheets. This sort of software is used when planning and making strategic decisions. Since the DSS will often be used by a non-specialist user, it may require an interface that makes accessing the data easy, such as a data base management system or fourth generation language. The output from a DSS would include forecasts and projections of what will happen if certain actions are taken. A DSS may be able to take certain decisions itself (eg in production planning), but is generally used to enable managers to make their own decisions more easily and safely. A DSS is valuable to anybody needing to make strategic decisions, but is of most use to senior management.

(4) **Expert Systems**

An expert system is used to provide specialist knowledge or to recommend particular decisions. Each expert system incorporates information about a specific body of knowledge. To build an expert system, a knowledge base and an inference engine (the rules by which decisions are taken) are input to the computer by someone who is an expert in the subject being stored. Non-experts are then able to access the knowledge that has been stored. Expert systems are valuable whenever expertise is scarce. There is a very wide range of potential applications, but examples are: medical diagnosis, the law, training, customer enquiries in a sales office, selecting particular production methods, allowing credit etc. The data used by expert systems are knowledge bases and decision rules, sophisticated expert systems are being developed that use the results of past decisions to refine future decisions. Outputs not only include decisions or recommendations, but also the reasoning behind the decisions. Expert systems are capable of making decisions in any situation where an objective decision can be made. They are used by senior management, specialists who need access to very specific bodies of knowledge, and by non experts that must make decisions. An example of the latter is the allocation of credit cards to individuals.

(b) **Applications in a production control department**

(1) Transaction Processing: purchasing of materials; production and maintenance schedules per machine; picking lists; cost accounting; processing orders.

(2) Management Information Systems: production levels per machine; materials usage; analysis of wastage; plant utilisation; factory performance; quality control reports.

(3) Decision Support Systems: forecasting; production scheduling; performance analysis; simulation studies; selecting suppliers; optimisation studies.

(4) Expert Systems: diagnosing machine faults; selecting suitable materials for products; quality control procedures; training operatives; selecting personnel; workplace laws.

14   BATCH PROCESSING

Answer Plan

(a) **Likely reasons for deterioration:** staff changes; training; motivation; quality of supervision; volume of work; hardware - insufficiency, reduction in reliability, changes in configuration; software - changes in operating system or compiler, modification to other software; transaction data - increase in volume, change in type of data not considered when system was created; master file - file corruption, records not fully sorted.

(b) (i) **Statement of requirements:** details of system; volumes; response times; organisational details.

(ii) **Proposal information:** hardware/software recommendations; terms; maintenance; security; standby facilities; documentation; training; levels of service; supplier details.

(a) The answer outlined below includes only the preliminary part of the report, which outlines the areas that the accountant would have had to investigate. In the absence of extra information, no conclusions can be drawn.

To: Chief Accountant
From: Anna Countant
Subject: Performance of the Sales Accounting System

Introduction

I have been asked to investigate the significant deterioration in the performance of the Sales Accounting System. The volume of faults reported by the validation program has risen from 4% to 15% over a six month period, and the operations staff are finding it difficult to keep to the established operating schedule. I have outlined below in a preliminary report some of the reasons why this may be occurring, and I strongly urge that a more detailed study should be carried out as a matter of urgency.

The following areas have been identified as possible causes of the problems:

(1)   **Staff:** there would be a loss of expertise if there have been a lot of staff leaving or changing jobs. Poor supervision is likely to cause a fall off in performance. There may be a need to retrain either the staff preparing the input documents or the data preparation staff. The volume of work may have been increasing gradually until existing staff levels are unable to cope. There may have been a deterioration in staff motivation. A change in the measures by which staff are judged may be required.

(2)   **Hardware:** the hardware configuration may have changed over the period being considered. Machinery may be less reliable due to old age. The volume of work may have increased to a point where there is not enough hardware to cope.

(3)   **Software:** changes in the system software - operating system, compilers, utilities - may be having unforeseen side effects. The data validation routines may not be competent to deal with the changes in data requirements (eg longer product stock codes). Amendments to the software may not be working correctly, or may have caused data corruption problems (see point 5 below). Other systems may have been changed, which has affected the Sales Accounting System. Occasionally, in computer departments where software has been evolving over a number of years and documentation and programming practices are not good enough, there are so many modifications to existing software that 'spaghetti code' develops. Changes in one system may require file structures to be modified, causing other systems to fail.

(4)   **Transaction data:** the data may have been changing over time until the current software cannot cope, with data being 'squeezed' to fit in with the existing validation requirements. An example of this would be an increase in the number of digits required for product stock codes, or stock codes having to incorporate letters as well as numeric digits. Increases in the volume of transactions have been putting undue stress on the staff (see point 1 above).

(5)   **Master file data:** the master file may have become corrupt, or the records may no longer be in sorted order. This could have been caused by the implementation of software modifications that have not been properly tested (see point 3 above), or by physical problems on the storage media. The file structure may have been modified to fit the needs of other applications without the system under question being modified accordingly.

(b)   (i)   **Contents of Statement of Requirements**

The statement of requirements must be clear and unambiguous. The following sections must be incorporated within the statement:

(1)   **Details of the system being replaced:** information flows (dataflow diagrams); inputs; outputs; input and output documents; screen listings; processing cycles; processing stages; current and required performance levels; coding systems being used.

(2)   **Volumes of data:** in order to properly quote, the supplier would need to know current and future volumes. This would include: file sizes; the number of each category of transactions; the frequency and timing of data input; the number and type of reports required from the system.

(3)   **Response times:** the required response time for different work stations and for different categories of transaction; the number of workstations; communications requirements; security requirements; required interface with other systems; specification of benchmarks.

(4)   **Organisational details:** the type of business; the number of employees; the organisation structure of the relevant parts of the business; the number and location of different offices or establishments; organisational standards for computer applications (eg must follow British Standards for documentation); resources available within IS & DP; current hardware and software used; implementation plans and required date for system completion.

(5)   **Formalities:** closing date for receipt of tender; contact names; address to which tender should be sent; what information should be contained within the tender.

(ii)   **Suppliers Response**

The company would expect to see the following information within the tender:

(1)   **Hardware recommendations:** specifications, speeds and costs of all hardware supplied - processor(s), terminals, storage, cabling, telecommunications equipment. Alternatives considered may have the same information recorded against them, with the reasons for rejection.

(2)   **Software recommendations:** a full description of all software to be provided; comparative performance levels (benchmarks) should be recorded where they are available; the software recommendations should be directly related to the statement of requirements, with any requirements which could not be met being identified.

(3)   **Maintenance agreements:** hardware and software maintenance available; location of maintenance facilities (showing how it relates to the location of different offices); contractual agreements; costs.

(4)   **Contractual terms:** total costs; payment terms; discounts available; warranty agreements; initial training availability.

(5)   **Training:** training facilities available, costs, location, frequency of courses.

(6)   **After sales support:** the level of support that is guaranteed.

(7)   **Capacity and expansion capabilities**

(8)   **Documentation:** hardware and software manuals, training materials.

(9)   **Delivery proposals:** time of delivery (related to initial statement of requirements documents), with explanations if initial requirements cannot be met.

(10)   **Development, testing and implementation proposals**

(11)   **Company information:** size of firm; length of existence; history of firm (if relevant); business experience; number of clients; demonstration facilities; availability of third party references; maintenance and support facilities.

15   SUCCESSFUL CONVERSION

Answer Plan

(a)   Implementation: a vital process; should be planned and controlled carefully; system testing; file conversion; training programmes; direct changeover; parallel running; pilot running; phased changeover.

(b)   Prototyping: the building of a model system; uses 4GLs; enables better system definition; involves users with development process; identifies problems; may be higher cost; needs to be controlled.

(a)   **Implementation**

The final implementation of a new system is one of the most important parts of its development process. Problems in implementation may cause users to lose faith in a system, which is likely to lead to the system falling into disuse.

To make sure that a system is successfully implemented, the following stages must be followed:

(1)   **Planning the implementation:** the implementation of a system must be properly planned and controlled. To do this one or more people should be made responsible for its success. Ideally a group or committee of people should share responsibility, with representatives from the systems development team and the user department(s). A set timescale for each activity should be produced, with regular checkpoints and reviews to ensure that things are going to plan. A formal project planning system such as Critical Path Analysis may be adopted for complex projects.

(2)   **System testing:** individual programs will have been tested as they were completed, but a comprehensive test of the complete system is important. Users will lose faith in the system if there are any teething problems. Testing of the system should involve users as well as the systems analyst and programmers.

(3)   **File conversion:** data from the old system has to be converted into a form suitable for the new system. If the system being replaced is a manual one, the conversion process will involve manual data entry. This will place an increased workload onto existing staff, so temporary labour may need to be hired. An existing computer system can usually have data put into the new file structure by means of a program, but extra information may well need to be added. The conversion process will require data to be validated and/or verified before the new files can be accepted. There are likely to be logistical problems in file conversion, with new data constantly arriving, and it is often useful to delay file conversion until the last possible moment.

(4)   **Training:** users must be trained in how to use the system before it is implemented. The timing of the training is crucial - too early and they will forget how to use the system by the time it is implemented, too late and the system will not operate efficiently. The training program for each individual should be carefully designed, with a general education programme preceding specific training. Training materials (manuals, hand-outs, on-line help screens etc) should be available before the training program starts. File conversion is often a useful part of the training process.

(5)   **Changeover procedures:** there are various methods of changing over from the old system to the new, and the most appropriate method of changeover should be selected. **Direct changeover** is the complete replacement of the old system by the new on a given data. It is less expensive than the other methods, but is risky. If any system bugs or hardware faults have remained unidentified, then the result can be disastrous. **Parallel running** involves both old and new systems running side by side until everyone is confident that the new system will be a success. It is much less risky than direct changeover, but is more expensive. Temporary staff may be needed to cope with the extra workload. **Pilot running** is similar to parallel running although the timings are less crucial. Data for a period of time is run on the new system and results compared with the old system. This method of changeover will also require the use of extra staff to cope with the increased work. **Phased** changeover is carried out in segments. It may involve different logical parts of the system being implemented at different times, or it may involve different parts of the organisation implementing the system at different times. The penalties of hardware or software faults are reduced, and the implementation process can be streamlined as more is learned.

(b)   **Prototyping**

Prototyping means the production of a working model of a system. Working models are used in many areas of business, from the production of new cars to the training of pilots to fly expensive planes. The use of prototypes minimises the risks that the item being designed will not fit its needs. Computer prototypes are used to help users define their needs more easily and precisely. Prototypes of computer systems are often built using fourth generation languages (4GL), which enable software to be produced quicker than by using a traditional third generation language. The working model which is produced is demonstrated to the user, who will be able to understand how the final working system will operate. Using prototypes, the analyst and user can develop the computer system on a dynamic basis.

Three advantages of prototyping are described below:

- **The final design can be guaranteed to fit the user needs.**

  It is often very difficult for untrained users to visualise what the computer can do for them and define what they require. By having a series of concrete examples, it is easier to visualise what the computer can do for them and to define their needs fully and precisely.

- **Employees are more involved in the systems development process.**

  Because of the dynamic nature of the systems development process, employees working in the user department are fully involved in the development process. They are more likely to identify the system as being their system. This will make sure that the system is properly defined, and will reduce the likelihood of dysfunctional behaviour.

- **Identification of problems**

  Once a full system has been developed, it is very expensive to eradicate any bugs or difficulties that are introduced. The systems analyst can identify any problems or omissions and eliminate them. The analyst will also be able to make sure that the system is as user friendly as possible.

  There are some disadvantages with the use of prototypes. 4GLs are very hungry for computer processing resources and are often expensive to buy. It is possible for the development process to become sloppy and unstructured, which wastes money and resources and makes planning difficult. With suitable controls, many of these disadvantages can be overcome.

---

16   FEASIBILITY AND PROJECT PLANNING

(a)   **The feasibility study**

An investigation carried out to provide information in order to justify the use of a computer for a specific application. It is NOT a full-blown study, but is normally a vital part of the systems development life cycle, because of the potentially wider implications to the organisation.

It has the following objectives:

(i)   to decide whether the stated objectives are attainable;

(ii)   to define the major problems existing in the area under study;

(iii)   to assess the potential that exists for savings in money, staff and effort;

(iv)   to estimate the time required, and the cost of, a full investigation;

(v)   to develop and briefly examine outline alternative solutions;

(vi)   to identify any requirements for specialist staff;

(vii)   to produce a precise and straightforward report covering the aims of the study and recommending further actions.

The feasibility is concerned essentially with three aspects of the proposed new computer system:

(i)   Technical feasibility

        This addresses the question of whether the proposed system will perform to the required specification. The analyst must find out whether current computing resources are adequate to cope with the new system, whether they can be upgraded, or added to, and, if none of these are feasible, whether the technology exists to meet the specifications. The answer here is normally 'yes', and then the question becomes an economic one.

(ii)   Economic feasibility

        Covers the question of whether the benefits of the new system are greater than the costs involved. Both development costs (staff time, hardware and software, etc) and operational costs (maintenance, consumables etc) must be taken into account.

Both tangible ie, those for which a financial estimate can be made, and intangible benefits ie, those which cannot be quantified in finanical terms, must be considered.

(iii)   Operational feasibility

This is dependent upon determining human resources for the project and is concerned with predicting whether the system will operate and be used once it is installed.

If the users are strongly in favour of the current system, see no problems with it, and are generally not involved with the move towards a new system, then resistance will be strong and chances for success remote unless the analyst can successfully erode such resistance.

But if the users themselves have expressed their desire for a new system, perhaps because of falling efficiency and availability, then the chances that the new system will be successful are much higher.

Determining operational feasibility requires both creative imagination and persuasive powers on the part of the analyst.

Judging the feasibility of systems projects is never clear-cut, or an easy decision, nor is it a decision made by the analyst, but by management, based on feasibility data rapidly and expertly gathered and presented by the analyst.

(b)   **Project planning**

The development of a computer system involves many different types of activities that together make up a project, which must be carefully planned if it is to be successful.

Planning includes the activities required to select the project team, identification of the tasks which need to be performed, assignment of members of the team to those tasks, estimating the times required to complete tasks, and installing feedback procedures to enable progress to be measured.

A structured approach is useful in breaking the project down into analysis, design and implementation. Then breaking analysis down into fact-finding, data flows, proposal preparation; design into data entry, input/out and data design; and implementation into file conversion, training, testing, changeover and evaluation. Subsequently the analyst takes each of the above and decomposes them further. The final level of detail reached depends on the project, but all critical steps need to appear in the plans.

Usually, the most difficult part of project planning is the crucial step of estimating the time it will take to complete each task. Experience is the key factor here. Uncertainty can be reduced by projecting most likely, pessimistic and optimistic estimates, and then using a weighted average formula to determine the expected time a task, or activity, will take.

Two commonly used techniques for scheduling are:

(i)   Gantt charts

This is essentially a chart on which bars represent each activity, the length of the bar representing the relative length of the task. The main advantage of the Gantt chart is its simplicity - not only is it easy to use, but it also lends itself to communication with users. Another advantage is that the bars representing activities are drawn to scale.

(ii)   PERT (program evaluation and review technique) diagrams

A project is represented by a network of nodes and arrows, then evaluated to determine the critical activities, improve the schedule if necessary, and review/revise once the project is under way. PERT is useful when activities can be done in parallel rather than in sequence. The longest path through a PERT network is referred to as the critical path; this is the path which will cause the whole project to fall behind schedule if any delay is encountered on it. Unlike other paths, there is no leeway, or slack time.

As well as managing time and resources, the analyst must also manage people, this implies the ability to communicate both to the project team and to users, with the need to motivate both groups high on the list of priorities.

Productivity goals have to be set for team members which reflect both the nature of the activity and the ability and experience of the team member.

Motivation is also very important, and can be at least partially achieved by acceptable goal setting.

17   FINANCE FUNCTION

Answer Plan

(a)   Costs of Development: personnel costs; software and hardware; systems investigation; training; changeover methods; security; dysfunctional behaviour; maintenance; leases and licenses; help desk; control system.

Benefits from Development: reduced costs; increased speed and accuracy; better cashflow; improved customer service; communication; better information; opportunities for other systems.

(b)   Cost-Benefit Analysis Techniques: payback period; ROI; ROCE; IRR; NPV; risk analysis.

(a)   **Costs and Benefits**

(i)   **Costs of Development**

The costs associated with producing the system can be divided into three categories - the building of the system, its initial implementation, and ongoing running costs.

Building the system

- **Costs of personnel:** various people will have to be co-opted onto a project team. Each member of staff in the project team will have to dedicate time to the investigation. Their salary costs and expenses are a major part of the development costs. The project team will contain representatives of each interested group - sales management, one or more members of the sales force, marketing, the finance function, the sales office, the systems analyst, the person currently responsible for the entry of orders, etc. There will also be personnel costs of the people who will be developing the system - the analyst, programmers, operating staff, salesmen. A 'wastage' factor must be built into these costs to cover eventualities such as illness and holidays.

- **Extra personnel:** some people with expertise in the kind of system being adopted may need to be hired, or consultants used.

- **Software costs:** the computer programs to run the system will have to be acquired. Some software may be produced in house, and some may be purchased from outside. If software is purchased, it is likely to need tailoring to fit the precise needs of the organisation. Bought-in software must be licensed. Software requirements will include the order entry programs and communications software. The computer time on the existing machines that will be used for development will needs to be paid for.

- **Hardware costs:** a great deal of hardware will need to be acquired (purchased, leased or hired). This will include portable computers for the sales force, communications equipment, and possibly a mini-computer or large micro-computer to act as a front end processor, linking the sales order system to the main computer. Costs to be considered are not only the purchase prices of the machinery, but also the cost of financing the capital expenditure.

- **System investigation:** in order to define what is needed from the system in question, an investigation is needed. Information is gathered by the systems analysts using interviews, questionnaires and observation. Various documents will need to be printed, and the time of interviewees and interviewer will cost money.

Implementing the System

- **Printing costs:** various manuals, training materials and stationery required for the operation of the system will need to be printed.

- **Training:** both sales staff and operations staff must be trained in the operation of the system. The training costs and the cost of lost time for trainees must be included in a cost-benefit analysis.

- **Changeover costs:** the changeover from the old system may involve parallel running - where both old system and new run concurrently - until the system has been proven. This will lead to a temporary doubling of staff requirements. The system is not likely to be adopted for the whole company simultaneously, a safer way of implementation is to phase in a region or sales force at a time. This implies that the old system and the new will run together for some time.

- **Redundancy costs:** some existing staff may lose their jobs. They will need to be paid redundancy money, and facilities provided to help them get new jobs.

- **Security costs:** allowing external access to the company's computer system has many implications for security. Procedures will have to be set up to make sure that no unauthorised person can 'hack' into the machine.

- **Dysfunctional behaviour:** this is behaviour where employees work against the interests and objectives of the organisation because they are antagonistic to the new system. Procedures and schemes to encourage the sales force to be positive towards the new scheme must be adopted. Any such schemes are likely to cost money but are extremely important.

Ongoing Costs

- **Maintenance costs:** all hardware and software will need to be maintained. Typical external maintenance costs are 12% of the initial purchase price per annum. Because the system will be so vital to the success of the business, it is essential to ensure that any down time is minimised. In order to ensure that no sales person is without a machine, there will need to be 'redundant' machines available for immediate replacement of any that go wrong or are damaged by the rough treatment that they are likely to receive. Hardware must be replaced as it becomes worn out.

- **External running costs:** there is likely to be lease or rental costs for hardware and communications equipment. There may also be annual software license fees. Telephone costs will be incurred each time a sales person accesses the main computer system. Upgrades to hardware and software may be required as they become available.

- **Help desk:** because the sales force will be relatively unskilled at using computers, personnel should be available to answer queries and solve problems.

- **Control mechanisms:** systems must be in place to ensure that the sales orders are being processed correctly. Security must be tight to prevent unauthorised access. Access must be prevented not only from non employees but from people who leave the company after the system has been set up.

(ii)   **Benefits from Developing the System**

It is more difficult to quantify the likely benefits from a system than it is to quantify costs, but it is important to do so as accurately as possible. Benefit may be quantified by comparing the increase (or avoided decrease) in market share due to the new system.

The benefits are likely to include:

- **Reduced labour costs:** a complete series of processes, filling out order forms and sending them to head office, will be eliminated.

- **Increased accuracy:** because the sales person recording the sales will be familiar with the customer, there are likely to be less errors provided that the sales person has been properly trained.

- **Improved cash flow:** the process of recording sales is speeded up. This will mean that the money will be received quicker and the company's cash flow improved.

- **Better customer service:** the customer will receive goods quicker. On-line access to the main computer will avoid the taking of orders which cannot be satisfied because stock levels are too low. Customer satisfaction will be improved by the elimination of promises that cannot be kept being made.

- **On-line credit reference:** before a new customer is accepted, a credit reference must be available. A credit reference database can be accessed on line, and the customer order can be taken (or refused) without delay.

- **Improved communication:** other uses can be made of the portable computers. An electronic messaging system can be used to communicate with sales persons, and sales leads can be transmitted directly without delay.

- **Computerised customer record cards:** among the other systems that would be possible once the customer order system is adopted is a computerised record card system. This would record details of existing customers, potential customers and indirect customers (those supplied through distributors).

- **Improved information:** information would be available faster, which would improve the quality of decision making. Other information can be made available that would not be possible under the old system because of time factors. The sales person can be made aware, for example, of major traffic hold ups on his or her likely route.

(b)   Cost-Benefit Techniques

Once all costs and benefits have been evaluated, it is then possible to carry out a cost-benefit analysis that will assess if the investment in the new system is justified. A cash flow analysis will be prepared. Once it has been established that the project will yield a positive cash flow the project's payback can be examined and compared with that of competing projects. Some techniques for comparing paybacks are:

- **Payback period:** this measures the length of time that a project will take to break even. The shorter the payback period the better. This minimises the risks of unforeseen eventualities.

- **Return on Investment (ROI) and Return on Capital Employed (ROCE):** these evaluate the investment in terms of a percentage return per year. The calculation of these indices is fairly simple, and the investment with the higher percentage will be the preferred option.

- **Discounted cash flow:** inflation and the cost of borrowing mean that it is better to receive money now than in a years time. A technique that takes into account when money will be generated as well as how much is discounted cash flow. The value of an investment can be estimated using such measures as Internal Rate of Return (IRR), and Net Present Value (NPV). In order to evaluate these, it is necessary to know the cost of capital for the firm.

- **Risk analysis:** the returns from the system are not certain, there is a risk associated with each category of benefit. By assigning a probability to different levels of return, the accountant can calculate the expected value of the return.

18	HUMAN RESOURCES

Answer Plan

(a)   Factors affecting whether or not reduction in staffing costs can take place: management; application; usage of computer system; structure; level of slack ; capacity of computer system to aid strategic decision-making; effectiveness of the new system.

(b)   Managers underestimate the value of their HR; staff turnover; hiring & firing mentality; HR problems; recruiting good personnel; keeping them; getting correct mix, and maintaining it.

(c)   Personnel development programme; performance management; manpower planning

Tutorial Note: be careful to allocate your time correctly to each part of the question. Part (b) is shorter than part (c) but is worth more marks.

(a)   One of the prime incentives for transferring to a computer-based system was that costs could be significantly reduced. Savings were anticipated in staffing costs, as activities undertaken by people would be superceded by computer operations.

This premise may not necessarily be sound; the ability to achieve reductions in staffing costs is dependent on several factors, some of which are listed below:

(i)   the perspective of the relevant manager, and his position within the organisation;

(ii)   the attributes of the computer system. A computer application which facilitates the automation of a production line, for example, will impact significantly on staffing levels;

(iii)   the use to which the computer facilities are put. If the requirement for the formation of a computer installation emerges, this will require staffing;

(iv)   whether a centralised or decentralised structure is adopted. In general, centralisation results in lower staffing requirements than decentralisation;

(v)   the consequential generation of staffing requirements following the installation of a computer system; data preparation is one typical area where staffing levels may need to rise;

(vi)   the amount of slack present in the system to accommodate growth;

(vii)   the system may successfully provide information not previously available and facilitate analysis for strategic decision-making. This may result in new opportunities arising for the organisation;

(viii) the extent to which the new system may be considered effective in two respects: its operational efficiency and the extent to which user needs are met.

(b)   As advances in technology continue to be made, it is fundamentally important that the technological skills of the personnel in information systems are developed at the same rate. Nevertheless, many organisations overlook the value of effective human resources management; this is typically due to the fact that IS managers miscalculate the potential of this resource.

Staff turnover provides an expensive dilemma for the IS manager.

It is essential that IS personnel are kept fully conversant with new technology, and that the appropriate staff are selected to work with new technologies as they are instituted. But attempting to achieve this can in itself be self-defeating; as staff gain new technological knowledge, they may find that there is an attractive market for their skills outside their present workplace, or they may find that the introduction of new technology renders their skills incompatible with the functions they are being expected to perform. In either case, leaving their current job often ensues.

Computing personnel accept that their careers will be based within the computer industry, rather than within an organisation. Movement from organisation to organisation has become acceptable practice. IS managers acquiesce to this trend by adopting a policy of hiring and firing staff to overcome any staffing difficulties, rather than developing a human resource development strategy.

As a result of these practices, the area of human resource management within the information technology function experiences difficulties which other sections of the organisation would not endure. For example, the level of turnover of staff is higher than elsewhere in the organisation, which results in a lack of continuity; it is an arduous task maintaining a balanced mix of skills and, as the organisation develops, technological development is inhibited by the absence of in-depth user knowledge by IS personnel.

IS managers need to consider four key factors:

(i)   What methods to adopt to ensure recruiting "good" personnel? The attributes of a 'good' IS person is dependent on the requirements appertaining at the time.

(ii)   What methods to adopt to ensure retaining "good" personnel? If the conditions of employment are unsatisfactory, for example a lack of career development opportunities, or there is no evidence of long-term security, then good personnel will leave.

(iii)   How to achieve the correct balance of skills? The information systems within an organisation are ever changing and, therefore, the requisite mix of skills will also change; taking on new staff with the appropriate skills may only solve the problem in the short-term, but may produce difficulties in the future.

(iv)   How to maintain the correct balance of skills, once this has been accomplished?

It should be possible to achieve this by retaining staff once they possess valuable skills.
Satisfactory solutions to the potential problem areas described above should ensure that the majority of problems related to human resources within information systems will recede.

(c)   The environment for personnel within the IS department needs to be stable and effective, and this can be achieved by means of a two stage programme.

Initially the organisation will need to instigate a personnel development programme, which is concerned with staff recruitment, engagement and training. This may entail:

(i)   establishing IS processes
(ii)   in-depth job analysis - identifying what the job entails
(iii)   in-depth identification of skills required
(iv)   establishing minimum acceptable levels of performance
(v)   comparing these requirements with those currently possessed
(vi)   using the above results to identify training and recruitment requirements
(vii)   gauging performance
(viii) delineating career course
(ix)   identifying and producing apt rewards in terms of career advancement.

The second stage should involve the introduction of performance indicators, against which actual performance should be compared to establish an individual's level of achievement against an agreed acceptable level. This procedure should highlight training needs, and any difficulties at an early stage.

This process might entail:

(i)   establishing IS processes
(ii)   in-depth job analysis - identifying what the job entails
(iiii) the establishment of minimum acceptable levels of performance
(iv)   establishing means of measuring performance
(v)   carrying out regular surveys
(vi)   adjusting staffing accordingly

A personnel development programme should be conducted alongside a manpower planning programme. The latter may entail:

(i)   the preparation of an annual plan
(ii)   a listing of jobs and skills
(iii)   anticipated skills deficiencies
(iv)   monitoring of performance
(v)   arranging training and recruitment

In practice these programmes are rarely embarked upon by IS management.

19   MEASURING COSTS AND BENEFITS

Answer Plan

Part (a)   (i) Non-DCF methods: payback; return on investment. DCF methods: NPV, IRR.
            (ii) costs: building; installation; operational and maintenance. Benefits: tactical
                 and strategic
Part (b) prices higher than anticipated; benefits lower; scenarios.

Tutorial Note: Part (a) (i) of this question requires you to describe TWO cost-benefit methods. Your answer might therefore include ONE of the non-DCF methods referred to in the solution and ONE of the DCF methods.
Part (a) (ii) of this question is looking for the specific problems associated with measuring the costs and benefits, therefore avoid just describing what the costs are.
Part (b) is not looking for a description of how to undertake a risk analysis, but rather a discussion of what factors should be considered.

(a)   (i)   **Cost-benefit analysis techniques**

Techniques of cost-benefit analysis fall into two main categories: those which ignore the time value of money (TVM), and those which take into account the TVM. First, we will consider two techniques which do not take into account the TVM.

Payback period

This method measures the number of years taken by the project to recoup the initial investment. Obviously, the shorter the payback period (PP) the better. The PP is used frequently by companies because it is easy to apply and comprehend. Use of the PP does, however, have a number of drawbacks. The determination of the cut-off period is essentially an arbitrary decision. The PP ignores cash flows which occur outwith the cut-off date; it also ignores the timing of cash flows within the PP itself. As a result, viable projects may easily be rejected.

In its favour, the PP does allow for risk and uncertainty by attempting to recover the initial outlay in as short a period as possible.

Return on investment

Using this method, the benefits of the project are expressed as a return on investment in terms of a rate per year.

This technique assumes that the investment is repaid over its economic life in a straight-line way. As with the PP method, it is easy to apply and comprehend but it, too, does not take into account the time value of money. It does, however, provide a useful indicator; organisations obviously seek to invest scarce resources where they will derive the highest return.

Discounted cash flow (DCF) methods take into consideration the time value of money.

We will consider the two principal DCF methods of project appraisal: Net Present Value (NPV) and Internal Rate of Return (IRR).

Net Present Value

This method takes the discounted present value of the future cash flows generated by the project, less the initial outlay. If the NPV is equal to, or greater than, zero the project should be considered as it will at least attain the required rate of return; when greater than zero it will enhance the value of the firm. When using this method to compare projects the one with the largest NPV should be selected.

Internal Rate of Return

This method identifies the rate of return which produces an NPV of zero for the project. If the IRR of a project is greater than the firm's required rate of return (usually the cost of capital), it should proceed with the project.

(ii)   **Measurement of Costs**

Some categories of costs associated with a computer system can be quite precisely ascertained, while others are less easily defined. The main costs related to information systems are those of building the system, installation costs, and operational and maintenance costs.

The costs associated with building the system include staff costs (the average salaries for all levels of staff participating in the project; lost time due to sickness, holidays etc.; staff training where the use of new software or hardware is necessary, and travel expenses incurred when making associated trips to suppliers etc.)and computer-related costs (computer time incurred during system development, and any new equipment which may need to be bought). Many of these costs cannot be accurately defined, but can only be estimated.

The cost of installing the system, which may include recruitment and training, commissioning and installation, conversion of files, user training, parallel running or phased implementation etc., may be easier to quantify. Operating and maintenance costs, (usually contributing to as much as 70 per cent of the total cost of the system) would include the costs of financing the system, maintenance contracts etc. These costs are often predetermined, and therefore their measurement is less problematic.

Measurement of Benefits

Tactical benefits are those which enable the company to continue functioning in the same way, but at a lower level of costs, or with increased profits. These can be moderately straightforward to define, although the accuracy of any estimations will be determined by the effectiveness of the new system, and its ability to accomplish the required functions.

Strategic benefits are those which enable the company to enter new markets, either offering a new product/service or reaching new customers, or both. These are of fundamental importance, yet are so difficult to predict, or quantify.

The improved system will enable better use to be made of information, which should enhance decision-making and the productivity of managers. Monitoring and quantifying these could present difficulties.

The information system may help in attracting new customers and retaining existing ones; and it should improve stock and credit control. Again, attempts to quantify and classify these benefits may be problematic.

(b)   The majority of investments are exposed to at least some element of risk. Risk may be categorised as systematic (factors that affect all organisations) or unsystematic (events that affect one project).

Most managerial decisions involve an element of uncertainty, and are therefore subject to some level of risk. Identifying, and being able to quantify, the risk factor is of great consequence.

Management want to have their vulnerable assets identified, their security requirements outlined, and protective measures delineated. The costs of safeguarding against risks can then be balanced against the estimated costs which would be incurred if the event took place. The project may be affected by prices which are higher than anticipated. This may be caused by:

(i)   bankruptcy of hardware suppliers
(ii)   high turnover of staff on the project team
(iii)   technology not meeting expectations
(iv)   opportunity being lost
(v)   unforeseen problems with contractors, unions etc.
(vi)   inadequacies in the project team
(vii)   instability in the economic environment
(viii) unforeseen costs/overheads
(ix)   inadequate information from the users with regard to their needs of the system

The project may equally be affected by anticipated benefits which do not emerge:

(i)   the users may experience difficulties or apprehension in adopting the new system; delays or disruption may ensue as a result

(ii)   projected increases in the market share may not occur

(iii)   the system may not be capable of performing at the level estimated, resulting in lower productivity than predicted

(iv)   the benefits derived from the information being produced by the new system may not be discernible

Risk assessment often involves scenario-based methodologies, which may involve preparing three scenarios: worst case, best case, and expected case.

20   INVESTMENT OPPORTUNITY

Answer Plan

(a)   levels of expenditure on IT - advantages of higher levels of expenditure; suggest reasons for viewing as a future investment; discuss implications (management control of IT etc.) and the reality;

(b)   Responsibility accounting - factors to be considered; type of responsibility centre: service centre, cost centre, profit centre and hybrid centre. Basis for chargeout: service centre, cost centre, profit centre or hybrid centre; criteria to be satisfied.

Tutorial Note: This type of question requires the development of reasoned arguments. In (a), for example, having explained the proposition made, it is helpful to discuss the implications of treating IT as an investment rather than as an expense.

(a)   The level of expenditure on information technology varies among organisations, but is generally between 1 and 5 per cent of sales revenue, and rising.

The rate of growth of expenditure on IT is probably greater than of any other area of activity within the organisation.

Many organisations, particularly those spending proportionately larger amounts on IT, view IT as a means of gaining strategic ascendancy.

The benefits derived from low levels of expenditure on IT are disproportionately lower than the gain enjoyed by organisations making a significant investment in IT. Financial analysis supports this view, and suggests that higher IT expenditure can assist in the organisation attaining superior profitability in its sector. If we accept these views then IT, in many organisations, should be viewed as future investment rather than as current expenditure.

On this basis, management control of IT must be readjusted; this has repercussions on aspects such as funding issues; project appraisal; responsibility accounting and measurement of performance.

Of particular importance are the areas of:

(i)   project appraisal: correct techniques must be used to ensure that the best project is selected

(ii)   financial planning must occur, to guarantee that funds are available to fund the IT project

(iii)   as capital investment is a means of instituting strategies, strategic concerns require consideration

(iv)   once the investment decision has been taken, it is important to review the payoff on that investment via competent implementation and acceptable returns

(v)   IT expenses will need to be charged out using an alternative method.

Approaching IT expenditure as an investment, rather than an expense, has not been taken up extensively, although it is suggested that in theory there will be funds available for investing in financially rewarding IT projects.

In reality, the 'soft' rationing of capital occurs. This means that Head Office imposes constraints on the permitted level of IT expenditure; this may be to quell over-enthusiastic expenditure on IT, or to institute priorities across the organisation as a whole.

'Hard' rationing occurs where capital markets are imperfect, or where firms are in financial difficulty, or have problematic relationships with their investors. In these circumstances IT projects, as well as other capital projects, will be hampered due to insufficient funds.

If IT is recognised as an investment rather than an expense, it should be funded in the same way as other capital projects. Therefore, where capital rationing exists, cost-benefit analysis techniques should be utilised to ascertain which project(s) should be selected.

Other issues which necessitate consideration are:

(i)   self-financing applications. In these cases, the effect on cash flow in the short-term is the only funding concern.

(ii)   decentralisation, where IT investment decisions would be placed with users and devolved business units. Soft rationing may result.

(iii)   concern of senior management. Supporting numerous IT projects may cause apprehension within senior management that the IT function (an area where they may have little knowledge) may be mushrooming out of control.

(b)   This second proposition is embracing the theme of responsibility accounting - in this case, the relationship between the IT function and the remainder of the organisation.

Some factors which should be considered are:

(i)   whether the IT function should be run as a business within a business, and whether it should be managed as a profit centre

(ii)   should it be run as an investment centre?

(iii)   on what basis IT services should be charged out (eg, at market prices, or cost-based)?

(iv)   can the chargeout procedures aid user involvement, and avoid the requirement for specialist control?

(v)   the method for linking the chargeout procedures and IT accounting with the principle management control system.

Also to be considered is the type of responsibility centre which the IT function might become. The four main options are a service centre, a cost centre, a profit centre or a hybrid.

Service centre

In this case users do not receive cost allocations for resources used, but neither are they charged for IT usage. The emphasis is placed on non-financial rather than financial goals with regard to the use of IT, and IT is funded from sources other than revenue or cost recovery.

Cost centre

The costs of IT are charged to users, which means the users must be conscious of the costs they are incurring. In this case decisions to invest in IT may be influenced by cost benefit analysis, but IT projects may not necessarily be funded out of cost recovery.

Profit centre

Services provided by the IT function in this case are charged out at cost plus or market-based prices. In this situation, the IT function is subjected to market forces, and must be customer oriented; it is set up as a business venture and may be funded by capital injection, with an expected return on that investment.

Hybrid centre

In this case a mixture of the above is utilised; users may be charged for some services, while others may be part-funded centrally. The IT function faces clearly identified financial objectives.

The basis for chargeout may be cost-based, market price, dual method, or no price. Whichever mechanism is adopted, several criteria should be satisfied:

(i)   both parties understand the charging system, and can predict to some extent what the cost will be
(ii)   where performance is measured, this must be fair to both parties
(iii)   where consumption is reflected, this should be realistic
(iv)   it must accommodate the selected responsibility accounting system
(v)   the interests of the organisation should be accommodated
(vi)   the mechanism must avoid the creation of entire new units to be administered

21   PRODUCTIVITY, RELIABILITY, MAINTABILITY

Productivity

This is perhaps the most visible problem facing the system development team today. The problem has two apsects: the number of new systems that need to be developed (the backlog), and the length of time required to build a new system.

In most organisations there is a backlog of several years, with the backlog consisting of three different types of system:

(a)   visible backlog, consisting of new systems which have been approved and funded, but not started because of lack of resources;

(b)   invisible backlog, consisting of new systems which users know they want, but have not bothered to ask for officially, because of the length of the visible backlog;

(c)   unknown backlog, which will be identified as soon as concrete progress is made in backlog reduction.

The length of time required to build a system is of concern to users:

(a)   because often a new system is associated with a perceived business opportunity, which has a limited window, or time period, after which the opportunity is lost and the new system no longer required;

(b)   because they worry that by the time a new system is built, the business environment will have changed so drastically that the original requirements will no longer be valid.

A third reason for the productivity problem is the number of projects that are cancelled before they are finished, for various reasons, such as technical and managerial problems, inexperienced staff, lack of user involvement, inadequate systems analysis, etc.

Solutions to the productivity problem include:

(a)   hiring more programmers and analysts;
(b)   hiring more talented analysts and programmers and giving them better working conditions;
(c)   letting users develop their own systems;
(d)   better programming languages;
(e)   attacking the maintenance problem;
(f)   use of software engineering disciplines;
(g)   use of automated tools for systems development.

Many of these can be used together, because they involve complementary concepts and techniques. There is no dobut that, used selectively, and with care, these approaches can significantly alleviate the productivity problem.

Reliability

Low productivity plus the amount of time spent testing and debugging systems, might be acceptable if the end products were reliable and easily maintained systems. The evidence is that systems produced over the past 30 years are very far from error-free, and often almost impossible to change.

Software errors range from the trivial, where correct output is not formatted exactly as the user requires, through to situations such as where the system refuses to accept certain types of input, which the user can circumvent, to errors which cause the entire system to grind to a halt.

The number of errors in a system may never really be identified; after the system has been handed over, there will initially be few errors found, because users are feeling their way; as they gain confidence, the number of errors met will rise; only after considerable use will the system stabilise and the users find fewer and fewer bugs. By that time, however, the system is a patchwork quilt, with some areas the subject of numerous corrections; and those corrections in turn introducing other errors.

A final problem is the difficulty of resolving software errors; once an error is discovered, the analyst and/or programmer must identify the nature of the error and find out how to correct it. This is not easy to do!

Maintainability

Software maintenance is a major problem for most organisations; between a half and three-quarters of the work done in most systems development departments is associated with the revision, modification, conversion, enhancement or debugging of a computer system created some time earlier.

In many organisations, systems that were built a number of years ago simply cannot be modified to reflect a changing business environment; it is diffcult enough simply resolving errors!

The cost of replacing such monolithic systems is likely to be prohibitive, with the result that they continue to be used, and to deteriorate.

The problem is compounded by the frequent lack of reliable documentation describing both what the system is supposed to do, how it does it, and what amendements have been carried out over the years. It is essential that an accurate up-to-date model of every system exists - this is the responsibility of the systems analyst.

22	COMPUTER SECURITY

Answer Plan

(a) (i) Potential Threats
Threat   *Precaution*
Fire   detectors; gas flooding; training; inflammable materials;
                  backups elsewhere
Water   waterproofing, location,
Weather regular inspections; lightning conductors; anti-surge equipment;
Physical environment separate area; dust control units;
Access:Control:entrances, guards,conventional/cipher keys; card reader & lock,
voice/signature recognition
(ii) Contingency Plans: multiple DP
sites; reciprocal agreement;computer bureaux; empty/equipped rooms;relocatable
computer centres
(b) unauthorised access; unauthorised access with intent; unauthorised modification

Tutorial Note: Note the allocation of marks, section (a)(ii) carrying 40% of the marks for this question. Allocate your efforts appropriately. Also note that you are asked to address three specific points in each of (a)(i) and (a)(ii). In part (b) be sure to specify the permitted penalties as well as the three offences.

(a) (i) **Potential Physical Threats:**

Fire

Fire is perhaps the most serious physical threat to a computer system.

Precautionary measures would include the use of appropriate building materials and installation of fire doors; adequate detection; appropriate extinguishers; training of staff in the principles of fire safety, and adopting suitable fire prevention procedures; utilisation of fireproof safes; and implementing practices such as retaining back-ups of data in an alternative physical location.

Water

Water can also provide a serious threat. Damage from water can ensue after firefighting operations elsewhere in the building; as a result of burst pipes and from natural flooding.

Precautionary measures may include waterproofing ceilings and floors and adequate draining, and avoiding locating computer equipment near water pipes, or in basement - or even ground floor - accommodation.

Weather

The weather provides a persistent threat to buildings: rain, wind and storms all contributing to the damage, which may be caused by rain leaking through the roof, wind causing structural damage, and by lightning or electrical storms, causing electromagnetic interference.

Precautions may involve regularly inspecting the building, installing lightning conductors and fitting anti-surge equipment. Comprehensive protection against power surges or failure would include an uninterrupted and a stand-by power supply.

Physical Environment

Fluctuating temperatures, and excessive amounts of dust and static can also be harmful. Precautionary measures would include providing a stable temperature for the equipment and, where appropriate, computer equipment should be located in a separate area. Air conditioning, dust control units and antistatic carpeting may be necessary.

Access Control:

Entry Control

Protection against intruders will be facilitated if the number of entrances to the centre is kept to a minimum.

Receptionists and guards

Entry should be controlled by guards and/or receptionists, positioned at entrances. All members of staff and visitors should wear badges.

Conventional or Cipher Locks

Conventional keys may be appropriate in a small establishment with few employees, but in a larger organisation cipher locks (requiring a code to be entered on a key-pad) may be appropriate. Locks can be inconvenient if the doors are in regular use.

Card Reader and Lock

Using this system, entry can be controlled by the user requiring a card. There are also several systems available which allow automatic entry by means of badges worn by members of staff, or by voice or signature recognition.

(ii)   **Contingency Plans**

Purpose

A contingency plan is prepared so that the response to any potential disaster, such as the loss of part of the computer system, is managed.

As computing increasingly becomes an important element of a business, the effects of a breakdown of the computer system are potentially ever more damaging. Also, the computer system is increasingly exposed to the potential threat of "hackers" and the introduction of computer viruses.

For the duration of the downtime, losses can be expected to escalate; it is therefore essential that the time when the computer system is unavailable is kept to a minimum.

A number of standby plans may merit consideration; the final selection being dependent upon the estimated time that the concern would function adequately without computing facilities:

(i)   creation of multiple data processing facilities on separate sites, with the smallest site being capable of supporting the crucial work of at least one other site during the calculated recovery time. This strategy requires hardware and software compatibility and spare capacity. It is calculated that approximately only 20 per cent of computer usage is critical, so the volume selected for temporary transferral can be kept to a minimum

(ii)   reciprocal agreement with another company. Although a popular option, few companies can guarantee free capacity, or continuing capability, which attaches a high risk to this option

(iii)   a more expensive, but lower risk, version of the above is the commercial computer bureaux. This solution entails entering into a formal agreement which entitles the customer to a selection of services

(iv)   empty rooms, or equipped rooms. The former allows the organisation access to install a back-up system, which increases the recovery time but reduces the cost. The latter can be costly, so sharing this facility is a consideration

(v)   relocatable computer centres. This solution involves a delay while the facility is erected and assembled, and larger computers cannot usually be accommodated

(vi)   The effectiveness of the contingency plan is dependent on comprehensive back-up procedures for both data and software.

The appropriately detailed contingency plan must identify initial responses and clearly delineate responsibility at each stage of the exercise, from damage limitation through to full recovery.

The greater the effort invested in the preparation of a contingency plan, the more effectively the organisation will be able to mitigate the effects of a disaster.

(b)   **The Computer Misuse Act 1990**

Three offences were defined in this Act:

(i)   **Unauthorised access**

This offence makes it unlawful for any person to cause a computer to perform an operation without the consent of the computer user. For the offence to be committed the person has to knowingly attempt to gain unauthorised access to a computer system.

To establish that an offence has been committed, the prosecution needs to ascertain what operation was executed; what were the bounds of authority of the accused and whether the operation fell outwith these bounds; and whether the accused was aware of these limits.

It is sufficient to prove that an attempt was made to gain unlawful access; it is not necessary for the attempt to have been successful.

The penalties for this offence is a fine of up to £2,000 or imprisonment for up to six months, or both.

(ii)   **Unauthorised access with intent**

This offence covers the situation where a person gains unauthorised access with the intention of committing and then facilitating a further crime. The intention may be to commit blackmail, for example, having gained access to personal information, or theft by means of redirecting a transfer of funds.

The necessity is to establish the intent to commit a further crime; that the further crime was not committed, or even possible, is not a defence. This offence is more serious than the previous one, and therefore carries a heavier penalty. An imprisonment of up to five years and/or an unlimited fine can be imposed.

(iii)   **Unauthorised modification**

This offence is committed when the person knowingly causes an unauthorised modification to any computer, with the intention of vitiating its operation in some way. It is not necessary to establish that the accused knew which computer systems would be affected or in what way. This wide-reaching offence covers intentional modification or deletion of computer-held data, as well as the deliberate introduction of a computer virus into a system. This offence is viewed as being as serious as the second, with similar penalties.

23   CONTROL EVALUATION

Answer Plan

(a)   Disaster recovery: backups; contingency plan; standby scheme; manual fall back;

(b)   Environmental controls and physical security: precautionary measures against fire; water damage; storm damage; interruption of power supply; back-up for air-conditioning system; access control (entrances; to computer facilities); safe storage of data and programmes; password control; back-up facilities; support for hardware.

(c)   Input, output and file controls: to ensure data is timely, complete and secure.
(d)   Operations - regulating work of operators.

Tutorial Note: Be careful that you address both aspects of the question, namely describing the main objectives of each of the four procedures and suggesting areas for particular scrutiny.

(a)   **Disaster Recovery**

Main objective: to ensure that, in the event of a failure of any key element of the organisation (hardware/software/an application/personnel/power), crucial processing will proceed unimpeded.

Areas to be scrutinised:

(i)   Whether there exists a backup copy of the computer files, including programs, and also the run documents. These should be kept in a strongroom at a different, secure site.

(ii)   Whether the backups are sufficiently comprehensive to restore the situation should information be lost from the computer system.

(iii)   The contingency plan. This should be developed, tested and maintained to ensure the continuation of processing based on different scenarios.

(iv)   Whether there exists a standby scheme which provides replacement facilities. These would be used while the contingency plan is implemented to restore computing operations.

(v)   Whether there exists a manual fall back system to be implemented during short disruptions or during the early stages of a large disruption.

(vi)   Whether there exists a contingency plan associated with each application.

(vii)   Whether user departments have been involved in the devlopment and testing stages of the contingency plans.

(b)   **Environmental controls and physical security**

Main objective: to minimise the risk of losing data processing facilities.

Areas to be scrutinsed:

(i)   Whether there are appropriate precautionary measures against fire; these might include the use of appropriate building materials and installation of fire doors; adequate detection and appropriate extinguishers; fire drill which undergoes regular testing; training of staff in the principles of fire safety, adopting suitable fire prevention procedures; utilisation of fireproof safes etc

(ii)   Whether there are appropriate precautionary measures against the threat of damage from water. These may include waterproofing ceilings and floors and adequate draining, and avoiding locating computer equipment near water pipes, or in basement - or even ground floor - accommodation.

(iii)   Whether the risk from storm damage has been evaluated and whether appropriate precautions have been taken (regularly inspecting the building; lightning conductors etc.)

(iv)   Are appropriate measures in place to deal with an interruption in the power supply (eg, a stand-by generator; batteries; uninterrupted power supplies)? This ensures that computers, air-conditioning etc. continue to function in the event of a mains failure. The back-up power supply should be activated automatically, and tested regularly).

(v)   The existence of adequate backup for the air-conditioning system.

(vi)   The existence of access control at all entrances (which should be kept to a minimum), and at the outer perimeter.

(vii)   Is access to the computer facilities limited to only those who need it?

(viii)   Are data and programmes stored safely to guard against unauthorised access?

(ix)   Is an adequate system of password control being applied to guard against teminals being used by unauthorised persons?

(x)   The existence of back-up facilities for the computer system, and whether any arrangements reached with a third party have been recorded.

(xi)   Whether there is adequate support for hardware, in the event of equipment failing, to ensure an internal processing capability.

(c)   **Input, output and file controls**

Main objective: to ensure that data, both received and distributed, is accurate, timely, complete and secure; to preserve the integrity of all media where files are stored, and safeguard the media from unauthorised modifications.

Areas to be scrutinised:

(i)   Is the group responsible for input/output separated from other responsibilities?
(ii)   Are job handling procedures prescribed?
(iii)   Does the scheduling of computer processing come under the responsibility of the control section?
(iv)   Do cut-off dates receive adquate attention?
(v)   Are controls enforced over the submission of data to and issuing of data from the computer system?
(vi)   Are there strict controls in place to restrict access to the file storage library?
(vii)   Is the environment where the file storage library is located satisfactorily controlled?
(viii)   Are files of a confidential nature stored in a secure location?
(ix)   Is the distribution of tapes and discs strictly regulated?

(d)   **Operations**

Main objective: to regulate the work of operators to ensure that productive computer time is optimised, to minimise the risk of mistakes and fraud, eradicate unauthorised operations and to ensure the confidentiality of information.

Areas to be scrutinised

(i)   Are programmers permitted to operate the computer?

(ii)   Are operators permitted to work single-handedly?

(iii)   In the event of an application failing, is the operator permitted to restart the program without the intervention of a supervisor?

(iv)   Are procedures prescribed for controlling the handling of the console log?

(v)   Is the database administrator distinct from the operators?

(vi)   Are tapes and discs strictly controlled?

(vii)   Are the running of sensitive programmes confined to normal working hours, and performed under tight scutiny?

(viii)   Are precautions taken to prevent disks from being overwritten unintentionally?

(ix)   Do instructions exist for the running of each application; are they reviewed and amended on a regular basis, and are they observed by operators.

24   DATA PROCESSING

(a)   **Data validation**

Techniques include:

(i)   visual checks;
(ii)   data verification;
(iii)   test for missing data;
(iv)   test for correct field length;
(v)   test for class or format;
(vi)   test for range or reasonableness;
(vii)   test for invalid values;
(viii)   test for comparison with stored data;
(ix)   check digit validation;
(x)   use of hash totals;
(xi)   sequence checks;
(xii)   transactions counts;
(xiii)   batch controls.

(b)   **Computer-based auditing techniques**

Where the auditor is faced with either a complex computer system, or one where the volumes are high, it is only sensible to utilise the power of the computer to carry out much of the checking involved in audit work. There are various methods by which this may be achieved:

(i)   Standard utility programs

These are essentially report generators, enabling the average user to access files to generate specified reports, and thus check data accuracy. As the program is a utility, there will be no doubt that it will run on the users machine; and because the users are making use of it, there will be some expertise available. Its use will not cost the auditor anything, and is less likely to be regarded with suspicion by the users.

(ii)   Computer audit programs

These perform essentially the same functions as the utility program, but have been purpose-built for the task for auditing. As such, they may offer a wider range of facilities and enable more complex calculations to be carried out.

(iii)   Test packs

The purpose of a test pack (a set of data), is to ensure that a program is working correctly; they are less used than audit programs because of problems relating to protability, secure storage of data, data entry difficulties, testing programs further down the program suite, and the effect on the files which will be accessed and probably updated, (probably requiring the construction of dummy files).

Other more advanced techniques are also available to the auditor; they are less commonly used and require greater machine and programming knowledge. They include:

(i)   computer program examination;
(ii)   use of file dumps;
(iii)   snapshop technique (known also as tagging and tracing, and audit hooks);
(iv)   integrated test facility.

25   FOOD WHOLESALER

Answer Plan

(a)   Administrative controls: efficient day to day running; control of staff; control of data; security.

Systems development controls: satisfactory standards for all stages of system design; steering committee; project committees; structured design; standard documentation; performance indicators.
Processing controls: ensure complete and accurate processing of data; verification; validation; distribution of outputs.

(b)   Computer assisted audit techniques: to ensure systems do what they are supposed to; to check data processed accurately; to identify fraud; data retrieval; simulation; embedded routines; test data; program review and comparison; statistical analysis.

(a)   **Controls Within the Computer Department**

(1)   **Administrative Controls**

The objectives of administrative controls are to ensure that there is an acceptable level of efficiency and discipline in the day to day running of the department. The word 'acceptable' would be defined to fit a measurable set of objectives for a specific computer department.

The following routines would be used to ensure departmental efficiency:

- A clear demarcation between the roles of the different groups of staff within the department. Each staff member would have a formally defined and agreed job description.

- An organisation chart, with everybody in the department having access to the information summarised on the chart.

- Clear lines of communication between different people within the department. There should be regular formal meetings as well as informal relationships.

- Document flow should follow strict guidelines, with the relevant staff receiving the documents in time for them to be able to adhere to the given timetables.

- Access to financial and other secure information should be restricted only to those people authorised to see it.

- There should be rules for the physical security of the computer installations, with back up procedures in the event of problems.

- A member of maintenance staff should be on duty or on call (with a bleeper) at all times. Other staff members could be on call as appropriate (operations management, systems management etc).

- Physical access to restricted areas (such as the computer room) should be kept to authorised personnel, with entry being controlled by an electronic locking system.

- Fire regulations should be strictly followed.

- Security back ups of data and program files should be kept in a separate and secure location.

- Staff members should not be allowed to have unsupervised access to information that can be amended to their advantage (salaries, expenses, attendance logs).

- Regular job rotation will ensure that members of the department can operate efficiently and can develop their careers within the organisation.

- There should be a minimum of two operators on duty at any one time. One operator should be designated as shift leader on each shift.

- There should be a rotation of operations duties.

- The relevant operations documentation should be available at all times, with operating procedures and standards being followed rigorously (documentation should be amended if a change is required).

- All operator interventions should be noted on a log.

- The librarian should keep strict control over access to and modification of data files.

- Specific user groups should be designated as the owners of specific sets of data, and modification of data should only be made by them or with reference to them.

- The database administrator should centrally control access and amendment to the data dictionary and to the central database.

- Screens displaying secure data should be shielded to prevent electronic eavesdropping from outside the building.

- Data being transmitted over public communications network should be encrypted to protect against industrial espionage. Procedures should be in place that can identify where data has been altered (by line interference or by hackers) during transmission.

- Standby procedures should be available in case of breakdown, with the ability to reconstruct data files.

- Security procedures should be set up. User numbers and passwords would be used to prevent or restrict access. Terminal 'handshake' procedures would identify special terminals that could access certain applications. Physical security could prevent unauthorised access to those terminals.

- Passwords should be regularly changed. They should be memorable to a user, but difficult for someone to guess. A secure procedure should allow a particular user to find out his or her password when it been forgotten. If a password is written down, it should be kept in a secure location.

- Terminal and system usage should be logged. This can be used to allocate costs or to identify suspicious changes in usage patterns. There are computer algorithms that can identify automatically when usage patterns change suspiciously - they are currently used to identify credit card fraud.

(2)   **Systems Development Controls**

These are designed to ensure that there is a satisfactory standard at each level of the systems development process, including the analysis of needs, design of the system, project management, program specification, program writing, program testing, system testing, system implementation and documentation. Methods of ensuring good quality are:

- A steering committee could be used to help allocate priorities for system developments. This would also be responsible for defining and enforcing systems development controls.

- A structured methodology such as SSADM could be followed in analysing, designing and developing a system.

- Specific projects would be carried out for individual project teams, which would be managed by a project management committee.

- A project time-schedule would be set up, with control deadlines being overseen by the project management committee.

- Members of the department would be encouraged to build relationships with the users of systems, and should encourage users to become aware of the facilities that the computer makes available.

- Each program would be thoroughly tested, with a test log showing what conditions have been tested and what the result of the test was.

- The completed system would be comprehensively tested, with a test log being kept as above.

- Documentation would be created according to one of the published sets of standards (the relevant British Standard, the National Computer Council standard). Documentation should show what action should be taken in any eventuality (all types of errors should be foreseen and recovery procedures designed).

- Performance indicators should be built into the system, and a procedure designed for correcting any situation where the system is not meeting its objectives.

- All modifications to the system should be designed and documented to the same standard as the original. All original documentation should be updated to take account of the modifications.

(3)   **Processing Controls**

The purpose of processing controls is to ensure that all data used by a system is accurately and completely processed from point of origin and that all data files are accurately maintained and updated.

Each application would have its own appropriate set of control procedures. A batch system would use different control procedures than an on-line system. Control procedures include:

- Checks that the initial documents are correctly completed.

- Verification, which will check that data has been correctly entered. An on-line system will display the data on a screen and ask the user to verify that it is correct before it is stored. A batch system may require data to be entered twice.

- Batch totals will ensure that all data has been entered, and that it has been entered correctly. If the total being computed is meaningless (such as the sum of different account numbers), it is called a hash total.

- Batch listings are produced. These can be manually checked against source documents.

- Data can be validated (checked by the computer). Different techniques are used - check digits, reasonableness, existence, format etc.

- Redundant data can be entered into the system. If the price per unit and number of units sold are entered, then it should be unnecessary to also enter the total cost, but this is sometimes used as a cross-check that the first two items have been entered correctly.

- Audit trails may be used to ensure that files are updated correctly, and that they can be reconstructed in the event of system failure.

- A log of runs on a particular system can be used to identify problems when they have occurred.

- Procedural controls are set up so that it can be ensured that output reports are complete, accurate and distributed appropriately.

(b)   **Computerised Audits**

The auditor should be able to objectively show whether the system is doing what is required of it, whether data has been accurately and completely processed, and when computer fraud has occurred.

Software that is useful for auditors includes:

(1)   **Data retrieval software:** this is used to extract data from files, and to prepare reports. These reports can be compared with the original data and processes that have been carried out since the last audit.

(2)   **Parallel simulation:** the auditor's own code is used to duplicate the results from the system being audited.

(3)   **Embedded audit routine:** auditing procedures are included within the original program routines. They may produce an audit trail of transactions for later analysis, or may be used to display the procedures that are in operation within the program.

(4)   **Test data:** this is often used by the auditor to ensure that the program is producing the results that are expected.

(5)   **Program review:** programs exist that will build structure diagrams from the original code. This will allow the auditor to make sure that the program performs according to its specifications, and that no undocumented modification has occurred. Programs also exist which can 'decompile' compiled programs into source code.

(6)   **Program comparison:** this involves the automatic comparison of two versions of the same program to show where unauthorised or undocumented changes have been made.

(7)   **Debug programs:** these can show a dump of what is happening in the memory of the computer as the program is being run.

(8)   **Statistical analysis and consistency analysis software.**

26   INTERNATIONAL INVESTMENT SERVICES LTD (IIS)

(a)   The term **real-time system** is used to describe a system that has to react rapidly to input as and when it occurs and then generate appropriate output. The actual time scale will vary according to the application; so, for example, a computerised system controlling a chemical process may need to react to temperature and pressure changes within fractions of a second. In IIS's circumstances, an effective system would need to capture information from the financial institutions and process it at least as quickly as its competitors so that IIS's staff have the very latest information to act upon.

Some aspects of decision making in the areas of investment and financial management can be automated so that, for example, the sale or purchase of stocks and shares is automatically triggered by specific circumstances such as a particular rise or fall in the share price or a share index. Substantial and significant changes in the financial markets often happen very quickly and are often exaggerated by these sorts of automated decisions - so it is important that IIS have a system which can react without significant delay in these circumstances.

The main features of a system designed to support IIS's real-time processing needs are:

•   suitable communications links. The data from the financial institutions can be transmitted via the telephone system and, since the link will need to be permanently in place during trading hours, they should be high-speed leased lines which are solely used by IIS

•   high-specification computer systems with a high-speed processor, or possibly several processors operating in parallel, and fast-access, large-capacity storage in the form of magnetic disks or some of the emerging optical-disk technology

- back-up and security facilities which can be provided by a second system on 'hot standby' or by using a distributed processing system which has sufficient spare capacity to cope if one part of it fails. Uninterruptible and back-up power supply equipment should also be used

- multiple access for users, possibly with each user having a high-performance workstation which allows information to be processed quickly and shown clearly using graphical displays.

(b)   The purpose of an expert system is to provide specialist advice in order to emulate the analytical and choice processes undertaken by human decision makers. In order to do so, it needs to incorporate a knowledge base and choice criteria.

An expert system combines:

- a database of information about a specific topic

- a set of rules for dealing with particular sets of circumstances

- a user interface which allows the user to interrogate the system and receive the resultant output, which will usually be either a recommended course of action or the system actually taking responsibility for making the decision.

The development of expert systems draws upon the research into artificial intelligence (AI) systems which seek to simulate human activity and decision making. The increasing power of modern computer hardware has led to more rapid progress in the field of AI than has been the case in preceding years, but it is only now that AI is being harnessed in commercial applications and then in fairly narrow areas. Typical areas are:

- in the setting up and operation of credit control systems

- legal systems, such as English case law, where vast amounts of data need to be searched and analysed before relevant cases can be identified

- financial markets, where Frank Heinman, IIS's Senior Investment Executive, has identified potential applications.

The main features of an expert system to handle data from the financial markets which could be of benefit to ISS are:

- the ability actually to make decisions in some situations, thus allowing IIS to reduce staffing levels or free experienced staff for less routine activities

- speed of reaction, which is improving as the power of hardware increases. Speed of reaction is important to IIS as a delay of only a few seconds can see factors like share prices change radically

- consistent reactions to situations where different humans may vary in their decisions

- the fact that they do not suffer many of the adverse reactions to pressure situations that humans experience.

However, IIS need to be aware of some drawbacks with expert systems:

- The quality of programmed decision making relies on the quality of the information fed to the system and the programming itself. A human may be aware of additional facts which have not been included in the expert system and often these facts are not directly related to the markets - for example, the effects of strife between governments can trigger a chain of events which a computerised system could not be expected to handle.

- Many successful financial decisions are made on the basis of a human's 'gut feeling' which cannot be replicated by an automated procedure.

- IIS may become totally reliant on the system, which means IIS must take great care over security and backup facilities.

- Human supervision of the decision making of an expert system is still needed but, in the long term, the availability of expertise based on years of experience will become scarce.

(c)   Structured Systems Analysis and Design Methodology (SSADM) is a systems development methodology which concentrates on the early stages of the life cycle of a system's development. Initial versions were developed in the 1970s and it is the preferred methodology for UK government work.

It is highly structured in that there are six main stages, each broken down into steps which are further decomposed into tasks. It requires the use of graphical representations of three aspects of the analysis and design of a system:

- Processes are modelled using data flow diagrams (DFD) which can be broken down into different levels to show more detail; this is called functional decomposition.

- Entity-relationship models (ERM) are used to show the data items that are of most interest in the system and the relationships between them.

- The events which can occur in the system are modelled by entity life histories (ELH).

Each of the stages of SSADM produces products which become the starting point for the next stage. A typical version of SSADM has the following stages:

Stage 1:   analysis of current requirements and problems to enable the boundary of the system to be defined, to identify the data that will form the basis of the new system, and to allow users and developers to build up an understanding of the system and of each other's working practices

Stage 2:   the requirements specification stage, where the logical requirements of the new system are defined and outlines produced of the business systems which could satisfy that design

Stage 3:   production of an outline of hardware and software for a suitable system and consideration of the technical, operational and economic feasibility of various options before recommending one option to continue with

Stage 4:   logical data design, concentrating on what is required rather than how it will be achieved

Stage 5:   logical process design, expanding on the required processes identified at stage 2

Stage 6:   physical design, where the outputs of Stages 4 and 5 are combined and a specification of a new computer-based system is produced.

An important aspect of SSADM is the separation of logical and physical design - so that by considering logical design first, the users and developers can establish the requirements without being constrained by preconceived ideas about the physical system.

John Kline, the Information System Director, is aware that users have expressed dissatisfaction with the information systems staff and the systems and support that they provide. A common failing of many systems is that they fail to satisfy users' requirements and this is often caused by a lack of mutual understanding and communication between users and information systems specialists. This can lead to the users feeling that the specialists do not understand their business requirements and are reluctant to demystify the terminology and working practices to make them more accessible to non-specialists. In turn, the information systems specialists feel that users do not understand the complexity of computerised systems, not do they appreciate the difficulty of modifying systems to suit the users' changing needs. Another factor to take into account is, in systems theory terms, the entropy that can arise because each functional department or sub-system has its own objectives which may conflict with those of other sub-systems and may not be fully aligned to the overall systems high-level goals.

The more traditional or 'hard' systems approach to the development of computerised information systems borrowed from the existing methodologies used for engineering projects. These projects were usually aimed at producing a physical system whose requirements and objectives could be clearly defined and stated. The development would proceed through several sequential stages and progress could be monitored against well-defined criteria. Thus, once a basic requirements specification had been obtained, the systems developers could carry on through the stages and present the users with the completed system.

Advocates of 'soft' systems methodologies, such as Checkland's SSM, claim that there are many situations which are fuzzy and ill-structured, particularly human-activity systems, which need a different approach - this is not aimed specifically at information systems development but many computerised information systems are to be used in contexts where the soft systems approach could apply. The soft systems approach concentrates on getting the users fully involved in the development and accepts that different people involved with the system will have different attitudes, requirements and perceptions of the system. It is important to realise that all the people involved with the system, the stakeholders, should be included in a series of iterations to develop a rich picture of the system which can be adapted at each iteration until agreement is reached that the envisaged system is most appropriate to the situation.

John Kline can try to instil greater understanding between the systems developers and the users by involving the users more heavily in the early stages of development and encouraging them to regard the development activities as presenting shared problems which need to be approached by users and technical specialists in partnership. Modern development tools are becoming more sophisticated and, in many instances, less technical in nature so the non-specialist can more readily use them and understand how they work. So it may be possible for users to do most of the development work on small-scale systems with specialists acting as advisors; for larger systems the users can still play a major role, particularly in specifying requirements, producing test plans, etc. The information systems staff at IIS should remember that their department provides a support service for the organisation's primary activities, and that any satisfactory system must take account of the needs, views and attitudes of all staff involved with it.

IIS can continue to use SSADM as their development methodology but adopt some of the attitudes of the soft systems and build up a development team from all the people involved with the system. This may involve users in having training in development techniques and management will need to accept the importance of user involvement and make allowances for the time and effort needed to allow users to contribute effectively.

(d)

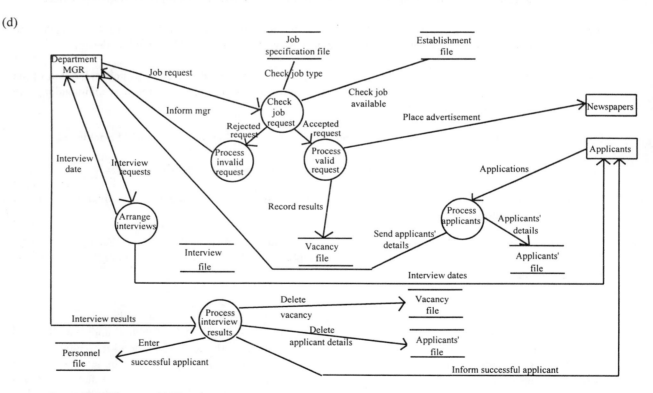

Data flow diagram (DFD)

(e)   Prototyping is the process of building a working model of part or all of the envisaged system early in the systems development life cycle. The model provides a test of design ideas and allows users and developers to see a tangible example of what the end-results could look like. Users and developers can discuss the features of the prototype and the development becomes a dynamic process as they can discuss enhancements and developments from the evidence provided by the prototype. Compared with the completed system it will be relatively inexpensive to make changes to the prototype, which is gradually refined until users are satisfied that it will meet their requirements.

Using a prototyping approach has other benefits in that it provides an initial focus for the development project, can give users valuable computing experience and encourage teamwork between the users and developers - although analysts and designers may be reluctant to share or relinquish their role as experts.

There are some problems associated with prototyping:

- project planning and costing can be difficult because of the constant modification and discussion of the prototype

- users may get a false impression of the ease and speed with which the final system can be produced

- inefficiencies and shortcomings may be acceptable in a prototype but there is the risk that they will; not be properly rectified, particularly if there is a lot of pressure to get the system delivered quickly or at reduced cost

- documentation is difficult to keep up to date if the system is constantly changing.

The use of a prototype could appeal to John Kline and ISS because, as well as the general benefits mentioned:

- user-friendly prototyping tools such as fourth generation languages (4GLs) and screen generators help to speed up development and it seems that IIS need a system quickly if they are to remain competitive

- the final system is more likely to satisfy users' requirements - which is something the users have been dissatisfied with previously

- it will provide the opportunity to build up teamwork and help to reduce the gap between users and the information systems department.

The investment appraisal system is a form of expert system and the prototyping approach could be used by starting with a prototype of an aspect of the expert system, such as the user interface, the report generation facilities or the 'inference engine' which performs the analysis and applies the programmed rules to the given situation. Work could proceed on all three aspects in parallel with prototypes of the different aspects being combined as they become available.

Graphical user interfaces (GUI) are becoming increasingly popular for many applications. Many GUIs are based on the 'WIMP' components of windows, icons, mouse and pull-down menus, which are claimed to offer a much easier-to-use method of interacting with a computer system. They provide an interface which is more intuitive for non-specialists and remove the reliance on keyboard skill once the user has mastered the art of manipulating the mouse or similar device. GUIs require more processing power and disk capacity than traditional command line interfaces, but the technological improvements of recent years have led to computers which are sufficiently powerful to support GUIs and sufficiently inexpensive to make them available to most commercial computer users.

For many applications, such as word processing, spreadsheets and computer-aided design, the use of GUIs is claimed to have greatly increased user productivity. However, IIS should select a style of user interface which is most appropriate to the application itself, an investment appraisal system, and to the users of the application, who are likely to be experienced financial analysts.

As well as a GUI, alternative styles of user interface are:

- menus

- command line - where the user types commands at the keyboard

- screens laid out in a format similar to paper forms and documents

- query languages, which often use a subset of ordinary language but in a well-defined, structured form

- screen dialogues, where the system presents the user with a series of questions to which the user responds.

It may be that two or more alternative forms of interface would be appropriate for IIS's system. For example, expert users who will spend a lot of their working hours using this application could become more efficient using a command line or a query language, since they will get to know the particular commands and will become familiar with abbreviations and short cuts using special keys. For novice users or staff who use the application less frequently, perhaps a screen dialogue style of interface will be more appropriate, since it can help to lead the user through the application by selecting the relevant questions without confusing or distracting the user with unnecessary details until they are required. A third option could be the use of a screen format reflecting the layout of IIS's existing documents, which could be an effective style of interface for staff who have a lot of routine operations to perform on the system.

27   BETTER BLOCKS LTD

(a)   The term 'end-user computer' refers to the use and control of computerised information systems by the system's users rather than by information systems specialists. More organisations are able to adopt a policy of end-user computing because:

- Computer hardware is becoming smaller, cheaper, more powerful and more suitable for operation in the physical environment of an ordinary office.

- More powerful hardware, particularly in the form of personal computer systems, enables the software developers to incorporate sophisticated techniques into the human-computer interface and into mass-produced applications which allow them to be more easily used and more readily adapted by non-computer specialists.

- Users are becoming more aware of the use of computer systems and more adept at using them.

- There has been a backlog in the development of applications software and many users have been dissatisfied with the applications developed for them by information systems specialists.

- Computer communications systems, in the form of both local and wide area networks (LAN and WAN), allow users to share some data whilst still being able to work independently without necessarily affecting other users of the system.

The main benefits claimed for end-user computing include:

- increased productivity
- better response times (since users can access data directly)
- better information, since users can access and adapt data to suit their requirements.

These benefits come about because:

- Users are able to access and work on data directly without the need for the intervention of information systems specialists and other personnel such as data entry staff. This is particularly the case with modern user-friendly software packages.

- End-user computing allows users to develop their own small-scale applications and also to become more actively involved in the development of larger-scale applications. Thus, the end result of a development is more likely to satisfy the users' actual requirements.

- Users feel more sense of ownership of, and commitment to, a system or application which leads to more positive attitudes to the system and a better understanding of its purpose and operation.

If Better Blocks introduce end-user computing in their local sales offices then the staff at these offices could:

- use wordprocessors and desk-top publishing packages for letters and marketing materials
- analyse sales forecasts and budgets using spreadsheets
- analyse data about customers and products using databases
- prepare presentations to customers using presentation graphics packages
- use other packages for work planning and diary systems.

However, there will still be a need for centralisation of some data (such as customer accounts) so, as well as computer facilities in the local offices, there are benefits in connecting all the local offices to the central mainframe so that up-to-date customer account information is accessible from the local offices.

Bill Keane has noticed that the managers of the local sales offices are purchasing computer equipment but trying to hide the nature of the equipment from the central purchasing system. This would indicate that at least some of the staff are keen to use computerised systems but also highlights the problem that end-user computing requires careful planning and control. If it is not carefully controlled then there are dangers, such as:

- duplication of effort
- neglected opportunities for sharing data
- lack of standards in hardware and software leading to incompatibilities
- under-utilisation of resources and uncontrolled expenses which do not prove cost-effective
- risks of unauthorised access to data
- risks of loss of data and ineffective backup procedures.

In addition to these dangers, Janet Carlton will need to consider the general problems associated with changing staff working practices, particularly if the policy involves the sales offices compulsorily adopting end-user computing in a wide range of their activities.

Janet Carlton should initiate a feasibility study to look in detail at the options and carry out a cost-benefit analysis, although estimating and quantifying the costs and benefits may be difficult.

(b)   The justification for the current policy, advocated by George Carlton, is that centralisation allows tighter control of the organisation's data and cost-effective use of staff's specialist skills. However, the continuing efforts of many computer hardware and software developers are towards more compact but easier-to-use systems which reduce the need for specialist skills. So the justification that data entry is best carried out centrally by trained, full-time data entry staff carries less weight.

The main benefit to Better Blocks of decentralisation of the data entry of delivery notes and other basic transaction data is that it will allow data to enter the system much more quickly, which should in turn speed up customer invoicing. This should then improve the cash flow and credit control, and provide much better information about customers for the sales staff to act upon.

Currently all computerised data processing is carried out using the mainframe as a batch processing system. This allows for:

- careful control over the data entry with the opportunity for data verification and validation
- control of access to the system during critical update and backup procedures
- spreading of the loading on the system by carrying out some processing outside of office hours
- ideal opportunities for backup at the beginning and end of a batch run.

Janet Carlton's idea of decentralisation of data entry entails the costs of providing the builders' merchants, quarries and local sales offices with computer equipment such as terminals, and communications equipment such as modems to allow them access to the central system. Staff will have to be trained and new procedures devised.

However, the logical extension of Janet's idea is that these same facilities will provide for other activities such as enquiries and reporting from the data held centrally, as well as other possibilities such as electronic mail. This goes beyond Janet's original ideas but highlights the need to take a high-level view of information systems and not concentrate on single applications in isolation.

A major consideration will be whether the existing batch processing is still appropriate or whether on-line processing should be used to allow Better Blocks to capitalise on having up-to-date information more readily available in most areas of the organisation. If on-line processing is chosen then the factors to be considered include the following:

- Can the existing software be adapted for on-line use or will new software be required?

- If new software is required, can it be purchased off-the-shelf or will Better Blocks need to become involved in a software development project?

- Will the increased workload on the system mean that new hardware is required; to be effective, on-line processing facilities will need to be available during normal office hours?

- What sorts of security features will be required to guard against unauthorised access - and will additional backup procedures be required if the computer systems become a more essential part of the information system?

Compared with batch processing, on-line processing makes some operations more difficult, such as:

- checking that data entry and processing are carried out properly
- controlling access to the system and data
- taking backups
- spreading the loading on the system.

However, there are advantages to on-line processing, such as:

- reduced staffing costs as specialist data-entry staff are not required
- cash flow and credit control can be improved
- there may be other, less tangible benefits, such as improved image and better customer relations.

(c)   Better Blocks currently have a functional, hierarchical organisation structure: each department is responsible for carrying out a particular set or related functions. This allows staff who are doing similar activities to be grouped together within levels in each department as is felt necessary to identify sub-functions. The further down the hierarchy a staff member is, the narrower their responsibilities are and the lower their status is. The organisation's primary activities relate to producing the raw materials (the Quarries function) and selling, either through the builders' merchants or direct to construction companies (the Sales function). The other three departments provide support functions to enable Better Blocks to carry out its primary functions.

This is a traditional structure found in many organisations but, in systems theory terms, it may be prone to entropy if the various sub-systems (the departments) are not appropriately linked or if the goals of the sub-systems become incompatible with the overall system's goals. Feedback may be delayed, resulting in poor monitoring and control of activities. For example, the Sales sub-system may be aware of large orders being placed - but there may be no simple mechanism for alerting the Quarries sub-system in order that appropriate changes to output schedules can be made in time to satisfy the increased demand.

In order to reduce the entropy, thereby making Better Blocks more likely to achieve its overall objectives, some changes to the organisation structure will be required. Instead of grouping staff according to the actual activities they normally carry out, it may be more effective to group some of them in line with the organisation's primary activities, irrespective of the actual tasks each staff member carries out. This would result in a structure which more resembles a matrix.

Matrix structures are typified by organisations that group staff according to a particular organisational objective - so, in a manufacturing organisation, the objectives are the making and selling of products. Therefore staff groups may be regarded as teams rather than departments: a team has responsibility for a particular product line, carrying out manufacturing, selling, accounting and providing information relating to that product line.

If Better Blocks adopt Janet Carlton's ideas for end-user computing at the sales offices and for decentralisation of much of the data entry work, then some of the work on support activities will be best handled by staff at the sales offices, and also at the quarries and builders' merchants if they are included in the decentralisation. There will be less work for the Finance and Administration staff, since tasks such as typing, data entry and producing reports can be carried out away from the central building in Leeds. Similarly, end-user computing at the local sales offices will entail support and development work being taken away from the central building, which will reduce the need for information systems specialists in the Information Systems department. This should mean that Better Blocks can reduce their staff at their central office but that more staff will be needed to work at the sales offices, builders' merchants and quarries. For example, instead of grouping primarily sales staff at the sales offices, the staff will form a team with more diverse activities that will include data entry, word processing and the other tasks that have been decentralised. In effect, Better Blocks should develop a hybrid structure combining elements of both hierarchy and matrix. This may lead to an overall reduction in staffing levels throughout Better Blocks.

There will still be the need for central staff to operate and manage the central mainframe system but many organisations that have adopted end-user computing have also set up an information centre to help users and to control and co-ordinate users' computing activities. Some of these staff may be allocated to support one or more sites and may spend only a little time at the central building.

(d)   The information technology and systems to assist retail operations like Better Blocks builders' merchants have been available since the 1970s and are still evolving. Many organisations are now dependent on information technology. The three main applications are:

Electronic Point Of Sale (EPOS)

These systems involve having data about each product encoded in some way on the product - typically using a bar code. The codes are read with a scanner which may be fixed in the sales checkout or hand-held. The scanner, or bar code reader, transmits the code to a computerised till that checks the details of the product and can display them in human-readable form, either on a visual display unit (VDU) or on a printout. The till automatically adds up the price of goods and generates a till receipt for the customer.

The EPOS system could be linked to a stock control system so that quantities of goods in and out are automatically fed into the stock control system, which provides up-to-date information about stock levels and can be processed to give useful information about sales trends. Better Blocks could consider setting up a central warehouse for some goods with electronic links to the builders' merchants so that information about sales and stock requirements can be processed centrally. This should allow Better Blocks to take advantage of bulk buying and fewer but larger deliveries from suppliers to the central warehouse. This would bring under Better Blocks' control the distribution of products from the central warehouse and allow reduction of stockholding at the builders' merchants. Better Blocks would have better information about current stock levels and requirements, thereby reducing problems with stock-outs and unnecessarily high stock levels. It may enable them to hold a wider range of stock and lead to an improvement in customers' perceptions of the organisation.

Electronic Funds Transfer (EFT)

An electronic funds transfer system is fed with the details of a customer's purchases. It reads the customer's bank details (usually from a swipe card) and, using electronic communication links, passes details of the transaction to both the customer's and the retailer's bank accounts. This speeds up the transfer, reduces the retailer's paperwork and gives customers an easier payment method than traditional cheques or credit cards.

EFT and EPOS systems can be combined so that the amount of manual work involved in making a sale is considerably reduced and, if properly managed, they reduce the risk of data entry errors.

Electronic Data Interchange (EDI)

EDI is a general term used to describe the many ways that organisations can exchange information electronically - so EFT, EPOS and electronic mail systems are all forms of EDI. However, it is often used to describe the use of the electronic systems to ease communication between, for example, a supplier and its customers. If Better Blocks have regular customers and/or suppliers then there is the possibility of using EDI to transmit purchase orders, invoices, etc. To use EDI both the sending and receiving organisations must have compatible data processing systems; this has slowed down the adoption of EDI. Better Blocks should investigate the possibilities of using EDI before settling on a system, since it may be very difficult to incorporate EDI once a system is in place.

At its builders' merchants, Better Blocks could use an integrated system combining EPOS, EFT and stock control to maximise the amount of useful and up-to-date information that is available and to allow data to pass automatically between the systems. In addition, EDI could be established as Better Blocks' preferred method of carrying out transactions with external organisations.

(e)   Better Blocks currently uses traditional methods and structures with its centralised support departments and extensive use of manual methods. It seems that the organisation could greatly benefit from better use of modern computerised information systems and may actually be dependent on their introduction for its survival. The ideas that Janet Carlton and Bill Keane are interested in would involve a major systems development.

Many major developments cause dissatisfaction when the completed system is actually delivered and put into use. The main criticisms are that systems are over-budget and overdue and do not satisfy users' requirements. It has been acknowledged that increased user involvement can help to reduce these problems by ensuring that the developers and users have a clearer picture of each other's requirements, so that the system more closely matches user expectations and the reasons for delays and additional expense are better understood. In Better Blocks' case the dangers are particularly relevant, as the majority of staff do not use computer systems in the normal course of their duties, or they use them in a very traditional setting.

The benefits of user involvement are:

- The final system is more likely to satisfy the users' actual requirements, since users have the opportunity to explore their requirements and the ways that the system can be built to suit them.

- Users are more committed to the success and effective use of the system if they have been part of the development and feel a sense of ownership.

- Users have the opportunity to gain knowledge and insight into the system and can make better use of it when it is operational.

The traditional systems development methodologies can be considered 'hard' systems methodologies, based upon tools and techniques used in development projects where the end result can be clearly stated and defined and agreed; an example is the introduction of a new production line in a manufacturing plant. However, computerised information systems are often introduced into 'fuzzy', people-based situations where different users have different requirements and views of what should be achieved and how to achieve it. This has led to the adoption of some of the ideas of 'soft systems methodologies' (SSMs) such as Checkland's SSM. These acknowledge that in many situations it may be difficult to specify actual requirements and that the best approach is for developers and users to work together to look at the complete situation from all points of view and reach agreement on requirements through a series of consultations and suggested solutions. This will be particularly important in Better Blocks' situation if a comprehensive information system is introduced, since it will affect almost all the staff's working practices.

Tools and techniques which can be used by Better Blocks to encourage user involvement include:

- Fourth-generation languages (4GL) and development tools, which are designed to enable systems to be developed without the need for highly specialised programming techniques and languages. 4GLs enable users and systems analysts to develop systems designs together.

- Prototyping - a technique where a working model of some or all of a system is produced quickly and early in the development. Users gain a better understanding of what the system will be like, so they can suggest changes early in the development which can be implemented much more easily than after the full system is delivered. Prototyping often takes the form of using screen generation facilities to rapidly produce data entry and output screens whose suitability can be discussed by users without their having to acquire expert knowledge of the system's inner workings. This would be very useful, since much of Better Blocks' system will be based on data entry and output screens for a variety of purposes.

- Query languages enable users to satisfy their own small-scale requirements or use a system in a more flexible way.

The increasing power and sophistication of modern computer systems allow the use of computerised development tools to carry out many of the low-level tasks of systems development and enable users and developers to concentrate on the higher-level or more overt features of the system. Better Blocks' management need to be aware that there are large benefits to be gained from a suitable computerised system. They should be prepared to set up a steering committee and allocate some of their own staff to work closely with the developers.

28   JOHNSONS SPECIALIST BOOKS LTD

(a)   Probably the two most obvious techniques used for assessing the economic feasibility of computer-based projects are initial costs, payback period and net present value (NPV) using discounted cash flows (DCF). These measures can be calculated but Johnsons will also have to consider some overall objectives. Is the aim to minimise investment or maximise profit? How cautious should Johnsons be? Is the system necessary for the organisation's survival regardless of its cost?

We have been told that this system (Option A) was selected because of its lower initial costs compared with the other options. This may be an overwhelming consideration if the initial cost of other options exceeds Johnsons' capability for expenditure. However, it may mean that potentially more profitable options are rejected.

To calculate payback and net present value further calculations are required, as shown in the following table. The top section of the table shows the five years' data given in the feasibility study report. For each year the quantified costs and benefits are shown and the net cash flow calculated. From this the cumulative cash flow is calculated.

The lower section shows the discounted cash flows (DCF) which are used to calculate the net present value (NPV) of the system. These take the time value of a cash flow into account. The NPV of a future cash flow is calculated by discounting it, using a suitable discount factor. In this case the figure is 12%, which Johnsons take to be the cost of capital. Note that cash flows are assumed to occur at the end of the year in which they are listed.

Johnsons Specialist Books Ltd
Discounted cash flow analysis for proposed new computer system - Option A

End of year	1	2	3	4	5
Costs	93	37	37	37	37
Benefits	23	89	64	52	42
Net cash flow	-70	52	27	15	5
Cumulative net cash flow	-70	-18	9	24	29
* Discount factor	0.89	0.80	0.71	0.64	0.57
Discounted cash flow	-63	41	19	10	3
Cumulative discounted cash flow	-63	-21	-2	8	11

Cost of capital = 12.00%. All figures in £'000.

* The discount factor shown is $\left(\dfrac{1}{1+0.12}\right)^n$ where n is the year.

From this table we can calculate the payback period. This is the time it will take for the system to pay for itself in terms of recouping the initial investment. The shorter the payback period, the more favourably the system is regarded. The cumulative net cash flow figures show that the system starts to generate a profit in Year 3. A reasonable estimate would be that the payback period is 2 years and 8 months. However, this does not take into account the time value of future cash flows. If we look at the cumulative discounted cash flow figures we see that it is not until Year 4 that the system shows a profit. A reasonable estimate would be that the payback period is 3 years and 3 months.

It is usually sensible to use a discounted cash flow figure, since this calculation will take some account of the time value of money. However, the method assumes that the discount factor remains constant for the span of the analysis, which is unlikely actually to be the case. For a system of this sort a two- or, three-year payback may be considered reasonable and it is relatively easy to compare the payback period of several options. A major drawback of using the payback period as a measure in isolation is that it ignores the pattern of cash flows - a system may be slow to recoup the initial investment but show large potential profits in the long run.

The same table can be used to show the **net present value (NPV)** of the system. In this case the NPV of the system over five years is £11,000, which would probably not be considered very favourable. However, it should be remembered that the figures are only estimates - the costs and, particularly, the benefits, of these sorts of comprehensive computer system can be difficult to predict.

A further consideration is whether a five-year analysis is appropriate for a system of this sort. Whilst it may be reasonable to plan to replace the system in five years' time, the future costs and benefits become increasingly difficult to estimate with any confidence. For example, requirements can change and lead to high maintenance costs if the system is modified to keep it in line with requirements. Taking more than a five-year timescale is probably not reasonable and, even within the five-year analysis, it may be better to look not just at the final figures but also at the pattern of cash flows. For example, it may be possible to determine when the anticipated annual profit, or positive cash flow, starts to diminish, which could indicate when the system is nearing the end of its useful life.

(b)

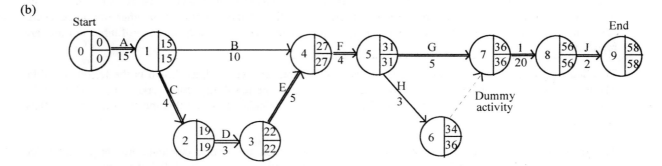

Network chart for Johnsons Specialist Books Ltd new computer system - Option A

The network of the activities listed shows the overall project duration is 58 days, and that activities A, C, D, E, F, G, I and J form the critical path, shown as a double line - any delay in their completion is likely to extend the overall duration of the project unless measures can be taken to reduce the duration of other activities on the critical path.

Alan Baker is probably right to feel concerned about the probability of getting the project completed smoothly and on time, for several reasons:

- There is already pressure because Alan was late starting his employment. This can easily lead to hasty decisions and increases the temptations to skimp on activities like testing.

- Activity B, 'modify software', is not on the critical path - there is two days' slack compared with the other path through the network that must be completed before installation and testing of the software. However, software development or modification needs to be carefully planned and controlled and it is often difficult to monitor its real progress until some actual results are generated by it. If problems show up at this late stage then it will be difficult to correct them without significantly extending the activity and disrupting the overall project.

- In addition, it is not clear whether or not the four days' allocation to Activity F, 'installing and testing the software', includes any provision for fixing any problems that are shown up by the testing - and this activity is on the critical path

- Since the software modification is not under Alan's direct control, he may not be able to allocate extra resources to the activity in order to speed it up.

- The critical path actually involves all but two of the activities, and one of them, 'modify software', is liable to delays. So delay in almost any activity is likely to extend the project's duration.

(c) The UK Data Protection Act 1984 relates to the storage and use of personal data by electronic equipment - principally computers. It was introduced in response to pressures from the civil liberties lobby and to bring the UK into line with some of its trading partners that already had similar legislation. The increasing use of electronic data communications is regarded as increasing the need for such legislation.

The Act defines:

- **personal data** as data about a living individual from which the individual can be identified

- **data subjects** as the individuals to whom the personal data relates

- **data users** as the people or organisations who electronically store personal data with the intention of processing it

- **computer bureaux** as places which store and process data on behalf of data users.

Data users must register with the Data Protection Registrar, giving details of the kind of data they hold and the purposes it is used for. The Act lays down eight data protection principles which data users should apply to personal data. These include, for example, that personal data must be:

- held for one or more specified and lawful purposes
- adequate, relevant and not excessive for these purposes
- accurate and, where necessary, kept up-to-date.

The Act provides data subjects with some rights which allow them, upon request, to be informed of personal data held by data users and to be supplied with a copy of it. It also provides the right to have inaccurate data corrected and for compensation for harm caused by loss of data or inaccurate data.

There some exemptions from the Act. Some of the most important exemptions are:

- Data held for some government functions is excluded from the Act where this is felt to be in the public interest - for example, where disclosure of data would impede investigations of crimes.

- Basic information held by clubs about members, such as name and address lists, is excluded, provided it is used only for purposes such as collecting subscriptions and circulating information to members.

- Data held solely for statistical and research purposes.

- Data in the form of basic records held for ordinary business activity such as payroll, pension and accounts. This is an important exemption which data users must interpret carefully, as it applies only to basic transaction data. Registration with the Data Protection Registrar can be a complex procedure and the exemptions may relieve a small business from having this additional administrative task.

The last exemption mentioned here could allow Johnsons to use a computerised accounting and/or payroll system without having to register under the Act. However, organisations claiming the exemption should realise that any change of use or purpose may mean that their data is no longer exempt. For example, if Johnsons use their accounting data to check on customers' creditworthiness then this goes beyond the limited scope of the exemption and Johnsons would have to register for this use of the data.

While data held simply for payroll purposes may be exempt under the Act, it is likely that Johnsons will use other data about their staff, such as an individual's performance review information. If this data is processed or stored on computer then Johnsons will have to register it under the Act.

If Johnsons use computerised systems to maintain records of customers' requirements they will have to register under the Act if it includes personal data such as the research work the customer has requested or their particular areas of interest.

(d)   The main areas which Alan Baker should consider when assessing the risk of unauthorised access to the new system are:

- access to the mini-computer from within Johnsons' offices

- access to the data held on the researchers' portable computers

- the communications links allowing the researchers to access the mini-computer over the telephone lines

- problems associated with staff being made redundant, who may be disgruntled and tempted to take malicious action on the computer system.

The steps that can be taken to combat these risks include the following:

Physical security

Modern mini-computer systems require less stringent environmental conditions than their earlier counterparts and they can be used in general office environments. However, since the mini-computer will be central to Johnsons' operations, it is important that direct physical access is strictly controlled by keeping the system isolated from the general office areas, with entry to the area controlled by keypads or swipe card readers.

Only operations staff should be allowed into the area. Most organisations employ general security measures to prevent public access to their work areas, but these should be reviewed because of the ease of access to large amounts of data on the new computerised system.

Johnsons should adopt a policy on the use of portable computers which includes keeping the power on/off mechanism locked and storing them under lock and key when not in use.

There should be a firm policy on the use of storage media such as floppy disks. Staff should not be allowed to use their own media unless it has been virus-checked and the use of the data has been properly authorised.

Division of responsibilities

Johnsons should allocate duties in a way that ensures that no one person operates a complete process where there is a risk of fraud or of sensitive information being tampered with. For example, computer operations or development staff should not have access to original accounts documents.

Logical access

Johnsons should operate a strict password system on their mini-computer, with procedures which require that passwords should be non-obvious, of a minimum length and regularly changed. Most modern computer systems allow for passwords to be applied at three stages: general access to the system, access to particular applications programs and access to particular data files. Access permissions can be used to prevent access or to provide read-only access. Users can be allocated various access permissions, depending on their work and level of responsibility, so that they can only legitimately access those parts of the system that are needed for their work.

Similar facilities may be available on the personal computers but the researchers should be made aware of the need to operate strict security arrangements and not to hold data on their systems unless strictly necessary. The personal computers should be subject to regular audits of the data and programs held on them.

Communication procedures

The researchers will need to use modems to access the telephone system and link up with the mini-computer. These links should be carefully controlled and not left open. Data encryption techniques can be applied on the data passed over the links.

Guarding against disgruntled staff

Alan Baker will have to consider carefully the effect that the possibility of redundancy may have on staff. The issue should be discussed by Johnsons' management, since if disgruntled staff work on the changeover to the new system or have access to the new system then they may have the opportunity to corrupt or destroy data, either directly or by leaving computer viruses or 'time bombs' in the system. Such precautions may be difficult to achieve, since it may not be possible to dispense with staff until the new system is fully operational.

Management support

It is important that Alan Baker explains the risks and the need for security arrangements to Johnsons' management and gets full management support so that awareness of the need for security permeates the whole organisation.

9 NEW SYLLABUS EXAMINATIONS

JUNE 1994 QUESTIONS

FIVE questions ONLY to be attempted

29 (Question 1 of examination)

The chief accountant of a company marketing agricultural products is extremely concerned at the length of time a feasibility report suggests it is likely to take to replace the current old computer-based sales accounting system by a new and more sophisticated system.

As the accounting department representative on the steering committee, he has called you in to demand:

(a) An explanation as to why the activities involved in developing new systems take so long;

(6 marks)

(b) Whether greater use of computers might both improve control of the project, and enable the project team to work more efficiently;

(7 marks)

(c) Whether future systems should involve greater user participation, and if so, how.

(7 marks)

How would you respond to each of these demands?

(Total: 20 marks)

30 (Question 2 of examination)

(a) In the light of the three categories of management information - strategic, tactical and operational; and three types of decision - structured, semi-structured and unstructured, briefly define and describe the differences between:

- a transaction processing system
- a management information system
- a decision support system
- an executive information system
- an expert system. **(10 marks)**

(b) Suggest ONE application of each of the system types listed in part (a) above for each of the following functional areas of business:

- sales and marketing
- finance. **(10 marks)**

(Total: 20 marks)

31   (Question 3 of examination)

The general manager of a large organisation has asked you to draw up a document identifying no more than 10 important system characteristics against which managers can evaluate the success of an information system, together with a brief explanation of each.

What would your document contain?   **(20 marks)**

32   (Question 4 of examination)

The context dataflow diagram below shows a system used to process orders in a manufacturing company in its most generalised form:

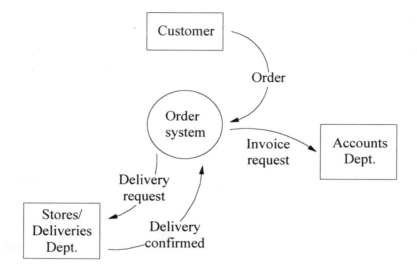

(a)   (i)   Produce a possible Level 1 dataflow diagram which 'explodes' this process order system, whilst still retaining a Level 1 symbol labelled 'process order'.   **(5 marks)**

       (ii)   Produce a Level 2 'explosion' of the Process Order process.   **(5 marks)**

(b)   What process specification tools might you now need to use to further expand on the logic of the system?
                                                                                                (10 marks)
                                                                                        (Total: 20 marks)

33   (Question 5 of examination)

You are required to carry out an internal audit of a production control system which was implemented just six months ago. This has consistently failed to achieve its specified performance-criteria in terms of both throughput and response times. It has also had to have a significant maintenance effort devoted to it.

(a)   (i)   Discuss the need for and the nature of the various types of maintenance.   **(6 marks)**

       (ii)   What reasons could you put forward to explain the excessive maintenance requirements and substandard performance of the system?   **(7 marks)**

(b)   From the auditing point of view, explain the need for documentation, and the nature of documentation which should exist for the system.   **(7 marks)**
                                                                                        (Total: 20 marks)

34   (Question 6 of examination)

The managing director of a distributor of motor accessories is convinced that the retail outlets to which they sell see them as a 'staid and stodgy' organisation and that new computer systems could help change that image by the production of new look invoices and reports for the outlets. This is despite the fact that there are currently no substantial problems with the existing computer systems. So convinced is he that he calls in the information technology manager and asks him to briefly analyse the situation and report back in person a week later.

The IT manager duly returns as requested to report that most users who have substantial contacts with the computer systems are happy with them. The IT department staff agree that the technology is readily available to update the systems. The IT manager himself is of the opinion that just because it can be done, doesn't mean it should be done.

However, the managing director requests that a feasibility report be produced, and you are asked to carry out the preceding feasibility study.

(a)   (i)   How would you assess the feasibility of this project?   **(6 marks)**

       (ii)   Outline-the likely contents of a formal feasibility study report for the managing director.
                                                                                                                 (6 marks)

(b)   Assuming that the managing director decides to proceed with the project, discuss the various fact-finding techniques you might now make use of to collect all the necessary information about the existing system and the new requirements.   **(8 marks)**
                                                                                                       (Total: 20 marks)

35   (Question 7 of examination)

Briefly discuss the following assertions in the context of information systems:

(a)   Computers can quickly and conveniently provide managers with all the information they desire;
                                                                                                                 (5 marks)

(b)   More information for managers will be welcome, and will result in improved decision making.
                                                                                                                 (5 marks)

(c)   Computers cause unemployment;   **(5 marks)**

(d)   Privacy is a more significant issue with computer systems than with manual systems.   **(5 marks)**
                                                                                                       (Total: 20 marks)

EXAMINER'S COMMENTS

It is intended that questions in this paper will become increasingly practical in nature. In this first examination session under the new syllabus, some steps have been taken in this direction. The results indicate that descriptive questions have been satisfactorily answered by all candidates. However, it has been noticed that some candidates have experienced problems with the practical questions. These candidates are reminded that as practical questions are becoming increasingly significant in future diets, they should work on this important area.

Question 1 was a relatively straightforward scenario-type question which required candidates to demonstrate knowledge of the following: in part (a), the systems development lifecycle; in part (b), the project control tools such as CASE, PERT, Gantt Charts, spreadsheets; and in part (c), why user participation is important and how tools/techniques such as 4GLs and prototyping might be made use of.

Part (a) was generally well answered. In part (b) very few candidates read the question carefully enough to realise that a discussion of project control tools was required, not how the use of computers might benefit the entire organisation. In part (c) the 'why' was often adequately answered, but not the 'how'!

Question 2 required candidates: in part (a), to explain the relationships of the various types of information systems to both levels of management and types of decision; and in part (b), to relate each system type to sales and marketing, and to finance.

The majority of candidates attempted this question and the standard of their answers for what is essentially a descriptive question was very high; in many cases the marks gained here compensated for the lower scores on the more practical questions.

Question 3 required candidates to identify and explain ten system characteristics against which managers can evaluate the success of the information system.

This question was neither popular nor well answered. Many of those who attempted it restricted their response to a discussion of the qualities of good information (as opposed to an information system), which is only one aspect of the topic. A good answer should additionally have covered areas such as cost, efficiency, effectiveness, reliability, acceptability, compatibility, etc. However, there were many answers of ten lines, each containing a few words, which were not an adequate response.

Question 4: part (a) required candidates to apply their knowledge of a common computer application (order processing), and an equally common systems development tool (dataflow diagrams) to a simple situation. Part (b) required candidates to refer to process specification tools; decision tables, decision trees and structured English.

This was the least popular question on the Paper, and was generally poorly answered. In part (a), most candidates had knowledge of either order processing or how to produce a dataflow diagram, but not both. Similarly, many could not apply their knowledge. In part (b), the well prepared candidates produced good answers. It was very apparent that some candidates only attempted the question because they could cope well with part (b).

Question 5: part (a) required candidates to discuss the need for and the nature of various types of maintenance. Part (b) required candidates to explain both the documentation and the nature of that documentation.

This produced a mediocre performance. In part (a) candidates failed to gain marks due to not discussing all aspects of maintenance such as hardware, software, adaptive, corrective and perfective. Instead, candidates concentrated on hardware. There were many good answers to part (a) (ii), which asked for an analysis of why this particular system might require excessive maintenance; relevant points included insufficient user contact, inadequate testing, hardware problems, systems management, user training and change in environment. In part (b) many candidates explained either the need for documentation or the nature of that documentation, but not both. Some answers restricted their responses to a (relevant) discussion of audit trail requirements, but failed to cover also the systems documentation aspects.

Question 6: part (a) (i) asked how the project might be assessed, and looked for a discussion, in the scenario context, of the operational, technical and economic aspects. In part (a) (ii), candidates were required to outline the contents of a feasibility study report. Part (b) required the application to the specific scenario of techniques such as interviewing, questionnaires, observation and document perusal.

In part (a) many answers covered one or two of the three required aspects (operational, technical and economic); fewer covered all three. In part (a) (ii) many good marks were gained, but a surprising number of candidates simply repeated the material already written down in answer to part (a) (i). Part (b) was generally well answered.

Question 7 required candidates to analyse assertions of interest to both company management and the computer community, such as production of information for management, computers and unemployment, and privacy.

Candidates who answered this popular discursive question generally gained up to half marks. However, it was disappointing to note the very low number of answers which achieved marks in excess of 60%. Few candidates were able to analyse each statement from more than one angle, and although it was not expected that they could cover all aspects, this obviously restricted the marks that could be awarded.

ANSWERS TO JUNE 1994 EXAMINATION

29   (Answer 1 of examination)

(a)   There are various stages in the systems development life cycle which, if the systems development is to be carried out effectively, might well consume significant amounts of time.

Even though the current system is computer-based, the activities implicit in the systems investigation, i.e. fact finding, must still be carried out, although the nature/bias of the techniques used here may well change compared to the situation where the existing system is manual in nature. For example, some interviewing of relevant staff will still be necessary, to discover both the faults in the existing system, and what requirements they have for the new system; but the number of interviews is likely to be significantly reduced, particularly if current documentation is available for the existing system. However, time will be required to interview computer operations staff, and to set up special test runs of the existing system.

Systems analysis and design are both time-consuming activities which must be undertaken here; this implies the production, in a structured environment of, for example, dataflow diagrams, entity-relationship diagrams, entity life histories, process specifications, structure charts, etc., culminating in a systems specification which forms the basis of the programming effort.

From this point, testing becomes an increasingly vital activity, in terms of module testing, program testing, systems testing, and using both test and live data. To attempt to shortcut this is to invite disaster!

The implementation stage of systems development is very complex, requiring, inter alia, the consideration and management of user training, documentation production, ensuring hardware availability, file conversion and actual changeover.

The project manager has the unenviable task of controlling the various stages in the systems development, and the project team personnel, as well as maintaining good relationships with users.

(b)   There are essentially two areas where use of the computer may be of assistance; project management techniques and tools, and CASE tools.

Project management techniques have been utilised for large projects, of any kind, for many years. They are essentially networking techniques, such as PERT (project evaluation and review technique), and CPA (critical path analysis). The use of Gantt (or bar) charts is also relevant here. Computer software packages are now available to enable rapid production of both networks and bar charts and also, importantly, the rapid updating of such diagrams.

Use of these tools enables the project manager to more accurately and closely evaluate and control the progress of the project; i.e. decide where more or fewer resources are required, identify what is behind or ahead of schedule, identify the critical path through the project, and paths where some slack exists, etc.

CASE tools (computer assisted systems engineering), are a more recent development. The widespread use of structured analysis and design does bring some disadvantages. A number of different graphical tools are called upon and, consequently, large amounts of paper are generated. The problems of incompatibility between the various models of the system that will be developed has also to be taken into account, and the implications of dataflow diagram decomposition.

It became obvious that the process of systems development needed some degree of automation; CASE tools were developed to carry out this purpose; essentially, they permit the analyst/designer/etc., to use the computer to draw the various diagrams, to carry out normalisation, to balance the various models, check for consistency in decomposition, and to create a central data dictionary. Other features are also often present; they may, for example, contain project management facilities, permit the generation of code, and/or enable the production of prototypes. All of these facilities, used properly, will enhance the efficiency and progress of the project.

(c)   The current trend in systems development is towards greater participation by users in the development of systems and, in many cases, towards users developing their own systems. This trend has two main root causes; a recognition that the backlog of systems awaiting implementation must be reduced; and that many implemented systems were failing to satisfy expectations because the needs of users were insufficiently taken into account during their design.

Consequently, computer software has now been developed with the objective of enabling users to play a greater part in systems development; Fourth Generation Languages enable analysts and users together to develop prototypes of the required systems; query languages enable users to satisfy their own small scale requirements. Organisations have in many cases set up information centres to help the users in this role.

For large scale projects, systems development methodologies such as ETHICS are aimed at enabling users to play a much greater part in the development of their systems. SSADM is a methodology which combines the structured approach with emphasis on user participation.

For these types of approaches to be of significant assistance in speeding up the systems development process, a number of key factors must be considered. They include hardware availability - some software will generate systems that are relatively inefficient in its hardware usage; the software packages must be acquired; and both computer staff and users trained in their use; those staff must be motivated towards their use; there must be careful consideration of exactly which systems will be best suited to these kinds of development; a significant amount of overt management support will be required; and, finally, the problems of controlling these new approaches to systems development!

30   (Answer 2 of examination)

(a)   Transaction processing systems (TPS) collect and store data about transactions and sometimes control decisions that are made as part of a transaction; they were the first computerised information systems. There are two main types of transaction processing; batch processing, where individual transactions are gathered together and stored for later entry into the computer system; and realtime processing where the transaction is processed as soon as it is gathered. The TPS is highly structured in nature, will only support highly structured decisions and is likely to be used only by those people who process transactions; it is essentially operational information.

Management information systems (MIS) convert data from a TPS into information for monitoring performance, maintaining co-ordination and providing background information about the organisation's operation. MIS reports provide summary information rather than details of individual transactions. Typical users are managers at the tactical level, making unstructured or semi-structured decisions. The concept of the MIS emerged essentially as a response to the shortcomings of the TPS, which provide little information for management. The transaction data remains essential, but is focused for management. However, the reports commonly produced by an MIS are inflexible.

A decision support system (DSS) is normally an interactive system that helps people make decisions, use judgement and work in ill-defined areas. It supports decision-making in semi-structured and unstructured situations and provides information, models, or tools for manipulating and/or analysing information. It enables managers to focus on the real business problems, by automating the process of gathering, summarising and analysing information relevant to a particular decision area, and enables one off *ad hoc* problem situations to be resolved. Its most likely usage is in the area of producing information to aid in tactical decision-making.

An executive information systems (EIS) provides managers with flexible access to information at the tactical and strategic levels, for monitoring operating results and general business conditions. In some ways it resembles, in outcomes, the DSS, but whereas the DSS provided tools that required significant expertise to use, the EIS is designed to help managers find the information they need whenever they need it, and in the most appropriate format. For both DSS and EIS, the TPS/database will be the source of raw information. The EIS is a high cost facility, and therefore its use is likely to be limited to high-level management functions.

An expert system (ES) differs from the DSS, which essentially provides usable information for managers. The ES supports the intellectual work of professionals who are working in complex situations requiring expert knowledge in a well-defined area. The ES captures the special knowledge of experts, and makes it available to others who have less knowledge or experience. Such knowledge is captured not only as facts, but also in the form of the reasoning processes the expert would go through in solving the problem. Use of an ES may guide the decision-making process, ensure that all key factors are considered, and help an organisation make consistent decisions. Its users in our context, are likely to be people working in areas where expert knowledge exists, who may be operating at the tactical or strategic levels, and it will often be used in conjunction with a DSS; the resultant hybrid is known as an intelligent DSS.

(b)   Obviously, the following are suggestions only - there are many other equally/more valid applications!

Sales and marketing

Transaction processing system - point of sale system for sales transactions;
Management information system - weekly sales report by product and region;
Decision support system - marketing data and model to analyse sales;
Executive information system - flexible access to sales data by region and product;
Expert system - system to develop sales strategy against competition.

Finance

Transaction processing system - processing of credit card payments;
Management information system - receivables report showing invoices and payments;
Decision support system - system displaying portfolio breakdown for stockbroker;
Executive information system - flexible access to corporate financial plan;
Expert system - system to support granting of credit applications.

31   (Answer 3 of examination)

Cost of ownership

The cost of any system includes the cost of acquiring the system, (either bespoke, or tailor-made), together with the cost of implementing, operating and maintaining it. Implementation is often a significant aspect here. Any system will have been developed on the basis that the building, implementing and operating costs would prove to be significantly less than the benefits which it would provide over its working life. The new system must be evaluated soon after at periodic intervals, to ensure that these costs and benefits are in the former case not being exceeded, and, in the latter case are, at least, being achieved.

Efficiency and effectiveness

These are complementary characteristics; effectiveness is the extent to which a system accomplishes its objectives, whereas efficiency is related to achieving those objectives in the right way. The efficiency of an information system is usually relatively easy to quantify using measures such as the cost per transaction or the cost per unit of information stored. An information system that generates vast numbers of weekly and monthly reports, very efficiently, but which are not required by users, is not operating effectively. Early information systems tended to concentrate on efficiency, to the exclusion of effectiveness; recent systems are developed to enhance the effectiveness of the organisation, as well as its efficiency. To ensure effectiveness, it is essential that the right tasks are being performed, and the required outputs generated.

Delays

Delays are time lags between different events that occur in an information system. An important benefit of more recent systems is that they integrate various subsystems and therefore reduce delays.

Capacity

Capacity of an information system is essentially the amount of work it can do; its capacity can be measured relative to the organisation's work, e.g. a system might process 500 transactions per hour to support 250 customers; at a more technical level, its capacity can be measured relative to the amount of work done in capturing, transmitting, storing, retrieving, manipulating and displaying data. The amount of work a system can support is usually measured at either average or peak load; the latter is especially important for systems that must maintain their performance at all times.

Reliability

Reliability is the extent to which a system can be depended upon to remain in service and not fail. Measures of reliability include average time to failure and percentage up time or down time. Reliability can be improved/increased in several ways. An expensive approach is to engineer its performance beyond that which is ever likely to be required. Another, more realistic, is to build in extensive backup and redundancy. Systems which are designed to be loosely rather than tightly coupled are usually more reliable. Tightly coupled systems are complex, highly integrated with little slack, require continual attention and are prone to disaster. Loosely coupled systems are decentralised, have some inbuilt slack, and are inherently more flexible; failures tend to be more localised and resolved more quickly. The idea of graceful degradation is essential to reliability: the design of systems that can continue to operate, albeit in a limited manner, despite the failure of some system component.

Complexity

A system's complexity is a function of the number of different components and interactions between those components. As complexity increases, systems become more difficult to develop and manage; they become harder to understand, and to evaluate the consequences of changes to the system. Obviously, this is also related to the concepts of coupling referred to above.

Operator error

Research suggests that 60 to 80% of accidents in complex systems can be attributed to operator error. Factors contributing to operator error include flawed design, poor training, and poor quality control.

Compatibility

Compatibility refers to the degree to which the standards and logic of two systems are consistent, and is often overlooked. Incompatibility can effect the ability to use information systems developed in other countries; format differences across data stored in different computers will cause problems; similarly with programs written in different languages and/or for different machines.

Controllability and adaptability

Controllability refers to the ability of the user to immediately influence or change what a system does. Adaptability is the user's ability over time to modify the system as business conditions or other requirements change. Ideally systems should be both controllable and adaptable. Many, particularly older, systems are difficult to control; they generate the same reports every week/month, and it is almost impossible to change the nature, format or content of those reports. Information systems become more difficult to control, the older they get, mainly because of the large amounts of maintenance and 'patches' they have been subjected to.

Acceptability and usability

The concepts of efficiency and effectiveness, however well applied, may well count for nothing if the system as implemented, does not have the acceptance of users. Lack of acceptance may be caused by a number of factors; users may never have accepted the need for the system in the first place; they may not have been adequately consulted as regards their particular need, opinions, etc.; the standard of documentation and training may well have been inadequate; they may find it difficult to use. Whatever the cause, lack of acceptance will frequently result in the system not being used to the required degree, to users finding alternative methods of work, and to problems of staff morale.

32   (Answer 4 of examination)

(a)   (i)   **Possible Level 1 dataflow diagram**

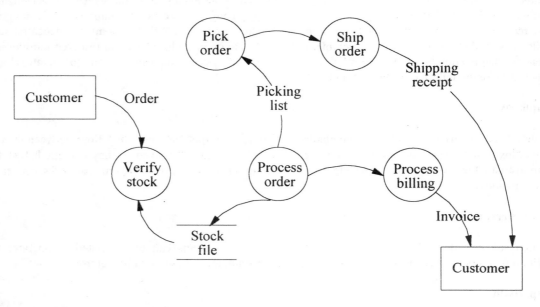

(ii)   **Possible Level 2 'explosion' of Process Order**

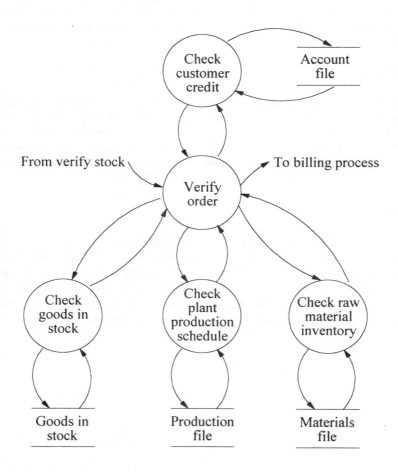

(b)   **Process specification tools**

Three tools are commonly used to describe exactly what goes on within each of the processes shown in the dataflow diagram - decision tables, decision trees and structured English.

A decision table is simply a guide to making decisions and defines a number of situations and the procedure(s) appropriate to each. Each situation is defined as a number of conditions and each procedure as a number of actions. Most decision tables have several conditions and several actions.

The task of defining each situation and listing the corresponding actions helps the analyst to identify shortcomings in knowledge, and suggests the questions to ask. Because they are unambiguous and easy to use, decision tables are very suitable for systems analysis.

Decision trees may be used where the user finds a decision table difficult to understand; if this proves to be the case, then the same logic can be presented in the form of a decision tree, which is generally easier to understand. A decision tree lies somewhere between a flow diagram and a family tree, a structure with which almost everyone is familiar, which displays the information in a linear fashion.

People generally find it easier to understand decision trees; however, decision tables are better in that it is easier to notice if a particular combination of rules has not been considered. Also, if there are a large number of actions, a tree will become too large and difficult to interpret; the table will grow larger but no more complex.

Structured English aims to be a concise and precise way of describing processes and attempts to remove the complexity from English by only using a subset of the language. The result must still be English, so programs should not be written in the specifications.

Structured English is an approach rather than a set of rules; in some cases the result may be very structured and appear very close to a programming language; in cases where the users would react very unfavourably to such a specification it may have to be rewritten in such a way that it appears as normal English, while retaining all the structure and exactness of the original.

Summary of the most appropriate situations for the use of decision trees, decision tables and structured English:

- decision trees are best used for logic verification or moderately complex decisions which result in up to 10-15 actions; also useful for presenting the logic of a decision table to users;

- decision tables are best used for problems involving complex combinations of up to 5 -6 conditions; can handle any number of actions; large numbers of combinations of conditions can make decision tables unwieldy;

- structured English is best used whenever the problem involves combining sequences of actions with decisions or loops.

---

33   (Answer 5 of examination)

(a)   (i)   The term maintenance is normally used to describe the process of modifying a system after it has been implemented and is in use, i.e. to correct errors and provide new facilities.

Maintenance falls into three categories; these are:

- perfective maintenance, which encompasses changes demanded by the user; 65% of maintenance is perfective;

- adaptive maintenance, which is caused by changes to the system environment; 18% of maintenance is adaptive;

- corrective maintenance, which is the correction of previously undiscovered errors in the system; 17% of maintenance is corrective.

It is impossible to produce a system of any size and complexity which does not need to be maintained; over its lifetime, its original requirements will be modified to reflect changing needs, and obscure errors will emerge. Because maintenance is unavoidable, systems should be designed and implemented so that maintenance problems are minimised.

(ii)   In the context of a system which has only been in operation for six months, it is not likely that adaptive maintenance plays a significant part - it is too soon, given no substantial changes in the environment, for this to arise.

If the system has been implemented without sufficient liaison and contact with users, and they were not given the opportunity to finally approve the systems, then it is quite possible that in many ways it does not satisfy their requirements, or they find it difficult to use and they are now demanding changes.

Similarly, if the system has been implemented without adequate testing, then the first six months is the period during which this omission will become clearly apparent, as errors are discovered during operational running.

Three areas need to be examined to discover the cause of poor performance. In terms of hardware, a particular component may well be of crucial importance; and may well act as a bottleneck in a particular system, e.g. the printer in a system requiring a lot of high quality printed output, or the CPU in a system carrying out many complex mathematical calculations. Other typical hardware bottlenecks include the speed of communications links and disk drives.

A second area is that of software performance, which may be affected by the number and complexity of the programs; the amount of memory required, the accuracy and precision of the programs making up the system, and the ease of maintenance of the system.

Finally, the operation and management of the system may have an effect on the performance of the system. Relevant factors here include the way the system is configured, the complexity of the security procedures for the system, and the attitudes and abilities of the computer operations staff.

(b)   The nature, size and scope of a system determine the optimum amount and scope of documentation. The following points summarise the case for good system documentation:

-    to enable analysts, programmers, users and computer operations to communicate;
-    to assist in the detection and correction of errors in the system;
-    to facilitate revision or modifications to the system;
-    for use in the training of users and operations staff;
-    to ensure consistent application of maintenance throughout the system;
-    to assist auditors in the computer audit process.

Documentation can be categorised into:

-    systems documentation, which describes the overall function and data flow in a system;

-    program documentation, which includes program specifications, program listings, and sample input/output;

-    operations documentation, which relates to the day-to-day running of the system, and provides operators with guidelines on how to run the system;

-    user documentation, which provides users with the information required to properly interface with the system.

34   (Answer 6 of examination)

(a)   (i)   Feasibility of a project is assessed in three main ways; operationally, technically and economically. A feasibility study is not a full-blown study; it gathers just sufficient information to enable management to make informed judgements on whether to proceed.

Technical feasibility relates to the adequacy of the existing technical resources, from the viewpoints of both equipment and technical expertise, to cope with the proposed system, or the ease with which those resources can be upgraded.

Technically, this project is feasible; the people in the system have the expertise, and the computer system can be updated to meet the new requirements.

Economic feasibility is the second aspect to be considered. Consideration is required here of the various costs that will be incurred in the development and operation of this system, and the monetary benefits that the system will bring to the organisation.

In this context, there is no pressing needs for the new system, nor is there likely to be an immediate reduction in operating costs or efficiency. Depending on the final design, it is possible that some long-term benefits may be forthcoming, but they are intangible, and unlikely to justify the costs of systems development. The proposed system is therefore not economically feasible.

Finally, operational feasibility must be reviewed. This is dependent upon a review of the human resources required for the project and the new system. It implies consideration of whether the system will both operate and be used, once it is implemented. User attitudes are crucial here.

Based on the information available here, it would seem that resistance to the new system will be high, because users have expressed satisfaction with the existing system, and it is known to be operating satisfactorily.

From the above discussion, it is apparent that the new project does not justify a full systems development exercise. It is technically feasible but lacks economic and operational feasibility. That is not to say that a senior manager with 'a bee in his bonnet' might not succeed in pushing the proposal through regardless!

(ii)   The feasibility report should contain the following:

-      introduction

-      terms of reference
       i.e. how the systems was selected for the study, and details about the scope of the study

-      existing system
       i.e. a description of the system currently operating

-      system requirements
       i.e. derived from the existing system, and, for new requirements, from management, users and operators

-      proposed systems
       i.e. an outline logical system, including input and output definitions; highlighting the differences between old and new systems; identifying hardware, software and staff requirements

-      development plan
       i.e. a suggested project plan, and how it will be implemented

-      costs and benefits
       i.e. detailed analysis of the costs that will be incurred in developing, installing and operating the system; and the monetary value of the various types of benefits that the new system will bring

-      alternatives considered
       i.e. identification of the various alternatives that have been considered, together with explanations of why they have been rejected in favour of the recommended approach

-      conclusions and recommendations
-      appendices.

(b)   Given the decision to proceed, despite the adverse feasibility study report, then there are a number of techniques which the project team might utilise in order to gather detailed information. It is usual practice for staff involved in the earlier feasibility study to be members of the project team, as they will bring with them a nucleus of knowledge about the systems.

Analysts have to make a decision on two key issues:

- which of the many items of documentation associated with the system should be concentrated upon?

- which people should analysts seek information from?

Information from documents

Analysts need to examine the 'hard data' contained in both quantitative and qualitative documents, i.e. reports, documents, financial statements, procedure manuals and memos. These provide information unavailable from any other fact-finding techniques. However, the analyst must always bear in mind such problems as accuracy, how up to date a document is, completeness, etc.

Interviewing

A major source of information about both existing and proposed system. The analyst listens for goals, feelings, opinions, and informal procedures, and attempts to sell the system and widen the knowledge of the interviewee. The interview may be structured in three basic ways:

- pyramid, where the interview begins with detailed questions and then broadens into more generalised questions;

- funnel, which is the reverse of pyramid;

- diamond, which combines the two.

Questions can be of two types: open, which leave all responses open to the interviewee; and closed, which limit the range of valid responses.

Interviews should be recorded, and reports written immediately afterwards to confirm what was said.

Questionnaires

These are useful if the people from whom the analyst needs to gather information are numerous and/or widely dispersed. They are most valuable when the information can be elicited by the use of simple, possibly multiple choice, questions.

The validity and reliability of the questionnaire is a problem of which analysts must be aware. Great care must be taken in their design, and they should be subjected to pilot test runs before being sent out.

Managers should have been consulted, agreed their use and made public their support for the technique in the particular context.

Observation

This technique provides analysts with an insight into what is actually done; they see at first-hand the relationships between the various types of users; they perceive the day-to-day activities which together make up the system, and may differ markedly from what documents or interviewees may reveal. It is essential that the analyst understand the nature of what he/she is observing.

The analyst can make use of event or time sampling, observe decision-making activities, and body language. There are various methods of recording observations, e.g. category systems, checklists. etc.

Prototyping

A useful information gathering approach, which may replace several stages in the traditional systems development life cycle. It enables user reactions, suggestions, innovations and revision suggestions to be obtained, to improve the prototype, and system plans to be modified with minimum disruption and expense. It will require the use of a Fourth Generation Language with which to build this prototype.

A disadvantage of this approach is that managing the process is difficult because of the many iterations and the speed of the process. The user may pursue requests when the systems already fulfil the specified requirements. Sometimes an incomplete prototype may be pressed into service, and become regarded as the complete system.

Prototyping enables systems to be changed more easily during development; enables development to cease at an early stage if it becomes apparent that it is not progressing as required and will result in a system that more closely addresses the requirements of the user.

---

35   (Answer 7 of examination)

(a)   The more senior the manager, the greater the amount of information they require will be external to the organisation; it is becoming increasingly possible to access external databases, but there is still much information that will not be readily available.

Even within the organisation, it is unlikely that all information will be stored within the corporate database, and it must therefore be collected before it can be processed. In order for that processing to take place, it is very possible that new computer procedures will have to be developed before it can be readily accessed in the required form.

If the required information is stored in some form within the database, then access to it in the appropriate format may still not be very easy. If the organisation makes use of decision support systems and/or executive information systems, then it is very possible that managerial requirements can be satisfied within the required timescale.

If management information is supplied via a management information system, then there may still be difficulties, in that such a system will provide routine reports on a regular basis, but will not lend itself to easy amendment, particularly for *ad hoc* requests.

(b)   The tendency to produce vast amounts of information for managers has long been a problem, and may result in a deterioration rather than an improvement in decision-making - the manager cannot see the wood for the trees!

To provide information when it has not been requested is obviously inefficient. It is unlikely to be made use of, and will certainly not enhance the manager's opinion of the system. Often, more information may reveal that an operation is being poorly managed, may be threatening and may, therefore, be resisted by managers.

To provide information on request may also not be valid, without first ensuring that the manager concerned realises exactly what it is he/she is asking for; particularly as there is a tendency for managers to 'play it safe' and ask for more information than they really need.

To continue providing information indefinitely, without periodically checking that it is still required can result in the production of surplus information - which was initially only required for a short period of time.

To be valuable to managers, information, as well as representing their requirements in terms of content, must also satisfy other criteria, e.g. it must be accurate, timely, and in the required format.

Even if we assume that management are being given precisely the information they require, there is no guarantee that decision-making will improve. They may not be aware of the best way to use the information to make the best decision, or they may persist in managing by instinct with minimal reliance on information provided.

(c)   There are situations where this assertion can be regarded as true, situations where it is possibly true, and situations where it is untrue. An analysis is therefore required of the differing nature of the computer applications which can lead to such diverse results.

Given the use of machine tools on a production line currently operated by human beings, with minimum use of computers, and then the subsequent replacement of equipment by computer controlled machinery, then it is obvious that such a move, however profitable to the organisation, is going to result in redundancies in the workforce.

In a business context, the replacement of manual systems by computer-based applications might, prima facie, be seen to result in staff losses in the departments affected; indeed this may often be the case. However, the creation of the new computer systems will also create new jobs, in terms of, for example, data entry, data control, and general user interface to the system. It will almost certainly have a greater capacity for work than its predecessor, creating opportunities for employment.

Finally, two scenarios where it might be claimed that jobs are likely to be created. Firstly, the decision by an organisation to invest in new computer systems may well result in new jobs being created in computer operations, user support, programming and systems analysis. Secondly, computers systems are increasingly being utilised to carry out applications which were not previously feasible; the jobs associated with these applications would not exist without the introduction of the computer.

(d)   Privacy might be defined as:

'the right of an individual to participate in decisions regarding the collection, use and disclosure of information personally identifiable to that individual.'

Civilised societies have always kept records about their members for administrative purposes; electoral rolls, medical records, police records, and many more, have been in existence for centuries. Such records have always been open to abuse, but such abuse has been restricted by the inefficiency of the filing systems used, and the disciplines imposed on those holding the information. The advent of computer files has meant that these controls are no longer sufficient.

It has been claimed (by Sieghart), that computers have changed information in the following ways:

-       more transactions are recorded
-       records are kept far longer
-       information is given to more people
-       data is transmitted over public communication channels
-       fewer people know what is happening to the data
-       data tends to be easier to access
-       data may be manipulated to provide information unavailable without the use of computers.

Increasingly, the computer databases holding personal information are being linked together, so that it is technically possible for information gathered for one purpose, to be transferred/used in conjunction with other files which are- being maintained for a totally different purpose.

In the United Kingdom, legislation has been introduced to preserve individual privacy where personal information is held in a computer system. It restricts the holding, disclosure, and usage of personal information; it attempts to ensure accuracy; provides access and rights of correction to individuals. There are significant exemptions, and many feel that this has drastically restricted the effectiveness of the legislation. However, the principles the legislation attempts to embody are not dissimilar to that of other countries across the world.

DECEMBER 1994 QUESTIONS

FIVE questions ONLY to be attempted

36   (Question 1 of examination)

A company which designs and manufactures marine engines regards customer service, i.e. the ability to respond effectively and in a timely fashion to service calls, as critical to its well-being.

Initially field engineers inspect faulty machines. Currently three quarters of faulty engines are referred to the repair centre, to be mended by repair centre engineers, resulting in a turnaround time of up to 10 days. The company has decided to investigate the possibility of carrying out more field repairs, with the aid of a portable expert system, in order to reduce the turnaround time.

The prototyping approach was used, and evaluation of the final prototype made it clear that an expert system, used in conjunction with laptop microcomputers would improve the situation to the extent that only 10% of engines would need to be returned to the repair centre, with the majority of repairs being carried out at the customers' premises by the field engineers.

(a)   Define what is meant by an expert system, and explain how it might be of use in this context;

(7 marks)

(b)   Define what is meant by prototyping, briefly comment on the advantages and disadvantages and explain how and why this approach is used;   **(7 marks)**

(c)   Discuss the changes that would take place if the expert systems was implemented in terms of the position, status, tasks and responsibilities of engineers at the organisation's repair centre and in the field.   **(6 marks)**

(Total: 20 marks)

37   (Question 2 of examination)

(a)   Define and distinguish between:

   (i)   structured, semistructured and unstructured decisions   **(3 marks)**
   (ii)   operational, tactical and strategic control.   **(3 marks)**

(b)   Suggest a classification by type of decision and type of control for each of the following information systems:

   -    accounts receivable
   -    warehouse location
   -    budget preparation
   -    new plant construction
   -    inventory control
   -    loan approval
   -    executive recruitment
   -    research and development planning
   -    short-term forecasting.

(5 marks)

(c)   A decision support system has been implemented by a landscape and garden maintenance company. Part of the system is designed to report on unusual problems reported by the various work crews. Some problems, such as a dying tree, may be important and require attention as soon as possible. This may mean reassignment of crews and extra expenses in terms of equipment, chemicals, etc.

(i)   Briefly describe the three phases which are commonly considered to make up the decision-making process and identify which phase in the part of the decision support system referred to above is being supported.

(5 marks)

(ii)   Explain how the decision support system described might support the two phases of decision-making that you did not identify in part (c)(i) above. State any assumptions necessary about the company.

(4 marks)
(Total: 20 marks)

38   (Question 3 of examination)

(a)   Define and distinguish between and explain the relevance to business information systems, using examples wherever feasible, of each of the following:

- deterministic and probabilistic systems
- closed and open systems
- dynamic equilibrium and entropy
- positive and negative feedback

(12 marks)

(b)   Show diagrammatically the operation of feedback control in a basic accounting system.

(8 marks)
(Total: 20 marks)

39   (Question 4 of examination)

A manufacturing organisation classifies each department as a cost centre. Consequently, each department pays for the computing services received.

A number of departments are purchasing microcomputers without reference to the information technology manager, who is becoming increasingly concerned about this situation.

(a)   Suggest some reasons to explain the action of these departments.

(6 marks)

(b)   What aspects of the above situation are likely to be of particular concern to the information technology manager?

(7 marks)

(c)   What steps might be taken in an attempt to resolve this situation?

(7 marks)
(Total: 20 marks)

40   (Question 5 of examination)

A small chain of four department stores is located in and around a major metropolitan area. It is about to implement, in all stores, a point of sale system with linkages to a central computer. The stores all currently use conventional cash registers. You have been asked to assist in the conversion to the new system.

Produce:

(a)   An evaluation of the various approaches to the system changeover.

(8 marks)

(b)   A checklist, in sequence, of the activities likely to be carried out during implementation.

(4 marks)

(c)   Suggestions as to how the new system might be evaluated after three months of operational running. **(8 marks)**

(Total: 20 marks)

41	**(Question 6 of examination)**

(a)   Briefly describe, with the aid of examples, any FIVE tools or techniques commonly used in structured analysis and design.   **(15 marks)**

(b)   What is a CASE tool, and what contributions can a CASE tool make to the development of information systems?   **(5 marks)**

(Total: 20 marks)

42	**(Question 7 of examination)**

A small but expanding mail order company specialising in the sale of silk garments is contemplating the purchase of microcomputers and software to help with supplier and customer accounting. The company is based in a small isolated town and staff have little or no computer knowledge.

You are a consultant brought in to advise them of the best ways forward.

Produce a report covering the following:

(a)   A list of the factors that the company should take into account for the selection of hardware and software.
                                                                                           (7 marks)

(b)   An analysis of the financial techniques the company might adopt to assess the potential profitability of the proposed system.   **(7 marks)**

(c)   An analysis of the main alternatives available for the financing of the acquisition of hardware.
                                                                                           (6 marks)

(Total: 20 marks)

EXAMINER'S COMMENTS

General comments

This is the last diet before the paper format changes to one wherein candidates have to answer compulsory questions based on a case study. A number of candidates struggled with the problem-oriented questions on this paper, failing to relate their answers to the given scenario, and consequently losing marks.

Question 1: Part (a) required candidates to demonstrate knowledge of various terms and to discuss the relevance of an expert system in a given scenario.

Many candidates were unable to satisfactorily identify the above elements. Rather more saw the relevance of an expert system to the scenario.

Part (b) concerned the use of prototyping to produce a working model of an application. Candidates were also asked to comment on the advantages and disadvantages of this approach.

Answers to this part were significantly better than to the other parts of this question.

Part (c) concerned the possible effects the introduction of an expert system might have on the engineers mentioned in the scenario.

The material to answer this part of the question could be found in the question paper; however, many candidates seemed unable to make use of this material.

Question 2: Part (a) asked candidates to define and distinguish between various terms.

This was answered well by many candidates; however, a significant number failed to define the terms and only related them to levels of management.

Part (b) asked candidates to apply the knowledge demonstrated in part (a) by classifying a number of information systems by type of decision, and by type of control.

In the main, candidates coped well with this question. Various answers were accepted providing they showed evidence of logical thinking and consistency.

Part (c) asked candidates to identify the three phases which commonly make up the decision-making process and then to explain how, within the given scenario, a decision support sytem might support the design and choice phases of decision-making.

Overall this was poorly answered with candidates demonstrating little knowledge of decision support systems.

Question 3: Part (a) asked students to define and distinguish between four pairs of terms used in systems theory.

Candidates answered this part satisfactorily.

Part (b) asked candidates to show diagrammatically the operation of feedback control in a basic acccounting system.

Many candidates failed to use a diagram; rather more failed to apply their answer to the required area.

Question 4: Part (a) asked candidates to explain why user departments in an organisation might decide to buy their own microcomputers without reference to the information technology manager.

A wide variety of valid responses were possible here; in general, this part was well-answered.

Part (b) asked why the information technology manager should be concerned about this trend.

Again many possible responses; but many answers failed to come to grips with such important aspects as compatibility, costs, control and security, support.

Part (c) asked how the situation might be resolved.

This part was answered less well; aspects such as co-ordination, information centres, prototyping, favourable contracts with suppliers, frequently were not covered.

Question 5: Part (a) Required candidates to evaluate various changeover approaches.

The majority of candidates answering this question produced satisfactory descriptions of the above. However, many lost marks by failing to discuss them in the context of their suitability for the given scenario.

Part (b) asked for a sequential checklist of implementation activities.

It was expected that answers would cover topics such as timetabling, personnel involvement, training, equipment delivery and testing, software installation and testing and documentation. Very few answers covered all of these activities; still fewer placed them in an appropriate sequence.

Part (c) asked for suggestions as to how the new system might be evaluated after three months.

Suggestions might have included timings, costs, performance, accuracy, security, morale and customer reactions. Many answers lost marks because these were not placed within the scenario of the question.

Question 6: Part (a) required a brief descrilption of five tools or techniques commonly used in structured analysis and design.

Some very good answers were produced for this part.

Part (b) invited candidates to demonstrate their knowledge of CASE tools.

Many candidates could get little further than identifying that CASE stands for Computer Aided Software Engineering, and had little insight into the assistance such a tool might provide in terms of diagramming facilities, access control, consistency checking, etc,.

Question 7: Contained three parts based on a simple scenario, within which all answers should have been framed.

Part (a) asked for relevant factors concerning hardware and software acquisition. Many candidates produced good responses here, but not all were placed in context.

Part (b) required an analysis of the financial techniques that might be appropriate in determining the potential profitability of a proposed system.

Candidates who identified areas such as payback period, return on investment and discounted cash flow produced good answers. Others provided irrelevant answers or covered the ground required for part (c).

Part (c) asked for analysis of how to finance a hardware acquisition. Many good answers were produced; but many others were spoilt by failure to keep within the given context.

ANSWERS TO DECEMBER 1994 EXAMINATION

36   (Answer 1 of examination)

(a)   An expert system is a sophisticated computer program that manipulates knowledge and expertise in a given problem area. It allows a user to create a *knowledge base*, which consists of rules which use facts, both supplied by the user. Thus a computer program makes that knowledge or expertise available to the non-expert. An expert system will have an *inference engine*; this is the part of the system which governs how the facts in the knowledge base should be dealt with and what inferences should be drawn from a given set of facts. It is crucial that the *user interface* should be well designed; presentation to the user of questions, prompts, explanations and conclusions must be free of ambiguity and open to interrogation.

Well known examples of expert systems include:

MYCIN: a system to diagnose infectious diseases and select appropriate therapy;

PROSPECTOR: acts as a consultant to aid geological explorations for ore deposits, by assessing the likelihood of discovering a particular type of deposit;

XCON: developed by Digital Equipment Corporation to recommend an appropriate computer configuration, from the vast number of products available, for a specific customer order.

In the scenario given, it is clear that, in the current system, field engineers are unable, in the majority of cases, to diagnose a fault from their own knowledge and experience, and from literature provided.

The expert system constructed might contain in its knowledge base the combined expertise and experience of all the engineers, both from the field and the repair centre; an inference engine would have been constructed to access this knowledge, or possibly an expert system shell made use of, with an appropriate man-machine interface. This would provide, for a particular problem, both a fault diagnostic and possible solutions, via an appropriate user interface, for the field engineer.

The entire system would have been constructed to fit onto a machine both portable and robust enough to accompany the field engineer on visits to sites.

(b)   The satisfactory working of a new computer system is the most important consideration for the end user. The traditional approach, getting the complete system right first, with user friendliness playing a subsidiary part, has often not achieved the desired results.

One solution is to involve the user in the design process; in the past the user's lack of technical expertise has often made this very difficult.

Prototyping is a more recent solution to these problems, and involves the use of software such as Fourth Generation Languages which permit the systems analyst, in conjunction with the user, to produce a working model of an application.

User and analyst can then work together to improve the model's ability to meet user's needs and the information processing requirements of the organisation.

The major advantages of prototyping include:

-    users gain experience and technical knowledge
-    prototyping is an efficient fact finding technique
-    user participation generates commitment to the new system
-    training occurs during development rather than after completion
-    development time can be reduced
-    the design approach is sufficiently flexible to accommodate changing user requirements
-    the traditional barriers between users and computing staff are broken down.

The major problems with prototyping are associated with resource requirements and project control.

In the scenario given, the use of a prototype should ensure that the new system reflects the needs of the field engineers in terms of user friendliness and accessability.

The fact that the system was developed in conjunction with them should result in a willingness to make use of the system in the field.

If the prototype system was initially introduced in a very limited manner, before an operational version is developed, then there will be opportunity to evaluate its performance, in the knowledge that a new version can be relatively simply developed.

Because the use of this approach will almost certainly result in a lower workload for the repair centre engineers, it is important that the system is also developed in conjunction with them.

(c)   The implications of the new system in relation to repair centre engineers refer firstly to changes in job position and status; because their workload will be significantly diminished, their job security must be called into question.

Relationships between field and repair centre engineers may well deteriorate. The former are able now, given the expert system knowledge, to carry out work formerly carried out by the latter. The former also now have available a tool not available to the latter.

As a consequence of the new system, job responsibilities may well have to be redefined; new criteria evolved for performance appraisal and evaluation; new procedures developed for co-ordination activities between field and repair centre engineers.

The question of control is also relevant; the new system is far more decentralised, i.e. less reliance on the repair centre, and fewer contacts with them. Consideration needs to be given to both the control of distant field engineers, and the procedures for dealing with both hardware and system faults which may develop.

37   (Answer 2 of examination)

(a)   (i)   *Structured decisions* are those where all or most of the variables are known and can be totally programmed; decisions are routine and require little human judgement.

Unstructured decisions are 'fuzzy' complex problems for which there are no clear cut solutions; very often they are resistant to computerisation and depend primarily on intuition.

Semistructured decisions fall somewhere along the line between structured and semistructured; they involve both standard solution procedures and individual judgement.

(ii)   *Operational control* is essentially the efficient and effective execution of specific tasks; operational managers oversee the operating details of an organisation; they make decisions using predetermined rules that have predictable outcomes when implemented correctly.

Tactical control relates to the short-term planning decisions made by middle management, i.e. how resources should be acquired and allocated to best meet organisational objectives. The decision-making area can be characterised as part operations and part strategic, with constant fluctuations.

Strategic control relates to the long-range objectives and the formulation of policies for resource allocation; decisions made at this level will guide managers on other levels in the years to come. Strategic managers operate in a highly uncertain decision-making environment.

(b) The following table shows a likely classification for the systems listed:

Type of control / Type of decision	Operational control	Tactical control	Strategic control
Structured	Accounts receivable	Short-term forecasting	Warehouse location
Semistructured	Inventory control	Budget preparation	Building new plant
Unstructured	Loan approval	Executive recruitment	Research and development planning

(c) (i) The three phases of decision-making are:

intelligence: awareness of a problem or opportunity; the decision maker checks for decisions to make, problems to solve, or opportunities to examine;

design: the decision maker formulates the problem and analyses several alternatives for potential applicability;

choice: the decision maker chooses a solution to the problem identified in the intelligence phase, from one of the solutions identified in the design phase.

The part of the decision support system identified is supporting the intelligence phase of the decision-making process, by creating awareness of an environmental problem, i.e. a dying tree threatening houses.

(ii) *Design phase*

The decision support system would help the company to develop and consider alternatives for reassignments of crews from other tasks, and analyse extra costs likely to be incurred by the company in terms of chemicals, equipment, etc.

Choice phase

The decision support system would help the company choose the most appropriate solution, concerning the crews and other costs; it would also help to implement reassignment of crews once a decision has been made.

---

38 (Answer 3 of examination)

(a) A *deterministic system* operates according to a predetermined set of rules. Its future behaviour can therefore be predicted if its present state and operating characteristics are accurately known. A computer program is a deterministic system, but business systems are not deterministic because they interface with a number of indeterminate factors. A *probabilistic* system is governed by chance events and its future behaviour is a matter of probability rather than certainty. Business systems are probabilistic; information systems are deterministic in the sense that given inputs result in known type and content of information.

A *closed system* is one that does not interact with its environment, i.e. it has no input or output. It is completely self contained and will continue in a state of equilibrium throughout its existence. This concept is more relevant to scientific systems; examples in the business context are rare. An *open system* does interact with its environment; this interaction may be in the transfer, to or from, of materials or information. Most business systems are open systems and the ability of a business system to adapt to an ever changing environment is a significant factor in its success. Obvious examples are sales, purchases, stock control, etc.

Dynamic equilibrium is a steady state condition in which the system readily adapts to environmental factors by reorganising itself. In a manufacturing company, this might be material purchase and product manufacture/marketing. *Entropy* is a measure of disorganisation; open systems tend to increase their entropy unless they receive 'negative entropy' in the form of information from their environment, i.e. increased material costs.

Feedback: the system output is sampled, measured and fed back to the input with subsequent modification, if necessary, to the output. Feedback systems are typically called closed loop systems; systems without feedback are called open loop systems. The type and amount of feedback is important to system stability and equilibrium. The process by which a system is regulated is called *negative feedback*; without negative feedback, a system would become increasingly disorganised, i.e. in an accounting system debts would increase and more bad debts incurred. *Positive feedback* is where the control signal tends to increase the difference between output and standard, i.e. an increase in bad debts as more customers are permitted to exceed their credit limit.

(b) Feedback control in a basic accounting system

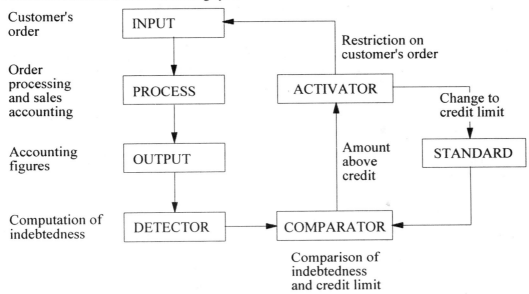

39   **(Answer 4 of examination)**

(a) A user department may take such action for a variety of reasons including:

- the reduction in costs of both computer hardware and software over the past few years;

- the wider range and increasing user friendliness of software packages available;

- more knowledge available in user departments;

- the backlog in getting new systems implemented by the information systems department, resulting in possibly unacceptable delays to user departments;

- once the new system is operational, then payments to the information technology department for computing services received may well diminish, or at least hold steady;

(b) An information technology manager might be concerned because:

- as a cost centre, this approach implies that the revenue currently received from user departments will reduce, with resultant implications for information technology staffing and resources;

- microcomputers purchased by various departments may well lack compatibility, making data transfers, etc. difficult;

- extra costs may be incurred by the organisation overall by the duplication of resources;

- decisions concerning choice of equipment may well be made by staff with inadequate knowledge of hardware and software, resulting in unsuitable systems being acquired;

- increasing amount of time being devoted by information technology staff to resolving problems of user departments who have taken this route;

- problems of control and security for a wide variety of hardware and software sited across the organisation;

- any attempt to establish centralised decision support/executive information systems will be severely hampered by the wide range of stores of possibly useful information.

(c)   Steps to resolve the situation might include:

- establish a co-ordinated approach/policy for the acquisition of hardware and software; this should aim at ensuring standardisation for user based systems;

- the information technology manager might consider taking steps to reduce the systems development backlog by introducing tools/techniques to reduce the time taken to develop new systems, e.g. CASE tools, prototyping, Fourth Generation Languages;

- possible establishment of an information centre to provide aid and advice to user departments concerning new systems development;

- introduction of computer familiarisation courses to widen the information technology knowledge in user departments;

- negotiation of contracts with suppliers at terms likely to be more preferential than those obtainable by user departments, who are then much more likely to acquire that hardware or software; a degree of standardisation can then be achieved with, possibly, an element of profit for the information technology department;

- consider, if the reduction of revenue generated internally is severe, the possibility of offering systems development services to other organisations.

40   (Answer 5 of examination)

(a)   Essentially, there are four approaches from which to choose:

Direct changeover

The existing system is abandoned for the new at a given point in time. Prima facie this seems an economical approach, but this is balanced by the risk that the new system will not work perfectly. Furthermore, there will be no safety net, in terms of existing procedures and staff, with which to recover the situation. It is not suitable for large systems crucial to the well-being of the organisation. If the new system bears little or no similarity to the old, this may be the only route. In the context of the department store, it should be obvious that this is not a viable option; if the new system collapses, then the store potentially loses all sales until it is remounted.

Parallel running

This involves the running at the same time of both old and new systems, with results being compared. Until the new system is proven, the old system will be relied upon. A relatively safe approach, which also allows staff to consolidate training in the new system before live running commences. It is expensive, however, because of the extra resources required to run two systems side by side. Parallel running is necessary where it is vital the new system is proven before operation. In the case of the POS system, this would be the most suitable method of changeover.

Phased changeover

Here the new system is introduced department by department, or location by location. This is less drastic than direct changeover, and less costly than parallel running, although each department may still be parallel run. For the department store group it might well be a sensible approach to introduce the new POS system into just one store, initially, and parallel run at that store first, before switching to phased changeover, and subsequently to implementation at all other stores.

Pilot changeover

This is another compromise approach, involving the running of the new system, or functions/subsystems thereof, on a sample of users, transactions, files, etc. in parallel with the new system. This might be followed by full parallel running, or a switch to phased changeover. Care must be taken with the choice of sample. The nature of the new system here, makes it unlikely that this approach could be adopted.

Whichever approach, or combination of approaches, is adopted, good management control, including thorough monitoring, will be essential if the new system is to be successful.

(b)   Checklist of implementation activities should include:

- development of a changeover timetable
- involvement of all affected personnel in planning
- advance notification to employees, followed by periodic progress bulletins
- development of training programme
- consider possible needs for external resources
- delivery of POS equipment
- testing of equipment
- installation and testing of software
- completion of documentation
- training for systems operators
- system trials
- changeover period
- acceptance of new system
- operational running.

(c)   *Systems evaluation*

This is a vital and important part of system implementation. Its objective is the systematic assessment of system performance to determine whether the established goals are being achieved.

A number of criteria are commonly used to measure the performance of the systems:

Time, i.e. the time required for a particular action to be performed. Response time is the time that elapses before a system responds to a demand placed upon it; for the POS system, this must be measured in seconds. Turnaround time is the length of time required before results are returned; for a POS system, little processing is done, and this may not be significant.

Costs, sometimes the only measure applied, are used to determine whether the various parts of the system are performing to financial expectations, and include labour costs, overheads, variable costs, maintenance costs, training costs, data entry costs, data storage costs, etc. For the POS system, all of these should be considered.

Hardware performance should be measured in terms of speed, reliability, maintenance, operating costs and power requirements. The performance of the POS devices in the various store departments, the central computer servicing the POS system and any networking components must be evaluated.

Software performance should be measured in terms of processing speed, quality and quantity of output, accuracy, reliability, maintenance and update requirements. Again, this is necessary for all software involved in the POS system.

Accuracy is a measure of freedom from errors achieved by the system and can be measured in several ways; but it is important that the type of errors as well as volume is analysed to ensure that serious errors are quickly identified. In the POS system, it is essential, for example, that the prices charged to customers are accurate.

Security means that all records are secure, that equipment is protected and that unauthorised or illegal access is minimised. It is important that the central database containing product prices is not corrupted, for example.

Morale is reflected in the satisfaction and acceptance that employees feel towards their jobs. Absentee rate and employee turnover are two factors that can be used to assess morale of the POS operators in the stores.

Customer reactions are an important factor in the context of the POS system; large numbers of complaints from customers would indicate that the system is not performing satisfactorily.

All the data gathered from the various components of evaluation should be studied to assess the success or otherwise of the system and, if the latter, to help pinpoint the reasons why performance is not reaching expectations.

41 (Answer 6 of examination)

(a) Some structured analysis and design tools and techniques

Dataflow diagrams are graphical representations of the flow of data between functional areas of an organisation or system. They are widely used in structured system development to illustrate where data originates, the process which transforms it to output, and where it is stored. The dataflow diagram is normally used in four phases; the old physical dataflow diagram describes the existing system, the old logical dataflow diagram reduces that existing system to a more abstract form by ignoring physical constraints; the new logical dataflow diagram is produced as a result of the incorporation of desired changes, and the new physical is the final model of the new system taking into account the availability of physical resources. Dataflow diagrams are normally hierarchical in nature; the topmost diagram is called the context diagram, the next level, level one, etc. Example context diagram:

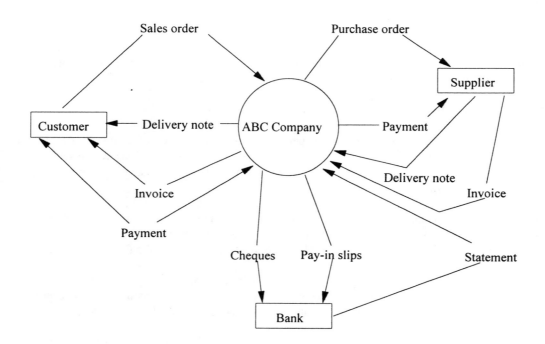

Decision trees provide a diagrammatic method of representing process logic; they clearly identify the condition or conditions which lead to an action or series of actions. Generally a question or condition can yield only two outcomes. A simple example is given below:

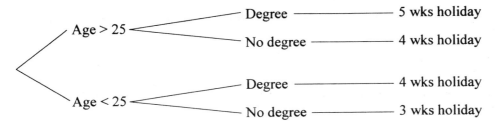

With the addition to the tree of the probabilities associated with each decision path, it may be possible to define more efficient software procedures. This technique is used to define in more detail the process logic identified in a dataflow diagram, but is less suitable than a decision table or structured English for complex situations.

Decision tables are simply a guide to which decision should be made, given the existence of certain conditions. The table defines the range of possible situations and the procedures appropriate to each, singly, or in combination. Each situation is defined as a number of conditions and each condition has a number of actions. The table structure is:

CONDITION STATEMENT	CONDITION ENTRY
ACTION STATEMENT	ACTION ENTRY

Three main types of table exist: extended entry, limited entry and mixed entry. Only limited entry provides the unambiguity and precision necessary for structured systems development; condition entries are limited to Y, N and -, action entries to X for 'take this action' and blank for 'do not take this action'.

Structured English aims to reduce the ambiguities and omissions which result from describing a process using the English language. It aims to be more concise and precise and to retain simplicity by using only a subset of the English language. It is an approach rather than a set of rules. Example:

ADD PRODUCT RECORD

READ Product record

MATCH Product number with Product number in file

    IF matched, reject Product record input

        Print reject product record

    ELSE insert Product record on file

        Add Product-Name, Product-Price, Stock-Qty

Note the use of upper case, the omission of all frills and the use of indenting to make the logic more apparent. Structured English is best used when the process involves combining sequences of actions with decisions or loops.

Normalisation is a technique used in data analysis to provide for the flexible use of data held in a database, whilst reducing or eliminating the effect of system changes on the file structures. A normalised record can be described as one which is independent, because it has no external dependencies and stable, because it is in its simplest form. The technique involves subjecting the data to several stages of analysis or redefinition, the three most significant of which are:

(i)   First normal form; study the data contents of the record and establish separate structures for repeated groups;

(ii)   Second normal form; remove to a separate record those items which are not wholly dependent on the primary key;

(iii)   Third normal form; remove items which can be derived from or are dependent on other non-key items in the records.

A data dictionary is used to define the data used in a system, and the flow of that data. Over the life of a system, the main purpose of a data dictionary is to provide a source of reference for analysts, users, etc. In general, everything for which a special name has been created in the system should be included in the data dictionary; such names could refer to dataflows, files, processes, entities or records. The dictionary may be maintained on a computer package, or as a set of index cards; the former is the more normal and the more useful! The following detail might be provided for a data item:

Data item (e.g. employee number)

-   type
-   aliases
-   format
-   origin
-   users
-   volumes
-   access rights
-   where kept
-   etc.

Entity modelling portrays the relationships that exist between the data stores identified in the dataflow diagram. Entities are 'things' the business needs to store information about, and are sometimes described as 'people, places, things and events'. Relationships exist between entities, i.e. between a customer and the order he places. Attributes are information about an entity, i.e. the order number. Once all entities and relationships for a system have been identified, then an entity diagram can be drawn showing graphically all the links that exist. This diagram then forms the basis for decisions about how information about the system should be stored in the database.

Entity life histories highlight the time dependent behaviour of a system, i.e. the effects of time on the system, and the various states that an entity can legitimately be in. Life cycle analysis also identifies the functions in which the entity type is involved and discovers any functions that have not been identified elsewhere. The diagram provides a pictorial method of communication that enables users to easily validate the accuracy of the system. It must always contain a start point, which sets the entity in its original state, and should always contain an end point, to complete the life cycle.

(b)   CASE stands for computer-aided software engineering. A CASE tool is a software tool which helps to reduce paperwork, enforce standards, and keep specifications updated. All of this is necessary in the context of structured systems development. A CASE tool helps the analyst construct graphical diagrams, and ensures the consistency of the model being built. The right tool in the right environment should result in more rapid and efficient systems development, and significant improvements in systems maintenance. Major facilities that a CASE tool should offer include:

-   support for the structured methodology in use
-   good diagramming facilities
-   a central data dictionary
-   access control
-   consistency checking
-   prototyping facilities.

42   (Answer 7 of examination)

(a)   Factors to be taken into account in hardware and software evaluation include:

-   proposed system workloads
-   benchmark tests
-   volume capacity of system
-   memory available
-   transaction processing time

- type of computer
- data storage devices
- quality of vendor support for:
  - installation and training
  - maintenance
- financial stability of vendor
- ease of system extension
- compatibility with other manufacturers equipment
- software effectiveness
- software efficiency
- ease of software use
- software flexibility
- quality of software documentation
- quality of suppliers support
- software licensing.

All of these are important, but for the mail order company those associated with vendor support, software usability, quality of documentation, are probably more significant.

(b)   Cost-benefit techniques

Cash flow analysis

The objectives are to ensure that the project will result in a positive end-balance, and to identify how well the investment will pay off. The normal way of portraying a cash flow is in tabular form.

Payback period

Simply measures the number of years it is expected to take for the project to recover the initial investment. The shorter the payback period, the better. When applied according to strict criteria, this approach may result in projects being rejected simply because, by their very nature, they have a long payback period, although their profit-making potential may be very high. In an unstable economic situation, it can be argued that because payback period attempts to recover outlay as soon as possible, it thus reduces exposure to risk and uncertainty.

Return on investment

An expression of benefits returned by a project in terms of a rate per year. The common approach is to assume that at the start of the project the total investment is outstanding, whilst at the end of the economic life, the investment is totally repaid. Return on investment does not take the time value of money into account, does not differentiate between large and small investments, or flow of profits. The approach does,however, focus on identifying which projects will give the highest return on investment.

Discounted cash flow

Stems from the notion that money is worth different amounts depending on when you get it. Future money is therefore reduced by a discount factor normally derived from the interest that can be obtained from an investment. The required rate of return is necessary to know what a firm's cost of capital is - this is the discount factor. The net present value is the present value reduced by the project development costs. A profitability index can be used to permit ranking of competing projects by degree of profitability; it is defined as the present value of an investment divided by its development costs.

(c)   Funding hardware acquisition

The company has essentially four methods available:

Cash payment from resources; this should be avoided if it is likely to cause cash flow problems. However, microcomputer hardware and software are the most likely choice for this company, and cash purchase may well be the most appropriate method.

Cash payment using a bank loan/overdraft facility/venture capital etc. prevents unnecessary strain on cash flow, and will result in ownership of the equipment; interest charges may be excessive but tax advantages may ensue.

Leasing is a popular method of acquiring a larger computer; the client takes out a three to five year lease for the required machine from a finance company. With a full payout lease, where the amount paid equals or exceeds the total cost of the equipment, the lessee will normally be able to rehire the equipment at a nominal rate. An operational lease runs for less than the expected usefulness of the machine; the lessee is then able to keep at the leading edge of the technology. Not a suitable arrangement for this mail order company at this stage in its development of computer systems.

Rental is useful for short-term hire, but an expensive method of acquiring a complete computer system; its use for a single peripheral may be advantageous. It does have the advantage that the arrangement is actually with the supplier rather than a third party such as a finance company.

Essentially, therefore, the method chosen depends upon the cost of the purchase, the cash position of the company, and the tax situation currently pertaining, which is likely to change from budget to budget and may make a particular approach more or less attractive.

JUNE 1995 QUESTIONS

Section A – ALL FIVE questions in the section are compulsory and MUST be attempted

Read the following case study carefully and then attempt all questions in this part

A maximum of 55 marks are available

You should spend no more than half the available time on this part of the paper

43   (Question 1 of examination)

Case study

The Mediserve Health Centre is located in a small market town with a population of approximately 10,000 plus a further 5,000 people in outlying farms and villages. The centre provides general medical care plus limited support services such as a small operating theatre for minor procedures, a laboratory for specimen testing and a radiography unit for X-rays. Medical care is on a day care only basis there being no facilities for overnight hospitalisation. Longer stay medical care is provided at the regional hospital some 30 miles away.

The centre is staffed by 10 doctors on a shift basis, who also provide emergency cover when the centre is closed on Sunday and during the night. The doctors are supported by four nurses. Administrative systems which includes patient records, staff records, and substantial correspondence between doctors, patients and consultants are undertaken by two full time and four part-time secretaries. The centre operates an appointments system for patients seeking non-urgent treatment. The system is operated by 12 part-time receptionists working on a shift system.

In addition, a radiographer works at the centre for three days per week and three laboratory technicians for two days each. The laboratory technicians are also responsible for ordering, maintaining and issuing drugs from the stocks held at the centre.

The centre also acts as the headquarters for the community health service which includes eight district nurses, ten health visitors and four midwives and is the base for the child vaccination and immunisation recording and monitoring system (vaccim). The health visitors maintain card based vaccim records, issue reminders, and administer the appointments system.

Proposed changes in the organisation of the national health service will lead to substantial local autonomy for the Mediserve Centre including full responsibility for its own financial affairs. At the present time the payroll, income receipts and expenditure payments procedures for the Mediserve Centre are undertaken on the mainframe system at the regional hospital computer centre.

All centre administrative, text and record keeping procedures are operated manually. There is, however, a terminal link between the centre and the regional hospital which is used to input accounting transaction data, order drugs and transmit medical statistical data used for national health monitoring. The lack of computerisation and office automation at the centre is not from choice but has been due to the absence of funding support from the regional computer centre. This has now changed with the delegation of financial responsibility to local medical centres. The senior doctors at Mediserve see this as an opportunity to computerise not only the financial systems which will now be necessary but many of Mediserve's administrative and record keeping procedures.

The doctors are fully supported in this initiative by the nursing and administrative staff. The support staff feel overwhelmed by the present volumes of paperwork but are very apprehensive at the prospect of taking responsibility for Mediserve's financial and associated systems.

Required

1   Describe what you believe would be the various problems currently experienced by all staff working at Mediserve as a result of the reliance on manually based systems.   (8 marks)

2   Identify the potential processes and functions suitable for information technology investment at Mediserve indicating any important linkages between applications.   (7 marks)

3   An initial investigation of other medical centres similar to Mediserve has revealed that some have adopted an information technology approach based on networked personal computers while others have opted for a minicomputer supporting a series of terminals. Explain these two configurations and discuss their suitability for Mediserve's operations.   (10 marks)

4   'It is one thing to have ownership of your own computer systems but another to accept the responsibilities of ownership such as data integrity, security and overall risk management.' This was a statement made at a recent medical conference attended by one of Mediserve's doctors.

     Explain what the statement means and indicate how Mediserve would ensure that its 'responsibilities of ownership' are properly carried out.   (15 marks)

5   Convert the following information for a child vaccination and immunisation system from its textual format into a data flow diagram (DFD).

     'There is a legal obligation upon local health authorities to provide facilities for vaccinating people against disease. Treatment normally commences when a child is one month old and registration of each child for their course of vaccinations is initiated by the birth of the child.

     'The system operated by Mediserve Health Centre requires information from which it can produce a program of vaccination notifications for the parents and the health centre staff. This information is obtained from the birth registration form. A consent form is completed by the health visitor and signed by the parent or guardian when visiting the child around the tenth day after birth. Protection is available against a variety of diseases and parents may agree to all, none or some of the scheduled immunisations and vaccinations. If all are accepted, separate courses will be scheduled between one month and 16 years.

     'A diary appointment system must be maintained which notifies families at the appropriate time and checks that parents are not notified if treatment has already taken place or, more distressingly, if the child has died. The system must provide facilities for adding and deleting children to and from the vaccination program if they have transferred in or out of the health centre's area (or if they have died) and provide a record of completed appointments.

     'Doctors are paid for immunisations and the system facilitates automatic payment.'   (15 marks)

                                                                                                    (Total 55 marks)

Section B – THREE questions ONLY to be attempted

44	**(Question 6 of examination)**

---

6   Explain what steps an organisation might take to facilitate identification and selection of computer projects and ensure a planned approach.   **(15 marks)**

45 (Question 7 of examination)

7   An organisation which operates solely by mail order uses the following procedure when an order is received for a product:

> If the product is in stock, then the goods are shipped at once, the stock level checked, and an order issued on suppliers if necessary. When the product is out of stock it is ordered from the suppliers unless an order has already been placed. Where the item has been discontinued, a substitute is dispatched. Customers are notified if an item cannot be dispatched immediately.

(a)   Use any *two* of the following techniques to describe the logic of the above order processing procedure:

    (i)   a structured English description
    (ii)   a decision table
    (iii)   a decision tree.   (10 marks)

(b)   Comment on the relative suitability of each technique for the order processing procedure outlined above, and explain the part these techniques play in the systems development process.   (5 marks)
                                                                      (Total 15 marks)

46 (Question 8 of examination)

8   (a)   Briefly define and distinguish between:

    (i)   analytic and heuristic decision-making;
    (ii)   unstructured, semi-structured and structured decisions.   (5 marks)

(b)   A production supervisor makes routine decisions about production schedules, has input into purchase decisions for ingredients and manages line workers.

    (i)   Briefly explain why you should deny the production supervisor's request for a decision support system

    (ii)   What changes in the decision-making situation might make a DSS appropriate?
                                                                          (5 marks)

(c)   The owner of a small chain of auto-accessory shops in five different towns inputs sales figures into a computer model that displays buying trends for each store. She uses her observations from visits to shops and information gained from the model, to make ordering decisions for each store.

    (i)   Are the ordering decisions she makes structured, semi-structured or unstructured?

            Briefly explain the reasons for your choice and outline what product related variables are involved in the decision

    (ii)   What features of the information systems she is using support the assertion that it is more of a DSS than a traditional MIS?   (5 marks)
                                                                      (Total 15 marks)

---

47   (Question 9 of examination)

---

9   (a)   A new on-line order entry system is currently being developed in your organisation. As part of the implementation procedures, users of the new system will require a number of training activities. The following table lists the activities, their duration, and the most appropriate sequence.

Activity	Preceding activities	Estimated duration
A	–	4
B	–	3
C	A	6
D	B	8
E	C, D	3

(i)   Produce a network chart from this information, identifying the critical path through the network.

(ii)   Explain how a Gantt chart might also be of use in this context, and identify any extra information which would then be required.   **(9 marks)**

(b)   What other activities are necessary during the implementation stage of a new system?

(6 marks)
(Total 15 marks)

---

48   (Question 10 of examination)

---

10   (a)   (i)   In the context of the acquisition of new hardware and software, identify the information you would expect to find in an invitation to tender and explain how such information might be obtained.

(ii)   Having received tenders from a number of suppliers, what steps should be taken before any final decision is made regarding the final choice of supplier?   **(9 marks)**

(b)   Briefly describe and evaluate the various financing methods by which an organisation with an existing but ageing computer installation might be able to upgrade its current computer applications to more up-to-date hardware.

(6 marks)
(Total 15 marks)

ANSWERS TO JUNE 1995 EXAMINATION

43 (Answer 1 of examination)

Examiner's comments and marking guide

Question 1: tested the candidates' understanding of the shortcoming of manual systems.

It was generally well answered although some candidates tended to give general answers and not apply their points to Mediserve.

Identification of general problems with manual systems (1 mark)
Identification of specific problems:
Patient records (2 to 3 marks)
Other four application areas (1 to 2 marks each)   (in total 8 marks)

Step by step answer plan

Step 1 Read the question again and make sure that you focus on precisely what is required.

Step 2 In question 1 describe the disadvantages of manual systems as against computerised systems. The examiner does not require a general discussion: he wants application to the specific circumstances of Mediserve.

Step 3 Question 2 is not about investment appraisal, or about systems development, two common misunderstandings noted by the examiner. You need to specify which areas of operations and records can benefit from automation.

Step 4 Question 3 requires both general discussion and application to Mediserve.

Step 5 In question 4 the approach is indicated by the wording of the question: take each of the three areas (data integrity; security; risk management) and explain the meaning of each, before specifying measures needed to attain them.

Step 6 The three paragraphs of question 5 in which the system is described provide an indication of the main areas to be included in the DFD: maintaining children's details, scheduling appointments, and controlling payments.

Step 7 Now review your answer plan and ensure that it does precisely answer the question as set.

The examiner's answer

1   Manual clerical and administrative procedures typically suffer a number of disadvantages against computerised systems – poor labour productivity, slow processing where significant data volumes are involved, potential for a great incidence of errors, limited flexibility of information access and retrieval and a generally lower quality of text presentation. In particular at Mediserve we would expect to find the following:

    (i)   Paper-based patient records. Currently patient records are held on a paper-based system. This would be very bulky and occupy a lot of space. Access to the records could be difficult, for only one person could have access to the medical notes at any one time and, if not replaced, for example, left in a pending tray, access could be totally restricted. If there is an emergency and a doctor is called out overnight, for example, the patient personal history and details might not be instantly available.

    (ii)   A paper-based appointments system affords only limited accessibility to the data, could be difficult to read, difficult to update, and might not ensure the optimum use of doctors' and nurses' time.

(iii)   Correspondence. Manual systems are very slow particularly where text corrections are needed or slightly differing versions of the same basic text is required. The presentation quality is not always very professional.

(iv)   Manual staff records and payroll systems could be inaccurate and insecure; it could be difficult to optimise use of resources, for example, staff replanning due to sickness. Similar accuracy, security and optimisation problems would arise in manual financial systems and drug recording systems.

(v)   Statistical data would be very difficult and time-consuming to produce from paper-based systems.

Did you answer the question?

In a case study like this, make sure that you refer to the specific situation and company in the question.

Examiner's comments and marking guide

Question 2: asked candidates to identify appropriate areas of computerisation at Mediserve.

This question was generally well answered although some candidates did not sufficiently stress the linkages between applications or apply their answers to Mediserve. However, there were also two relatively common misinterpretations of the question. Some candidates described investment appraisal methods (perhaps because of the word investment in the question) whilst others described the processes required to identify and design applications - the systems development life cycle.

Identification of application areas:
(up to 0.5 marks for each area identified)
(1 to 2 marks for indications of linkages between applications)   (in total 7 marks)

The examiner's answer

2   Integrated specialist software packages are generally available which removes any requirement for Mediserve to develop their own application software. Such application software typically provides the following facilities:

- Patient medical records*
- Appointments*
- Prescriptions*
- Drugs database**
- Recall services (further injections, screening etc)*
- Communication (electronic mail to colleagues, into hospital networks for booking patients in, test results, diagnosis database and referrals to specialist)***
- Stock control**
- Accounts**
- Research aid; clinical trials***
- Private patient accounting**
- Statistical analysis*
- Work scheduling; staff notes***

*/**/*** Indicates areas of potential integration of applications. In addition Mediserve would be able to utilise general purpose packages such as speadsheets, word processing, database and graphics.

Did you answer the question?

This question does not ask for investment appraisal but the processes for IT investment. Read the question?

Examiner's comments and marking guide

Question 3: had two parts. The first required candidates to give a simple explanation of two hardware configurations.

Generally this was satisfactorily answered although candidates from some centres showed a lack of knowledge about networked PCs.

The second part required the candidate to consider the suitability of each solution at Mediserve.

This was often ignored or given cursory treatment. Consequently marks were fairly low on this question, candidates scoring between 2 and 4 marks for their descriptions, but often 2 marks or less for their discussion about the suitability of each to Mediserve.

Simple description of LAN attributes (2 marks)
Explanation of LAN suitability (3 marks)
Simple description of mini systems attributes (2 marks)
Explanation of mini systems suitability (3 marks)
Explanation of hardware overlap (1 to 2 marks)   (in total 10 marks)

The examiner's answer

3   A local area network (LAN) consists of a small number (usually 2 – 20) microcomputers connected together by special cable and utilising networking software. There are a variety of different network architectures although most consist of one or more microcomputers (file servers) dedicated to holding files and programs used by other microcomputers in the network and therefore controlling the interactions between them. However individual microcomputers are also capable of functioning autonomously and running their own application independently. If only a few users need access to data or peripheral devices such as a high speed printer at any one time then a LAN would be appropriate. The LAN is generally most effective for users that have largely independent applications and with light requirements for data transfer. This will probably not be the case at Mediserve. A LAN system permits considerable flexibility – it is relatively cheap and is easily enlarged to spread the initial start-up costs or cope with changing levels of patients. Control of the central patient database could be difficult to achieve under LAN architecture.

In a system where a minicomputer was being used by terminals, Mediserve would be totally dependent upon the central processor for their processing power and if this 'crashed' all users would be affected. Most minicomputer based systems also however allow the user to employ microcomputers as terminals. This approach then affords the advantages of both modes of operation, functionality of independent workstations for carrying out local processing needs along with network access to the minicomputers more powerful processing and storage capabilities where necessary. At Mediserve this would ensure faster processing, support more users and provide better security over the data. It should also ensure standardisation of procedures and reduce the chance of duplication of data and systems.

It should be noted that the borderline between the two is not clear cut: a small minicomputer system will generally outperform a large micro-based system but will require a larger initial expenditure. On the other hand the initial start costs of a LAN based system are generally less but the incremental costs of adding machines to the LAN is generally higher. Note that both systems would be able to support data access from portable computers if these were to be supplied to the doctors.

Examiner's comments and marking guide

Question 4: was designed to test candidates' understanding of the 'responsibilities of ownership' with respect to data integrity, security and overall risk management.

This question was often poorly answered, with answers often badly structured, listing issues and counter-measures in no particular order - data validation, passwords, virus checking, security locks etc,. The comments on security were often limited to a two page explanation of the Data Protection Act and few candidates demonstrated their knowledge of risk management.

Correct definition of data integrity (1 to 2 marks)
Illustration of how controls ensure integrity (4 to 5 marks)
Correct definition of security (1 to 2 marks)
Illustration of systems security (4 to 5 marks)
Explanation of each of the three stages of risk management (4 to 5 marks)   (in total 15 marks)

The examiner's answer

4   The privacy issues associated with the extremely sensitive data held on the computer system about their patients will obviously be a very important consideration for the doctors. The statement highlights three important aspects:

Data integrity is the term used to describe the accuracy and correctness of data during and after processing. Systems controls are designed into a system as procedures to maintain the integrity of the data and are incorporated at all stages in the system's operation. Typically systems controls perform the following functions:

–   recognising when problems occur

–   finding and eliminating errors

–   ensuring that all data is processed

–   maintaining the correct timing and sequencing of input and output processing

–   restarting the system efficiently when a breakdown occurs or when data files have been corrupted

–   providing a record of all processing operations

The security of information relates to all aspects of protecting information from unauthorised access, sabotage, accidental loss or damage, fraud and physical damage. Systems security seeks to provide protection against the following:

–   the security risk of unauthorised users gaining access to the system;

–   the accidental loss of data stored on computer files, for example due to operator error or updating the wrong file;

–   the deliberate sabotaging of a system;

–   the risk of physical damage to computer files caused by dirt, water, fire damage and explosion.

Managing the risk associated with computer security essentially involves reducing the risk profile of the medical centre to the lowest feasible level. Risk management involves three stages as follows:

Risk assessment – arises from a full examination of all security factors. It should be noted that risk is specific to an organisation at a point in time and will change as applications are changed, new hardware introduced, location moved etc.

Risk minimisation – is the action the organisation takes when it has identified its exposure to risk and is the most critical aspect of the exercise. The process is often termed computer security and will cover a multitude of aspects such as the provision of standby facilities and disaster recovery procedures.

Risk transference – recognises that it is impossible to eliminate all risk however effective the computer security is. The uncovered elements of risk can be transferred through the medium of insurance to an insurer.

Did you answer the question?

The question asks for overall risk management. You must tackle this in your answer.

Examiner's comments and marking guide

Question 5: required the construction of a Data Flow Diagram (DFD).

These have been regularly tested in this examination (and its predecessor). Some of the answers in the examination were exceptional, earning 13 marks or over. However, many were very poor. Many candidates did not even attempt this compulsory question or else used flowchart symbols, layout and conventions. Candidates must look at this part of the syllabus and at least attempt one or two examples before taking the examination.

Identification of three main processes (3 marks)
Identification of four data files (4 marks)
Identification of data flows (6 marks)
General format and layout (2 marks)   (in total 15 marks)

The examiner's answer

Did you answer the question?

Read the question: it wants a data flow diagram, not a flowchart.

5   Data flow diagram for the child vaccination and immunisation system:

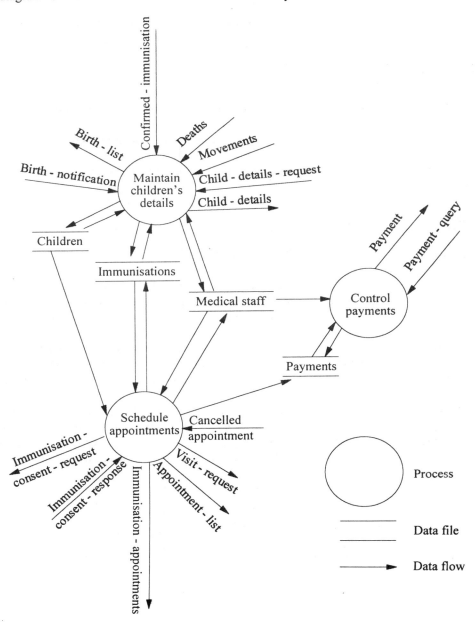

44   (Answer 6 of examination)

Examiner's comments and marking guide

Question 6: aimed at getting candidates to explain how computing projects should be identified, prioritised and planned within an organisation.

Many candidates limited their answers to describing the systems development life-cycle of a particular project. Some marks were available for this in the Marking Scheme, but it meant that answers of 4 or 5 pages restricted to this approach only scored 4 or 5 marks. Candidates must ensure that they answer the question that is set.

Answers should reveal understanding of:

-        the importance of information technology to the organisation
-        the need for strategic planning to take IT into account
-        the preferred methods of organising the IT department
-        the selection and development of computer applications.

The suggested answer contains eight points.

Award a maximum of two points for each valid point made; allocate the remaining mark to the quality of organisation of the answer.

Step by step answer plan

Step 1   Read the question again and make sure that you focus on precisely what is required.

Step 2   Proceed in turn through general strategic issues and detailed operational procedures.

Step 3   Now review your answer plan and ensure that it does precisely answer the question as set.

The examiner's answer

6   The following aspects all are pertinent to the question:

–   It is not appropriate for strategic decisions regarding information technology to be taken solely by the managing director; the company should consider the possibility of appointing an information technology director, or at least designating such a responsibility to a senior member of staff.

–   Traditionally, the computer department's first 'home' has been within the accounting function; as the use of information technology spreads, it might be better for it to be treated as a separate department in its own right, with a departmental management structure and defined roles and responsibilities.

–   Similarly, how are the services provided by the computer department to be regarded? Does the department provide a free service? Are user departments charged for the services provided? Is the computer department expected to make a profit? Can it move into the open market and offer its services to other organisations? What it should not be is the personal 'toy' of the managing director!

–   Ascertain the view of senior management regarding the role of information technology in the organisation.

–   Develop a strategic plan for use of information technology, and incorporating steps which, as a consequence, need to be taken with regard to information technology.

– Take decisions regarding the functions and composition of a steering committee and setting up of same.

– Develop procedures for project evaluation, such as creation of assignment briefs, carrying out feasibility studies and cost-benefit analysis.

– The establishment of systems development procedures, including user participation, statements of requirements for suppliers, systems investigation, analysis and design, the use of modelling tools, CASE tools, testing and implementation.

Did you answer the question?

Even when the requirement of a question seems very short, you must give it adequate thought to ensure you cover the whole topic.

---

45   (Answer 7 of examination)

Examiner's comments and marking guide

Question 7: required candidates to produce two process description models and to discuss the relative suitability of each model and where it might be used in the development life-cycle.

Most candidates seemed to know what a decision table or tree looked like (Structured English was unpopular) but the detail within the answer was often disappointing. However, marks were relatively satisfactory for this question although candidates did not often 'explain the part these techniques play in the systems development process' required in part (b) of the question.

(a)   Answers do not have to use the conventions adopted in the suggested answers, but must be a recognisable and acceptable form.

There may well be other valid solutions!

Award a maximum of six marks to each of the solutions proffered.

(b)   Award a maximum of three marks for an explanation of the suitability of the tools selected.

Award a maximum of three marks for an understanding of how/where these tools are used in the systems development process.

Step by step answer plan

Step 1   Read the question again and make sure that you focus on precisely what is required.

Step 2   Choose the two techniques that you are most at home with out of the three alternatives.

Step 3   Describe the logic of the situation using each of your chosen techniques in turn.

Step 4   Don't be tempted to overlook the easy marks available for part (b).

Step 5   Now review your answer plan and ensure that it does precisely answer the question as set.

The examiner's answer

7   (a)   Possible solutions:

(i)   *Structured English*

IF <u>product</u> is stock-item

THEN DO ship <u>product</u>

IF <u>stock-level</u> LT <u>reorder-level</u>

IF no <u>back-order</u>

THEN DO reorder product

ELSE IF <u>product</u> is discontinued

THEN DO ship substitute

ELSE DO order <u>item</u>

DO notify <u>customer</u>

(ii)   *Decision table (condensed)*

Stock item	Y	Y	Y	N
Stock LT Reorder level	Y	Y	N	–
Delayed dispatch	N	Y	N	Y
Back order exists	Y	N	–	–
Discontinued product	–	–	–	Y
Ship product	X	X	X	
Reorder product		X		
Ship substitute				X
Notify customer		X		X

(iii)   *Decision tree*

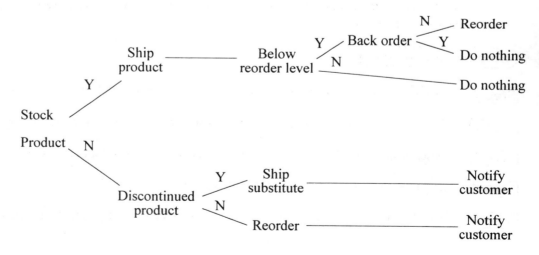

(b)   Structured English is neither easy to use or understand and may complicate the solution.

The decision table can be constructed by following a set procedure, is checkable, easier to understand, and lends itself to automation.

The decision tree is not so easy to construct and involves some repetition.

For this problem, either the decision table or the decision tree are acceptable.

The above techniques are known generically as process tools and are used in structured analysis and design to amplify the logic in the dataflow diagram bubbles, and in the structure chart modules. More informally, they are frequently used by the systems analyst during a systems investigation to check understanding and completeness of procedures, often in conjunction with users.

---

46   (Answer 8 of examination)

Examiner's comments and marking guide

Question 8: examined aspects of decision making and decision support.

It was generally well answered although there was a tendency to connect the type of decision making (structured, unstructured, semi-structured) with management decision levels (operational, tactical and strategic) and then to regurgitate information on the latter.

(a)   (i)   Award two marks for the definitions of analytic and heuristic decision-making.

      (ii)   Award three marks for the definitions of structured, semi-structured and unstructured decisions.

(b)   (i)   Award three marks for understanding why this is not a DSS situation.

      (ii)   Award two marks for suggestions of how it might become a DSS.

(c)   (i)   Award one mark for correct identification of decision type.

             Award one mark for the explanation of the choice.

             Award one mark for identifying two/three appropriate variables.

      (ii)   Award one mark for each DSS feature identified, to a maximum of five.

Step by step answer plan

Step 1   Read the question again and make sure that you focus on precisely what is required.

Step 2   Part (a) is simple (assuming that you have studied the topic!). Just define each term in a way that brings out the distinctions between them.

Step 3   The key point in part (b) is the nature of the decisions being taken by the production supervisor: they are routine and well structured.

Step 4   Part (c) is straightforward.

Step 5   Now review your answer plan and ensure that it does precisely answer the question as set.

The examiner's answer

8   (a)   (i)   An analytic decision maker relies on information that is systematically acquired and evaluated and makes a choice that is information based. Such a decision maker learns by analysing a particular situation, is methodical, and values quantitative information.

                An heuristic decision maker may make use of guidelines, but decisions will generally be experience based. Such a decision maker uses trial and error to find a solution, and relies on common sense to guide them.

(ii)   Structured decisions are those where all or most of the variables are known and can be totally programmed. They are routine and require little human judgement.

Unstructured decisions are those that are resistant to computerisation and depend mainly upon intuition.

Semi-structured decisions fall between the two; they are partially programmable, but still require human judgement.

(b) (i)   Decision support systems (DSS) are designed to assist managers make semi-structured, complex decisions; routine decisions do not warrant a DSS; information here will normally be provided by a management information system (MIS). The nature of the decisions made by the production supervisor are in the second category – an MIS is more appropriate.

(ii)   If the role of the production supervisor becomes far more complex, because of uncertainty and risk, then a DSS might become appropriate.

(c) (i)   The auto-accessory shop owner is making semi-structured ordering decisions; there are multiple criteria and human judgement is required.

Variables involved might include: sales, length of car ownership, popularity of customising kits, oil brands, etc.

(ii)   The features which make her system a DSS rather than an MIS include:

- addressing semi-structured problems
- many variables are considered
- what if capabilities are a possibility
- there is no correct solution
- human judgement is necessary.

Did you answer the question?

Do not fall into the trap of reproducing all you know about the topic you would like to have seen. Stick to the examiner's requirements.

47   (Answer 9 of examination)

Examiner's comments and marking guide

Question 9: was in various parts.

Part (a) asked the candidate to draw a network chart. This was generally well answered with a substantial number of candidates gaining full marks.

The explanation of the Gantt Chart was also satisfactory although some answers would have been enhanced by an example diagram.

The final part describing other activities necessary during implementation was well answered although a disappointing number of candidates included training - which was the subject of part (a) of the question and so could not be an *other* activity.

(a) (i)   I do not believe that there is any other valid solution other than that in the suggested answers - but I may be wrong!
Answers must take the form of a PERT/CPA network.
Award a maximum of six marks for a correct solution.
Deduct one mark for each omission ie, failure to identify the critical path, numbering of events, etc.

(ii)   Award a maximum of two marks for an explanation of the possible uses of the Gantt chart in this context.
Award a maximum of two marks for identification of the extra information that might be required.

(b)   Award one mark for each valid implementation activity identified, to a maximum of six.

Step by step answer plan

Step 1   Read the question again and make sure that you focus on precisely what is required.

Step 2   Sketch out a network diagram in rough, and when you are happy with it produce a fair copy.

Step 3   In part (a) (ii), some of the discussion is fairly general. As for the extra information required, this concerns resource estimates.

Step 4   In part (b) a simple list is required.

Step 5   Now review your answer plan and ensure that it does precisely answer the question as set.

The examiner's answer

9   (a)   (i)

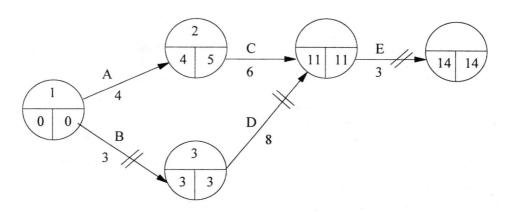

Critical path is B, D, E.

(ii)   A Gantt chart is a straightforward method of scheduling tasks; it is essentially a chart on which bars represent each task or activity. The length of each bar represents the relative length of the task. Its advantages lie in its simplicity, the ready acceptance of it by users, and the fact that the bars are drawn to scale.

In this context, before a Gantt chart can be used, estimates must be made of the resources required for each of the various activities - in terms perhaps of training personnel, or equipment requirements. Once the chart is constructed, it will at once become apparent where there are shortfalls or excess of those resources.

(b)   Apart from the training aspects, other components of systems implementation are:

–   systems testing, including the construction of test data;

–   acceptance testing, including verification validation and audit testing;

–   building and testing networks;

–   database creation;

–   file conversion;

–   changeover procedures ie, direct changeover, parallel running, pilot running and phased changeover;

- production of documentation ie, user guides, systems documentation, operations and training manuals;

- systems evaluation or audit.

Did you answer the question?

Notice that the requirement is for **other** activities, thereby excluding topics you have already covered.

---

48 (Answer 10 of examination)

Examiner's comments and marking guide

Question 10: was in two parts.

The first part of this question asked about the contents of an Invitation to Tender. Unfortunately many candidates described the contents of a tender document itself not an Invitation to Tender.

Few candidates explained how such information might be obtained.

Part (ii), the choosing of a supplier, was poorly answered with few candidates making valid points. The financing part of the question was fairly well answered although a surprising number of candidates again took the opportunity to describe investment appraisal in depth, rather than financing alternatives.

(a) (i) Award a maximum of four marks for identification of the contents of an invitation to tender.
       Award two marks for discussion of how such information might be obtained.
     (ii) Award up to three marks for description of the steps which should be taken on receipt of tenders.

(b) To gain full marks answers should briefly describe each of cash payment, rental, lease and outsourcing.

     Award a maximum of one and a half marks for each method; but no half mark answers, please!

Step by step answer plan

Step 1 Read the question again and make sure that you focus on precisely what is required.

Step 2 Begin by explaining the types of information needed and the sources from which it might be derived.

Step 3 Then list the likely contents of the invitation to tender.

Step 4 In part (a) (ii) a list of points with brief description is required.

Step 5 Four basic possibilities in part (b): cash payment; leasing; renting; outsourcing.

Step 6 Now review your answer plan and ensure that it does precisely answer the question as set.

The examiner's answer

10 (a) (i) **Invitation to tender (ITT)**

              In general terms, the ITT provides formal requirements, ground rules for responses, and, usually, a standard format for the proposal responses (the tenders).

              Before such a document can be formulated, the system requirements must be determined ie, the technical alternatives must be researched. This task identifies criteria that are important to the hardware/software to be selected. Criteria includes response times, ease of use/learning, throughput, licensing arrangements, training, etc. This information can be obtained from various sources, such as trade publications, manufacturers brochures, internal company standards, information services etc. This activity should also identify potential suppliers to whom the ITT may be sent.

Likely contents of the ITT include:

- introduction, including background, brief summary of needs, explanations, actions required of supplier;

- information required about the supplier;

- standards and instructions, including schedule of events leading to contract, ground rules that will be observed when making the selection decision;

- requirements and features, including the mandatory and desirable features and criteria for hardware, software and services;

- technical questionnaires;

- financial requirements;

- conclusion.

(ii)   Upon receipt of tenders from potential suppliers, the claims made in each must be individually verified, and any eliminated that fail to meet mandatory requirements. Performance is best validated by a demonstration set up by the supplier.

Once the individual tenders have been validated, they must now be evaluated and ranked. The criteria should have been established before the ITT was sent out. The evaluation may be carried out on a points basis, or as a cost-benefit analysis exercise. Both technical and financial aspects should be considered.

Once the proposals have been ranked, the analyst usually represents a hardware and software recommendation for final approval. When that is obtained, a contract must be negotiated with the selected supplier, in conjunction with accountants and lawyers. Out of courtesy and to maintain good relationships, a debriefing of the unsuccessful bidders should be provided.

(b)   Four basic methods are available. Briefly, they are:

- cash payment from resources; this should be avoided if it is likely to cause cash-flow problems; a medium to long-term asset such as a computer is normally funded by debt; gives the purchaser freedom to modify the system to meet the specific organisational requirements;

- leasing; a popular method of acquiring a larger computer which involves acquisition from a leasing company for an agreed number of years – usually three to five; a machine is thus available at once which can be funded out of future earnings, and with predictable payments;

- renting; useful for short-term hire, but an expensive way of acquiring equipment; has the advantage of being with the actual supplier rather than with a third party; the customer is responsible for providing the appropriate environment for the equipment; the charge made consists of a fixed rental and a variable charge for maintenance; now a less common method than leasing;

- outsourcing (facilities management or FM); this may take various forms, but can be interpreted in this context as either a FM company running user applications on the FM equipment at the user site, or at the FM site; this somewhat drastic step has recently increased in popularity; it gives some degree of certainty over the cost of computing over the period of the FM contract; it removes the responsibility for the staffing and day-to-day running of the computer installation; it may create staff dissatisfaction.

The method selected will depend upon the financial position of the company, the cost of the purchase, the current taxation arrangements, and the degree to which senior management regard computing as a core company activity.

DECEMBER 1995 QUESTIONS

Section A - ALL FOUR questions in this section are compulsory and MUST be attempted

Read the following case study carefully and then attempt all questions in this part.

A maximum of 55 marks are available.

You should spend no more than half the available time on this part of the paper.

49   (Question 1 of examination)

Case Study

Introduction

A large public authority is responsible for providing the following services to a town and its surrounding areas:

Housing. Provision of publicly owned houses which are rented out to local people at agreed rents. The authority is effectively the landlord of these houses and is responsible for allocation, repairs and maintenance of around 2,000 houses and flats. Twenty staff are employed in the housing department, headed by the chief housing officer. The housing department is based at the authority's headquarters building.

Library services. The authority administers the town library, together with five smaller libraries in neighbouring villages. The library services department employs 30 staff, with the chief librarian based at the town library.

Environmental health. The authority is responsible for measuring air and water quality as well as inspecting restaurants, shops and other premises to ensure that they conform to certain regulatory requirements. The environmental health section has 12 employees and its chief officer is based in the authority's headquarters building.

Planning. This department gives planning permission to individual buildings and monitors the construction of these buildings. The department also develops the local plan for the authority, recommending road construction and upgrading, strategic developments such as supermarkets, and introducing protection measures for countryside and other sites of special interest. The planning department currently has 20 staff and is led by the chief planning officer based at the authority's headquarters building.

Administration. The headquarters building is also occupied by the administration department, responsible for accounting, personnel and legal aspects of the authority's work. The finance department includes a small information systems (IS) section headed by the IS manager. The department currently consists of 3 analysts, 9 programmers 4 operations staff and 2 secretaries. The authority leases a mainframe computer supporting 93 terminals. There are also 36 personal computers (PCs) in the authority. All of these are standalone, except in administration where 20 of finance department's PCs are linked in a local area network (LAN). The IS manager reports directly to the head of finance.

Hardware is currently distributed as follows:

	No. of terminals	No. of PCs
Housing	33	6
Library services	5	2
Environmental health	5	2
Planning	10	6
Administration	40	20

The information system (IS) section is currently under pressure for two main reasons.

1.   The authority is considering making its departments into autonomous business units with their own budgets. The IS section is currently treated as an overhead cost and its staff, hardware, software and other costs are split evenly across the five departments.

2.   A recent housing records project exceeded its time and budget by about 25%. User acceptance testing had to be stopped on three occasions because of major system failures and because it did not fulfil the department's requirements. The system is now live but staff are still concerned about its reliability.

A consultancy firm has been invited to look into the funding of IS as well as the problems surrounding the housing records project. They have begun the latter of these two tasks by requesting the views of the chief housing officer. His memo is reproduced below.

Memo

From

Chief Housing Officer

We have found particular difficulties dealing with information systems in this project. I have fisted the main problems below:

Communication problems between IS and housing department staff. The initial collection of our requirements seemed to be satisfactory and were well documented in the meeting notes produced as a result of our interviews. However, we had great difficulty in understanding how these requirements were going to be translated into the system that we were going to use on a daily basis. No intermediate documents were produced until we received the system specification. This appeared to concentrate on the hardware configuration of the new system and so it was impossible to tell whether it would support our business requirements. The language was very technical and we were unable to fully understand it. Although I approved the document I had little confidence that it correctly represented our requirements. In the light of current events I now regret agreeing a document that I did not fully understand.

Difficulties in project control. I have referred to this problem in the previous point. It was generally impossible to monitor progress of the project because there was such a long gap between collecting our requirements and the delivery of the system. In fact the system was a month late, but we were not made aware of this until one week before we were due to take delivery for user acceptance testing. I felt that the project was never really controlled and that the system only emerged when it did because we threatened to cancel the project. I suspected the software was not finished, a suspicion confirmed by its poor performance in the first week of the acceptance test.

Quality control. The poor quality of the first release is well documented. However, subsequent releases have not convinced me that sufficient quality procedures are being used in our software construction. Let me give three examples:

1.   The 'tenant profile report' worked correctly in Version 1.01, failed completely in Version 1.02 and finally worked - but produced incorrect results in Version 1.03. It has since been fixed in Version 1.04, but I still get one of the clerks to manually check all the figures to make sure the system is correct.

2.   On most screens we have to use the function key F2 to save the record we are entering. However, on the property entry screen we have to use F3 to save the record, whilst F2 is quit!

3.   The data items on the data entry screen for a housing application are in a different order to the physical application form.

System changes. Now the system has gone live we seem to be involved in constant meetings about changes. Most of the meetings seem to be concerned with debating whether our request is a change or a misunderstanding (by IS) of the original requirements. Not surprisingly, IS suggests that everything is a 'specification change' whilst we contend that most of the changes are to make the system do what we wanted it to do in the first place. The specifications seem to be ambiguous or open to interpretation, so most of these meetings appear to be quite fruitless.

I have two suggestions to improve the situation

1.   Decentralise information systems to the individual departments. Make IS part of each business unit answerable to the head of that unit.

2.   Improve our methods of specification, development and project control.

End of memo.

Required:

1   What do you understand by the term 'decentralisation' when it is applied to computer systems organisation? Describe three advantages such an approach would give department heads such as the chief housing officer.

                                                    (9 marks)

2   The IS manager is keen to stress the advantages of a centralised computing facility and she is writing a report to summarise these. What does the term 'centralisation' mean in this context and describe three advantages such a strategy would give to the authority.

                                                    (9 marks)

3   (a)   The consulting firm's study on IS funding is currently considering two options. Discuss the principles, advantages and disadvantages of each of the following two approaches:

               (i)   Running the IS department as a cost centre within the authority but improving the way costs are allocated to the departments.   **(8 marks)**

               (ii)   Setting up the IS department as a separate company free to trade both inside and outside the authority.   **(8 marks)**

    (b)   Which of the above two funding options for IS would you recommend for the authority and why? State any assumptions and conditions you make.

                                                    (4 marks)
                                            (Total: 20 marks)

4   (a)   Explain what is meant by 'structured methods or methodologies'.

                                                      (5 marks)

    (b)   Explain how structured methods help address the following issues identified by the chief housing officer in his memo.

             -        The communication problems between IS and Housing Department staff
             -        Difficulties in project control
             -        Quality control
             -        System changes.

                                              (12 marks)
                                          (Total: 17 marks)
                                          (55 marks)

Section B - THREE questions ONLY to be attempted

50   **(Question 5 of examination)**

5   An important system design objective is that the delivered software should be 'user-friendly' - easy to use. One of the features that makes software 'user-friendly' is the use of language familiar to the user. If the users call a function 'posting P23 forms' then that is how the system should refer to it - not 'updating master expense record' or some other message devised by the systems designer.

      Identify FIVE further software features that should make a system more 'user-friendly'. Describe why each feature makes the software easier to use.

                                                    (15 marks)

51   **(Question 6 of examination)**

6   (a)   Explain what a DBMS is and what it does.

                                                     (4 marks)

    (b)   Describe three advantages of the DBMS approach to data processing.

                                                     (6 marks)

(c)   An application requires that information is held about orders and customers, where a customer places many orders, but an order can only be placed by one particular customer. Each customer is identified by a unique account-number and each order has a unique order-number. List the likely content of the order and customer tables in a relational DBMS and explain how particular orders are linked to the customer who placed that order.

(5 marks)
(Total: 15 marks)

52   (Question 7 of examination)

7   (a)   Explain what is meant by negative feedback. Give an example of how this principle could be used in a business information system.

(6 marks)

(b)   Spreadsheets are often constructed and used by managers to help them make tactical decisions. Explain why spreadsheets are so appropriate for assisting managers to make this type of decision.

(4 marks)

(c)   Describe two possible problems that might arise in an organisation where end-users are extensively using spreadsheets for model building.

(5 marks)
(Total: 15 marks)

53   (Question 8 of examination)

8   Two practical tasks in systems implementation are testing and file conversion.

(a)   Describe the stages of testing and how each stage of testing should be carried out

(7 marks)

(b)   Discuss the issues that arise in data conversion when

(i)   Moving from a current manual system to a computer system
(ii)   Moving from a current computer system to a new computer system.

(8 marks)
(Total: 15 marks)

54   (Question 9 of examination)

9   The information systems section of a company is currently advertising for a systems analyst. It has received 400 applications and so the following procedure has been designed to compile the interview shortlist.

If the applicant is an accredited systems analyst then he or she is automatically given an interview. Accredited systems analysts with computer aided software engineering (CASE) experience will be interviewed on 29 November and those without CASE experience on 3 December. Applicants with CASE experience but without systems analysis accreditation will be placed on a waiting list.

All applicants without systems analysis accreditation but with Fourth Generation Language (4GL) experience will have their application form photocopied and sent to a nearby public authority who are currently looking for a 4GL programmer.

When the form is received at the authority, programmers with 4GL experience in the mainframe environment are automatically scheduled an interview whilst the others are placed on a waiting list.

All other applicants are rejected.

(a)   Document the above procedure with a decision table or tables.
(b)   Explain what a decision tree is.

(12 marks)
(3 marks)
(Total: 15 marks)

ANSWERS TO DECEMBER 1995 EXAMINATION

---

49   (Answer 1 of examination)

Examiner's comments and marking guide

Question 1: this question asked candidates to describe decentralisation and to give three advantages of this approach to organising information systems delivery.

This is a relatively straightforward question based on material found in most study texts and courses. Most candidates answered this question satisfactorily. However, some answers described networks and different network topologies, confusing the delivery of decentralised systems with its implementation. Some candidates also gave 5 or 6 advantages but credit was only given for three, as requested by the question.

3 marks for appropriate explanation of decentralisation
2 marks for each advantage

Step by step answer plan

Step 1   Read the question again and make sure that you focus on precisely what is required.

Step 2   In question 1, explain what is meant by decentralisation. Do not get bogged down in descriptions of network topologies, as some candidates did when the exam was set. Then list three advantages, specific to the scenario.

Step 3   In question 2, explain what is meant by centralisation. Do not get bogged down in descriptions of mainframe computers, as some candidates did when the exam was set. Then list three advantages, specific to the scenario.

Step 4   Question 3 is the largest item in this part of the paper. The examiner tackles it by, in effect, taking parts (a) and (b) together.

Step 5   In question 4, the requirement of part (a) is met by a very brief definition and description. In part (b), the discussion must be tailored to the requirements of the scenario.

Step 6   Now review your answer plan and ensure that it does precisely answer the question as set.

The examiner's answer

1   Decentralised or distributed systems allow information services to be provided from a number of points within the organisation. In this context this would be the ownership of information system equipment and staff by individual departments (such as housing) not by a centralised computer facility.

Decentralisation should provide:

-        better response to local changes in business requirements
-        a technical solution more appropriate to local requirements
-        a better fit with a profit centred approach
-        staff should identify with business requirements and operations rather than technical computing objectives.

Did you answer the question?

Don't give any more than the three advantages requested by the question. You will get no extra credit.

Examiner's comments and marking guide

Question 2: this question asked candidates to describe centralisation and to give three advantages of this approach to organising information systems delivery.

This is a relatively straightforward question based on material found in most study texts and courses. Most candidates answered this question satisfactorily. However, some answers described mainframes (contrasting them to the networks of question 1), confusing the delivery of centralised systems with its implementation. Again, some candidates also gave 5 or 6 advantages but credit was only given for three, as requested by the question.

3 marks for an appropriate explanation of centralisation
2 marks for each advantage

The examiner's answer

2   A centralised information system is one where all services are provided from a single point. In this context the information systems manager foresees the continued existence (and perhaps expansion) of her department providing a central point for services and expertise in the company. All computer equipment, services and personnel will be owned by this centralised facility.

Centralisation should provide:

-    easier to enforce standards and security
-    economies of scale in purchasing supplies and equipment
-    centralisation of computer staff allowing employment of specialists such as communication experts
-    clearly defined career paths for computing staff within the organisation.

Examiner's comments and marking guide

Question 3: this question was designed to give candidates the opportunity to show knowledge gained in other subjects and in their practical work experience as well as from the formal material included in the paper 5 syllabus.

In general, it was well answered with many candidates scoring 15 marks or more. However, some candidates did not seize the opportunity and a number of markers expressed their surprise that candidates seemed to lack a basic understanding of the principles of cost centres.

For sections (i) and (ii) I have not told the student how the eight marks are distributed through each part of the question. Hence I will leave it to your discretion with the proviso that none of the three 'parts' (ie, principles, advantages and disadvantages) is allocated more than 4 marks. The total of 8 marks for each section cannot be exceeded.

The final part of this question is looking for a coherent answer, rather than a 'right' one.

Give a mark to each valid point up to a maximum of 4.

The examiner's answer

3   The first part of this question requires a discussion on a fairer way of partitioning costs. For example, costs could be split on the basis of actual use. Possibilities include:

-    number of terminals/workstations in each department
-    use of CPU time
-    use of computer staff resources, such as programmers and analysts.

The main advantage of such an approach is that the cost reflects use, rather than an arbitrary division of an overhead cost.

Disadvantages include:

-    calculation of costs may be difficult for the user. For example, it is difficult for a user to estimate the CPU time used by a particular report or enquiry. The efficiency of the use of the CPU is determined by the way the programmer has designed the program. Most users are unable to comment on this design or suggest faster ways of doing things. The unscrupulous or incompetent programmer can make money for the department by writing poor programs!

- the user may only have the choice to accept a cost or reject it. They may not be given the opportunity to seek competitive quotes from elsewhere and so are unable to judge the fairness of the quote they have been given. This is particularly relevant to analysis and programming time. It is almost impossible for a user to question the time taken for a particular requirement unless they have access to an alternative quote.

- the overhead costs of the information systems department still has to be met, whether it has been used or not. Thus users can decide to not use computer systems and staff to save money but the company still has to pay the salaries of the computing staff.

The main advantage of making IS into a separate company is that it establishes a contractual arrangement between the provider and user of information systems. If users do not like the terms or cost of that contract then they can seek alternative suppliers.

Disadvantages include:

- lack of expertise in management. Many IS departments made into companies may struggle due to lack of financial and entrepreneurial skills in their new management. Running a company is very different from running a department.

- the costs will have to reflect that a separate company now has to make a profit out of providing a service. Thus daily rates are usually much higher than previous internal charges

- one of the most important resources (information provision) of the company is now subcontracted to another organisation.

Did you answer the question?

Make sure that you tackle all aspects of the requirement ie, (i) which options, (ii) why, (iii) assumptions and (iv) conditions.

Examiner's comments and marking guide

Question 4: this question asked candidates to briefly describe the principles of structured methods and then to show how such methods tackled some of the problems described in the case study.

The first part (describing structured methods) was reasonably answered. However the second part was answered very poorly. The four problem areas were directly related to the headings in the case study and there were clear pointers to the answer in the text of the case study. However, most candidates overlooked these pointers in preference to general answers with little relevance to structured methods. The answers suggested that candidates could describe structured methods but did not understand their application or relevance.

(a)   Give a mark for each valid point up to a maximum of 5.
(b)   Give a mark for valid point up to a maximum of 3 for each section.

The examiner's answer

4   (a)   Structured methods (or methodologies) are essentially collections of models, techniques and procedures showing the process of systems development. They define a systems development method, showing where standard models and other deliverables fit into the development life cycle. SSADM is a typical structured method. It includes both

Structure: Describing the framework of the methodology in terms of modules, stages and steps.

and *Techniques* such as data flow diagrams defining how the steps are carried out.

(b)   *Communication* with users is achieved through the development of graphical, logical models. These represent the blueprint of the system, and most methods require users to acknowledge their understanding and acceptance of the models by formally signing them off. The issue of communication was one of the main reasons for the original development of structured methods. Narrative text was tedious to write and read as well as being ambiguous. Technical physical implementation (such as in the example given by the chief housing officer) would not be a user sign-off in a structured method.

Project control. Structured methods normally define which deliverables have to be completed to finish a stage or step. The progress of the project can be monitored by the delivery of these models against the required set. The stage or step is only completed when all deliverables have been accepted and met their quality criteria.

Quality control. Each model has a set of defined quality requirements. For example, a data flow diagram must have each process uniquely named and a store cannot be connected to an external entity. Conformance to these quality criteria is checked by standards staff or internal auditors.

Change control. Many of the models unambiguously define the user's requirements. For example, a one to many relationship between customer and depot defines that a customer can have many depots but that each depot only belongs to one customer. Acceptance of a specification defining this relationship means that any subsequent discovery that a depot can be shared by customers is a change in business requirements and hence will consume cost and time.

Did you answer the question?

A case study question will usually give you relevant information to build into the answer. Try to use it, especially where the question specifically asks for it.

---

50   (Answer 5 of examination)

Examiner's comments and marking guide

Question 5: this question was concerned with the use ability of software. It specifically asked for software features. Pointers to the answer were also available in the case study where users suffered from inconsistency (in the use of the F2 and F3 function keys) and inappropriate data entry (the data items on the data entry screen were in a different order to the physical application form).

However, despite these clues, candidates often chose to describe hardware features. Furthermore, when candidates provided correct answers they often did not give enough detail to score more than one or two marks per point, concentrating on describing the feature rather than why it made the system easier to use. Consequently, many candidates scored low marks for this question.

Give a mark for each valid point up to a maximum of 3 for each feature.

Step by step answer plan

Step 1 Read the question again and make sure that you focus on precisely what is required.

Step 2 List five relevant software features.

Step 3 Show how each of your selected features makes the software easier to use.

Step 4 Now review your answer plan and ensure that it does precisely answer the question as set.

The examiner's answer

5   This question is concerned with software features, rather than the technology of the interface (mouse, touchscreens etc.).

Consistency of presentation and operation. Users are confused by arbitrary changes in phrasing, layout and format and this leads to anxiety, errors and lower productivity. For example, inconsistent use of a confirm key for data entry will lead to input errors and subsequent correction.

Conformity with other software. Experience shows that users often take their knowledge from one application to another and expect related systems to work in a similar manner. One of the benefits of the Windows interface is its consistency across applications allowing users to be in familiar territory when using new application software running in that environment. This reduces training time and costs and allows users to quickly become proficient and productive.

Provision of HELP facilities. Context sensitive HELP allows users to access screen-based information relevant to their position in the software. This should allow users to resolve problems more quickly and hence improve productivity.

Escapable. There may come a point where the user is unsure about the next command. A natural reaction may be to panic and switch off the machine or terminal, with unpredictable effect. An easy and obvious escape route reassures the user and ensures the integrity of the data. This escape facility (often, in fact, the <esc> key) should be consistent throughout the system.

Logical. If the software is concerned with data entry, then the positioning and order of the fields should reflect the physical form. Colour can be used to highlight the entry fields and to show where data values are mandatory. Entry screens that do not reflect the physical form lead to slower data entry and a greater possibility of errors.

Other issues that might be considered include:

- provision of default values to allow fast data entry

- appropriate use of colour and spacing

- icon driven, to permit menu selection without keyboard entry

- flexibility. Experienced users of a system may have 'fastpath' key commands in place of cumbersome menu selection.

Did you answer the question?

When a question asks about software, don't discuss hardware!

---

51 (Answer 6 of examination)

(**Examiner's comments and marking guide**)

Question 6: parts (a) and (b) of this question were fairly straightforward questions on the definition and advantages of the DBMS approach to data processing.

These parts were generally well answered, although some candidates did not restrict themselves to only three advantages. Part (c) was a more technical problem, allowing candidates to show that they understood how relationships were maintained in a RDBMS. The answers were quite good although many candidates also stored order-number in the Customer table, hence covering (incorrectly) all options!

(a)   1 mark for the definition data base management system (or software?)
         1 mark for explaining that it is software
         2 marks at your discretion for valid explanation/examples.

(b)   2 marks per valid benefit. Three benefits are requested in the question.

(c)   1 mark for showing the correct keys of the two tables
         2 marks for placing the foreign key in order
         2 marks for explanation of the link between the tables.

(**Step by step answer plan**)

Step 1   Read the question again and make sure that you focus on precisely what is required.

Step 2   Parts (b) and (c) are straightforward, and the examiner commented that they were answered well.

Step 3   Then think carefully about the logic of part (c) and describe the content of the required tables.

Step 4   Now review your answer plan and ensure that it does precisely answer the question as set.

(**The examiner's answer**)

6   (a)   DBMS stands for data base management system. A data base is a shared, formally defined, centrally controlled collection of data used in an organisation. The data base is organised and accessed through a generalised software package called a data base management system. The DBMS provides access to the data for different application programs and users. It will also provide security, rollback and recovery facilities.

There are three accepted DBMS models - hierarchical, network and relational.

Typical examples are IMS, IDMS, ORACLE, INGRES and DB2.

(b)   Typical benefits include:

-    better exploration of the company's data allowing different parts of the enterprise to use consistent shared data. In an application centred approach to systems development each application has its own private files. There is little opportunity to share data and so analyse information across the whole of the enterprises

-    easier enforcement of standards in systems development, data naming and program development. These issues are under the control of a centralised organisational unit (Data Base Administration) charged with the central control of data and responsible for deciding the information content of the data base, the storage structure, defining security and integrity checks and producing a strategy for backup and recovery.

-    controlled redundancy. Data used across several different application areas can lead to repetition of information, leading to inconsistency and duplicated data. The DBMS may hold redundant data for performance or application reasons rather than as a result of fragmented systems development.

(c)   A relational DBMS would define two tables order and customer and the key of customer (account-number) would be held in the order table. All orders for a particular customer (say, account-number 17) would be located by searching the order table for instances where account-number was equal to that value. Speed of access to this field is improved if this foreign key (in this case account-number) is defined as a secondary index.

Relational DBMS tables

·   CUSTOMER (account-number, customer-name,.....

ORDER (order-number, order-date, account-number.....

---

52   (Answer 7 of examination)

(**Examiner's comments and marking guide**)

Question 7: part (a) of this question asked for a definition of negative feedback together with an example of how this principle could be used in a business information system.

The definitions of negative feedback were satisfactory although some candidates interpreted 'negative feedback' as 'criticism'. The business example was less satisfactory and indeed many candidates elected not to give one.

Parts (b) and (c) concerned the application of spreadsheets and problems that might arise from their use. The latter issues (part (c) of the question) were answered satisfactorily and the Examiner was pleased to see candidates using their practical experience in the answers.

(a)   3 marks for the definition of negative feedback
3 marks for an appropriate business system example.

(b)   1 mark for each valid point up to a maximum of 4 marks.

(c)   2 - 5 marks for each disadvantage. Two disadvantages are requested in the question.

Step by step answer plan

Step 1   Read the question again and make sure that you focus on precisely what is required.

Step 2   Describe what is meant by negative feedback. For an example drawn from business, choose a production control system or similar.

Step 3   The main point in part (b) is the use of model building, with ability to change parameters in order to explore different outcomes.

Step 4   Part (c) is not about general shortcomings of spreadsheet modelling. It is about the use of such modelling by end-users, as opposed to a centralised system.

Step 5   Now review your answer plan and ensure that it does precisely answer the question as set.

The examiner's answer

7   (a)   Outputs of a system are measured by a sensor. This measures the magnitude of the output and communicates this to the control mechanism which contains a comparator. The comparator compares the actual with the required state and, if necessary, adjusts the output of the system so that the required magnitude can be achieved.

The most common example is that of a sensor (thermostat) measuring output magnitude (temperature) in the environment of the system (room). If this performance is inadequate (too cold) it will change the system's performance (by turning on the heating) so changing the magnitude of the output.

A production control system may have a sensor (on a machine line) measuring output magnitude (production). If this performance is inadequate to meet the desired production rate then the controlled variable (speed of the machine line) may be increased to meet the required production figures. In some instances the control mechanism might be a manager or supervisor. For example, sales may be measured by bar code scanning in a shop. If the required sales targets are not met then the variance is fed back to a sales manager. The manager can then attempt to boost system performance by reducing product price, increasing marketing spend, improving sales bonuses etc.

> **Did you answer the question?**
>
> If a question asks for an example, make sure that you provide one.

(b)   Spreadsheets are excellent tools for exploring tactical decisions because they allow simple and flexible model building. The models are based around parameters that can be changed (such as supplier costs, lead times and interest rates) allowing the manager to explore a large number of scenarios. Furthermore, most allow internal data to be downloaded (through an import facility) very easily so that operational data of the company can be used in the model.

(c)   Disadvantages of using spreadsheets for such model building include:

-     it is unlikely that developers will properly document their spreadsheet models. This makes it difficult for other staff (particularly successors) to use and modify the models

-     problems in writing and maintaining macros. The macro commands are often difficult to understand and are unsuited to writing structured programs

-     poor training in spreadsheets often leads to poor or under use. Thus systems are not designed or developed efficiently

-     lack of audit trails can lead to misuse. Spreadsheets operate in memory and changes made are not automatically recorded in an audit trail.

53   (Answer 8 of examination)

Examiner's comments and marking guide

Question 8: part (a) of this question concerned the stages of testing and how they might be carried out. The suggested answer looked for program, system and user-acceptance testing.

Although some candidates answered in this way, many others restricted themselves to discussing testing in the systems implementation stage. On reflection this is a perfectly reasonable interpretation of the question and so candidates answering in this way were not penalised - one mark was allocated for each relevant point up to a maximum of seven marks.

Part (b) concerned data conversion and generally it was not well answered, with many candidates repeating the same points for moving from a manual to a computer system as for moving from a current computer system to a new one. Parallel running, direct changeover and pilot implementation were also described. These have little relevance to this question.

(a)   2 marks for each testing stage
       1 extra mark at your discretion for any other valid point raised in the answer.

(b)   A mark for each valid point raised up to a maximum of 4 for each sub-section.

Step by step answer plan

Step 1   Read the question again and make sure that you focus on precisely what is required. See the examiner's comment on this question for the variety of approaches that are acceptable.

Step 2   In part (a) one approach is to discuss in turn: program testing; system testing; and user acceptance testing.

Step 3   Part (b) is very general: the term 'issues' may refer to procedures, problems or almost anything else. Be careful to select just a limited number of 'issues' that appear important, because only eight marks are available.

Step 4   Now review your answer plan and ensure that it does precisely answer the question as set.

The examiner's answer

8   (a)   Testing goes through three basic stages

Program testing

During the programming stage each programmer or programming team will perform their own program testing to the specifications laid down by the systems analyst. This stage is concerned with validating the internal code of the program making sure that it conforms to the standards of the company as well as performing the functional business requirements defined by the analyst. The testing is performed through manual 'walkthroughs' of the program as well as the production of test plans and their results.

Systems testing

This is designed to ensure that the sub-systems work properly together. This testing is performed against specification and uses test data and test results. Testing is performed over a single pass of data before progressing to cyclical tests (such as end-of-month and end-of-year routines), and volume testing. Testing may be performed by the systems analyst or by specialist quality and standards staff.

User acceptance testing

This is organised and performed by users. It is concerned with proving, to their satisfaction, that the delivered system meets the specification. The testing is again against test data with suitably prepared test results. The users check the outputs to prove the system against the day-to-day running of the system. User acceptance testing also allows for gradual user training and gives them experience of the system prior to implementation.

(b)   Issues in data conversion.

Current manual system to a computer one

-     Set up of master files. The task of file creation can be a daunting task. The resources of the department may not be sufficient or willing to undertake such activities on top of their daily work. The system is unusable until all such data is entered.

-     Entry of system derived fields. The operational use of the system may automatically create certain data values. For example, the date-of-last-order on the customer file might be posted into the field on receipt of order. However, at the start of the system this field will be blank in all the established customer records. Thus specially written file creation programs may have to be written to capture historical information into the system.

-     The lack of historical data may restrict use. For example, reports running off the date-of-last-order field introduced in the previous section, may be of little use until the second or third year of the system's use.

Computer system to another computer system

-     Technical feasibility of moving from one system to another. The developer has to investigate whether it is possible to technically take data from one system and put it on the target machine. It may not be possible to move information from a Prime machine to a Hewlett-Packard.

-     Data mapping and program testing. If it is possible to move from one machine to another then the developer has to carefully map the fields on the current system to the proposed one. For example, the field delegate-name may currently sit on a course file and this has to be transferred to a student record on the new system. The developer will have to formally map these relationships and write a program to move the data from the old to the new system. This program has to be tested and the test results carefully examined.

-     Dirty data, different field lengths and empty fields. Problems can be caused by the transfer of incorrect data values, differences in field lengths between the new and old systems, and empty fields in the new system that have to be populated by specially designed data creation programs.

54   (Answer 9 of examination)

(Examiner's comments and marking guide)

Question 9: this was a decision table question.

The question hinted that tables were required and so candidates who produced two tables, linked in a hierarchy, could score two marks more than candidates who chose to produce one large table. The original marking scheme for this question also gave two marks for a reduced decision table but these were withdrawn on later consideration and re-distributed to the main table. The question was well answered with some candidates producing perfect or near-perfect solutions. Part (b), concerning the decision tree was also answered satisfactorily. A few candidates produced a decision tree or data flow diagram for part (a). Unfortunately this gained no marks.

Decision Table A (8 marks)
(2 for conditions, 1 for actions, 1 for the perform Table B action, 4 for correct combinations and action ticks)

Decision Table B (2 marks)
Reduced Decision Table A (2 marks)

Candidates with only one decision table can only score a maximum of 9 marks (7 marks for Decision Table A and 2 marks for Reduced Decision Table A).

Step by step answer plan

Step 1   Read the question again and make sure that you focus on precisely what is required.

Step 2   Clearly the hard work is in part (a) and you should study the logic of the situation closely. Draft your answer very quickly in rough before preparing the final version.

Step 3   Three easy marks are available in part (b). Be sure not to overlook them.

Step 4   Now review your answer plan and ensure that it does precisely answer the question as set.

The examiner's answer

9   (a)   *Decision Table A*

	1	2	3	4	5	6	7	8
Accredited analyst?	y	y	y	y	n	n	n	n
CASE experience?	y	y	n	n	y	y	n	n
4GL experience	y	n	y	n	y	n	y	n
29.11	✓	✓						
3.12			✓	✓				
Waiting list					✓	✓		
Do Decision Table B					✓		✓	
Reject								✓

Reduced Decision Table A

	1	2	3	4	5	6
Accredited analyst?	y	y	n	n	n	n
CASE experience?	y	n	y	y	n	n
4GL experience	-	-	y	n	y	n
29.11	✓					
3.12		✓				
Waiting list			✓	✓		
Do Decision Table B			✓		✓	
Reject						✓

Decision Table B

	1	2
Mainframe experience?	y	n
Interview	✓	
Waiting list		✓

(b)   A decision tree is another way of showing the alternative actions that can take place as a result of different combinations of conditions. The diagram resembles a fallen tree, with a root on the left hand side and branches representing each decision. The tree is read from left to right and the actions to be undertaken are recorded down the right hand side of the diagram.

Did you answer the question?

Part (a) requires a decision table and part (b) concerns decision trees. Read such questions carefully to ensure that you discuss the correct topic in the correct part.

JUNE 1996 QUESTIONS

Section A - ALL FOUR questions in this section are compulsory and MUST be attempted

55   (Question 1 of examination)

Case Study

Introduction

Four years ago the government introduced a Certificate of Proficiency in Information Systems. All information systems staff with over five years practical experience are eligible to sit for certification. Candidates have to take three examination papers and pass all three at one sitting. Successful candidates are allowed to call themselves Certified Information Systems Practitioners. Examinations are set in April and November and are conducted in centres all over the world.

The task of organising the certificate was given to a new organisation called ISEC (Information Systems Examination Centre).

ISEC

-     publishes and maintains the examination syllabus
-     appoints examiners, markers and invigilators
-     processes scripts and results
-     publishes statistical analyses of examination results.

ISEC is set up as an independent trading company and it has to record a profit.

It was originally forecast that ISEC would have to deal with about 3,000 candidates per annum.

However the success of the scheme, particularly abroad, has meant that over 11,000 scripts had to be processed in the last sitting of the papers.

ISEC has a chief executive who has three department heads reporting to her. The departments are:

Administration department

The administration department has seven staff. They are responsible for:

-     Storing and acknowledging applicants for the examination

-     Sending examination instructions to candidates

-     Receiving examination scripts from the examination centres and distributing these to examination markers

-     Receiving marked scripts back from the markers and recording the results

-     Sending examination marks to candidates and publishing statistical analyses of the results.

The head of section has produced a simple single-user spreadsheet for recording applicants, receipt of examinations and final results. The spreadsheet records:

-     Applicant registration number and the date of application

-     The date the examination instructions were sent to the candidate

-     The date the candidates completed examination script was received from the examination centre

- The date the examination script was sent to the marker and the name of the marker

- The date the marked examination script was received back from the marker

- A record of the marks for each question for the candidate

- The date marks were sent to the candidate

- Simple statistical analyses of results, by paper, marker and question.

Copies of application forms have to be passed to finance and administration who raise an invoice for the examination fee. Details of successful candidates are passed to education department who produce a certificate and add the candidate to the Member's Register. The spreadsheet automatically produces a total of the number of scripts marked by each marker. These details are also passed to finance and administration.

Education department

The education department has five staff and is responsible for:

- Defining and publishing the examination syllabus

- Scheduling and organising examination centres and organising invigilators

- Appointment of external examiners

- Checking that examinations set by the external examiners are of the required standard

- Auditing examinations to ensure that examination marking has been fair and consistent

- Producing membership certificates and maintaining a Membership Register.

There are three stand-alone personal computers (pcs) in this department used for word processing. Details of the examination schedule and examination centres are passed to the administration department. External examiner details are passed to finance and administration who pay the examiners an annual fee.

Finance and administration

The finance and administration department has three staff. It is responsible for:

- Payment of external examiners and markers

- Receipt of payments from candidates

- Payment of full-time staff

- Maintenance of the accounts ledgers.

The department has a single user personal computer running standard purchase, sales and nominal ledgers together with payroll.

Although each department is computerised there is no link between any of the pcs either within or between departments.

ISEC are currently considering a project to integrate the three departments of the company. A software house specialising in examination systems has suggested a solution based on a local area network with a dedicated file server based in the administration department. It is proposed that this will support three personal computers (pcs) in the education department, three pcs in finance and administration and a further four pcs in the administration department. The software might be a standard package or a system specially written by the software house for ISEC.

ISEC are considering the costs and benefits of such integration.

1   (a)   Describe three benefits that are likely to arise at ISEC from integrating the current systems.

(9 marks)

(b)   Describe four types or categories of cost (actual values are not required) that will be incurred if the current systems are integrated using the solution suggested by the software house.   (8 marks)

(Total 17 marks)

2   In examining the economic feasibility of the project the organisation will have to consider methods for evaluating costs and benefits of the application. The chief executive is not familiar with these methods.

(a)   Describe what is meant by each of the following two methods and give TWO advantages and ONE disadvantage of each.

(i)   Payback period or time to payback   (5 marks)
(ii)   Discounted cash flow (net present value and internal rate of return).   (6 marks)

(b)   Briefly comment on the difficulties associated with applying such methods in assessing the economic feasibility of an information systems project.   (3 marks)

(Total 14 marks)

3   In looking at the technical feasibility of the system it has been agreed that the accurate, fast and cheap collection of data for examination scripts is essential. For each examination script the system needs to record:

-   The candidate who has written that examination script

-   The marker of that examination script

-   Which paper that examination script is for

-   The centre the candidate sat the examination paper at

-   The questions they attempted in their script

-   The marks given for each question by the marker

-   The total marks for each examination script.

(a)   Given that 99% of all candidates registered attend and sit the examination what information could almost certainly be pre-recorded on an examination answer book? Identify any problems associated with pre-recording such information.   (8 marks)

The following data collection methods have been suggested for the examination system;

-   Optical mark recognition
-   Optical character recognition
-   Bar coding.

(b)   Briefly describe ONE of the data collection methods given above.   (3 marks)

(c)   For the method that you have selected in part b, describe its potential application in the examination system, highlighting where it would be particularly appropriate and where it would not.   (5 marks)

(Total 16 marks)

4   A feasibility study should consider the operational feasibility of a project.

(a)   Describe two issues that should be examined in determining the operational feasibility of a project.

(4 marks)

(b)   Suggest and briefly explain what operational issues might arise at ISEC.   (4 marks)

(Total 8 marks)

Section B - THREE questions ONLY to be attempted

56   (Question 5 of examination)

The entity-relationship model (or Logical Data Structure) shown in Fig 1 has been provided as a part of a functional specification document. The entities in this diagram are shown as rectangular boxes.

(a)   Explain the meaning of the model shown in Fig 1 using a set of English statements.   (4 marks)

(b)   Describe the basic principles of the entity-relationship model and identify its role in systems development. Why is it particularly important that users should understand such models?   (7 marks)

(c)   The model shown in Fig 1 contains a likely flaw in the relationship between invoice and payment. What should the relationship be?   (1 mark)

(d)   Many methodologies decompose such relationships. Decompose (or break down) with a brief explanation, the relationship between invoice and payment.   (2 marks)

(e)   What data items could be contained in the newly determined entity?   (1 mark)

(Total 15 marks)

Fig 1 Information Analysis

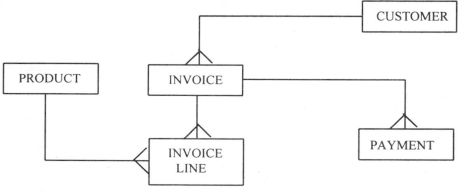

57   (Question 6 of examination)

The development of computer systems is a project based activity. The development project has a start and, once it has met its objectives, an end.

(a)   At the start of many projects a document, sometimes called a project initiation document (PID), is produced. List and briefly describe the typical contents of such a document.   (7 marks)

(b)   Explain how computer software can be used to help the planning, estimating, monitoring and reporting of project progress.   (8 marks)

(Total 15 marks)

58   (Question 7 of examination)

(a)   Explain what a CASE tool is   (3 marks)

(b)   The following issues are important in systems development

-        Producing and maintaining documentation
-        Adhering to development standards
-        Maintaining a logical data dictionary
-        Prototyping.

With reference to the four issues above, explain what advantages a CASE tool offers the systems developer compared to systems development using manually produced and maintained diagrams, standards and documents. (12 marks)

(Total 15 marks)

59 (Question 8 of examination)

A small equipment hire company is considering its information systems strategy. A consultant has produced a comprehensive requirements specification which is now being used to select appropriate software. Two alternatives are currently being examined.

The first proposal is from a company that has suggested that their software package fulfils 90% of the company's requirements. They have proposed that the company purchases the package and that further work is commissioned to tailor it to the company's specific requirements.

(a)   Briefly explain three advantages of adopting a software package solution. (6 marks)

(b)   Comment on any dangers you can see in accepting the proposal of tailoring the package to the company's specific requirements. (3 marks)

(c)   The second alternative is to commission a local software house to build a bespoke or tailored solution. The software will be designed to fulfil the exact needs of the equipment hire company.

Briefly explain three advantages of adopting such a bespoke or tailored solution to the company's requirements. (6 marks)

(Total 15 marks)

60 (Question 9 of examination)

Data validation and verification are concerned with improving the accuracy of data entry.

(a)   Describe, with examples, three different types of data validation checks that might be made when data is entered from a keyboard. (6 marks

(b)   Some data entry procedures use a check digit. Describe, with an example, what is meant by a check digit and explain what sort of errors it is designed to detect. (5 marks)

(c)   Explain what is meant by data verification and why it might be necessary even when data validation checks are to be made on entered data values. (4 marks)

(Total 15 marks)

ANSWERS TO JUNE 1996 EXAMINATION

55   (Answer 1 of examination)

1

Examiner's comments and marking guide

Question 1: this was a gentle introductory question defining costs and benefits that computerisation would bring to the case study organisation. It was generally well answered.

(a)   Up to three marks for each valid benefit. Three benefits required.

(b)   Up to two marks for each valid cost category. Four cost categories required.

Step by step answer plan

Step 1   Read the question again and make sure that you focus on precisely what is required.

Step 2   In question 1 focus on the obvious duplications in the current system. Then rely on 'bookwork' knowledge to describe the categories of expense that will be incurred. This is a straightforward question which the examiner says was well answered.

Step 3   Question 2 again demands mainly 'bookwork' knowledge, but note that in part (b) you are required to apply your knowledge to a specific situation.

Step 4   In part (a) of question 3 a systematic approach is to consider each item of data in the list and decide whether or not it can be preprinted. Parts (b) and (c) can be tackled together.

Step 5   Question 4 is worth only eight marks in total, and this should make it clear that only brief description is required.

Step 6   Now review your answer plan and ensure that it does precisely answer the question as set.

The examiner's answer

(a)   Benefits that are likely to arise from integration will include:

-    The current arrangement requires certain data to be entered separately into different systems to satisfy the needs of individual departments. For example, candidate details are entered in both the administration department (for acknowledging and monitoring applicants) and in finance and administration (for raising invoices and processing payments). Integrating the systems will lead to time (and hence cost) savings as the data will only have to be entered once.

-    The same data held across different systems introduces the chance of inconsistency. For example, a change of address of an external examiner, acknowledged and stored in the education department, may not be notified or entered into the finance and administration department's system. This leads to the annual cheque being sent to the wrong address! Integrating the systems will eradicate such inconsistency and should lead to a reduction in errors.

-    The integration of the systems will provide a foundation for flexibly retrieving data currently stored across three departments. This should provide consistent and useful management information. This information is available in the current systems but it would be difficult and time-consuming to produce and differences in definition may lead to inconsistencies and misinterpretation.

- The integrated system should provide a more robust, documented and standard solution than the three sub-systems that are currently being used. Integration will require the definition and standardisation of certain terms and fields as well as requiring a defined and documented design to fulfil the requirements of all three departments. In the current situation there is unlikely to be agreed naming and other standards across all three departments and the spreadsheet used in the administration department is probably undocumented and not constructed to any company standards.

(b)   Four categories of cost will include:

Hardware: there are currently five PCs in the organisation. The software house's suggestion is for a further five pcs together with a further high performance pc as the dedicated file-server. Network cards will have to be placed in each pc. Printer requirements will have to be investigated and fulfilled.

Specification: the current system will have to be documented and the requirements of its successor investigated and listed. This requirements specification will form the basis of the evaluation of software packages or a starting point for the bespoke design of the system. A feasibility study will also incur costs.

Software: the company may elect to develop bespoke software or to purchase a package off-the-shelf. Network software will also have to be purchased. Multi-user versions and licences will have to be bought for standard applications such as the word processing package.

Training: training will include both software and network training. There may also be a need to repeat training on standard packages (such as the word processing) particularly if it interacts with the application software.

Conversion: converting data from the current systems into the new one. Data may be manually re-entered or converted via specially written file conversion programs. Such programs have to be designed, tested and documented.

Infrastructure: infrastructure costs include cabling, ducting, installation, furniture and stationery.

Staff: it may be necessary to recruit or re-grade a member of staff as network manager. This person will have to attend appropriate network management courses. Individual staff in the departments may need to be re-graded to reflect their new responsibilities and competencies.

2

(Examiner's comments and marking guide)

Question 2: this question concerned economic feasibility of the computerisation. It was a fairly straightforward 'bookwork' type question and could be answered without particular reference to the case study.

Many candidates scored well on this question and have made appropriate points in part (b) where they were asked to comment on applying the methods to information system projects. However, many markers were also surprised about the large number of poor answers to this question given the general importance of these methods in accountancy.

(a)   (i)   Up to two marks for the explanation. One mark for each valid advantage and disadvantage up to a maximum of three marks.

      (ii)   Up to three marks for the explanation of NPV and IRR.
One mark for each valid advantage and disadvantage to a maximum of three marks.

(b)   One mark for each valid comment up to a maximum of three marks.

The examiner's answer

(a)　(i)　Payback period or time to payback. This is the period taken for the cash inflows of the project to equal its cash outflows. Usually the project with the shortest payback period is selected or the organisation defines a payback period which all projects must achieve.

Advantages include:

Simple to calculate and understand
Favours quick return projects which produce faster growth and improve corporate liquidity.
Quick return projects also reduce uncertainty due to time. Longer payback projects tend to be riskier because more changes can take place in the project's environment during the proposed payback time.

Disadvantages include:

Payback does not consider cash flows after the payback period and so does not consider the overall worth of the project.
Payback may disguise important differences in the timing and relative values of the cash flows.

(ii)　Discounted cash flow (DCF)

Net present value: (NPV)

The NPV method calculates the present value of expected cash inflows and outflows to determine whether the present value of cash inflows is greater than the present value of cash outflows. The present value for each net cash flow is calculated by multiplying the value by a discount figure which reflects the time value of money. These discount figures are recorded in standard tables.

The internal rate of return (IRR) is the discount rate which yields an NPV of zero for a project. The IRR can then be compared with the actual cost of capital to determine if it is viable. For example, a project may yield an IRR of 9%. If the current interest rate or cost of capital is greater than this then the project may not be considered to be viable.

Advantages include:

Discounted cash flow takes into account the time value of money.
All cash flows within the life of the project are considered.
Simple criteria exist for accepting or rejecting a project proposal.

Disadvantages include:

Although DCF reduces the value of net cash inflows that take place later in the project, they are (unlike the payback period approach) taken into consideration. This may cause short-term liquidity problems and increases the uncertainty associated with time.

(b)　Difficulties include

-　Problems with quantifying 'untangible benefits', such as the value of not having to apologise for as many order errors.

-　Uncertainty at the timing and amount of quantified benefits.

-　The benefit is often due to a joint effort of a number of departments in the organisation. It is very difficult (and perhaps fruitless) to try to assess the computer's contribution.

Difficulties in estimating costs reduces the accuracy of the cost-benefit analysis.

Did you answer the question?

The requirement of this question is very well-structured and you should ensure that your answer matches.

3

Examiner's comments and marking guide

Question 3: this question concerned data capture methods. It invited candidates to describe one of three common data collection technologies (part (b)) in the context of the cast study (part (c)). The first part of the question asked candidates to define what information could be pre-recorded given certain conditions.

Some candidates misinterpreted 'pre-recording' as meaning 'filling in by a candidate at the time of sitting the examination but before being processed', so that their answers talked about having boxes/spaces on the script to fill in questions answered etc. Some candidates also felt that pre-recording the marks was a good idea! Candidates often failed to identify where their chosen data collection method might be inappropriate in the examination system and others just re-described the technology they had written about in part (b).

(a)   One mark for each valid item (candidate details, examination centre, desk number, paper name and marker code) up to a maximum of five marks.
One mark for each valid point about potential problems up to a maximum of three marks.

(b)   One mark for each valid point up to a maximum of three marks.

(c)   One mark for each valid point up to a maximum of five marks.

The examiner's answer

(a)   With such a high attendance rate it should be possible to pre-record candidate details, examination paper and centre details on the answer book so creating an individual answer book for each candidate in advance. A problem would arise if a candidate needed two or more answer books to complete his or her scripts. The system could produce two answer books in advance for each candidate but this is likely to be very wasteful as most candidates probably complete examination papers within one book. There are a number of simple solutions to this problem and an agreed policy would have to be formulated and documented - for example, each subsequent book is completed by the applicant on the day and is attached to the first book with an appropriate tag.

It may be possible to record marker code details in advance if the marker is allocated to a script prior to the examination. This is possible but unlikely, but it must be checked with the user. It is not possible to pre-record which questions the candidate will attempt (even if they are all mandatory) or what marks they will achieve!

(b) & (c)

Optical mark recognition (OMR). OMR readers recognise hand or machine printed marks on forms. The user fills a lozenge-shaped box that represents the value they wish to record.

Optical mark recognition is not particularly suitable for pre-coded data, such as the candidate, centre and examination paper details, unless the lozenge-shaped boxes are completed automatically under a printed version of the information.

However, OMR could be used in the examination system for the candidate to indicate the questions he or she has attempted and, later in the procedure, for the marker to enter details of the mark for each of the attempted questions. A column for total mark might also be recorded as a quality check against the individual marks. Errors in filling in the individual marks might be trapped by them failing to add up to the total mark allocated by the marker.

The marker might also fill in an appropriate marker code to record which marker has marked that paper.

Optical character recognition (OCR). OCR readers scan documents pre-printed with a stylised font. They are particularly effective in reading pre-printed information (such as candidate details, examination paper and centre) and these are produced in a form that can be read by the user - rather than a series of filled in lozenge-shaped boxes. OCR can also be used to read hand-written documents, although they usually have certain tolerances. Consequently most systems have an associated keyboard where unrecognised characters can be displayed and re-entered.

OCR may be appropriate for the examination system but may be subject to problems due to poor handwriting of both candidates (entering which questions they have answered) and markers.

Bar codes: a bar code is a pre-printed series of bars which uniquely identify each candidate, examination centre and paper. The bar code is scanned by a bar code reader permitting fast, cheap and accurate data entry. Bar codes are ideal for information that can be pre-recorded and so appropriate codes can be printed on each paper. Markers could also be allocated a set of bar codes which they could stick on to each paper they have marked, so identifying the marker of each paper. The problems lie in recording which questions have been answered and how many marks have been given for each answer. Many bar code systems have to record such unpredictable numerical data by entering it through the numerical keypad of a hand-held terminal.

4	·

Examiner's comments and marking guide

Question 4: most writers agree that there are three feasibility issues - technical (question 3), economic (question 2) and operational (question 4). The required answer should have considered personnel and organisation structure.

Unfortunately, this question was poorly answered. Far too many candidates offered commentary on feasibility in general and failed to apply the answer to the case study.

(a)   Up to two marks for each valid issue. Two issues required.
(b)   One mark for each valid point up to a maximum of four marks.

The examiner's answer

(a)   Operational feasibility is concerned with the human, organisational and 'political' aspects of the system.

It will consider such issues as:

Job changes. The proposed system may affect the jobs of current employees. This may lead to the re-definition of responsibilities and the re-negotiation of wages. Some staff may have to be made redundant, and for these correct procedures must be followed and the direct and indirect costs of their redundancy reflected in the cost-benefit analysis. New staff may have to be recruited to fill newly created jobs and the costs of recruiting and employing such staff must again be recorded in the cost-benefit analysis.

Training and other re-skilling costs have to be reflected in considering operational feasibility. This will include identifying the skills required, organising and delivering appropriate training and testing the acquisition of these new skills.

New systems may also disturb established organisational structures and the hierarchy and status of individuals associated with those structures. This has to be assessed and tackled.

(b)   The main issues at ISEC appear to be

Staff training. Staff appear to be relatively inexperienced, perhaps limited to standard packages in a single-user environment. Hence comprehensive training will have to be carried out.

Issues that arise from sharing data. Data which only used to belong to one department may now be shared across the company. This may lead to 'political problems'.

The Head of section of the administration department may resent having his or her private spreadsheet taken away. They may currently enjoy high status, conferred on them by their ownership of the examination data.

Did you answer the question?

Always try to relate your answer to the specific requirements of the question.

56   (Answer 5 of examination)

Examiner's comments and marking guide

Question 5: entity-relationship modelling has been tested in previous examinations. In this question the emphasis was on the interpretation of the model and it aimed to reflect the role of an accountant who may need to sign off a formal requirements specification. The latter part of the question required some technical knowledge (the decomposition of many to many relationships) but this is covered in most text books covering this syllabus.

The question reflected the Examiner's desire to test comprehension and interpretation rather than the construction of the model. The technical orientation of the question was also expected to appeal to candidates who prefer these types of question to narrative, essay questions.

Many candidates attempted this optional question but answered it as if the model was a Data Flow Diagram. This led to many poor answers. There is a clear distinction between a Data Flow Diagram and an Entity-Relationship Diagram, both in notation and purpose and candidates should know this distinction.

(a)   0.5 mark for each valid statement up to a maximum of four marks.
(b)   Up to three marks for the basic principles of the model.
        Up to two marks for its role in systems development.
        Up to two marks for the need for users to understand it.
(c)   One mark for the flaw.
(d)   Up to two marks for correct decomposition.
(e)   One mark for data items.

Step by step answer plan

Step 1   Read the question again and make sure that you focus on precisely what is required.

Step 2   In part (a), look carefully at each entity-relationship (invoice-customer, invoice-payment etc) and describe in turn what each signifies.

Step 3   Part (b) is in essence subdivided into two: first discuss the basic principles, then explain the importance to users.

Step 4   Parts (c), (d) and (e) require only very brief comment.

Step 5   Now review your answer plan and ensure that it does precisely answer the question as set.

The examiner's answer

Although there are established naming conventions (such as in SSADM) looser textual descriptions have been used in this booklet. If the candidate used the more formal method of SSADM then full allowance would have been given. Optional relationships have not been built into the examination example because different methods use different notation. Consequently all relationships are mandatory.

(a)   English statements

        Each customer receives one or many invoices
        Each invoice is sent to only one customer
        Each invoice has one or many invoice lines
        Each invoice line is for only one invoice
        Each invoice is paid through one or many payments
        Each payment refers to only one invoice
        Each product is on one or many invoice lines
        Each invoice line is for only one product.

(b)   The entity-relationship model or logical data structure shows the fundamental entities or objects of the system. Each entity (or more properly - entity type) represents something which the enterprise wants to store information about. So, for example, the entity-relationship shown in Fig 1 suggests that the company wishes to hold information about the entity type invoice, for which there will be many individual instances or entity occurrences, with each occurrence identified by a particular invoice-number. The relationships (shown by the connecting lines) give the business relationships that take place between the entities. So, for example, each customer entity occurrence is linked to one or many invoice occurrences, but each occurrence of invoice (say invoice no 3452) is linked to one and only one occurrence of customer (say account no 23). The main role of the model is to unambiguously state these relationships and entities. It provides a clear statement of what things are important to the enterprise and shows how these things are connected. It can also provide a basis for subsequent file and database design.

Such models are important to the user because:

They represent the business rules and assumptions on which the system will be constructed. Only the users know these rules and assumptions and so they must be charged with the responsibility for signing off such documents.

If the system does not fulfil business requirements then the entity-relationship model is one of the documents that can be reviewed to see if the requirements have been correctly implemented. If the diagram shows a one to many relationship between invoice and payment and it has been implemented with this assumption then the responsibility lies with the user because he or she has singed off a business model that was incorrect. However, if the diagram shows a many to many relationship and the software does not support this then the developers are at fault. Responsibility for mistakes becomes critical when discussing who is going to pay for 'changes' in the system requirements.

(c)   The relationship should probably be many to many

(d)   The many to many relationship should be decomposed into two one-to-many relationships with a new intermediate entity probably called allocation (or invoice/payment will do).

(e)   The likely contents of this entity are
Payment-number (the key of payment)
Invoice-number (the key of invoice)
Amount.

Payment-number and invoice-number will be the dual key of this new entity.

Did you answer the question?

The question clearly did not require a data flow diagram

---

57   (Answer 6 of examination)

(**Examiner's comments and marking guide**)

Question 6: this question concerned project management. It asked for the contents of a document that would be produced at the start of any project.

Unfortunately many candidates wrote standard Systems Development Life Cycle (SDLC) material. Others produced long answers on the Feasibility Study and, although missing the point, did gain some marks because there is some overlap between the two documents. Part (b), examining how software can help in estimating, planning, monitoring and reporting project progress, often lacked structure and relied on word processing and spreadsheet packages rather than describing the more appropriate facilities and features of project management software.

(a)   One mark for each valid point up to a maximum of seven marks.
(b)   Up to two marks each for planning, estimating, monitoring and reporting.

Step by step answer plan

Step 1   Read the question again and make sure that you focus on precisely what is required.

Step 2   Part (a) is very straightforward: a list with very brief explanation where necessary.

Step 3   Part (b) should be tackled as four separate questions: planning; estimating; monitoring; reporting.

Step 4   Now review your answer plan and ensure that it does precisely answer the question as set.

The examiner's answer

(a)   There are no standard contents for a project initiation document (PID). However they will typically cover the terms of reference of the project and so include:

Business objectives.
Project objectives.
Scope. What is to be considered by the project and what is not.
Constraints. These may refer to standards, suppliers or time scales.

Authority or client of the project. The ultimate customer of the project. This is the person who will resolve conflict between users and ultimately accept the project.

Resources. These are the facilities made available to the project manager to achieve the project's objectives. This will include staff, technical and financial resources.

Risks. A risk analysis of the project.

Project plan
Some PIDs also cover (as separate sections)
Project organisation and management
Configuration and change control procedures
Purchasing and procurement policy.

(b)   **Planning.** Project management software can be used to enter activities, estimates, precedences and resources to automatically produce a network diagram, showing the critical path and a Gantt Chart showing resource use. These diagrams are difficult to manually produce and maintain and the software also allows the simple what if? experiments (adding resources, changing estimates, re-setting precedences) with the objective of meeting the required delivery date. Resource profiles can be printed off as a planning tool for staff used on the project.

Estimating. Project management software allows the entry of actual data - the hours or days actually taken to complete a particular task. Many of these task are the same in systems development across different projects, for example; interview users, construct a logical data structure, and so a considerable amount of information can be collected about the time taken to complete common tasks. This can be used to improve future estimates. A computer may also be used to support the actual estimating model itself.

Monitoring. Project management software allows the entry of actual data which can be used to monitor the progress of the project and to re-plan the rest of the work. During re-planning the critical path may change and this is important to know.

Reporting. Most project management software packages have comprehensive reporting requirements which allow managers to print out the progress and status of the project. This means that standard progress reports can be produced automatically and so ensure that precious project time is not wasted in producing such reports.

58   (Answer 7 of examination)

Examiner's comments and marking guide

Question 7: this question examined the definition and facilities of a CASE tool.

It was not expected to be a popular or well answered question. However, pleasingly it was both popular and well answered! The Examiner considers CASE tools to be central to the future development of information systems.

(a)   One mark for the definition of CASE.
       Up to two marks for the definition of the overall concept.
(b)   Up to three marks for valid points for each of the four issues.

Step by step answer plan

Step 1   Read the question again and make sure that you focus on precisely what is required.

Step 2   Part (a) requires only a brief definition and explanation (note that only three marks are on offer).

Step 3   Part (b) should be treated as four separate questions.

Step 4   Now review your answer plan and ensure that it does precisely answer the question as set.

The examiner's answer

(a)   CASE stands for computer aided software (or system) engineering. A CASE tool is a software package that supports the construction and maintenance of logical system specification models. Many CASE tools are designed for a specific methodology and so support the rules and interaction of the models defined in that methodology. More sophisticated CASE tools permit software prototyping and code generation.

(b)   **Producing and maintaining documentation.** The graphical editing facilities provided by all CASE tools means that high quality, easily read documents can be produced. Furthermore changes to those documents can easily be made and the charts and models re-printed. Such editing is particularly useful with diagrammatic models, such as dataflow diagrams and entity-relationship models. It is very difficult to maintain manually produced versions of these diagrams.

       Adhering to development standards. Standards define how development will be carried out. Individual models have standard rules of construction. For example, a data store cannot be directly linked to an external entity in a dataflow diagram. However, there is nothing to stop the designer making such a connection in a manually produced example and it will not be picked up until it is assessed in a quality review. A CASE tool cannot produce such a diagram because it is not allowed. In this way the CASE tool ensures that standard construction rules are adhered to.

       Maintaining a logical data dictionary. A logical data dictionary stores information about the constituent parts of the logical systems specification. There will be logical data dictionary entries for dataflows, data stores, entities, processes, external entities and individual data items. A manually compiled example (say on reference cards) is difficult to maintain and to analyse. A CASE tool will hold all this information in a computerised data dictionary. Reports and analysis will be available. For example, it will be possible to list all the dataflows where a particular data item is used. The logical data dictionary also supports the consistency checks performed by the CASE tool; cross-referencing for instance, the logical data stores of the DFD to the entities of the entity-relationship diagram.

       Prototyping. CASE tools can support prototyping in one of two ways. The first is through developing screens and output prints for the input and output dataflows of the system. Each dataflow is defined in its logical content in the data dictionary. The CASE tool may allow these logical contents to be displayed on a demonstration screen and to link these screens together using menus and other dialogue structures. Thus the user sees a demonstration of the system through the CASE software. A second possibility is for the CASE tool to offer program and data generation. Such tools convert the process descriptions of the logical data dictionary into programs and the data stores/entities into files and databases. The user can then experiment with the software. Any changes in requirements are made in the definition of the models and the system re-generated for further experimental use. In this approach the models and the actual system are always in harmony.

59   (Answer 8 of examination)

Examiner's comments and marking guide

Question 8: the advantages and disadvantages of software package versus bespoke development was the theme of this question.

It was generally well answered. However, although many candidates can define advantages sufficiently well, their idea of a disadvantage is to point out what might go wrong if the work is badly or inappropriately done. The answer should discuss the disadvantages *inherent* in an idea not that the work (in this case tailored development) may be carried out by a bad programmer doing a bad job.

(a)   Up to two marks for each advantage. Three advantages required.
(b)   One mark for each valid point up to a maximum of three marks.
(c)   Up to two marks for each advantage. Three advantages required.

Step by step answer plan

Step 1   Read the question again and make sure that you focus on precisely what is required.

Step 2   From this point on the structure of your answer is closely determined by the sequence of instructions in the question. Just tackle each subsection in turn, remembering that a few relevant remarks on each will pick up important marks. Don't omit any part from your answer. Most of the requirement is concerned with basic bookwork knowledge about the pros and cons of off-the-shelf versus bespoke software.

Step 3   Now review your answer plan and ensure that it does precisely answer the question as set.

The examiner's answer

(a)   Advantages of a software package solution includes:

Early delivery. The package is ready to use, it just requires data. There is no delay while the system is designed, written and tested.

Proven product. The package is a tested proven product. Earlier users have found the bugs and the problems. Bespoke systems are usually affected by program errors in their first few months of operation.

Cheaper price. The package has been developed on the principle that its development cost will be recouped over a number of sales achieved over time. The complete cost of a bespoke solution falls upon the commissioning company and so it is unlikely to be as cheap.

Quality documentation. Packages are usually accompanied by high quality documentation and training. This documentation can be assessed before the product is purchased.

(b)   There are two main problems that can arise from this approach.

The cost of fulfilling local requirements may be very costly and so reduce the cost advantage of buying a packaged solution. The advantage of early delivery may also be lost.

The software house will have to ensure that future upgrades take into account the tailored requirements. Failure to do so may lead to unpredictable side-effects. Recognition of the need to take into account such requirements may also be reflected in higher maintenance charges.

(c)   Advantages of a bespoke solution include:

Complete fulfilment of the company's requirements. The software will fulfil at the needs listed in the Requirements Specification.

Ownership of the software. The software belongs to the organisation.

Changes to requirements can be accommodated. The future direction of the company may be unpredictable. It may develop into areas not supported by enhancements to the software package.

Competitive edge. All the companies that use a particular software package are unlikely to have any information systems competitive edge. Organisations that choose a bespoke solution may be able to offer a service that few of their competitors can match.

---

60   (Answer 9 of examination)

Examiner's comments and marking guide

Question 9: this was a relatively straightforward question on data validation, verification and check digits.

Unfortunately it was poorly answered with many candidates unable to differentiate between validation and verification and confusing check digits with parity bits.

(a)   Up to two marks for each valid check. Three checks required.
(b)   Up to three marks for the example and description.
         Up to two marks for the errors it is trying to catch.
(c)   Up to two marks for describing data verification.
         Up to two marks for recognising the necessity of such a check in certain circumstances.

Step by step answer plan

Step 1   Read the question again and make sure that you focus on precisely what is required. As the examiner's comment indicates, you need to be clear about the distinction between data validation and data verification.

Step 2   Select three checks and describe them.

Step 3   Describe the use of a check digit. Note that an example is required.

Step 4   Part (c) is straightforward provided you are familiar with the distinction between data validation and data verification.

Step 5   Now review your answer plan and ensure that it does precisely answer the question as set.

The examiner's answer

(a)   Validation checks include:

Valid range check

Range checks determine whether the entered data value lies within the acceptable value range. For example, customer-account-number lies between 200 and 500. It is a relatively imprecise check.

Valid value check

A value check determines whether the entered value is acceptable. For example, there may be six valid employee grade codes - 1, 3, 9, 14, 18 and 21. A value check would only pass entered figures that matched one of these valid codes. This is clearly more precise than a range check (accepting all values from 1 to 21).

Valid format check

This checks that the data always conforms to a specified format. Thus a product code designated as two letters followed by four numbers must always be entered in this way (format XX9999). Thus the entered values A4352 and AT433 would both be rejected. Thus the format check also ensures that the entered value is of the correct length.

Consistency check

Two entered data values may be checked against each other to check their validity. For example if the reason for leaving is given as 'pregnancy', then the value of sex should not be 'M or male'. In the United Kingdom a large company sent calendars to customers who were 'deceased'.

(b)   **Check digit**

A check digit is a number added to a code to allow the rest of the code to be checked for transcription or transposition errors. For example, a company uses six digit product numbers. The addition of a check digit will create a seven digit code and allow the rest of the code to be checked. A simple example is the modulus 11 check digit. The example below shows its application to the original product code 345213.

Product code	3	4	5	2	1	3
Multiplier	6	5	4	3	2	1
Product	18	20	20	6	2	3
Product sum	69					
Divide by 11	6 remainder 3					

The remainder is added to the product code to create the code 3452133

Everytime a product code is entered the software undertakes a modulus 11 check to validate the check digit. If the last entered figure is 3 and the rest of the code is correct then the input is permitted. A simple transposition error shows how mistakes can be identified.

Product code	3	4	5	1	2	3
Multiplier	6	5	4	3	2	1
Product	18	20	20	3	4	3
Product sum	68					
Divide by 11	6 remainder 2					

The check digit is incorrect and hence an error has been made.

(c)   Data verification is concerned with the double entry of the same data. Thus data values are entered by two different operators and checked against each other by the software before being subjected to validation checks. Verification is particularly important for data where only range and format checks are possible. A transcription error may not be found by such checks. Check digits are only useful for pre-coded data and there are many circumstances (for example, entry of sales figures) where this is not possible.

Did you answer the question?

Even if a question seems fairly short and covers specific topics, do make sure that you give it some thought to make sure you are discussing the right technical terms.

DECEMBER 1996 QUESTIONS

Figure 1

Data Flow Diagram

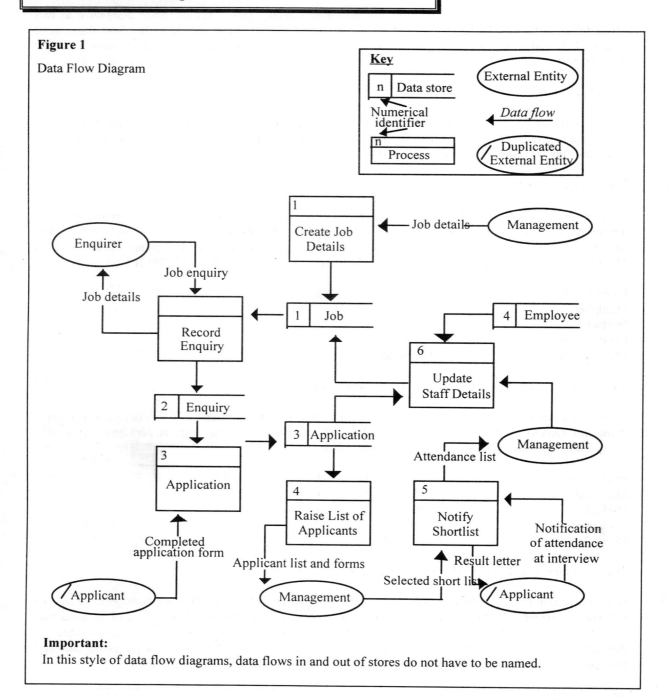

Important:

In this style of data flow diagrams, data flows in and out of stores do not have to be named.

Figure 1

The Data Flow Diagram opposite shows the proposed system. It contains six processes.

1   **Create job details**

     This creates the details of a particular job or post and records details about grade and the closing date for applications on the Job store.

2   **Record enquiry**

     Potential applicants send in job enquiries in response to advertisements placed in local and national newspapers. All enquiries are logged on the Enquiry store for later statistical analysis. Details of the job are retrieved from the Job store and sent to the potential applicant together with a blank application form.

3   **Record application**

     People who complete and return application forms are known as Applicants. Each application is cross-checked against each Enquiry. The management wish to know how many Enquiries are translated into firm Applications. Details of applicants are recorded on the Application store.

4   **Raise List of Applicants**

     On the closing date for applications a list of applicants is automatically raised and sent (together with the application form) to management.

5   **Notify Shortlist**

     Management consider the applicants and decide which candidates they wish to shortlist. Each candidate is sent a letter notifying them about their success (or failure) of their application. Applicants who are on the shortlist must notify their willingness to attend the interview. The applicant result (shortlist and attend, shortlist but not attend, not shortlisted) is recorded on the Application store. Finally, an attendance list for the interview is sent to Management.

6   **Update staff details**

     Details about the selected candidate are returned to the system once they have accepted the job. The details of the successful applicant are transferred from the Application to the Employee data store and the Job Store is updated with the information that it is filled.

Section A - ALL FOUR questions in this section are compulsory and MUST be attempted

---

61   (Question 1 of examination)

Case Study

A large hospital is considering the computerisation of its recruitment system. The hospital has a small in-house IS (Information Systems) department who administer the internal systems and have written bespoke software for the hospital in the past. However, the hospital management committee have decided that all future developments will be outsourced (i.e. sub-contracted to an external software company). The internal department will be restricted to supporting current systems and will eventually be phased out altogether.

The first outsourcing project is the recruitment system. In the first phase of this project the software house has produced a Functional Specification (Figure 1 is extracted from this) defining the requirements of the system. The software company has also put in a bid to write a bespoke system to fulfil the requirements. They propose a client-server solution based on a recently developed Fourth Generation Language (4GL). The hospital administrator has surveyed a number of packages but believes that none of them completely fulfil the Functional Specification. He has proposed that the hospital should jointly build the software with the software house and, after successful implementation, sell it to other hospitals. The hospital management committee have agreed in principle with his suggestion and have given the go-ahead to proceed with the bespoke development.

1   The Data Flow Diagram (Figure 1) has been given to you for checking. You have been asked to ensure that the diagram is consistent with the textual descriptions of the processes (also in Figure 1) and with the conventions and notation of drawing Data Flow Diagrams.

Identify *six* errors in the Data Flow Diagram (Figure 1)   **(12 marks)**

2   (a)   The Data Flow Diagram (Figure 1) is an example of a standard document produced in systems development. There are many such standards at all points in the systems development lifecycle.

Describe why such standards are important in information systems development by explaining what roles they play in assisting successful systems development. Emphasise why such standards are particularly essential in the development of the recruitment system within the hospital.   **(8 marks)**

(b)   The accuracy and quality of Data Flow Diagrams is often assessed at 'structured walkthroughs'.

(i)   Explain what structured walkthroughs are and why they are a particularly appropriate method for examining a specification document such as a Data Flow Diagram.   **(3 marks)**

(ii)   Define the roles of *two* of the participants in a structured walkthrough.   **(4 marks)**
(Total: 15 marks)

3   The proposed recruitment system will hold personal information about applicants and there is some concern in the hospital about this information being misused or passed on to employees outside the personnel department.

(a)   Data protection is concerned with ensuring the privacy of this personal data. Identify four basic principles of data protection and explain their relevance to this system.   **(8 marks)**

(b)   Describe what measures and procedures could be used to ensure that the computer system developed for the recruitment system conforms with each of the four principles that you have identified in part (a).   **(8 marks)**
(Total: 16 marks)

4   Several members of the hospital management committee are worried about the manner in which this project is being set up and conducted. They believe that it is exposing the hospital to considerable business risk. Consequently they have asked you to undertake a risk analysis of the project.

Identify three risks associated with the project and for each risk explain what measures might be taken to overcome or reduce it.   **(12 marks)**
(Total: 55 marks)

Section B - THREE questions ONLY to be attempted

62   (Question 5 of examination)

Four elements of Office Automation are listed below;
-    Electronic Mail
-    Word Processing
-    Teleconferencing
-    Spreadsheets.

Briefly describe *three* of these elements. For each of the three, identify two ways in which it has impacted on the operation and organisation of office work.   **(15 marks)**

63 (Question 6 of examination)

The following techniques can be used to investigate the operation of a current information system and to identify requirements for its successor.

- Interviews with users
- Observation
- Questionnaires
- Document analysis

(a) Briefly describe *two* of these techniques, listing three advantages of each technique you have described.

(10 marks)

(b) The four techniques listed above are traditionally used for investigating a current manual system. Briefly suggest other fact-finding opportunities that would be available if the current information system was already computerised. To what extent would these opportunities affect the application of the traditional techniques?

(5 marks)
(Total: 15 marks)

64 (Question 7 of examination)

In the context of systems development:

(a) Explain what is meant by a prototype.

(3 marks)

(b) Describe two advantages and two disadvantages of using a prototyping approach to systems development.

(8 marks)

(c) Select two facilities usually found in a Fourth Generation Language (4GL) and explain their application in developing a prototype system.

(4 marks)
(Total: 15 marks)

65 (Question 8 of examination)

(a) A small company has one accountant. One of her responsibilities is to decide whether to offer credit to a customer, and if so, to determine an appropriate credit limit. This credit decision depends upon such factors as bank references, order value and customer location. This example demonstrates how information must be **relevant** to the decision-making process. Relevance is an important quality of information.

Define five further qualities of information and describe their application to assessing the credit-worthiness and credit limit of a customer.

(10 marks)

(b) Does the decision to offer credit and set an appropriate credit level fit into a structured, semi-structured or unstructured decision type? Define the decision type that you have chosen and explain why the credit example fits into this category.

(5 marks)
(Total: 15 marks)

66   (Question 9 of examination)

A manufacturing company has issued an Invitation to Tender requesting proposals for a replacement to its current inventory control software. The hardware is not being replaced. Three proposals have been received offering competing software package solutions. The manufacturing company wishes to compare the three solutions to decide which (if any) they should buy.

(a)   Describe five issues that will have to be considered in evaluating each proposal. Briefly explain why each issue is relevant and must be included in the evaluation.   **(10 marks)**

(b)   Initial evaluation suggests that none of the proposals provides the perfect solution. What methods can the company use to assess the strengths and weaknesses of each proposal and hence choose the most effective solution?   **(5 marks)**

                                                                 (Total: 15 marks)

ANSWERS TO DECEMBER 1996 EXAMINATION

61 (Answer 1 of examination)

1

Examiner's comments and marking guide

Question 1: This question asked candidates to identify errors in a Data Flow Diagram, comparing the graphical model with a textual description. It reflected the Examiner's wish to examine the interpretation of a model rather than its construction.

In general the question was either done well or badly. It is suprising after the format of earlier examination papers, that many candidates have little knowledge of data flow diagrams and their conventions. Weaker candidates questioned the scope and business rules of the system or made general comments on the presentation of the diagram. Others suggested 'improvements' that did not conform with the conventions of DFD construction (eg, data flowing directly from one store to another) or using conventions taken from flowcharting.

Two marks for each error. One mark may be given for a debateable 'error'
Six errors are required giving a total of 12 marks

Step by step answer plan

Step 1 Read the question again and make sure that you focus on precisely what is required.

Step 2 In question 1 you simply have to work carefully through the text and the diagram and hope to pick out errors.

Step 3 In question 2 you need to explain both the 'bookwork' aspects of standard documentation and their relevance to the specific system under consideration.

Step 4 In part (a) of question 3 you need of course to know (at least) four of the data protection principles. If you know more than this, choose the four which will best enable you to answer part (b).

Step 5 In question 4 identify three possible risks and discuss them in turn. The examiner's solution covers: first outsourcing agreement; using relatively unproven software; becoming a supplier of software to other organisations; internal staff dissatisfaction.

Step 6 Now review your answer plan and ensure that it does precisely answer the question as set.

The examiner's answer

Figure 1 - errors and possible errors

Process 2. Record enquiry
       Error: The process should have an identifier - number 2
       Possible error: The data flow to the Enquirer should show the blank application form
       Possible error: There should be a data store of Application Forms

Process 3. Record application
       Error: The process name does not include a verb
       Possible error: Updating Enquiry store with the information that an application form has been received.
       Possible error: A further data store is required showing physical application forms

Process 5. Notify Shortlist

      Error: The process should write to the Application store with the applicant result.

Process 6. Update staff details
      Error: The data flow into the process is not named.
      Error: The Employee data store is written to, not read.

Overall
      Error: The Management external entity is not shown as duplicated.

```
2
```

(Examiner's comments and marking guide)

Question 2: It was originally intended that question two would pick up the standards theme from question one, asking candidates to elaborate on the roles of such standards in system development and to relate these to the development of the hospital recruitment system.

The role of standards in communicating requirements should have been evident from question one, however a significant number of candidates used the question to describe, sometimes at great length, **specific** standards (such as entity-relationship diagram). Many further explained why that **specific** standard was essential in the development of the recruitment system. It was decided at the marker's meeting that the question may have been ambiguous and so candidates were given marks for answering it in this way. However, even with such marking flexibility, the answers were still disappointing.

Part (b) of the question concerned a **structured walk-through**. In doing so this continued the theme of question 1 - the Data Flow Diagram would probably be assessed at such a walk-through. Very few candidates answered this question successfully, often confusing a structured walk-through with structured English.

(a)   One mark for each valid point up to a maximum of eight marks
(b)   (i)   Up to two marks for the definition of a structured walkthrough. One mark for an explanation of why it is particularly appropriate for the review of a Data Flow Diagram - total 3 marks
            (ii)   Up to two marks for the definition of each role
                   Two roles required - total 4 marks

(The examiner's answer)

(a)   Standards can be used for

      Communication The Data Flow Diagram presented in Figure 1 is an example of a standard model primarily used for communicating the scope of the system to the user. It is important that users are able to interpret such diagrams as they represent the functionality of the system that will be delivered by the developer. This is particularly significant in the recruitment system because the hospital is using an external supplier. In these circumstances the functional specification represents a contractual agreement and so changes in requirements will have to be paid for. There are a number of standard models that will be used to communicate requirements and features and these will be needed in the future if the system is offered as a software package.

      Providing a work framework The standards manual defines how the development method should proceed. This gives a framework for the task and so it should always be clear how far development has progressed and hence the status of the project can be monitored. This will be important for the hospital management committee as they will need to carefully track the project as it is the first development they have undertaken with an external supplier.

      Documentation The standards should document the system. Documentation will be important in the development of the software and it will also be used in demonstrating the design and construction of the system to potential customers. Documentation will also be needed for estimating and planning modifications required in the future.

Quality The standards defined in the development of the software should improve its eventual quality. The developers of the system are also able to demonstrate and document their construction method. This should allow the organisation to be accredited for quality standards (such as ISO9001) and such a quality mark should be an advantage in selling the software to potential customers.

(b)   (i)   A structured walkthrough is a formal review meeting. It can be used to consider products at all stages of a project. Such walkthroughs focus on the *product* and not the person who has produced that product. The meetings are attended by people who have defined roles (see below) and the results of the meeting are formally documented. A structured walkthrough is particularly appropriate for assessing a Data Flow Diagram because *it cannot be tested any other way.* Unlike program code, it cannot be executed to see if it works.

        (ii)   Roles include:

The chairperson
The chair is responsible for the management and running of the walkthrough. In order to ensure that standards are met the chair should have sound technical knowledge and be thoroughly familiar with the quality standards that apply to the review. The chair will also have the normal procedural responsibilities of setting up a meeting; issuing invitations, checklists and the agenda. During the meeting the chair must ensure that the focus remains on the product, not the person who has developed it. The final sign-off of the product will also be the responsibility of the chairperson.

The presenter
The presenter is often the author of the product. It is the responsibility of the presenter to ensure that a product is ready for review and that it is submitted to the chairperson in time for distribution to the reviewers. The presenter will *walkthrough* the product at the meeting, noting comments and follow-up actions. The presenter may have to re-submit products if they fail to satisfy the chairperson.

The reviewer
Reviewers are required to help improve the quality of the product. Before the meeting they will be supplied with review checklists and details of the quality criteria that the product should meet. Their role is to detect non-conformance of the product with these criteria. An error list is produced before the meeting and sent to the chairperson and the author. Reviewers attend the meeting to clarify any points they have made and to review any subsequent changes made as a result of their pre-meeting comments.

Other roles might include;

User representative
A representative from internal audit

Did you answer the question?

Think before you start to write; a structured walk though is not the same as structured English.

```
3
```

Examiner's comments and marking guide

Question 3:   **The principles of data protection are an established and fundamental part of the syllabus. However, many students appear to have been unprepared for a question on this area, perhaps because they have never featured prominently before.**

Part (a) (concerning the principles of data protection) was straight-forward however very few candidates scored well. Many answers were incorrectly concerned with passwords, locks on doors and backup systems.

Part (b) (concerning measures to enforce the principles) was slightly better answered, although in many scripts the same information was given as for part (a). However, too many part (b) answers were unrelated to the principles defined in part (a) and were not presented in the context of the recruitment system.

(a)   One mark for each valid principle. One mark for relevant example.
        Four principles required giving a total of 8 marks
(b)   Up to two marks for measures and procedures attached to each principle
        Four principles required giving a total of 8 marks

The examiner's answer

(a)   There are a number of data protection principles defined in textbooks and Study Manuals. Five of these are defined below;

Personal data held shall be held for one or more specified and lawful purposes.
The data held about applicants must be defined and the purpose of each data item must be specified. For example, the age of the applicant is required to ensure that the applicant is old enough to do the job. However, this purpose must not be illegal. In many countries age must not be used to discriminate against an applicant.

Personal data held for any purpose or purposes shall be adequate, relevant and not excessive in relation to that purpose or those purposes.
Irrelevant data should not be stored on the system (for example, there should be no need to store information about the applicant's pets). Irrelevant data may be defined as information that is unlikely to be used in the selection process.

Personal data shall be accurate and, where necessary, kept up-to-date.
Personal data, such as current salary and qualifications should be accurate as these will be important factors in the selection process. If the applicant details are to be used in future job selection it must be ensured that any changes in qualifications must be reflected in the system.

Personal data for any purpose or purposes shall not be kept for longer than is necessary for that purpose or purposes.
If the data is held for processing applications for a particular job, then applicant details of unsuccessful applicants must be deleted after the job is filled.

Personal data held for any purpose or purposes shall not be used or disclosed in any manner incompatible with that purpose or purposes.
The purpose of collecting certain data items must be defined. In the recruitment system the information is being collected to support employee selection. It may not be acceptable for customer details such as name and address to be used in mail-shots for health care insurance.

(b)   Personal data held shall be held for one or more specified and lawful purposes.
It is difficult to use computer-based procedures to ensure this particular principle, because the system has no control over how data is used by the selection committee. Hence management procedures may have to be established to ensure that staff do not use information inappropriately. It may be useful to include reports in the software analysing successful and unsuccessful applicants by age and sex to demonstrate fairness in the selection procedure.

Personal data held for any purpose or purposes shall be adequate, relevant and not excessive in relation to that purpose or those purposes.
It is important that each data item stored in the system must be fully justified and defined. The data must be adequate and relevant for the purpose (what information is required to make the selection decision?) Information which might be 'nice to know' or 'may be useful in the future' may not be collected.

Personal data shall be accurate and, where necessary, kept up-to-date.
One way of ensuring that personal data is accurate is to make sure that such information is provided by the applicant not by a third party. Accuracy of data entry can be improved by data verification and data validation procedures. It is difficult to keep information up-to-date unless copies of the data are periodically sent to the applicant who is asked to return changes in the data.

Personal data for any purpose or purposes shall not be kept for longer than is necessary for that purpose or purposes.
The rules for the deletion of the information can be built into the software. For example, if the rule is that all unsuccessful applicant records must be deleted after the appointment of the successful applicant, then this can be written into the system hence ensuring that this principle is upheld.

Personal data held for any purpose or purposes shall not be used or disclosed in any manner incompatible with that purpose or purposes.

It is difficult to control this. A certain amount of control can be achieved through passwords and security in the system. For example, not permitting the marketing department to access applicant address information for mailshot purposes. Internal procedures must be in place to ensure that these rules are adhered to.

4

Examiner's comments and marking guide

Question 4: attempted to extend the theme of the case study to commercial risk.

Most candidates answered too generally - considering risks in any project rather than risks in this particular one - and this was reflected in the marks. Achieving budgetary targets and timescales appear to be the favourite risks and these would be present in any project, rather than specifically in the hospital recruitment system. The case study scenario did provide fairly obvious clues *(eg, the internal department will be restricted to supporting current systems and will eventually be phased out altogether, . . . solution based on a recently developed Fourth Generation Language, . . . the first outsourcing project).* Candidates are reminded to apply their answers to the case study rather than theoretical descriptions of marginal relevance to the question.

(a)   Up to two marks for identifying the risk.
Up to two marks for risk reduction suggestions
Three risks are required giving a total of 12 marks

The examiner's answer

Risks might include:

First outsourcing arrangement. This project is to be the hospital's first outsourcing assignment. Previous systems have been developed by the internal information systems (IS) department and so the hospital management does not have any experience in contractually dealing with an external supplier. Risks of this sort can be reduced by drawing up formal supply contracts which include arrangements for dealing with changes, extensions, conflicts and finance. The contract must clearly establish what is to be supplied under its terms. Arrangements must also be made for such possibilities as the supplier going out of business.

Using relatively unproven software. The application is to be developed with a recently-developed Fourth Generation Language. This software is likely to be unproven and so it may still have errors and problems. It is also unlikely that there are many developers with experience of this development language and so contract developers may be difficult to find and expensive to employ. This risk can be reduced by an incremental approach to development so that facilities can be experimented with and parts of the system developed to allow 'proof of concept' and to demonstrate progress to the user. Risk can also be reduced by asking the software house to undertake parallel development with a more conventional software language, so that development can be swapped to a more proven language if the recently developed Fourth Generation Language proves to have insurmountable problems.

Becoming a supplier of software to other organisations. There are a number of risks associated with supplying a product that does not perform acceptably. The customer may enter into a legal dispute demanding consequential damages for business losses caused by the non-performance of the software. These risks can be reduced by

-     Legal disclaimers in the supply of the software.
-     Insuring against claims for damages.
-     Careful specification, development and testing to reduce the possibility of software failure.
-     Setting up the software supply side as a separate company which can be liquidated in the face of an award for considerable damages.

Internal staff dissatisfaction. Staff dissatisfaction appears likely given the fact that the internal Information Systems staff will not be able to develop bespoke systems in the future. This dissatisfaction may lead to efforts to undermine or discredit the external supplier. This is a difficult risk to reduce given the policy adopted by the management committee. One possibility may be to outsource the work of the IS department, perhaps to the same supplier.

Did you answer the question?

You must relate your answer to the facts of the case study itself.

| **62** | **(Answer 5 of examination)** |

Examiner's comments and marking guide

Question 5: This question asked candidates to describe three elements of Office Automation and to identify the impact of each element on the operation and organisation of office work.

This question was answered well by most candidates, although many answers were stronger on description rather than the impact of each element on the organisation.

Description of the element - up to two marks, Effect on office work - up to three marks
Three elements are required giving a total of 15 marks

Step by step answer plan

Step 1   Read the question again and make sure that you focus on precisely what is required.

Step 2   Choose the three elements that you are most familiar with, particularly those with which you come into contact personally.

Step 3   For each element chosen give a brief description, including two examples in each case of the element's impact.

Step 4   Now review your answer plan and ensure that it does precisely answer the question as set.

The examiner's answer

Electronic mail (or e-mail) is a system where messages are sent electronically. This provides an alternative to posting paper documents in external postal systems or sending memoranda through the internal mail. Each user has a mailbox where messages are stored until the user is ready to read them. E-mail can be used internally, using the mail facilities offered by a multi-user Operating System or Local Area Network (LAN) software, and externally through commercially available e-mail services provided by telecommunications companies. It has changed office work in a number of ways, including;

-    Speed of delivery. Messages are placed in the user mailbox immediately after they have been sent. Further time-saving is provided by multiple addressing using distribution lists set up in the system. All the sender needs to do is to specify the distribution list(s) to be used and a copy of the document is sent to each mailbox on the distribution list. This saves a considerable amount of distribution time and costs.

-    Proof of delivery and acceptance. The e-mail software records the fact that the message has been received at the target mailbox (hence preventing documents getting lost in the post) and also *shows whether the document has been opened and read.* The first of these facilities is provided by most surface mail systems (using recorded delivery) but not the second!

-    Reduced material costs. Documents may be written with a word processor and sent via the e-mail to many mailboxes (saving printing and photocopying costs). The users of those mailboxes will read the message but may not choose to print it out - thus again saving printing costs. This reduced printing also lessens the need for filing, filing cabinets and other methods of physical storage.

Spreadsheets provide facilities for the entry, manipulation and display of data. They have in-built financial and scientific functions allowing the relatively easy construction of sophisticated models.
Tabular and graphical output is supported and ease of exporting data to other packages (particularly word processors) is a key feature allowing users to insert tables and graphs into reports at the appropriate place. Most spreadsheets provide macro languages to allow users to program repetitive tasks and procedures.

Spreadsheets have changed office work in a number of ways, including;

- Relatively complex models can be built by end-users. Many of the problems modelled with spreadsheets are too small-scale to be suitable or economic for conventional Information Systems development. Before the development of spreadsheets there was little software to support this area and scale of problem and so it was largely neglected. Spreadsheet-based models are ideal for this class of problem and they may be passed on in the organisation so that similar problems can be solved elsewhere without reinventing the logic.

- The development of models allows users to undertake what-if? questions designed to see the effect of changing key parameters in the system. For example, the effect of different wage rises and prices on the profitability of the company. This was possible (by using a calculator) before the widespread use of these tools but was time-consuming and prone to error. Spreadsheet-based models allow decision-makers to explore the problem area more fully before making their decision.

- Spreadsheets can be used to produce high quality tabular and graphical documents. Extracts can be written into word processed documents allowing users to produce professional reports without using skilled typing and reprographics staff. The extensive formatting facilities of the software also allows professional output documents with tabular data properly aligned and displayed.

Teleconferencing allows geographically distributed participants to hold a meeting together. It may be either audio or video based and the meeting is under the control of a chairman who ensures that the meeting is effective. In audio based teleconferencing the participants use a standard telephone with microphones and loud speakers. In the video version cameras and television screens are used allowing the participants to see each other during the meeting.

Its effect on office work includes:

- Reduced travel costs. Moving geographically remote managers to one location is expensive in direct costs (such as flight and accommodation costs) as well as in the cost of the time that managers spend away from their base. Teleconferencing permits managers to remain at their base - solving daily problems - but allows them to easily keep in touch with issues, colleagues and corporate policy.

- Teleconferencing allows a rapid response to a crisis. The time-consuming tasks of setting up a meeting (getting a room, finding a date when all participants are free etc.) are removed. Teleconferences are particularly appropriate in quickly changing business situations where decisions have to be made immediately.

- Ordered meetings. Teleconferencing demands that meetings are better structured and controlled. Conventional meetings may be dominated by certain individuals, often reinforcing their dominance with body language and physical presence. Teleconferences may enforce an order of speaking (allowing as much time for the weak as for the strong) and a degree of control from the chairman that may be difficult to achieve in a conventional meeting.

Word processing is an important element of Office Automation (OA). Documents can be entered, stored, edited, merged and printed. Features are provided for enhancing the text (such as boldface and underlining) and a spell-checker may be provided to improve the accuracy of the document.

Word processing has changed office work in a number of ways. Three are listed below:

- It has brought increased productivity to the office by allowing staff to easily add, delete and change text before printing a new version. Documents produced on traditional manual typewriters usually had to be typed and re-typed to accommodate changes and corrections. Consequently word processing has led to time savings and improvements in the layout and accuracy of the content.

- The increased availability and improved usability of word processing software has led to their increased use by all staff, allowing them to enter, edit and print their own documents. Many organisations no longer employ specialised typing staff. Accurate, high quality documents can be produced without the delays and cost associated with the traditional 'typing pool'.

- Many word processing packages offer template facilities which allow the user to define how a document using that template will be laid out and structured. This permits the organisation to issue templates throughout the company ensuring that documents adhere to company standards. This allows relatively inexperienced staff to produce correct and standard documents without having to consult style manuals or submit their work to quality checks.

Did you answer the question?

The question asked for both description and impact.

---

63   (Answer 6 of examination)

Examiner's comments and marking guide

Question 6: **This question asked candidates to describe two fact-finding techniques and to suggest how fact-finding would be different if the current system was already computerised.**

This question was again answered well by most candidates.

(a)   Description of the technique - up to two marks,
Advantages - one mark for each advantage up to a maximum of three advantages.
Two techniques required giving a total of 10 marks

(b)   One mark for each valid point up to a maximum of 5 marks.

Step by step answer plan

Step 1   Read the question again and make sure that you focus on precisely what is required.

Step 2   In part (a) you should again choose the two most familiar techniques, because personal experience will lend authority to your answer. Don't forget that you are specifically required to list three advantages of each.

Step 3   Part (b) asks quite a lot, given that only five marks are available. The examiner's answer is fuller than you should probably attempt in the exam.

Step 4   Now review your answer plan and ensure that it does precisely answer the question as set.

The examiner's answer

(a)   **Interviews with users:** Interviews are meetings where the analyst can ask the user face-to-face how the current system works and about requirements the user has for its successor. The interview is a formal meeting with an agenda and objectives. The meeting is documented by the analyst and the resulting interview record is fed back to the user for confirmation.

Advantages include:

The interview allows the analyst the opportunity to build up rapport with the user. User's must feel confident about the understanding and competence of the analyst. These face-to-face meetings are important opportunities for establishing confidence and empathy.

The answers to some questions may require further investigation and clarification. In an interview such follow-up questions can be asked at once. This is not possible in a questionnaire.

Interviews allow the analyst to observe the tone of the responses and body language which accompanies their delivery. Gestures, facial expressions, eye contact and general posture will convey a great deal of information about values and opinions.

The meeting record is a formal agreement between the analyst and the respondent. Its contents define what was agreed in the meeting. If the respondent believes that significant facts are missing then these must be documented. The interview record is part of the contract between the information systems supplier and client.

Observation is concerned with watching the participants in a system go about their usual activities. In this instance the user is not *asked* about the way they do the work but are *observed* doing it. The analyst takes notes about the participant's activity and may supplement this with questions which clarify why an activity was done in a certain way.

Advantages include:

Allows the analyst to observe environmental conditions (such as dirt, space and noise). These will influence the technology and siting of the eventual information system solution.

Provides the opportunity for the analyst to cross-check information given in an interview. There may be important discrepancies between how someone *says* that they go about their work and how they *actually* do it.

Gives the analyst the opportunity to observe informal information flows that take place in the system. Most interviews tend to concentrate on formal information flows because these are the ones that come readily to mind and are (usually) supported by documents.

Provides excellent insight into the business operation which the analyst needs to understand if they are to provide an appropriate solution. Research shows that user's value analysts who demonstrate that they understand the business application.

Questionnaires. These are formal lists of questions which can be submitted to a user for him or her to answer at their leisure. It is likely that the questionnaire will be a mix of closed questions (to ascertain facts) and open questions (to describe feelings and opinions). Questionnaires may represent a first stage of data collection to be supported by later follow-on interviews.

Advantages include:

Provides an effective way of standardising questions so that they are not affected by interviewer inconsistency. Each participant has exactly the same question to answer presented in the same (preferably neutral) way.

Many participants have to look up factual information. The questionnaire can be used to ask for this information (such as - how many orders are processed in a day) and the respondent can investigate and respond at their leisure. It is unlikely that such questions will be answered as accurately in an interview where the respondent may be under immediate pressure to produce an answer.

Questionnaires may be used where the respondents are relatively few and geographically dispersed. Interviewing such users may be expensive and time-consuming and so the questionnaire provides a cheaper option.

The questionnaire can be used to provide anonymous responses. This may be important in some applications where significant job changes are being planned. There is evidence to suggest that respondents are more likely to give more accurate responses if the questionnaire does not have their name at the top.

(b)   If the current system is already computerised then a large amount of factual information about the present system can be found from the files and programs of the current system. For example, volume information about the number of customers, number of orders/day and order lines/order can be found by analysing data on the system - not from asking users. The functionality of the present system is traditionally found through interviewing. However, much of this can again be derived through using the current software, reading the program documentation and following the user manuals.

It will also be possible to discover information about the frequency of system use. For example, the number of times a particular report is requested, or a document is produced or an enquiry screen used. This provides factual information to support or refute user requests and statements. Special routines may have to be written to find this information but such *sampling* is much easier and cost-effective when the current system is already computerised. *Sampling* or *Special Purpose Records* are often included in textbooks as important fact gathering methods, but they become much more effective when the current system is computerised.

In current manual systems the scope of the documentation and access to it is controlled by the user. Analysts have to identify documents and ask for selected copies. It is difficult for them to know if all the relevant documents have been found or that the examples they have been given are representative. In a current computer system all the files and transactions are on display and are accessible to the analyst *without* the knowledge, intervention or selection by the user.

Interviews and Observation remain valid methods in the investigation of a system which is already computerised. However, it is likely that the number of interviews can be reduced and that they will concentrate on requirements rather than operational details of the present system. Observation will still be required but might focus more on the difficulties users have in using the current software. It is unlikely that fact based questionnaires will be required (because most of the information will be in the system) but anonymous open-question questionnaires may still be needed for capturing information about values, feelings and opinions.

64   (Answer 7 of examination)

Examiner's comments and marking guide

Question 7:   This question concerned prototyping and the use of a Fourth Generation Language in developing a prototype system.

This question was generally answered well by most candidates.

(a)   One mark for each valid point up to a maximum of three marks.

(b)   Up to two marks for each valid advantage and disadvantage
       Two advantages and two disadvantages required giving a total of 8 marks

(c)   Up to two marks for each facility and its application to prototyping
       Two facilities required giving a total of 4 marks

Step by step answer plan

Step 1   Read the question again and make sure that you focus on precisely what is required.

Step 2   Part (a): three marks available for a brief 'bookwork' explanation.

Step 3   Eight marks are available for part (b), so a fairly detailed discussion of two advantages and two disadvantages is required.

Step 4   For part (c) select two possibilities from the four identified by the examiner: integrated screen design tool; dialogue design tool; non-procedural programming code; object set.

Step 5   Now review your answer plan and ensure that it does precisely answer the question as set.

The examiner's answer

(a)   **Definition of a prototype**

A prototype is a working system that captures the essential features of a later implementation. It is usually used to verify parts of the system (such as requirements or dialogues) with users, or to prove (or disprove) some concept or idea. A prototype system is intentionally incomplete. It will be subsequently modified, expanded, supplemented or supplanted. Prototypes may be iteratively developed into the final system, so that each prototype represents a stage in the development of the finished product. Alternatively, prototypes may be 'thrown-away' after the objective of the prototype has been achieved.

(b)   **Advantages and disadvantages of a prototype**

Advantages might include:

Pleases users. Users have conventionally had to review paper-based screens and report layouts and sign off requirements and operations that they could not fully visualise. The prototype represents a tangible thing that they can touch and feel and the inputs and outputs of the system are represented in the medium in which they will eventually be used - on a computer screen not on paper.

Prototyping decreases communication problems. Training takes place incrementally through the development of the software. Furthermore, excessive documentation is not needed because users gain knowledge of the software through use rather than through reading user manuals.

Reduces marginal functionality. There is evidence to suggest that prototype systems produce less reports and screens programmed to meet the 'I think I need' requirements that often emerge in specified systems. Prototype systems usually contain fewer validations and unnecessary controls.

Prototyping provides tangible progress. The user can see the progression of the development through a series of usable systems, rather than through abstract diagrams and models.

Possible disadvantages

In most instances the prototype produces a less coherent design than a system that has been specified. The iteration of the development means that it is difficult to produce an initial design that is likely to be applicable to the final agreed system.

Prototypes can be oversold. By definition a prototype has limited capabilities and captures only the essential features of the operational system. Sometimes unrealistic user expectations are created by overselling the prototype, which may result in unmet user expectations and disappointment. The system looks ready, but it is actually very incomplete.

Prototypes are difficult to manage and control. Traditional life cycle approaches have specific phases and milestones and deliverables. These are established before project initiation and are used as a basis for project planning and control. Planning and control of prototyping projects are more difficult because the form of the evolving system, the number of revisions to the prototype, and some of the user requirements are unknown at the outset. Lack of explicit planning and control guidelines may bring about a reduction in the discipline needed for proper management (ie, documentation and testing activities may be bypassed or superficially performed).

It is difficult to prototype large information systems. It is not clear how a large system should be divided for the purpose of prototyping or how aspects of the system to be prototyped are identified and boundaries set. In most cases, time and project resource constraints determine the boundaries and scope of the prototyping effort. Moreover, the internal technical arrangements of large information systems prototypes may be haphazard and inefficient and may not perform well in operational environment with large amounts of data or large numbers of users.

(c)   Useful facilities in a Fourth Generation Language include:

Integrated Screen Design Tool. Allowing the quick construction of example screens. Many languages allow the developer to effectively construct the screen with the user; discussing field positioning, display and validation as they go along. This provides effective user involvement and also uses the medium (the VDU or PC) that will be used in the final system.

Dialogue Design Tool. A dialogue design tool will be used for the construction of menus, prompts and error messages. These often change during the development of the prototype and so the language must support flexibility and ease of amendment. To many users the dialogue **is** the system and so it must reflect the way users wish to go about their work.

Non-Procedural Programming Code. Most Fourth Generation Languages have their own development language. This language is usually concise and non-procedural allowing the quick development of programs that might later be discarded. Conventional programming languages are generally verbose and procedural and are time consuming to change and hence are not suitable for prototyping.

Object Set. Many Fourth Generation Languages include standard object sets which can be used in the development of the system. Thus a developer does not have to write a printer driver, merely select a printer icon from the object set. The code for printer control is already written in a program attached to this icon. This again allows fast system production.

65 (Answer 8 of examination)

Examiner's comments and marking guide

Question 8: Part (a) of this question asked candidates to define qualities of information. Part (b) asked candidates to define a decision type in the context of the example described in part (a).

This question was again well answered. It was generally a popular question. Some candidates tended to duplicate qualities of information ('simple to understand' and 'easy to interpret' seem rather close) and some of the examples were not relevant.

(a)   One mark for each valid quality of information. One mark for a relevant example.
        Five qualities required giving a total of 10 marks
(b)   Up to two marks for the explanation of the decision type. Up to three marks for the justification.

Step by step answer plan

Step 1   Read the question again and make sure that you focus on precisely what is required.

Step 2   As the examiner comments, part (a) is a relatively easy question to approach. The qualities of good information are routinely discussed in textbooks and it is simply a question of selecting five of them for brief discussion.

Step 3   For part (b), begin with an explanation of the three types of decision mentioned. Then analyse the particular decision under consideration and classify it as one type or another.

Step 4   Now review your answer plan and ensure that it does precisely answer the question as set.

The examiner's answer

(a)   Further qualities of information might include:

Timely The information must be provided at the correct time in the process. So, for example, the credit information must be available before the first order is processed so that goods are not reserved for a customer the company decides later not to supply. These goods could have been used to supply an established customer.

Up-to-date The information must be correct at the time of processing. For example, the setting of the credit limit may require information about the customer's bank account details at the close of business the previous day; not on information provided at month end. Out of date information may lead to a limit that is too restrictive (reducing that customer's trade with the supplier) or place the supplier's business at risk because the credit limit has been set too high.

Accurate The information must be accurate enough for the decision that has to be made. In some instances data has to be extremely accurate (down to three or four decimal points) because the process demands that precision. In the credit example the data has to be relatively accurate (perhaps to the nearest hundred or thousand pound) but details of unit pounds and pence are unlikely to contribute to a better decision.

Complete The information must be complete for the decision that has to be made. For example, the credit limit may be partly based on the customer's current bank balance. This may again lead to an unduly restrictive credit limit if the supplier is not informed that a number of incoming cheques have been presented but are not yet reflected in the balances. This information might have led to a more generous credit limit.

Understandable The information has to be presented in a clearly understood format. This means that significant values are highlighted and the source and units of the data must be clearly stated on the table or graph. Determining credit availability and limit may require the collection of standard key variables. The values of these variables must be easy to locate and interpret.

Cost-effective The cost of collecting the data must justify its value to the firm. Setting an incorrect credit limit leads to two kinds of risk.

A risk of undertrading with the customer so that the customer places orders elsewhere.

A risk of overtrading with the customer, who may go into liquidation owing large amounts of money.

This suggests that credit limits should be set very carefully and that thorough investigation is justified.

(b)   Structured decisions are those where all the variables required in the decision can be defined in advance. The decision-maker has to find the *values* of the variables for each instance and then apply them to a formula or compare them to a criteria. There is little need for human judgement.

There are companies which use structured decision rules for deciding whether to extend credit and to determine the credit limit. These usually apply where there are many customers applying for credit and so a procedure has to be worked out to deal with these in a standardised way. This may be the case in the company, although much will depend upon the management method, the character of the accountant and the number of customers involved.

Unstructured decisions are usually associated with fuzzy complex problems for which there is no clear structure and the result relies upon management's intuition. Some smaller companies may use this approach to the credit example, dealing with each case as a separate problem and making the decision upon "gut-feel". It is unlikely that this will be true in the company because of the risk involved but it might be. Some textbooks also defined unstructured decisions as everything that is not structured and so this definition may be appropriate to the company.

Semistructured decisions fall somewhere between the two. They involve both standard procedures and elements of individual judgement. It is likely that this fits the company. The accountant will take into consideration factual data provided by the customer, banks and credit-checking agencies. However, it is also likely that she will also use elements of judgement.

66   (Answer 9 of examination)

Examiner's comments and marking guide

Question 9: **Evaluating software was the focus of this question. Candidates were asked to describe five issues that should be considered in evaluating each proposal. The second part of the question suggested that none of the proposals provided the perfect solution and invited candidates to describe methods which could be used to assess the strengths and weaknesses of each proposal.**

This question was not popular with candidates. In general the first part of the question (the five issues) was well answered. The second part of the question was usually restricted to a points scoring system. Few candidates described simulation and benchmarking.

(a)   Up to two marks for each valid issue
         Five issues required giving a total of 10 marks
(b)   One mark for each valid point up to a maximum of 5 marks.

Step by step answer plan

Step 1   Read the question again and make sure that you focus on precisely what is required.

Step 2   Clearly there are many issues that could be discussed, so you should jot down five that you feel able to discuss in detail for part (a).

Step 3   For part (b) there are two main possibilities to consider: factor-weighting and benchmarking.

Step 4   Now review your answer plan and ensure that it does precisely answer the question as set.

The examiner's answer

(a)   **Issues in software selection**

Requirements Fit. It is important to assess the 'fit' of the software to the requirements of the manufacturing company. It is unlikely that any of the packages will fulfil all the requirements defined in the ITT and so the company has to decide to either make compromises and forgo certain requirements or to commission bespoke changes to produce a system that exactly meets its needs. The *flexibility* of the package may be an important issue in evaluating each proposal. Some packages allow menus, dialogues and reports to be tailored to each organisation's specific requirements. Some vendors will also build in changes at low cost in the understanding that such functionality can be passed on to other users, so that their product becomes more functional and hence attractive to other customers in the marketplace.

System performance. The functionality of the system must be supported by acceptable performance. The company must be sure that the system can cope with the volumes of data that will be processed and stored. Many suppliers have tables of performance statistics showing the response time of their software under different loadings and configuration. It may be possible to achieve acceptable performance by relatively cheap hardware upgrades and so it might be unwise to reject a package on system performance alone.

Compatibility with existing software. The company currently has inventory control software. This will be storing information about products, orders, despatch notes etc. which may still need to be accessed by the replacement system. Consequently the company needs to investigate issues of data conversion and compatibility and the willingness of the supplier to provide such facilities and their cost.

Usability. Many software packages offer very similar facilities because they are supporting the same functional area. Consequently, differences may be confined to the user-friendliness of the software - general screen layout, meaningful error messages, context-sensitive HELP, report layouts etc. In certain environments the package may be judged against de-facto industry standards (such as Microsoft Windows). Evidence suggests that users are increasingly expecting packages to be consistent across applications, so that they can take their skills from one area to another.

Security and audit. Many competing packages offer different emphasis on the security aspects of the software. Some may offer only rudimentary password facilities (perhaps on initial entry into the package) whilst others provide layers of passwords, supported by encryption and other measures designed to protect the data. The audit trail should also be inspected and its content discussed with internal auditors or external advisers.

Supplier factors. Package selection should include a general evaluation of the supplier. This might include an assessment of the financial strength of the supplier, their experience in manufacturing industry and the number of solutions they have supplied to this sector. The supplier might also offer flexible supply options (for example, allowing the customer to rent the package for three months before deciding to purchase). Training, support and documentation can also be examined and assessed.

(b)   **Weighted tables**

The most common approach to assessing the strengths and weaknesses of each proposal is to compile a number of important factors and to weight their importance in the selection process. For example:

Factor	Weighting
Functionality	10
Cost	8
Compatibility with existing software	8
Performance	7
User-friendliness	7
Flexibility	5
Security	5
Supplier issues	4

Each supplier is either given a rank or a score for each of these factors and a weighted total produced. The package with the highest figure is selected.

Benchmarks
Benchmark tests are undertaken by running competing software over the same data. The speed of response or function can be recorded and compared. There appears to be no plan to upgrade the current hardware in the manufacturing company. Consequently vendors can be invited to benchmark their software over the current configuration, providing statistics to supplement general tables of performance.

Did you answer the question?

The question refers specifically to inventory control software, so your answer should be geared to that.

JUNE 1997 QUESTIONS

Section A - ALL FOUR questions are compulsory and MUST be attempted

Scenario

. Amalcar Staffing Ltd is a company specialising in the supply of temporary staff on short-term contracts to several industrial sectors. Staff are employed (full-time or part-time) by Amalcar and then hired out to client companies. The clients are invoiced weekly for the hours worked by the contract staff. The staff are either paid weekly or monthly directly by Amalcar. Employee taxes and staff welfare are the responsibility of Amalcar.

The need to produce client invoices quickly and accurately led to the company developing a bespoke client billing system. This was written and installed two years ago by a software house specialising in staffing and recruitment systems. The system operates on a local area network (LAN) supporting four users in the billing office. Staff on contract return their weekly timesheets to the billing office, whose staff enter the time details into the billing system which produces client invoices.

Amalcar's rapid expansion led to the decision to sub-contract (or outsource) staff payroll processing to a computer bureau. Copies of the weekly timesheets are sent to this bureau which produces the payroll details and payslips for Amalcar. The contract with the payroll bureau is negotiated on an annual basis and is due for renewal in two months' time.

Six months ago the management of Amalcar decided to recommence payroll processing within the company and to discontinue the bureau contract. There were two main reasons for this decision:

- To improve access to information. Amalcar's managers increasingly require access to cost and income data to help them evaluate current contracts and bid for new ones.

- To reduce costs. The bureau has indicated that charges for the next contract will be 'substantially' larger than the current contract.

A small team was set up and an appropriate package selected and purchased. The selected package is well established with over 1,000 users in the country. There is an active independent user group which has a specialist payroll sub-group.

The task of implementing this package within the company is the responsibility of the billing office manager. The software will be installed on the LAN in the billing office and the system expanded to support six users. The number of staff employed in the office will also increase from four to six to cope with the new responsibilities. The billing office manager has attended the three day standard course to learn how to use and install the package. This course runs once per month at the software company's headquarters and costs £750 per delegate.

It is currently envisaged that details of hours worked will be entered separately into the billing (for invoicing) and payroll systems. A link between the two may be developed in the future, but it is not part of the current project.

The billing office manager has broken the implementation of the payroll package down into the following main activities:

A.   Produce project plan and terms of reference

B.   Attend training course (billing office manager only)

C.   Install payroll software

D.   Recruit two new employees

E.   Upgrade hardware

F.   Agree training objectives

G.   Agree training material

H.   Attend training courses (other staff)

I.   Prepare user documentation

J.   Create master files

K.   Prepare test plan

L.   User tests

The activities A and B have already been completed.

---

67   (Question 1 of examination)

The billing office manager is considering two systems implementation options:

- Parallel running
- Direct changeover

Required:

(a)   Explain what is meant by 'parallel running' and 'direct changeover' and give two advantages of each.

(12 marks)

(b)   Which option would you recommend for Amalcar? Briefly explain why you believe that your recommendation is the better approach to implementation.

(3 marks)
(Total: 15 marks)

(Question 2 of examination)

Training is an essential part of successful implementation. The billing office manager has included some elements of training in her initial project breakdown, but she would welcome your views on the training requirements for the new system and how they could be fulfilled. Four options are currently being considered. She points out that the usual everyday work of the billing office will have to continue during this training period.

The four options being considered are as follows:

- Sending each employee on the standard three day training course at the software company's headquarters.

- Running the standard three day course at Amalcar's offices and putting all employees on this course. The software company has quoted a price of £2,000 per course for a three-day course attended by up to 12 delegates.

- Using the billing office manager to teach employees individually, so spreading her knowledge through the organisation.

- Buying a CBT (computer based training) package available from an independent training company. This CBT package costs £40 for a single user licence and covers the facilities and installation of the payroll package.

Required:

(a)   Choose *three* of these training options. For each option chosen, give *two* advantages and *two* disadvantages.

(12 marks)

(b)   Each of the four training options could be justified for Amalcar. Recommend *one* of these training options, justifying your choice.

(3 marks)
(Total: 15 marks)

(Question 3 of examination)

The suppliers of the payroll software have sent the billing office manager details of a support (or maintenance) contract which they recommend should be taken out for their payroll software.

Required:

(a)   Explain what a support (or maintenance) contract is and what facilities and services should be included in such a contract.

(7 marks)

(b)   Explain why it is essential for Amalcar to subscribe to this contract.

(3 marks)

(c)   The billing office manager has also received information from an independent user group inviting Amalcar to subscribe to its payroll sub-group. Explain what is meant by a user group and what benefits there are for Amalcar in becoming a member.

(5 marks)
(Total: 15 marks)

(Question 4 of examination)

The project breakdown produced by the billing office manager represents her initial view of the constituent parts of the project. A colleague has suggested that these should be represented on a network diagram so that network analysis can be used to determine the critical path and the elapsed time of the project.

Required:

(a)   Identify what further information would need to be recorded about the activities before this network diagram could be drawn.

(4 marks)

(b)   Explain the terms 'the critical path' and 'elapsed time of the project' and explain why it is essential that the billing office manager knows which activities lie on the critical path.

(6 marks)
(Total: 10 marks)

Section B - THREE questions ONLY to be attempted

68   (Question 5 of examination)

(a)   Feedback is an important concept in a controlled system. Systems theory defines two types of feedback - negative and positive.

Required:

Define the basic components of a controlled system and explain (using an appropriate practical example) the principle of negative feedback.

(8 marks)

(b)   Some systems experience *positive feedback*. Explain what is meant by positive feedback. Give *one* reason (with an example) why it might occur in an apparently controlled system.

(3 marks)

(c)   Two system concepts are:

  (1)   Coupling and decoupling
  (2)   Entropy

Explain *one* of these concepts and give an example of how it can be applied in an organisation.

(4 marks)
(Total: 15 marks)

---

69   (Question 6 of examination)

A keyboard operator enters examination results into a computer system from information provided on a form compiled by the examiner. The following data is on the manual form:

  Candidate number
  Centre number
  Desk number
  Examination number
  Marker number
  Questions answered
  Marks for each question
  Total mark for the examination

The question paper for each examination is divided into two sections. The first section, Section A, is worth 55 marks and consists of four compulsory questions. The second section, Section B, has five questions from which the candidate must answer three. Each question in this section is worth 15 marks. 60,000 candidates sit the examinations at 150 centres.

Required:

(a)   Briefly describe *four* different types of check that can be used in examination mark data entry to improve the accuracy of the entered data. For each different type of check explain what entry errors it is trying to detect and give an example of its application in the examination mark data entry system.

(12 marks)

(b)   Explain *one* other general design principle that the developer could use to facilitate the speedy and accurate input of the examination mark data.

(3 marks)
(Total: 15 marks)

---

70   (Question 7 of examination)

A visiting computer salesman explains that his product is written with a 'relational database and supports SQL'. Your manager tells you later that he does not know what this means.

Required:

(a)   Explain the principles of the relational model.

(6 marks)

(b)   Explain what SQL is.

(3 marks)

(c)   The following relations (tables) have been defined for a relational application. The key of each relation (table) is shown in bold.

PRODUCT   **Product-code,** product-description, price
CUSTOMER   **Customer-no,** customer-name, customer-address
ORDER   **Order-no,** customer-no, customer name
ORDER LINE   **Order-no, product-code,** product-description, order-date

There are three likely errors in these tables which prevent them from being in Third Normal Form.

Identify, briefly explain and correct each error.

(6 marks)
(Total: 15 marks)

71   (Question 8 of examination)

(a)   Many organisations undertake a feasibility study before taking the decision to commit to a full-scale systems development.

Required:

(i)   Describe the main objectives of the study.
(ii)   Explain the different types of feasibility it will consider.

(9 marks)

(b)   A feasibility study will often commence with the terms of reference.

Required:

Briefly describe (with examples) *three* elements that are usually defined within the terms of reference.

(6 marks)
(Total: 15 marks)

72   (Question 9 of examination)

(a)   A manufacturing company is about to implement a bespoke inventory control system. The implementation team is keen to collect data that measures the quality of the delivered system. A HELP desk has been set up to support the users of the software.

Required:

Define and show the difference between *corrective* and *adaptive* maintenance.

(6 marks)

(b)   The implementation team wishes to monitor the user-friendliness and frequency of use of the system. They want to ensure that users find the software easy to use and that managers extensively use the enquiry and reporting facilities.

Required:

Suggest a total of *three* appropriate measures of user-friendliness and frequency of use and describe how such data might be collected, interpreted and acted upon.

(9 marks)
(Total: 15 marks)

ANSWERS TO JUNE 1997 EXAMINATION

67   (Answer 1 of examination)

Examiner's comments and marking guide

Question 1: Candidates were asked to define 'parallel running' and 'direct changeover' and to give two advantages of each. This is a fairly straightforward textbook subject and the question was answered well by most candidates.

Paer (b) of this question asked candidates to recommend the best implementation approach for Amalcar - the case study company. Although marks were given for a well justified answer suggesting parallel running, full marks could only be gained by recommending (with appropriate justification) the direct changeover method. The contract with the computer bureau expires in two months' time. The parallel running option would require a continued relationship with the bureau for a limited time perod and it is likely that this will be very expensive.

(a)   Up to 2 marks for the description. Up to 2 marks for each advantage.
         Two advantages required. Two options need describing - 12 marks.
(b)   One mark for each valid point, up to a maximum of 3 marks.

Step by step answer plan

Step 1   Read the question again and make sure that you focus on precisely what is required.

Step 2   In part (a) of question 1 you need just a textbook explanation of the two possibilities. Note that 12 marks are available, so a reasonable level of detail is required.

Step 3   Sensible advocacy of either method, in a limited space, will earn some of the three marks available for part (b) of question 1, so don't overlook this part of the question. As the examiner comments, the direct changeover is the only option likely to be feasible.

Step 4   In question 2, again most of the marks are available for textbook explanation in part (a), but easy marks can be picked up by devoting a few minutes to part (b).

Step 5   In question 3 notice that the maintenance contract relates to the payroll software; marks are not available for discussion of hardware maintenance.

Step 6   Question 4 is straightforward bookwork knowledge on network diagrams.

Step 7   Now review your answer plan and ensure that it does precisely answer the question as set.

The examiner's answer

1   (a)   **Parallel running**

                In this method the old and new systems are run simultaneously for an agreed period of time and results from the two systems are compared. Once the user has complete confidence in the new system the old system is abandoned and transactions are only passed through the new one. Parallel running places a large administrative overhead on the user department because every transaction effectively has to be done twice - once through the established procedures and then again through the new computer system. Results have to be cross-checked and the source of errors located. This will lead to system modifications if problems are discovered in the computer system.

Advantages

- This method does have the advantage of having a 'fail-safe' system to fall back on should the new system crash for some reason. System problems can then be sorted out and the parallel run resumed without suspending the operations of the whole company.

- Training can be phased throughout the parallel running period and problems of usability addressed. Mistakes made by the operators will be detected (through the cross-checking of results) and the reasons for these mistakes investigated and, if necessary, amendments to dialogues and controls suggested and implemented.

- Managers and users have complete confidence in the system when it becomes fully operational. Systems implemented by direct changeover often contain small faults which have to be repaired. During this period of repair the system is 'down' and as well as affecting the operations of the company it undermines the confidence of the users in the robustness and reliability of the software.

Direct changeover

This strategy is to implement the new system completely and withdraw the old without any sort of parallel running at all. Thus processing of the current system may end on a Friday night and all transactions pass through the new computer system from Monday morning onwards. There is no 'fail-safe' system to fall back on.

Where possible, direct changeovers should occur in slack periods and take advantage of natural breaks in the operations of the organisation, such as industrial holidays. It demands very thorough testing and well planned file creation and training strategies. All operations of the system must be understood at the moment of going live because the opportunity for gradual training and further testing does not exist. It is potentially cheaper but riskier than parallel running.

Advantages include

- Direct changeover has none of the cost and time overheads of parallel running. The time taken to enter values into two systems and then cross-check the results means that organisations often have to employ part-time and temporary staff, thus increasing the cost of implementation. Direct changeover is potentially cheaper.

- Direct changeover does not allow users to remain dependent on the old system. In many parallel runs the inconsistencies between the two systems are usually attributed to the new or replacement system and so there is often a temptation to revert to (and hence rely on) the old system. Problems still arise when the parallel run has been completed because difficulties have not been properly resolved in the parallel running period.

  In many systems there is no direct correspondence between the functions and features of the old and the replacement system. In such circumstances cross checking of outputs is not possible and so direct changeover is the preferred method.

(b)   The contract with the computer bureau expires in two months' time. This suggests that direct changeover is probably the preferred implementation option. The parallel running option would require a continued relationship with the computer bureau for a limited time period and it is likely that this will be very expensive as the bureau exploits the final months of a contract that will not be renewed.

Did you answer the question?

Apply the facts of the question to your answer.

Examiner's comments and marking guide

Question 2: asked candidates to describe and evaluate three training options for the implementation of the system at Amalcar. This question concerned part of the syllabus that had not been examined before.

On the whole, the answers were very good and seemed to indicate that candidates had studied and revised this part of the syllabus even though it had not appeared in previous papers.

(a)   Up to 2 marks for each advantage and disadvantage. Three options required - 12 marks.
(b)   One mark for each valid point up to a maximum of 3 marks.

The examiner's answer

2   (a)   The four training options are as follows.

To send employees on the standard three-day training course offered by the software company. The billing office manager has already attended one of the standard courses and so she is able to report on the effectiveness and quality of the course. Advantages and disadvantages of further employees attending such a course include:

Advantages

Training can be provided for one delegate at a time. Hence the majority of staff will still be in the billing office undertaking the daily routine business.

Each employee receives standard tuition of a known quality.

The delegate gets the opportunity to talk with other users of the software and so profit from their experience.

Disadvantages

Booking individual places will be more expensive than commissioning an on-site course. The cost of sending the remaining five billing office staff is £3,750 compared with £2,000 for an on-site course.

There are not enough presentations of the course to send one employee on each course before the deadline date. It appears that there will only be two further courses before the implementation date. Thus at least three employees will have to be sent on one course (perhaps causing some office disruption) unless Amalcar decide to train some of the employees after the system has gone live.

The course is unlikely to be appropriate to the managers who only wish to interrogate the data. Hence a different method of training will have to be employed to fulfil this training need.

To arrange an in-house course. This is the standard training course run at the customer's premises.

Advantages

This option is cheaper than sending all the employees on individual bookings on public courses.

The content of the course can be tailored to Amalcar's specific requirements, particularly concerning the training of the managers who will be discretionary users of the system. It may be possible to structure the course so that managers attend a self-contained session where all trainees learn about query and reporting facilities.

The users can all be trained before the proposed implementation date.

Disadvantages

It is likely that the billing department will have to be closed down during the course.

There is no opportunity to learn from users from other companies.

Some delegates may find it difficult to learn with their colleagues and may feel inhibited by the presence of their peers and managers, particularly if they are having some difficulties with the concepts and functions of the software.

Use the billing office manager to cascade the course throughout the department.

Advantages and disadvantages include:

Advantages

It is probably the cheapest option as it has no direct tangible cost.

Individual tuition can be provided so there is no need to shut the department down during the training period.

Tuition can be organised so that all employees are trained before the implementation date.

Disadvantages

The billing office manager is not a full-time trainer and may have no aptitude for training.

The billing office manager has only just learnt the software herself and so may feel uncertain about her ability to effectively present the course. She risks exposing her own limited knowledge to her staff.

The billing office manager will have to prepare training material and courses. It is unlikely that she will have the time or the expertise to complete these before the deadline date.

To use CBT software produced by the independent training company.

Advantages and disadvantages include:

Advantages

Employees can fit their learning in with their operational job. There is no need for individuals to go off-site for courses.

Better assessment method. Most CBT packages include tests which are used to control progression onto the next subject. Delegates must pass these tests before they can continue. This limit on progression is not usually possible in taught courses.

The material remains in the company and so it can be used for staff that join in the future.

Disadvantages

A personal computer (PC) must be available for running the CBT software and time must be allowed for undertaking the learning programme.

There is nobody to answer specific questions about the operation of the software if employees are unsure or confused by certain features and facilities.

There is no opportunity to meet staff from other companies who use the software and hence profit from their experience.

(b)   This part of the question requires a coherent justification. Each of the four options could be justified. For example, the company might elect to run an in-house course. This could be justified on the cheaper cost per delegate and it also ensures that all staff are trained before the system goes live. Training might be organised across two (or three) weekends to allow the continued operation of the department.

Examiner's comments and marking guide

Question 3: **Part a of this question concerned a support (or maintenance) contract for Amalcar. In the context of the case study this was a support contract for the payroll software not the computer hardware.**

Unfortunately many candidates included hardware maintenance features in their answer and credit could not be given for this. Many candidates also failed to start their answer by explaining what a support (or maintenance) contract actually is, preferring to list the facilities and services of such a contract.

Part b of this question asked candidates to explain why it is **essential** for Amalcar to subscribe to this contract. The key point here is that payroll is subject to unpredictable requirements defined by government. The company must comply with these changes.

The supplier of the payroll software must include such changes in their package to allow their customers to meet statutory requirements. This is why the subscription to the contract is **essential** rather than just desirable or recommended. Some candidates identified this and scored well on this part of the question.

The final part of this question required candidates to describe a **user group** and explain the benefits of Amalcar becoming a member. This was generally answered fairly well, although there was some confusion about what a user group actually was. Some candidates suggested that it was a steering group of users who would be consulted throughout the project.

(a)   One mark for each valid point up to a maximum of 7 marks.
(b)   One mark for each valid point up to a maximum of 3 marks.
(c)   One mark for each valid point up to a maximum of 5 marks.

The examiner's answer

3   (a)   Most software products offer a support or maintenance contract which is renewed annually for a given cost. This cost is sometimes a set percentage of the price of the original software.

Facilities provided might include:

Technical advice by telephone, telex or mail to resolve customers' difficulties in installing and using the software product. This advice is usually provided through a HELP desk which is usually available between set times defined in the contract.

Provide maintenance revisions of the software which rectify faults found and reported by users. Fixes to known errors are usually bundled together into a minor release which is made available (together with installation procedures) free of charge to registered users.

To provide revisions or procedures which allow the customer to comply with changes in legislative requirements. This is very important in this instance. Future changes in payroll procedures must be reflected in the software, otherwise it becomes unusable.

Purchase major upgrades at discounted prices. Upgrades are major changes or re-writes. They usually add significant functionality rather than just fixing problems. The upgraded product is the one offered to new customers. Users of the current software can upgrade at a much lower price than the purchase price requested from new users. Stationery may also be available at favourable rates.

Newsletter/fact sheets. Many support contracts include a subscription to a periodic Newsletter which offers advice, information and technical tips.

Legal definition. The maintenance contract will also have legal conditions concerning the:

Obligations of the customer. The software must be used on the correct hardware and copies restricted to those defined in the contract.

Liability of the supplier to consequential damage caused by the failure or incorrect operation of the software.

Force Majeure.
Termination and assignment procedures and restrictions.

> **Did you answer the question?**
>
> The question specifically relates to software, so it is irrelevant to discuss hardware.

(b)   Amalcar must take out a support contract because of the nature of the application. Payroll is subject to unpredictable requirements defined by government. These changes and requirements are not framed in the context of how easy they will be to implement in a package. Thus the onus for specifying, implementing, testing and releasing these changes is placed with the software supplier and this responsibility alone is worth the cost of the contract.

(c)   A user group is a group of people who use the same software product. In this case the group consists of employees from different organisations who have come together into a self-help group where members can assist each other to overcome problems with the standard payroll package.

It will be particularly helpful in this instance because the product has a well-established user base and it is unlikely that any difficulties encountered by Amalcar will not have been met before by at least one user in the group. Consequently the user group will be a valuable source of advice and guidance.

User groups also enable the software supplier to keep in contact with their customers and many suppliers will use the group to identify a wish-list of amendments and enhancements which may be incorporated into the next release of the product. As a member of the user group Amalcar will be able to contribute to the future development of the product.

Finally, the independence of the user group means that it can act as an effective arbiter in any disputes between individual users and the software suppliers.

Examiner's comments and marking guide

Question 4: asked questions concerning Critical Path Analysis and project management. **Part (a) of this question requested what further information would be needed to produce a network diagram.**

The answer was the precedences and time estimates for each activity. Unfortunately many candidates suggested new activities on the plan, budgets, resources available etc. Although these are essential parts of project management they are not needed to draw the network diagram.

Part (b) of this question asked candidates to explain the terms 'critical path' and 'elapsed time of the project' and to explain why it is essential for the manager to know which activities lie on the critical path.

Candidates appeared to know what was meant by the critical path but failed to explain how the manager would use this information. Very few candidates were able to successfully define the 'elapsed time of the project'.

The elapsed time of the project is defined by the Earliest Finish Time (EFT) of the last activity on the network diagram. It is not 'how much time has been used on the project so far'.

(a)   2 marks for precedences, 2 marks for estimates.
(b)   Up to 2 marks for the explanation of critical path.
        Up to 2 marks for the explanation of the elapsed time of the project.
        Up to 2 marks for reasons why the manager should know what lies on the critical path.

The examiner's answer

4   (a)   The following information would be needed to draw a network, and hence determine the critical path.

Three deliverables from the case study are used to illustrate the answer.

Precedences for each deliverable. For example, it may be necessary to finish both activities A and B before commencing C.

		Precedence
A.	Produce project plan and terms of reference	-
B.	Attend training course (billing office manager only)	-
C.	Install payroll software	A, B

Estimates of the time taken to undertake each activity. For example:

		Precedence	*Estimate*
A.	Produce project plan and terms of reference	-	2 days
B.	Attend training course (billing office manager only)	-	3 days
C.	Install payroll software	A, B	2 days

(b)   When the network diagram is complete, it is possible to establish the EST (earliest start time) and EFT (earliest finish time) of each activity. The EFT of the last activity on the network diagram defines the *elapsed time of the project.* This time is not the addition of all the individual estimates of the project activities because it is usually possible to undertake some activities in parallel. For example, if the project consisted of just the three activities defined above then the network would look like the diagram below and the elapsed time would be five days.

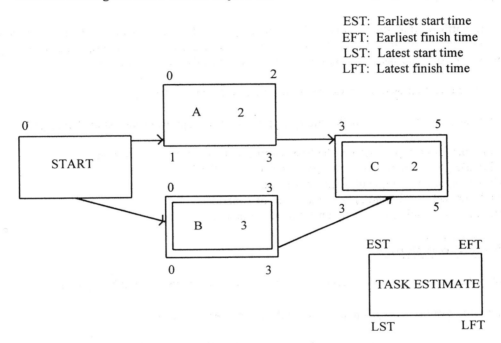

```
EST:  Earliest start time
EFT:  Earliest finish time
LST:  Latest start time
LFT:  Latest finish time
```

The earliest finish time of the last activity on the project determines the latest finish time (LFT) for that activity. The latest start time (LST) is then calculated by subtracting the activity duration from the LFT. This latest start time is the time each activity must start by if **the estimated elapsed time of the project is not to be increased.** For many activities there is a difference between the EST and LST showing the number of days of float or slack that exists for that activity. This gives how many days the start of a particular activity can be delayed by without affecting the overall elapsed time of the project. However, for some activities the EST and LST are the same. These activities are **critical activities** because their delay will increase the elapsed time of the project. Together these activities make up the **critical path.** In the example above B and C are on the critical path.

The billing office manager needs to know what deliverables are on the critical path so that she can:

-    Allocate these activities to her most experienced and reliable staff

-    Monitor their progress more carefully than non-critical activities

-    Re-investigate estimates to ensure that the elapsed time is correct

-    Examine possibilities for splitting these activities if the project elapsed time is unacceptable.

68   (Answer 5 of examination)

Examiner's comments and marking guide

Question 5: This question asked candidates to define elements of systems theory.

The components of a controlled system were fairly well described by most candidates. The better answers include a diagram cross-referenced to a practical business example. The principle of negative feedback was fairly well defined although some candidates focused on the identification of deviation rather than the corrective measures made to bring the system back into control.

Part (b) concerned *positive feedback.*

This is a fairly straightforward textbook subject. Unfortunately candidates did not define the term correctly, believing that the term meant praise or acclaim rather than a poorly constructed feedback loop causing the system to go increasingly out of control! The same mistakes were made last time this question was set.

The final part of this question asked candidates to define coupling or entropy.

This was generally answered fairly well with candidates providing appropriate organisational examples.

(a)   Up to 4 marks for an explanation of the basic components of a controlled system.
        Up to 2 marks for explaining the principle of negative feedback.
        Up to 2 marks for an example of negative feedback.
(b)   One mark for each valid point up to a maximum of 3 marks.
(c)   One mark for each valid point up to a maximum of 4 marks.

Step by step answer plan

Step 1   Read the question again and make sure that you focus on precisely what is required.

Step 2   Note that part (a) is very similar to Q7 of the December 1995 exam.

Step 3   Parts (b) and (c) offer a few marks for simple explanations of two systems terms (from three) one after the other.

Step 4   Now review your answer plan and ensure that it does precisely answer the question as set.

The examiner's answer

(a)   Most systems have to achieve defined objectives. For example:

-     A central heating system has to maintain a certain room temperature

-     A hospital admissions system has to keep within a maximum waiting time for outpatients' appointments

-     A stores system has to maintain a minimum stock level

These objectives define the **standard** which the system is aiming for.

Each system attempts to reach these defined objectives by a **process** of some kind that takes in inputs and turns them into outputs. The values of the outputs are measured by a **sensor** which passes this information to a **comparator** that evaluates the values of the system against the **standard** required. If the values do not conform to the standards required then the inputs of the system are changed by an **effector** that alters the input so that the process can produce outputs of the required value.

In a controlled system there is a feedback loop that monitors the outputs of the process and, if the output does not meet the standard, changes the input values to allow the process to produce the outputs required. This is an example of **negative feedback**: the system has recognised that it will not meet its targets and so has applied changes to allow it to meet its original objectives.

	Central heating	*Stock level maintenance*
Standard	Required temperature	Target stock value
Input	Fuel	Order goods
Process	Burning fuel system	Purchase order system
Output	Heat	Stock level
Sensor	Thermometer	Daily stock level report
Comparator	Thermostat	Purchasing manager
Effector	Thermostat	Purchasing clerk

In the central heating system the feedback loop will compare the actual output value with the required temperature and adjust the system accordingly. If the temperature is below the required value the inputs will be increased to raise the temperature. If the required value has reached the standard then the thermostat will reduce or shut off the inputs.

In the stock level maintenance system all goods below the re-order stock value will be reported on the daily stock level report. Re-ordering is authorised by the purchasing manager and actioned by the purchasing clerk. The received goods will bring the system back to its desired standard.

(b)   **Positive feedback** will take place when there is a poorly-constructed feedback loop which modifies the inputs to a system so that its performance deviates even further from its required standard.

The fault could be anywhere in the feedback loop. For example:

- The sensor may measure the wrong output. The output selected to monitor performance may be inappropriate. For example, many countries measure the performance of their health services through sickness and illness statistics. Many commentators believe that this is a negative and simplistic measure of 'health'. It leads to more resources being committed to treating (and re-defining) sickness rather than improving health.

- The standard set for the system may be inappropriate. For example, the target set for sales in an organisation may be too low and so exceeding sales targets may lead to a reduction in inputs (reduce marketing spend, sales commissions) because the targets have been met, so losing opportunities for further growth.

- The performance of the effector may be misunderstood so that it does not have the required effect on the process. For example, many projects are monitored against a required project plan. Failure to be on schedule leads to organisations adding extra resources and staff to the project in the hope that this will bring the project back on time. However, there is considerable evidence to suggest that adding resources to certain types of project (such as software development projects) and at certain stages in the project life cycle actually leads to additional project delays and so the project slips further behind schedule.

Did you answer the question?

Make sure in your own mind that you can define technical jargon before you commit yourself to paper.

(c)   **Coupling and decoupling**

Systems and sub-systems are usually linked in some way so that the outputs of one system become the inputs of the next. The assembly of many products is based on such principles. For example, specialist seat manufacturers produce car seats which they despatch to car manufacturers. These seats are inserted into the car at a defined stage in the assembly line. Management have traditionally been concerned to decouple these systems so that one sub-system is not unduly affected by failure in the other. So, for example, large stocks of car seats have been maintained with each seat passing through quality control procedures before its acceptance. The manufacture of the car then uses seats from the accepted stock and so will not be delayed by unavailability or unacceptability of components. The maintenance of stock effectively decouples systems but it does so at a cost.

The manufacturing supply strategy of just-in-time (JIT) is an application of close coupling. In JIT stock holding and handling costs (traditionally a costly area) are minimised by the manufacturer only taking delivery of raw materials and components a few days or hours before they are needed. However, failure of suppliers to deliver will lead to major problems because supply and use is closely or tightly coupled. Consequently co-ordinated planning, quality procedures and contracts have to be in place to reduce the potentially damaging effect of close coupling.

Entropy

Systems are often classified into open and closed systems. Closed systems have little interaction with their environment in contrast to open systems which continually process and react to information passed to them. In practice there are few completely open or completely closed systems, most systems are on a continuum between the two.

There is a tendency for closed (or almost closed) systems to become increasingly disorganised over time because they fail to take in and process relevant information from the environment. The term **entropy** is used to describe this uncertainty or disorganisation. Higher levels of entropy will be experienced until the very existence of the system is threatened. Systems cope with this by re-organising themselves to receive inputs from the outside environment (negative entropy) to reduce uncertainty and increase organisation in the light of new information and conditions.

Many businesses, political and social organisations tend unconsciously towards becoming increasingly closed organisations. Their perception of the outside environment becomes rooted at a certain time and subsequent staff are recruited who share this perception. In fact individuals who do not share the vision are weeded out as 'potential trouble-makers' or 'they would not fit in here' and so opportunities for processing new information from the outside environment are rejected. Entropy dictates that the increasingly closed organisation will lead to disorganisation and under-performance as it fails to react to changes in the environment. Eventually this is recognised (through financial performance, election results, poor attendance at meetings) and it is tackled by organising negative entropy (bringing in new management staff or leaders, hiring consultants etc). Some organisations are saved. Others do not survive and their entropy proves fatal.

---

69   (Answer 6 of examination)

(**Examiner's comments and marking guide**)

Question 6: asked candidates to describe four types of check to improve the accuracy of data entry.

Most candidates competently answered this. In some instances candidates failed to distinguish sufficiently between two checks. For example, providing two format checks as examples of two different *types* of check.

Part (b) of this question asked candidates to provide a general design principle to facilitate the speedy and accurate input of examination data.

Candidates seemed to focus on either direct data entry (via OMR) or the design of the data entry screen to reflect the sequence of data items on the form. These were acceptable answers and most candidates scored well on this part of the question.

(a)   1 mark for each valid check.
       Up to 2 marks for an appropriate example and understanding of the errors it is trying to detect.
       Four checks required - 12 marks
(b)   One mark for each valid point up to a maximum of 3 marks.

Step by step answer plan

Step 1 Read the question again and make sure that you focus on precisely what is required. Note the examiner's comment that two different format checks do not constitute two different types of check; they are just two different examples of a single type.

Step 2 The examiner provides six types of check. Choose four, and in each case provide a description, an explanation of the errors it seeks to detect, and an application to the scenario.

Step 3 Note that there are three fairly easy marks on offer for a few minutes devoted to part (b).

Step 4 Now review your answer plan and ensure that it does precisely answer the question as set.

The examiner's answer

(a)   Possible checks include:

Format checks

Each data field will have a specified length and format. Format checks ensure that the entered data conforms to these requirements. In this example, the candidate number may be specified as an eight digit numerical field. Thus invalid entries, such as AS546738 (which includes alphabetical characters) and 5473451 (incorrect length) will be rejected.

Valid value and range checks

Certain fields may only have a limited range of valid data values. For example, the examination will only be sat at a limited number of centres and so centre codes entered can be checked against a list of valid examination centres. Many systems now offer users a pull-down list of these valid values. The range check is a similar concept. The actual value of marks for each question cannot be predicted, but (in section B) it must lie between 0 and 15. Thus the software can check whether the entered value lies within this range.

Consistency checks

Consistency checks are concerned with verifying the relationship between two entered data values. For example both the candidate number and the centre number can have valid values and formats and hence pass the two previous tests. However, the combination of the two could be invalid because the candidate did not register at that centre.

Item counts and totals

The previous example concerned consistency between two sets of data held in the system. Calculated total and item counts are concerned with consistency between values at the time of data entry. For example the marks for each question must (when added together) equal the total mark for the paper and the number of questions answered must tally with the number of marks recorded.

Data verification

Data verification concerns the double entry of data values by different operators. For example, marks for individual questions may pass the range check (0-15) and so be valid but they may still be incorrect - an operator has entered a 6 instead of an 8). In data verification each candidate's mark is entered twice and the software compares the two sets of data values. Values that do not match are rejected for further investigation.

Check digit

Certain fields may have codes to which a check digit can be attached. This digit becomes the last character or number of the code. When the code is entered the check digit is recalculated and validated against the one entered by the operator. Check digits are particularly useful in supporting range checks. For example, the entered candidate number may have two digits transposed (71233452 instead of 72133452) and still pass the range check (70000000-80000000). However, if the code had used a check digit system to produce the last character then this transposition would have been picked up.

(b)   There are a number of general design principles that could be used by the developer. Two examples are given below.

Pre-recording data

It may be possible to pre-record some of the information before the candidate sits the examination and before the script is marked. For example, each candidate will have to be pre-allocated to a centre for a particular examination, otherwise they will not know where to sit the paper! This allocation could be extended to the desk number, so that candidates arriving at the centre have to sit at particular desks. If these details are recorded on the system prior to the examination, then the entry of the marks could use these as confirmation values. The operator enters the examination number and centre number and the expected centre name and desk numbers could be retrieved and displayed for confirmation.

Data entry order and layout matches the original form

The chance of fast accurate data capture is improved if the entry screen is similar in layout to the manual form and the order of data entry corresponds to the order of the fields on the form. Thus the operator can logically progress down the manual form without having to jump around the screen to enter the data items in a different order or at unfamiliar places.

---

70   (Answer 7 of examination)

(Examiner's comments and marking guide)

Question 7: This question was concerned with the relational data model. It examined a relatively technical part of the syllabus, giving candidates an opportunity (in part (c)) to apply their knowledge in a practical exercise. It was felt that candidates who wished to avoid discussion, essay-type questions, would also answer this question!

Not many candidates attempted this question. Those who did either did very poorly or very well. The poor answer usually described entity-relationship modelling in part (a), skipped part (b) (on SQL) and only found one error in the part (c) exercise. The good answers usually found all three errors in the part (c) exercise and usually scored above 11 marks out of 15 for the whole question showing excellent command of the subject.

(a)   One mark for each valid point up to a maximum of 6 marks.
(b)   One mark for each valid point up to a maximum of 3 marks.
(c)   Up to 2 marks for each possible error. Three errors are required - 6 marks

(Step by step answer plan)

Step 1   Read the question again and make sure that you focus on precisely what is required.

Step 2   There are six marks available in part (a), so you should provide a relatively detailed 'bookwork' explanation of the relational model.

Step 3   In part (b) a briefer description of structured query language will earn the three marks.

Step 4   In part (c) you simply need to analyse each line in detail to identify the likely errors.

Step 5   Now review your answer plan and ensure that it does precisely answer the question as set.

The examiner's answer

(a)   A relational data base views the data as a simple collection of two-dimensional tables called relations. Example order and customer tables are given below:

ORDER   **Order-no,** order-date
Example values
Order-no   Order-date
13452   12.12.96
17634   13.2.96
15673   15.1.97

CUSTOMER   **Customer-no,** customer-name, customer-address
Example values
Customer-no   Customer-name   Customer-address
A321   Ali-fazel   12 Lark Avenue
A345   Wong   14 Arcacia Way

All the values in a column (such as order-date and customer-name) are values of the same attribute type and contain only a single attribute value. Each column of the table must have a distinct name, called the attribute name, and consequently the order of the columns in the table is immaterial. Each row of the table must be distinct, so that a row can always be identified by quoting an appropriate combination of attribute values. Such a combination of attributes is termed a primary key. In the examples given above Customer-no and Order-no are the primary keys of the two tables. All information in the relational model is represented by attribute values, not by such methods as physical order and row order. Consequently the data manipulation language is much simpler.

Relationships between two tables in a relational database are implemented through keys. For example, in a particular application, a customer places many orders and each order is placed by only one customer. In a relational database this relationship is represented by placing the key of CUSTOMER in the ORDER table. Hence the order table becomes:

ORDER   **Order-no,** order-date, customer-no
Example values
Order-no   Order-date   Customer-no
13452   12.12.96   A321
17634   13.2.96   A321
15673   15.1.97   A345

The simplicity of the relational model makes it easy to understand and to use. The user does not need to be concerned with the physical structure of the database so user requests can be expressed non-procedurally using SQL (see below). The model provides a high level of data independence, so both the physical structure and the logical structure can be changed without affecting the application programmers on one hand or the users on the other.

(b)   SQL stands for structured query language. It is a data manipulation language for a relational database. SQL commands are English-like statements which are used to query, insert, update and delete data in the database. Commands are formalised. For example, finding all the orders placed for customer-no A321 would be written as

SELECT * FROM ORDER WHERE CUSTOMER NO = 'A321'

SQL can be used directly or embedded in a host language such as COBOL or C. SQL often needs such a host because it is not a complete programming language in its own right. For example, it has no constructs for branching or looping.

(c)   The three likely errors are:

Customer-name should not be in the ORDER table. Customer-no determines the name. It is unlikely that the customer will want different names associated with different orders.

Order-date should be in ORDER and not ORDER-LINE. All the lines of an order are likely to be placed on the same order-date.

Product-description should not be in ORDER-LINE. Product-code determines product-description. The product is unlikely to have a different description on different orders.

---

71   (Answer 8 of examination)

Examiner's comments and marking guide

Question 8: asked candidates to describe certain aspects of the Feasibility Study.

Although many candidates wrote long answers to this question they did not gain as many marks as they might have expected to because:

They failed to correctly identify the main objectives of the study. Many claimed that the objective of the Feasibility Study was to replace one system with another.

They failed to correctly identify the contents of a Terms of Reference. Many candidates listed the contents of a Feasibility Report rather than the Terms of Reference for the Feasibility Study. Consequently they wrote long answers concentrating on the wrong area and gained very few marks.

(a)   One mark for each valid point up to a maximum of 9 marks.
(b)   Up to 2 marks for each element. Three elements required.

Step by step answer plan

Step 1   Read the question again and make sure that you focus on precisely what is required. Note that in part (b) the examiner is looking for three items defined within the terms of reference, not just any three items from within a feasibility study as a whole.

Step 2   In part (a) divide up your discussion so as to cover economic feasibility, technical feasibility, operational and social feasibility.

Step 3   Now review your answer plan and ensure that it does precisely answer the question as set.

The examiner's answer

(a)   A **feasibility study** is used to determine whether a potential computer system application should progress to detailed analysis, design and development. The primary objective of the **feasibility study** is to identify the key technical and performance objectives that the system must achieve and to ensure that the technology exists to technically achieve these targets. The study must also determine the cost of achieving these targets. This cost information is fed into the economic feasibility assessment.

Further objectives of the study are to:

Determine whether the project is economically feasible

This demands that the costs of the project are identified and costed. Costs will include:

-        Capital costs for hardware and software

- Infrastructure costs for communications and accommodation

- 'One-off' revenue costs for consultancy, conversion and training

- Maintenance costs for hardware and software

- Staff salaries, stationery and financing costs.

The benefits of the system should be driven from the business case that identified this potential application in the first place. These benefits may be as a result of:

- Direct cost savings
- Increased capacity
- Improved quality of product or service
- Competitive edge
- Improved decision-making.

These benefits must be quantified so that they can be compared with the cost. A formal cost-benefit analysis will be undertaken which takes into account the **timing** of the costs and the benefits. The results of this analysis will be assessed in the context of the criteria used by the company to give the go-ahead to projects. For example, the organisation may state that all projects must pay back within three years, and failure to achieve this may lead to the project being deemed economically infeasible.

Determine whether the project is technically feasible

Most projects have to technically achieve certain targets. For example:

- An output has to be produced within a certain response time. For example, a customer receipt must be produced within 15 seconds of the completion of the transaction.

- Inputs have to take place within a restricted timescale. For example, all examination marks must be entered into the system by the 30 June.

- The system has to integrate with other software and pass data in a certain format.

Determine whether the project is operationally or socially feasible

This type of feasibility is concerned with ensuring that the project fits with the business and social organisation of the company. For example:

- The new system may require new skills and attitudes. The feasibility study must assess whether the current employees have such skills and, if they do not, whether they can attain these skills and the cost of attaining them (for use in economic feasibility). Redundancies may be necessary and the feasibility study should assess both the direct and indirect (for example; in terms of morale and motivation of remaining staff) costs of such a programme.

- The new system may cut across established organisational boundaries and structures. This is likely to lead to resistance and reluctance as employees see well-established procedures and career paths disappear.

Some of these operational feasibility issues can be directly costed (such as training costs). Others have less tangible effects that must be documented in the feasibility report.

(b)　Terms of reference might contain:

Objectives. What is expected at the end of the feasibility study. For example:

To produce a feasibility report which recommends whether the project should proceed or not and, if progression is recommended, to produce a detailed timetable for the next phase.

Scope of the study. The terms of reference should specify what is within the scope of the feasibility study. For example:

The feasibility study is concerned with investigating the procedures for dealing with customer complaints made directly to head office.

Constraints that apply to the study. The feasibility study may have to conform to company standards and its conduct and presentation has to take place in a prescribed way (perhaps to a certain quality standard). Other constraints may include time. For example:

The feasibility study must be concluded by 8 October.

Client of the study. The feasibility study and its eventual report must be **owned** by someone within the organisation. The client or authority will agree the other aspects of the terms of reference as well as monitoring progress and signing-off the final product.

Resources available to undertake the feasibility study. This defines the people, equipment and budget available for the study. For example:

The feasibility study will be produced by two analysts seconded full-time to the project. Two personal computers (PCs) will be allocated for their use. A sum of £5,000 is available to cover travelling, subsistence and other related costs.

Did you answer the question?

The terms of reference of a feasibility study are a very specific part of it. Do not stray off the subject.

---

72 (Answer 9 of examination)

Examiner's comments and marking guide

Question 9: The first part of this question asked candidates to distinguish between corrective and adaptive maintenance.

This was fairly well answered by most candidates.

The second part of this question asked candidates to suggest three appropriate measures of user-friendliness and frequency of use and describe how such data might be collected, interpreted and acted upon.

Unfortunately many candidates just described how to make a system user-friendly. This was not the question. The point of the question was how to determine whether a system was easy-to-use, not to suggest means of making it easier to use.

In this instance too many candidates answered the question they wanted to be asked - not the actual question itself.

(a)   One mark for each valid point up to a maximum of 6 marks.
(b)   Up to 3 marks for each measure. Three measures required.

Step by step answer plan

Step 1 Read the question again and make sure that you focus on precisely what is required.

Step 2 For part (a) you need a description of each type of maintenance, defined in such a way as to bring out the differences between them.

Step 3 In part (b) there are many possible measures. In choosing three, you should be aware of the need to describe frequency of use etc, so choose the three for which you are best able to do this.

Step 4 Now review your answer plan and ensure that it does precisely answer the question as set.

The examiner's answer

(a)   Corrective maintenance is the term often applied to the fixing of programming errors in the software. It can also be applied to hardware faults and to operational errors that cause the system to become unusable. Corrective maintenance is often required to return the system to a fully operational state. The system is 'down' until corrective maintenance has been completed.

Many companies log 'downtime' system failures. It must be determined whether these are due to operational problems (for example, the user switching the system off leaving files partially updated) or due to programming errors or mistakes in file use and updating. Each of these errors must be logged and investigated. The investigation must focus on the development and testing process so that it is understood how the error was introduced into the system in the first place. The results of the investigation may lead to changes in procedures and standards.

Adaptive maintenance is concerned with changing the software to reflect alterations in the business environment. These changes may be due to new user requirements or (more usually) refined user requirements in the light of experience in using the software. New user requirements are often triggered off by changes in the business environment or perhaps by new users! In most instances the system can still be used whilst adaptive maintenance is performed.

Measuring the number of functional user changes after implementation is useful as long as the changes are correctly diagnosed and categorised. For example, some changes will actually be 'what we wanted in the first place'. In such instances there has been an error of specification and so specification methods must be reviewed to reduce these problems. In other instances the user's understanding of the requirements has only become clear after experimenting with and using the software. These changes can be expected although there may be a case for seeing whether these might have been uncovered earlier in the systems development life-cycle, perhaps through prototyping. Finally, there may be amendments due to unforeseen changes in the business environment. Hopefully a flexible design will reduce the effect of such changes but in general these amendments are difficult to predict.

(b)   **User friendliness and the frequency of use of the software**

Appropriate measures might include

-        Calls to the HELP desk
-        Software monitoring of errors

Calls to the HELP desk must be categorised and the statistics produced analysed. It may emerge that problems keep recurring and the reasons for this must be understood. There may be confusion or ambiguities in the dialogue, training may have been unsuccessful or inappropriate, or the system may not be able to cope with the variety of circumstances met in practical use. The reasons must be investigated and remedies suggested - changes in dialogue wording and structures, refresher training courses, new documentation etc.

Software monitoring of errors records information about what errors have been made. It will include errors that never get reported to the HELP desk because the user has solved the problem themselves - after some confusion and wasted time and effort. Consequently the HELP desk statistics and the software monitoring of errors are important complementary sources of information. The overall usability of the software can also be assessed through:

-        Recording the time required for users to become proficient in the software. This may emerge from training courses, where users may still not be confident in the use of the software after the allocated course time. The trainers may also observe common problems and feed these back to the development team.

-        Suitable questions in a user-satisfaction questionnaire.

-        Software monitoring of the use of the system by discretionary users.

The last of these examples illustrates how software monitoring can be used to assess the use of the system. For example, the number of times a particular report is requested can be logged together with the user and the time taken to produce the report or fulfil the enquiry. This can be used to provide statistics of actual use.

This is very important with discretionary users such as managers who do not have to provide operational input into the system. Managers may elect not to use the system because:

- It does not provide useful information. Hence requirements must be reviewed.
- It is too difficult to use. This may lead to changes in dialogue wording and structure.
- It is too slow to use. This may lead to changes in programs or data structures.

```
DECEMBER 1997 QUESTIONS
```

Section A – ALL FOUR questions MUST be attempted

Scenario

Introduction

Elex is a supplier of electrical products. It is a private limited company. Elex has an in-house Information Systems (IS) department consisting of an IS Manager and eight development staff. The department is primarily concerned with supporting and maintaining accounts and payroll applications. These applications operate on a mainframe computer and are written in COBOL. The IS manager reports directly to the Financial Director. Ten years ago the IS department wrote a simple order processing system (again in COBOL) and until six months ago this had been operating on the mainframe supporting ten terminals in the Operations Department.

A year ago the Operations Director decided to replace the order processing system. He argued that the system written ten years ago no longer supported the procedures and volumes of his department. Furthermore, he wanted a more modern flexible system using personal computers (pcs) and operating in the Windows environment. Users would also have access to spreadsheet, word processing and management reporting software which would allow them to use their pcs to improve their overall effectiveness and efficiency.

The IS Manager suggested that the replacement order processing system should be developed in-house but the timescale she suggested reflected the lack of Windows and pc knowledge amongst her staff and this led to this option being rejected by the Operations Director. However, it was agreed that the IS department would purchase, install and support the personal computers and a new member of staff was taken on with this responsibility. The new member of staff was also given the task of training users in spreadsheet and wordprocessing software.

Software selection

The company decided to buy a software package to fulfil its requirements. A Steering Committee of the IS Manager, the Warehouse Manager and the Operations Director was formed to select the most appropriate package. At its first meeting the IS Manager suggested that a formal requirements specification should be developed using a structured methodology and this should be the basis of package selection. The other two members disagreed with her suggestion. The Warehouse Manager said, 'We know what we want. We want the facilities of the old system plus a few new requirements and a different user interface. We will know which package we want when we see it.' The Operations Director and Warehouse Manager agreed that they knew 'intuitively' what they wanted and asked the IS Manager to restrict her input to technical rather than business issues. No other employees were involved in the software package selection.

After this meeting the IS Manager resigned from the Steering Committee to be replaced by the Sales Manager. The new Steering Committee selected three companies and invited each company to demonstrate its product to the Steering Committee. It specified that each demonstration should take no longer than half a day. Only two of the invited companies attended. The first company was rejected on price and so the other company, a small software supplier (HR-SOFT) with a relatively new product, was selected. HR-SOFT provided a reference site (another customer who used the software) and the Operations Director telephoned the site to ask a few questions about HR-SOFT. The reference site (a dairy) confirmed that the software fulfilled their requirements and that generally it was reliable ('although we have not yet used all its facilities'). Some concern was expressed about the training organised by HR-SOFT. 'That's OK,' said the Operations Director, 'It costs too much. We are going to do our own training anyway.'

Software implementation

Six months ago the system was implemented on a twenty-user computer (pc) network in the Operations Department. The pcs were bought directly from a manufacturer. HR-SOFT recommended a minimum configuration of the pcs but was not involved in hardware purchase and installation.

Unfortunately the software has not been successful or popular. In fact software problems during implementation caused the IS Manager to telephone the reference site again. During that telephone call it emerged that the dairy was actually using a different version of the software product operating on a mainframe computer. In fact, as HR-SOFT later admitted, the Elex system was only the second implementation of the pc-version of the software. This system had been re-written in a relatively new programming language and some difficulties had been experienced. At the time of the presentation to the Elex Steering Committee, the first user of the pc version was experiencing reliability problems with the software and hence had not been used as a reference site.

Post-implementation review

Eventually the increasing problems and discontent with the software caused the Managing Director to organise a post-implementation review undertaken by external consultants. On receipt of their report the Operations Director resigned. A new Operations Director was then appointed.

The post-implementation review undertaken by the consultants specifically identified three main problem areas.

Functional shortcomings

The software package does not appear to support the procedures and requirements of the organisation. It is estimated that the package fulfils about 80% of the organisation's actual requirements. Furthermore it also has facilities and features that are not required by the company. These cause confusion to the users of the system.

Performance

The company receives 60% of its orders over the telephone. Entry of these orders is often affected by slow response times (confirming customer account details and product availability) and this leads to frustration, poor customer service and inefficient use of the telephone sales staff. This requirement had not been identified by the Steering Committee and no attempt had been made to assess system performance prior to implementation.

System down-time

There appears to be a significant amount of system 'down-time' when orders cannot be entered into the system. HR-SOFT accepts that there are some problems with the product (which will be fixed in a new version due in three months) but believes that a large number of problems are due to unreliable hardware and operational errors made by the telephone sales staff.

The consultants also undertook a user-satisfaction survey. It showed that many users have low confidence in the system because of its error rates and the fact that it does not support their operational procedures. One of the telephone sales staff commented, 'It just does not work in the same way that we do'. The survey also revealed that the planned training had not taken place. Instead users were expected to learn the software from the user manual. Twenty copies of the manual had been bought so that a copy could be placed next to each personal computer. However, as one user commented, 'It (the manual) is too large and too technical and it is impossible to relate its contents to our business procedures'.

Finally, the consultants commented on the lack of project management procedures and standards at Elex. They suggested that no employee had been made project manager for the project and hence responsibilities had become blurred and confused. In the end 'everybody thought that someone else was doing the work'.

73   (Question 1 of examination)

The post-implementation review identified three specific problem areas:

- Functional shortcomings
- Performance
- System down-time

For each of these problem areas discuss the likely reasons for the problems identified by the consultants, and describe what advice you would give to reduce the chance of making similar mistakes in future projects.

(15 marks)

74   (Question 2 of examination)

Three suggestions have been made for addressing the current problems with the software

- To purchase the source code of the software package from HR-SOFT and to bring future development in-house. The in-house team would make the changes required, remove unwanted features and support and develop the system in the future.

- To replace the software with a bespoke system developed in-house in COBOL. This would run on the mainframe system using dumb terminals.

- To commission HR-SOFT to make the changes required and to investigate the performance problems of the system and to recommend improvements.

Give one advantage and one disadvantage of each suggestion. **(15 marks)**

75 (Question 3 of examination)

The Managing Director of Elex has decided to establish a formal project to recommend the future direction and development of the order processing system. The project team will make their recommendations in six months' time. In the meantime, the Managing Director has asked whether there is anything that can be done in the short-term to improve the situation.

Suggest, with reasons, short-term actions that you feel the Managing Director should consider while waiting for the project team to make its recommendations. **(10 marks)**

76 (Question 4 of examination)

The new Operations Director is the project manager of the team set up to recommend the future direction and development of the order processing system. The Operations Director has asked for a brief description of the *responsibilities* of the project manager so that he understands his role before he takes on the project manager's job.

Briefly describe five responsibilities of a project manager. **(15 marks)**

Section B – THREE questions ONLY to be attempted

77 (Question 5 of examination)

An analyst investigating an order processing system has found the following rules are applied by order clerks:

All orders received by the company are checked by order clerks. The order clerk first calculates the value of the order and adds that value to the customer's current credit balance. If the credit balance exceeds the customer's credit limit then the current payment record is investigated. All such customers who have no invoices older than 30 days are notified that their order is 'on-hold' and that the order has been passed to the accounts manager who will contact them in the next three days. However, if the credit limit is exceeded and any invoice is older than 30 days, then the order is rejected. If the customer has not exceeded the credit limit then the current payment record is still investigated to find whether there are invoices older than 30 days. If there are, then the order is processed but a reminder letter is sent reminding the customer of the payment terms. In all other circumstances the order is processed without query.

(a) Construct a Decision Table for the process described above. **(6 marks)**

(b) Describe the above process using Structured English. **(7 marks)**

(c) What advantages does the Structured English description have compared with the Decision Table for this particular example? **(2 marks)**

(Total: 15 marks)

78 (Question 6 of examination)

A large insurance company is currently reviewing the way its information systems are provided. The company has traditionally developed its own systems in-house and the current Information Systems (IS) department has 250 staff and is headed by the IS Director.

(a) External consultants have suggested that the company should consider outsourcing technical support, the user help desk and new systems development. The IS department would remain in a smaller form and would mainly maintain established systems.

    (i)   Explain what is meant by outsourcing. **(2 marks)**

    (ii)   Briefly describe, from the perspective of an outsourcer (such as the insurance company), TWO advantages and TWO disadvantages of outsourcing. **(8 marks)**

(b) The IS Director, alarmed by the consultants' suggestions, has put forward an alternative proposal. He has suggested that the traditional hierarchical organisation of the department be replaced by a flat structure. Several management posts will be lost in this re-structuring and this will bring immediate cost savings.

    (i)   In this context, explain what is meant by a 'flat structure'. **(2 marks)**

    (ii)   Explain why a 'flat structure' is particularly appropriate to an IS department. **(3 marks)**

(Total: 15 marks)

79 (Question 7 of examination)

(a) Explain the difference between operational and tactical decisions. **(3 marks)**

(b) Information has the following four attributes:

- Accuracy
- Completeness
- Timeliness
- A source or origin

Describe each of these attributes. In the description of each attribute include one example from an operational decision context and one example from a tactical decision context, emphasising the difference between the two contexts. **(12 marks)**

(Total: 15 marks)

80 (Question 8 of examination)

(a) What is a Data Dictionary? **(3 marks)**

(b) Explain two roles of a Data Dictionary. **(6 marks)**

(c) Briefly describe three functions or tasks of the Database Administrator. **(6 marks)**

(Total: 15 marks)

81   (Question 9 of examination)

A small training company had decided to computerise its order, despatch and invoicing procedures and is currently selecting an integrated package to fulfil its needs. The owner of the company is concerned about the control and security procedures of the application and so he is particularly looking at the password and audit trail features of each package.

(a)   (i)   What are passwords and what is their primary function?   **(2 marks)**

(ii)   Briefly describe two potential problems with passwords.   **(4 marks)**

(iii)   Explain how each of these potential problems could be overcome.   **(4 marks)**

(b)   Briefly describe the operation, content and purpose of an audit trail in a software package.   **(5 marks)**

(Total: 15 marks)

ANSWERS TO DECEMBER 1997 EXAMINATION

Section A

73   (Answer 1 of examination)

Examiner's comments and marking guide

Question 1. This question asked candidates to comment on three specific problems identified in the case study organisation. These three problems; functional shortcomings, performance and system down-time were clearly indicated (under sub-headings) in the case study scenario. The question asked the candidate to discuss the likely reasons for each of these problems and to describe what advice might be given to reduce the chance of making similar mistakes in the future.

Most candidates answered this question relatively well, although there was a tendency to describe the problems (which was relatively easy to do given that they were described in detail in the case study!) rather than discussing the likely reasons for each of these problems. Unfortunately this led to some candidates writing a long description of the problems. Not only did this give them few marks it also created time problems later in the examination.

Marks

Up to five marks for each specific problem area. Within each problem area, one mark for each valid point. Three problem areas required giving a total of 15 marks   Max 15

Step by step answer plan

Step 1   Read the question again and make sure you focus on precisely what is required.

Step 2   Note in particular that you are required to 'discuss' the likely reasons and not just describe them or list them.

Step 3   Functional shortcomings. Poor specification would generally be the main problem here. Probably caused by poor analysis.

Step 4   The evaluation of the package was probably too brief.

Step 5   Performance. Poor analysis and documentation of the system. This should be discussed against the background of the scenario.

Step 6   Failure to visit actual sites and observe current procedures and note problems. Again, discuss against the background of the scenario.

Step 7   Systems down time. The software program is relatively new and would seem to have several problem areas. The scenario makes it clear that insufficient research was done and this should be discussed.

Step 8   Operational errors. Inadequate training is a frequent source of problems. Again, discuss against the background of the scenario.

Step 9   Now review your answer plan and ensure that it does precisely answer the question as set.

The examiner's answer

Functional Shortcomings

Possible reasons:

(i)   A failure to specify requirements before selecting the package. The IS Manager had suggested that the company should define a formal requirements specification using a structured methodology which could be used as a basis for package selection. This advice was rejected. Consequently packages were evaluated against a fuzzy requirement held in the heads of the Warehouse Manager and the Operations

Director. It is unlikely that such an informal evaluation will be successful. Users working without a formal document tend to evaluate the interface of the package rather than its functionality. Consequently it is recommended that all future projects involving package selection should be analysed properly and a formal system specification produced.

(ii)   A lack of formality in package evaluation procedure. It is unlikely that a package can be selected successfully on the basis of a half day demonstration and a telephone call to a reference site. It is suggested that a set of formal criteria is established for package selection. One of these criteria will be requirements fit. The formal requirements specification covered in the previous point can be used in evaluating competing packages so that both compromises in business functionality and additional unwanted functionality can be identified in the evaluation exercise – not when the system is first running live. Formal tenders should be issued requesting the design specification of the product. These can then be compared with the functional business requirement.

Did you answer the question?

Have you discussed the data in the scenario rather than simply described or listed it? Have you really selected details from the scenario and used them in your answer? Have you made recommendations?

Performance

Possible reasons:

(i)   Poor analysis. The Steering Committee appears to have failed to observe and document how the organisation currently worked or to recognise how this would be affected by the chosen package. Many managers believe they know how systems work without actually observing the operators of the system in action. In this case there appears to have been a reluctance to involve lower level employees in analysing the way the current system works and defining the requirements of its successor. It is important to understand the gap between how a business function works now and how it will work in the future. Managers need to appreciate the size of the gap so that they can help employees, through training and mentoring, to bridge that gap. It is recommended that all future projects should include detailed job analysis of current functions and the actual day-to-day users of the system should be involved in selecting and implementing a solution. They should also help design the future organisation of the work and establish the skills needed to make the transition from the current to the required work practice.

(ii)   Failure to visit a reference site or undertake any benchmarking. The poor response times associated with telephone order entry may have been discovered if the Steering Committee had visited a reference site rather than telephoned them. They could then have observed the system in action and noted any operational problems. Furthermore, there is no evidence that the software was benchmarked against the hardware configuration so that likely response times could be identified prior to system implementation. It is recommended that future reference sites are visited and observed and that benchmarks are requested or established, particularly for critical on-line operations. Performance criteria must be established for all systems and used in the formal evaluation of the package.

Did you answer the question?

Re-read the box above as the same points apply. In addition, note how the examiner in his answer is going beyond the bare scenario and developing some of the standard problems that are always being encountered in any IT practical application.

System down-time

Possible reasons:

(i)   Immature product. It is now clear that the product is a relatively new release of the software based on a hardware platform in which the software house is relatively inexperienced. It has also since emerged that the reference site was using a previous version of the software and was running it on a more established hardware platform. It is recommended in the future that the version and hardware configuration must be established and that only sites with the same version and hardware be accepted as suitable reference sites. This reinforces the value of visiting the reference site and seeing the system in operation. It would have been obvious in a visit that the favourable comments concerned a different release and operating environment. Furthermore, it might be useful if the reference site were a similar type of organisation. It is unlikely that a dairy has the same operational procedures and requirements as an electrical supplier.

(ii)   Operational errors. The planned training did not take place and users were expected to learn the operation of the system from user manuals. Hence it is likely that there are a large number of input errors and the facilities of the system are probably under-used. It is recommended that training is integrated into future projects and that operators become familiar with the system before it goes live. It may also be beneficial if the user manuals are presented as smaller operational guides tailored to the way the business operates. It is helpful if operational guides and HELP facilities are written by the operators who are going to use the system. There is also no evidence of a testing procedure for formal acceptance of the package and hence it is recommended that a formal testing method be devised for the future. Furthermore, the implementation appears unplanned with no parallel running. It is recommended that the file conversion and implementation of software must be more carefully planned in the future.

Did you answer the question?

Read the boxes above as much is applicable here. Clearly what the examiner is looking for is some detailed appreciation of the contents of the scenario, but also some common sense discussion about standard problems. Has your answer really given him that? Also, have you been making the recommendations he asked you for?

---

74   (Answer 2 of examination)

Examiner's comments and marking guide

Question 2. This question provided three suggestions for tackling the software problems of the case study organisation. Candidates were asked to give one advantage and one disadvantage for each suggestion. Most candidates had little problem with this question, although some answers tended to be too brief.

Marks

For each suggestion: Up to 2.5 marks for each advantage and disadvantage. One advantage and one disadvantage required giving up to five marks for each 'suggestion'. Three suggestions required giving a total of 15 marks.

Max 15

Step by step answer plan

Step 1   Read the question again and make sure you focus on precisely what is required.

Step 2   Source code – advantage. Note that you are only required to suggest one advantage and disadvantage of each suggestion.

Step 3   Source code – advantages. Users are in full control and obtain the system they require. Disadvantages. In house team will probably have no experience of the programming required.

Step 4   Bespoke system with COBOL – users will get system they want and are familiar with COBOL. Disadvantages – would need to specify the entire system again and this would cause delays.

Step 5   Commission software house to make changes. Advantages – the software house knows the product and maybe the problems have been in part due to the company's own shortcomings. Disadvantages – Part of the problems have been due to the software house and one has to balance their experience with past history of problems.

Step 6   Now review your answer plan and ensure that it does precisely answer the question as set.

The examiner's answer

The options are

To purchase the source code of the package and to bring future development in-house.

Advantages:

The users get the business functionality and user interface they want. Future developments can be tailored to the requirements of the business, rather than relying on the enhancements offered by the software house. The future development of the package may not reflect Elex's business requirements.

The development time should be relatively short (although the lack of experience of the in-house developers should be noted) because the developers are building on a product that fulfils about 80% of the user's requirements.

The in-house team gets to understand how the software works so that they can support the product effectively and tune the software to the hardware environment of the company. The physical design will then reflect Elex's requirements and configuration.

Disadvantages:

The in-house team probably has little or no experience in the development language and so software development estimates may be very optimistic. There is also evidence to suggest that there are relatively few programmers experienced in the product and so staff may be difficult to find and expensive to employ.

It is likely that the software house will cease support of the product (except on a time and materials basis) once the in-house team modifies the source code. This places extra demands on the in-house team as they also have to solve problems caused by errors in programs that they did not write. Evidence suggests that it will be difficult to interpret and de-bug these programs.

Did you answer the question?

The examiner's answer gives more than one advantage or disadvantage. However, note that you can't simply make a bald statement of an advantage in say one line and expect to earn the 15 marks for the question. To have earned the 5 marks here the examiner would expect some description of why the advantage might occur which might involve you in expanding your answer into something which could be interpreted as a second advantage. Certainly don't list two or three advantages, but don't restrict yourself overly in your description of the advantage.

To replace the software with a bespoke system developed in-house in COBOL.

Advantages:

The users would functionally get the order processing system they want. Future enhancements can be added to tailor the system exactly to how the business wishes to develop. The software is written specifically for the organisation. No compromises have to be made to take account of the data and program design of the package.

The in-house team has considerable experience in developing software in COBOL. Development estimates are likely to be fairly accurate. There is no need to develop new skills or take into account the time lag due to the acquisition and practice of these new skills.

The development language is standard and well known. A large pool of contractors should be available to add to the project team to speed up system development.

Disadvantages:

The time taken for system development. The organisation is, in effect, starting again. The system requirements need to be formally specified and agreed before the system is designed and coded.

Program development in COBOL is relatively slow. By the time the system is delivered the organisation may be at a severe competitive disadvantage.

The interface is unlikely to be as flexible and intuitive as the one supported by the software package. Using dumb terminals on the mainframe system may not be as attractive to users, particularly now that they have experienced a Windows environment.

Did you answer the question?

Note you are required to go a little beyond the scenario – just use some common sense understanding of the language being proposed and the likelihood of this being a success; disadvantages with the COBOL approach can be identified from your knowledge of the language rather than relying simply on what is contained in the scenario.

To commission the software house to make the changes required and to investigate the performance problems of the system and to recommend improvements.

Advantages:

The software house knows the design of the product well and is experienced in the programming language used to develop the product. Consequently changes should be implemented quickly and accurately.

Experience from future users of the package will be fed into the product bringing new opportunities to the firm at the relatively low cost of a software upgrade. This wider experience is not available with a bespoke in-house development.

The development and maintenance of the product is provided by a third party supplier at an agreed cost. There is no need to employ expensive internal resources to provide the same level of service. A third party supplier is paid for support and development as it is required. In-house staff are paid whether or not they are working on the project (or, indeed, on any project).

Disadvantages:

Dependence on software house. Experience to date has not been very favourable – for example; providing a reference site for a different release of the package running in a different hardware environment. The future direction of the development of the package is also unpredictable and is unlikely to be totally compatible with the requirements of one individual firm.

Cost of changes. The changes may be expensive to commission and so negate the original cost advantages offered by the package solution. Future changes (particularly if the needs of the company diverge from the product development by the software house) will also be expensive to implement.

Did you answer the question?

Read the boxes above as much is applicable here. In general, this is a straight forward question that requires some common sense understanding of typical problems rather than relying too much on the scenario as set. In particular, note the examiner's complaint that some answers tended to be too brief.

---

75   (Answer 3 of examination)

Examiner's comments and marking guide

Question 3. The Managing Director of the case study organisation has decided to establish a formal project to recommend the future direction of the software implementation. However, this team will not make their recommendations until six months time. This question concerned advice that could be given to the Managing Director in the meantime to improve the situation. The aim of the question was to focus on short term actions where short-term means the six months until the project team make their recommendations.

This question gave the candidate great scope for interpreting the case study situation and credit was given for any well-argued suggestion. There were also clear hints in the case study narrative (such as lack of training). Some candidates produced very good answers to this question. However, many other candidates produced very poor (and very short!) answers, which did not appear to reflect the fifteen minutes, which should have been allocated to this question.

Marks

Up to two marks for each valid point up to a maximum of 10 marks.   Max 10

Step by step answer plan

Step 1   Read the question again and make sure you focus on precisely what is required.

Step 2   Think carefully about the standard procedures that apply to all IT systems. In particular remember to use your common sense and not just rely on the scenario.

Step 3   One option is to revert to the old system.

Step 4   If the short term solution is to stick with the current system, then examine the following options: new documentation; record employees' performance and retrain; ensure hardware operates as well as possible; alter the way processes are undertaken.

Step 5   Now review your answer plan and ensure that it does precisely answer the question as set.

The examiner's answer

Valid points may be drawn from a number of areas. Five illustrative areas are given below.

Revert to the old system.

The old COBOL system is still available. It served the company for almost 10 years and was live until six months ago. The data will not be up-to-date and so transfer of data from the package to the COBOL system will have to be investigated and planned. However, the system itself is tested and its operation understood by the employees of the company. It will give important breathing space whilst the future of the project is being reviewed and it will take the pressure off finding a quick solution.

Produce new documentation and undertake training.

There is evidence to suggest that the documentation is not well presented or understood by users. Consequently, users could be encouraged to write their own documentation, concentrating on the operation of the business system rather than on the software. A series of small, function-based manuals should prove valuable. Similarly, user training could be reviewed, with users attending the courses they were denied in the original implementation. Many of the perceived problems of the package may be due to misunderstanding or a failure to explore all the features of the package. Certainly training should cut down the operational error rates.

Record and attribute errors.

It is still unclear whether the software 'down-time' is due to operational errors or software failure. The production of new documentation and training should reduce the operational errors. However, it is important that all down-time is properly logged and the reasons documented. A formal error reporting system could be established with the software house, so that software problems are diagnosed and immediately tackled.

Review hardware set-up.

The performance problems may be due to the way the current hardware and software is configured. Performance statistics should be collected and strategies for tuning hardware and software investigated and employed. The hardware and software was provided by different suppliers and this may need to be reviewed. It is easier to establish responsibility if the hardware and software is supplied by the same vendor.

Re-structure the way processes are undertaken.

The staff are currently complaining that the system 'does not work in the same way that we do'. An increasing number of organisations are electing to change their business processes to fit the package rather than the other way round. A short-term (maybe even long-term) solution would be to re-structure the way the company does business to fit in with the way the package works.

Did you answer the question?
Is your answer really worth 15 marks? Is it all just too brief? Have you concentrated on the short-term solutions? Have you looked in the scenario for clues (eg, training)? Have you used common sense to list out the points that the examiner has selected which are all fairly standard approaches to this type of question?

---

76   (Answer 4 of examination)

Examiner's comments and marking guide

Question 4. The theme of poor project management was continued in question four, which asked the candidate to briefly describe five responsibilities of the project manager. Each responsibility was worth three marks and so candidates could spend about five minutes writing about each responsibility.

Two points arose from this question. Firstly, candidates did not write enough about each responsibility to justify three marks. Candidates must use the mark allocation as a guide to how deeply they should answer a question. Secondly, many candidates wrote about the responsibilities of a systems analyst and used this question as an opportunity to write about the systems lifecycle. These candidates were awarded few marks. The combination of these factors meant that many candidates scored less than five marks on this question.

Marks

Up to three marks for each responsibility. Five responsibilities required giving a total of 15 marks. Max 15

Step by step answer plan

Step 1   Read the question again and make sure you focus on precisely what is required.

Step 2   You are asked for five responsibilities (3 marks each) of the project manager. Make sure you give the examiner five (not too brief) separate points. Make sure you are talking about the project manager and not some other person (like the systems analyst).

Step 3   Note the examiner's answer gives six illustrative responsibilities – remember you only need five.

Step 4 The responsibilities would be: agree the terms; plan the project; monitor the project; report on project progress; undertake post-project review; motivate the project team. Note how these are a very standard application of project planning in almost any scenario, not just IT.

Step 5 Now review your answer plan and ensure that it does precisely answer the question as set.

The examiner's answer

Six illustrative responsibilities are:

Agree the terms of reference of the project.

Every project should start with Terms of Reference describing the objectives, scope, constraints, resources and project sponsor or client. It is the responsibility of the project manager to compile and agree these Terms of Reference. In particular he or she must be confident that the project can meet its objectives within the time agreed (a constraint) with the resources available. The Terms of Reference may be expanded into a Project Quality Plan which will describe such issues as quality procedures, standards and a risk assessment. Producing the Project Quality Plan will also be the project manager's responsibility.

Plan the project.

The agreed project will have to be broken down into lower level tasks and activities, each of which will be given a time estimate. Precedences (which tasks must be completed before others can start) will also be agreed. The project task breakdown, the precedences of tasks, and task estimates will form the basis of the project plan. This will allow the project manager to determine the critical path and hence the elapsed time of the project. The project manager will also be able to see more clearly the resource requirements of the project. The project manager usually has the responsibility to produce and interpret the project plan, often using a computerised tool.

Monitor the project.

During the project the project manager must ensure that the overall project remains on target. Hence he or she will monitor the progress of tasks and record their completion on the project plan. Some of these tasks will over-run their original estimates and the consequences of this have to be carefully monitored and managed. The project will also be affected by new user requirements, staff illness and holidays and other external factors that cannot be predicted at the start of the project. The project manager has to reflect all these in the project plan and produce revised versions showing the effect of these changes.

Report on project progress.

It is usually the responsibility of the project manager to report project progress both upwards (to the project sponsor or client) and downwards (to the rest of the project team). Progress reports usually specify what tasks have been completed in the last period, what tasks have been started but not completed (with perhaps an estimate to completion) and what tasks are scheduled to start in the next period. Reports should also highlight problems and changes, showing the effect of these on the project plan and suggesting a course of action. The project sponsor can then decide whether such changes are implemented in the project or left until a later phase of the development. Project reports may also contain important cost and time information showing the overall cost of the project to date.

Undertake post-project reviews.

A post-project review usually takes place at the end of the project and it will be the responsibility of the project manager to organise and chair this review and report on its conclusions and recommendations. The post-project reviews will consider both the **products** of the project (such as the robustness of the software, the satisfaction of users etc.) and the organisation of the project itself. It may review the estimates of project cost and duration and compare these with actual costs and duration. Large variances will be discussed and analysed and any lessons learnt recorded and fed back into the project management method.

Motivate the project team.

Most projects are undertaken by a multi-disciplinary team brought together for the purpose of undertaking the project. Once the project is complete the team will probably be disbanded. During the project it is the responsibility of the project manager to motivate team members so that the tasks they are assigned are completed on time and to the required quality. Project managers have direct influence over the work that is assigned to the team members, the amount of responsibility individual team members are given and the recognition they are accorded on completion of their work. How the project manager goes about these management tasks will critically affect the morale and motivation of the team members.

77   (Answer 5 of examination)

Examiner's comments and marking guide

Question 5. The first part of this question asked candidates to construct a decision table for a narrative description. The decision table was relatively straightforward (it only had two conditions) and many candidates answered this part very well, with a significant number gaining full marks.

Part (b) asked candidates to express the same problem in Structured English. Structured English has been relatively neglected in recent examinations and so I was particularly keen to set this question. The answers were fairly good although, as I expected, not as good as the decision table.

Finally, part (c) asked candidates to state the main advantage of the Structured English over the decision table for this particular example. Very few candidates identified that the opening procedural sentences of the narrative could not be easily expressed in the decision table However, because there were only two marks for this section this failure did not have a tremendous effect on overall performance on this question.

Marks

Part a	One mark for each condition (two conditions)
	One mark for four correct columns
	Up to two marks for the action list
	One mark for the correct 'X's
Part b	One mark for the preliminary commands
	One mark for correct indentation
	Up to five marks for the structure of the Structured English
Part c	One mark for each valid point up to a maximum of two marks.

Max 15

Step by step answer plan

Step 1   Read the question again and make sure you focus on precisely what is required.

Step 2   Read the description of the process very carefully in the question and make sure that you pick up all aspects of it before attempting parts (a) and (b).

Step 3   Part (c) – focus on the procedural part of the process.

Step 4   Now review your answer plan and ensure that it does precisely answer the question as set.

The examiner's answer

(a)

	1	2	3	4
Exceed credit limit?	Y	Y	N	N
Any invoice > 30 days	Y	N	Y	N
Reject order	X			
On-hold Order		X		
Pass to Accounts Manager		X		
Process order			X	X
Send reminder letter		X		

(b)   DO Order entry

      Calculate order value

      New credit balance = Old credit balance + order value

      IF New credit balance > credit limit

          IF any invoice > 30 days

               Reject Order

ELSE (all invoices ≤ 30 days)
    On-hold Order
    Pass to Accounts Manager
ENDIF
ELSE (New credit balance ≤ credit limit)
    Process order
    IF any invoice > 30 days
        Send reminder letter
    ENDIF
ENDIF
ENDDO

Did you answer the question?

To some extent you can either do parts (a) and (b) or you can't do them. Re-read what you have written and make sure that it agrees with the description of the question.

(c) The procedural part of the process (calculation of order value and updating of the credit balance) is easier to express in Structured English. These statements can be added to the Decision Table but it is cumbersome as they are actions applied to every combination of the conditions.

Did you answer the question?

The examiner's comments rather dismisses the two marks for this part. But it is an easy two marks if you know it and could be the difference between passing or failing. Make sure you have had a go at saying something for part (c).

---

78   (Answer 6 of examination)

Examiner's comments and marking guide

Question 6. Outsourcing is a very significant trend in Information Systems (IS) delivery. In this question an insurance company is considering outsourcing and candidates were asked to describe what outsourcing means and to identify two advantages and two disadvantages of this approach to IS provision. This question was answered relatively well with many candidates providing examples from their own experience (including one candidate who named a well-known insurance company currently pursuing this approach!).

Part (b) asked candidates to explain what was meant by a flat organisation structure and to comment on why this was particularly appropriate for an IS department. This syllabus topic has not been examined in the past. Consequently I was keen to examine it. Most candidates produced good answers to part one (the explanation of flat structure – although more diagrams would have helped) but were less strong on the second part; why the flat structure is particularly appropriate to an IS department.

Marks

Part a (i) One mark for each valid point up to a maximum of two marks
     (ii) One mark for each valid point up to a maximum of two marks for each valid advantage and disadvantage. Two advantages and two disadvantages are required
Part b (i) One mark for each valid point up to a maximum of two marks
     (ii) One mark for each valid point up to a maximum of three marks   Max 15

Step by step answer plan

Step 1   Read the question again and make sure you focus on precisely what is required.

Step 2   Note that there are two lots of easy two marks for simple definitions, the bulk of the question being (a) (ii). Make sure you give (a) (ii) the weight of your efforts in constructing the answer.

Step 3 (a) (ii) – all fairly standard stuff that you should know. Advantages: reduction in staff development and training; systems development becomes a variable cost; cost efficiency; easier future planning. Disadvantages: loss of control over a key resource; loss of competitive edge; probably a long term commitment; potential high costs for services not envisaged in initial description.

Step 4 (b) (ii) Stress the distinction between 'jobs' and 'roles'. The IT department should be project oriented and the flat structure helps this.

Step 5 Now review your answer plan and ensure that it does precisely answer the question as set.

The examiner's answer

(a) (i) Outsourcing is the term used to refer to an arrangement where external agents perform one or more organisational activities of the host company. In this example the consultants have suggested that three functions within the IS department will be outsourced. Staff in these functions will be employed by an external company who will invoice the insurance company for work undertaken on their behalf. The external company is responsible for employment taxes, employment terms and conditions, and staff development and training of these employees.

(ii) Advantages

Staff development issues are passed on to the supplying company. Most organisations cannot justify a large internal IS department and so there is little opportunity for staff to progress up a well-defined hierarchy. In many instances advancement is through leaving the company, taking skills and knowledge the organisation finds hard to replace. In the outsourcing arrangement the employees work for a computer company where their skills are valued and their needs understood.

New skills can be harnessed quickly and cheaply. The cost of training and learning is borne by the outsourcing provider rather than by the employing organisation. Thus organisations can confidently employ new languages and technologies without depending upon the ponderous evaluation and re-skilling of their own staff. Many organisations have provided their staff with new skills and opportunities only to see these employed elsewhere as the employee uses his or her new skill to gain better paid employment.

Systems development is a project-oriented activity. Because the number of projects running at any one time is variable (depending on demand from the business) the demand for development staff is also variable. This is difficult and expensive to manage as an employee organisation. The number of full-time staff cannot be maintained at the peak of project demand and hence it is inevitable that many projects are delayed, or never started, causing frustration and complaints. In contrast, an outsourcing arrangement passes these problems on to the supplier. In principle, resources can be adjusted to fit demand without any of the commitments normally associated with full-time employees.

Cost-efficiency. Outsourcing often appears to offer cheaper costs. Internal IS departments do not usually have incentives to achieve low costs and high productivity. They exist to provide a service – not to deliver a demonstrably cost-effective service. Consequently costs are less well controlled and productivity less well understood than in outsourcing organisations whose survival and success depends upon effective management. Furthermore, the size of these companies often leads to them benefiting from economies of scale.

Easier to plan the future. In some arrangements a fixed-fee is set for a pre-specified number of services. The customer is guaranteed that these baseline costs will be fixed for the duration of the contract – typically five or ten years. This arrangement is often made more attractive by the supplier offering deferred payments, paying for staff redundancies and other financial inducements. Many organisations account for Information Systems as an overhead cost and so the long-term cost agreement makes planning easier and reduces the impact of future technologies. In general, many organisations see IS as a utility and so it must be 'cheaper to pay for the electricity rather than building the power plant'.

Disadvantages

Key resource passed to a separate company. Information is often an important resource of the organisation. In fact in some companies it is the key resource. There is some concern about passing this resource over to a separate company. Organisations have encouraged this by simplistic assertions that they 'are an insurance rather than a computer company', forgetting the vital role information plays in making them a successful insurance company. There is also the worry that confidential information is placed in the hands of a supplier who may also provide outsourced services to a competitor.

Lack of competitive edge. Some organisations use IT to provide a 'competitive edge' over their rivals. In many instances the impetus to use IS in this way has come from either the IS department or IT literate managers in other departments. Outsourcing IS may lead to a lack of internal knowledge about the capacities of IS as a competitive edge strategy and so lead to missed business opportunity.

Tie-in to a provider company. Many of the outsourcing contracts require a long-term tie-in to a provider. Problems may arise because of the management and strategy of the provider itself. For example, it may suffer financial problems or be taken over by a company whose philosophy and approach is less sympathetic. Furthermore, the tie-in may also encourage a dependency syndrome and customers eventually find themselves at a disadvantage during contract renewal.

Hide internal inadequacies. There is evidence to suggest that organisations outsource to rid themselves of the problem of controlling and using the internal IS department effectively. It may be that the savings promised by outsourcing could have been achieved (or exceeded) by establishing better procedures for costing and managing the internal IS department. The problems of using IS responsibly and effectively may have been passed on, rather than solved.

Contractual problems. Although costs are guaranteed for the base services, evidence suggests that excessive fees may be charged for services that are not covered by the base contract. The scope of the contract has also caused problems, with services that the customer believed to be included in the base contract emerging as extras. There are inherent difficulties in specifying unambiguous functional specifications and arguing about whether the requirement is a change or not causes friction and delay.

Did you answer the question?
You must make sure you picked up the two marks for (a) (i).
The advantages and disadvantages are easy enough to identify but did you write enough to satisfy the examiner to earn the 8 marks?

(b)   (i)   A flat organisation structure has few management levels and a wider span of control for those managers within the structure. Employees in the organisation can be combined in a number of ways to fulfil current work requirements. Flat organisations are more flexible than hierarchies but (without a good project management method) provide less opportunity for control.

    (ii) A large amount of the work of the IS department is project-oriented. The demand for resources at any one time is variable. A structure within the department based upon the traditional programmer, analyst, team leader, project manager hierarchy can lead to artificial bottlenecks (we do not have enough senior programmers for this part of the project) or problems (we do not have a project for this project manager to manage). The flat structure recognises that most 'jobs' are really 'roles' and that individual employees may be selected from a large 'pool' and placed into these roles as demand requires it. For example, at any one time we may only have one large project – so we only need one project manager. Other 'project managers' are slotted into other roles on this project. This emphasis on role rather than job also allows the organisation to employ large salary bands and partly relinquish the link between salary and advancement up the management hierarchy. This means that technically-oriented people can be adequately remunerated without moving into a management role which they are neither equipped for, nor desire.

Did you answer the question?
Make sure you picked up the two marks for (b) (i).
(b) (ii) You may not particularly have thought of this aspect before. Make sure you think quickly and make sure you get something down which is relevant and which can earn you some marks.

---

79   (Answer 7 of examination)

(**Examiner's comments and marking guide**)

Question 7. The first part of this question asked candidates to explain the difference between operational and tactical decisions. This was answered fairly well. The second part of this question asked candidates to describe four attributes of information; accuracy, completeness, timeliness and origin. Each description had to include an example from an operational decision context and a tactical decision context, emphasising the difference between the two contexts.

This should have been a relatively easy question. It is standard bookwork and requires no knowledge of computers. Unfortunately it produced very weak answers. Many candidates described accuracy and then basically stated that operational decisions required accurate data and tactical decisions required accurate data. This approach was repeated for all four attributes.

The point of the question was that each attribute has different characteristics in each type of decision (for example, tactical decisions require less precise data than operational ones).

Marks

Part a   One mark for each valid point up to a maximum of three marks

Part b   One mark for each valid point up to a maximum of three points for each attribute. Four attributes are specified.   Max 15

Step by step answer plan

Step 1   Read the question again and make sure you focus on precisely what is required.

Step 2   Part (a) – very straightforward for 3 marks – basic book learning.

Step 3   Part (b) requires you to describe and illustrate the attributes with one example from operational and one from tactical. Make sure you do that in your answer.

Step 4   Now review your answer plan and ensure that it does precisely answer the question as set.

The examiner's answer

(a)   Operational decisions are usually made by line managers to meet day-to-day schedules and targets. Procedures are set up and measures recorded to monitor short-term goals. Operational planning often requires many decisions to be made but the rules for making these are usually well defined (often by the tactical planning process) and so they become routine. Examples of operational decisions are:

- Responding to a request for a customer account

- Ordering products that have fallen below a re-order stock level

Tactical planning and control has longer term objectives and is usually pursued by middle-managers. Such tactical decisions are usually defined within the context of some overall strategy. These decisions are less routine in nature and usually require collecting and interpreting data from outside sources. Once the tactical decision has been made then operational procedures can be defined. Examples of tactical devisions are:

- Setting the rules for customer account acceptance

- Setting the re-order level and agreeing authorised suppliers

(b)   **Accuracy**. Operational decisions usually require precise and accurate data. For example, the decision to re-order goods is based on an exact comparison of the physical stock level and the re-order level. Tactical decisions can be based on less accurate (normally rounded) data. For example, the re-order level itself may partly be determined by forecast daily demand. This forecast is unlikely to be accurate and so a rounded daily average might be used.

Completeness. A complete set of information usually has to be available to support an operational decision. For example, all the delivery notes have to be available to schedule successfully tomorrow's deliveries. In tactical planning certain information may not be available but a decision still has to be made. For example, pricing levels and discount structures will be set without knowing the prices and offers planned by competitors.

Timeliness of data. Operational decisions normally require up-to-date information that is immediately available. For example, the delivery note information for today's deliveries **must** be available by 10.00 am – otherwise they cannot be delivered. Similarly, re-ordering of products must be based on the up-to-date stock position, not last week's! Tactical decisions can use more historical data. For example, the setting of discount structures may be partly determined by past ordering patterns. These are unlikely to have changed in the last month and so the data does not have to be completely up-to-date.

Source of the data. Most operational decisions are based on internally generated data. For example, the re-order level will be determined by historical patterns of use collected by the company itself. Tactical decisions will use internally generated data (usually in a summarised form) but will also use data from outside the company. This may be from suppliers (supply lead-times, prices) or from published statistics (population forecasts).

> **Did you answer the question?**
> It is easy in this question to simply not do what the examiner asked. Did you describe each of the attributes? Did you give an example relating to an operational decision for each? Did you give an example of a tactical situation for each? This question offers easy marks if you did what the examiner asked.

80   (Answer 8 of examination)

Examiner's comments and marking guide

Question 8. This question asked candidates to explain the term Data Dictionary, to describe two roles of a Data Dictionary and to outline three functions or tasks of the Database Administrator. This was not a popular question. However, most candidates attempting this question gained fairly reasonable marks (most scored 6 – 8 marks), although there was also a significant number of very good answers demonstrating sound knowledge of a relatively technical part of the syllabus.

Marks

Part a   One mark for each valid point up to a maximum of three marks
Part b   One mark for each valid point up to a maximum of three points for each role. Two roles are required
Part c   One mark for each valid point up to a maximum of two marks. Three functions required.

Max 15

Step by step answer plan

Step 1   Read the question again and make sure you focus on precisely what is required.

Step 2   If you know all about a data dictionary, this is a bit of a gift as it is for the most part, straight forward description.

Step 3   Part (b) – potential roles need be not only listed but fully explained to earn the six marks.

Step 4   A database administrator implements a physical file structure, prepares logical data models, improves the system performance, and maintains the data dictionary. Again make sure you don't just list these but write enough to earn 6 marks.

Step 5   Now review your answer plan and ensure that it does precisely answer the question as set.

The examiner's answer

(a)   A Data Dictionary records information about data. It can be used to hold information about the logical system – for example; the name, volume and content of each entity in the Logical Data Structure as well as data about the physical system – field names, field types, field lengths, default values etc. The Data Dictionary may be maintained on paper or index cards or by specialised Data Dictionary Software. Data Dictionaries are also used to underpin Database Management Software (DBMS) – holding the physical definition of fields and files – and logical data dictionaries are used in most Computer Aided Software Engineering (CASE) tools.

(b)   Potential roles include:

Documentation. The logical data dictionary is where the analyst stores information gathered in the fact-finding stage. For example, information about a particular document (say, order form) can be stored in the dictionary. This information will not only include information about the form itself (volumes, ownership, growth-rate) but also data about data on the form (the length, format and type of individual fields). The data dictionary is a convenient central location to store this information and is accessible to all users and developers working on the project. It also provides standard contents, so prompting analysts to ask for information to ensure the completeness of the analysis. If the dictionary is computerised it means that information can be readily maintained and updated ensuring that all developers working on the system have a complete and consistent view.

Production of the physical system. Most of the computerised Data Dictionaries have the facility to automatically produce a partial physical design. This is usually in the definition of physical files and fields. Logical entities are used as the basis of physical files and data items become fields. Attributes of the logical data items (such as length and format) are automatically transferred into the physical environment. Some data dictionaries also produce program code or (more usually) code frameworks, where the programmer writes the program within a defined standard structure.

Impact analysis. Data Dictionaries also allow the developer to look at the impact of system changes on the design of the software. Impact analysis is much easier if the data dictionary is computerised. However, it is also possible in a carefully maintained and cross-referenced manual system. Impact analysis may be restricted to changes in one field. For example, what files and programs are affected by a change in the field length and format of order-number? However, impact analysis is particularly useful in assessing and estimating the effect of functional changes requested by the user. For example, the implication of changing the way part-orders are handled by the system.

Control and Maintenance. In conventional programming languages, the rules for the validation of entered data are usually specified in the program. For example, the rule that all customer numbers lie between 001 and 999 is included in each program where validation of entered customer numbers is required. So, if this occurs at five different locations in the system, then five different programs may contain the validation program code. This creates a programming overhead as well as making maintenance more difficult. When the rules for validation change, they have to be changed in five places. Software supported by a physical data dictionary usually allows such validation rules to be defined in the data dictionary itself. When the entered data has to be validated it is checked against the central data dictionary definition. Furthermore, if the rules change, then the validation rules only have to be changed at one place.

Did you answer the question?

You are only asked for two roles so make sure you only give two, and make sure that you have fully explained them. The information analysis examiner keeps mentioning that candidates simply don't say enough to earn the marks available.

(c)   The Database Administrator (DBA) has a number of potential functions:

To implement physical file structures. In many organisations the DBA receives the Logical Data Structures and other supporting models prepared by the analyst for a particular application. The DBA converts these into appropriate physical files, taking into account the functional and performance requirements of the system.

To prepare logical data models. In some organisations the DBA is responsible for preparing logical data models for particular applications. So the DBA will undertake the analysis work producing normalised data models which will later be tuned in physical design (see previous point). If a corporate data model is produced it is likely that the DBA will also be involved in that task.

To improve system performance. The DBA will need to monitor the performance of the DBMS to ensure that the performance requirements of systems are achieved. Degradation in performance will lead to the DBA tuning the DBMS itself, changing software and hardware allocation and set-up, as well as changing the structure and content of the physical files.

To support and maintain the data dictionary. The central role of the data dictionary in holding information about data makes its maintenance one of the DBA's responsibilities. Most DBAs are responsible for the physical data dictionary that underpins the physical files and programs. Others also have responsibility for the logical data dictionary.

The DBA will also have a number of tasks concerning the management of staff, the training of users and programmers and the production of operating manuals. This will also encompass assessing hardware needs and ensuring the security and integrity of the database systems.

Did you answer the question?

Identifying the roles is straightforward. Once again, though, make sure you write enough to satisfy the examiner.

---

81   (Answer 9 of examination)

Examiner's comments and marking guide

Question 9. The first part of the final question asked candidates to explain the meaning and function of passwords. They were also asked to describe two potential problems with passwords and suggest how each of these potential problems could be overcome. Candidates competently answered this.

The second part of the question concerned the operation, content and purpose of an audit trail in a software package. This was not answered particularly well with candidates describing audit trails (and audit) in general rather than (as requested) in a software package.

Marks

Part a (i)   One mark for each valid point up to a maximum of two marks
        (ii) One mark for each valid point up to a maximum of two marks. Two problems required
        (iii) One mark for each valid point up to a maximum of two marks. Two problems need to be overcome.
Part b   One mark for each valid point up to a maximum of five marks   Max 15

Step by step answer plan

Step 1   Read the question again and make sure you focus on precisely what is required.

Step 2   Part (a) is straightforward. Potential problems in part (b): user being observed, easy to identify passwords, possibility of forgetting passwords; long lived passwords. Make sure you describe these fully and also the way they can be overcome.

Step 3   A very standard question on audit trail but make sure you answer it fully.
              Note you are asked to describe the operation, content and purpose. Make sure you did those three things.

Step 4   Now review your answer plan and ensure that it does precisely answer the question as set.

The examiner's answer

(a)   (i)   A password is a sequence of characters that must be presented to a computer system before it will allow access to the system or parts of that system. Passwords are designed to restrict user access to a system or part of that system.

        (ii) Potential problems with passwords include:

              The password may be observed when the user is entering it into the system.

              Unimaginative user-defined passwords may be easy to guess. Users may often choose their initials or use commonly defined passwords such as "Fred" or "Letmein". Access to the system can often be quickly gained by experimenting with likely values.

              Difficult to remember passwords. Computer generated passwords may be more difficult to crack (because they have no association with the user) but they are also difficult for the user to remember! Users may get over this problem by writing them down on a label and sticking them on the computer itself – hence defeating the whole purpose of the password.

              Long-lived passwords. Many passwords become common knowledge because they are used for a long period of time. Passwords are shared (I'll just go in under your sign-on – what's the password again?) and in some instances default passwords used in the software are never changed. Hence all users of the package have the same password.

        (iii) Potential problems may be overcome by:

              When passwords are entered the actual characters do not usually appear on the screen. Asterisks are often displayed to help the user confirm the length of the entered password.

              Unimaginative user-defined passwords may be easy to guess. Passwords should be computer generated. They should be case-sensitive and use numbers as well as letters to give greater variety.

Difficult to remember passwords. Mnemonic methods (making up a phrase such as Every Good Baby Deserves Favour for EGBDF) can help remember meaningless character strings. Shorter passwords are also easier to remember. Consideration might also be given to using passwords used by the user under other circumstances.

Password changes must be enforced. This may be through administrative arrangements (the IS department regularly issuing updates) or, more effectively, through software control. Software can detect the length of time a password has been in use and automatically generate a replacement code.

(b)   Valid points may be made in a number of the areas. Illustrative areas are described below. The audit trail records information about a sequence of transactions in the system. For example, information may be stored about an order, a despatch and a subsequent invoice. The audit team will want to check that all three elements of the transaction have been executed fairly and legally. An audit trail record will be created for each transaction and the three records (one for order, one for despatch and one for invoice) must be consistent with each other. Hence the audit team are able to tell if the amount despatched was equal to the amount ordered and, similarly, that the invoiced amount was correct (or that the despatch was invoiced at all!).

The audit trail usually includes

> Audit record-id
>
> The id of the user
>
> The time of the transaction
>
> The date of the transaction
>
> The terminal used
>
> The transaction type (order, despatch or invoice)
>
> Key information about the transaction (quantity, value etc.)
>
> Cross-references to related transactions

The audit trail is primarily used in the detection of fraud. The audit team is looking for irregularities and a failure to stick to agreed procedures. However, it can also be used to record user data entry errors and so suggest areas of the system where training or better user-interfaces are required.

JUNE 1998 QUESTIONS

Section A – ALL FOUR questions are compulsory and MUST be attempted

Case Study

CAET-IT provides electronic components for the Information Technology (IT) industry. The company has three main operational departments; Sales, Accounts and Dispatch. Computer systems are used in all three departments. There are no links between the three computer systems.

A brief description of each department is given below. The main information flows between the three departments are shown in Figure 1.

Sales

The company currently has eight clerks handling telephone and faxed orders. Each has a workstation linked to a small minicomputer operating in the UNIX environment.

Orders are only received by telephone or by fax. All order details are entered onto the computer system. A formal order confirmation is raised and faxed to the customer. At the end of the day a Daily Sales List, listing all orders received that day, is raised and sent to the Dispatch department.

The software used in Sales is a standard package bought five years ago. It stores customer account details. Order confirmations are only sent out if the customer is not on a credit stopped list. The system also holds product details because orders have to be priced and checked for stock availability. Order confirmations are dispatched only if the products required are in stock. There are procedures for dealing with out of stock items.

Details about dispatched and invoiced orders are received from the Dispatch and Accounts departments and are used to update the order details on the computer system.

Dispatch

The Dispatch department has a single PC operating in a Windows environment. The dispatch department software was written by a local software supplier and installed last year.

Dispatch receive the Daily Sales List from Sales and enter the order details into their system. The system stores these details on an Order data file.

One of the functions of the Dispatch software is to produce a standard Dispatch Note. This function uses information from the Order data file as well as using information stored on Product and Customer data files maintained in the Dispatch system. The Product and Customer data files are updated periodically with details of new customers, change of address of customers, insertion and deletion of products etc. Three copies of the Dispatch Note are produced. One copy is used by dispatch staff to pick the goods and is subsequently stored in the department. A second copy is sent with the goods to the customer and the third copy is sent to the Accounts department for invoicing purposes.

At the end of the day a Daily Dispatch List is sent to Sales listing the orders dispatched that day. This information is used by the Sales department to enter the dispatch date of the order on their computer system.

The quantity of each product in stock is held on both the Dispatch and Sales computer systems. It is generally accepted that the Dispatch system has the accurate figures (as they have access to the physical stock). Consequently, Dispatch periodically print out the current stock position on their computer system and send it to Sales so that they can check and update their stock details.

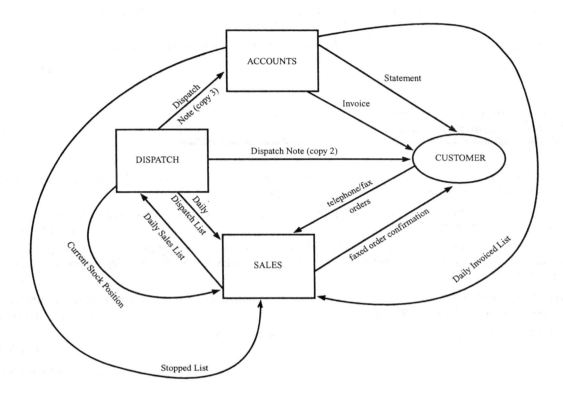

Figure 1
Main information flows at CAET-IT

Accounts

The computer system used in Accounts is a three-user DOS based PC network bought five years ago. The software is a standard accounts and invoicing system, supporting sales, purchase and general ledgers.

The copy of the Dispatch Note received from Dispatch is used to enter details into the accounts system. An invoice is raised and sent to the customer. Many customers pay on statement and so a weekly statement is also produced. Payment details are entered into the system and the accounts software maintains standard aged debtors and account details. Customers in arrears with their accounts are placed on a stopped list. A copy of this stopped list is sent to Sales who enter this information into their system. It is used in determining the credit-status of the customer.

Accounts also send a Daily Invoiced List to Sales who use it to record, in their system, that an order has been invoiced.

The integration project

A recent consultant's report identified the lack of integration of information systems as a major organisational weakness. Consequently, the company has appointed an Information Systems (IS) manager with the responsibility for justifying, defining and acquiring a new integrated information system. The company does not plan to employ any other IS staff. If the project is agreed, the system will be a bespoke development by an external software house.

CAET-IT employs an internal auditor who ensures that component manufacture complies with international standards. It has been agreed that the internal auditor will assist the IS manager in the integration project.

82   (Question 1 of examination)

The IS manager of CAET-IT has to produce a business justification for the integration project. This business justification will include a cost-benefit analysis of the proposed project.

Briefly describe *four* potential benefits to CAET-IT, of acquiring an integrated information system.

(16 marks)

83   (Question 2 of examination)

The IS manager is informed that the project must be cost-justified. Only projects which payback within three years when all cash flows are discounted are given the go-ahead.

(a) Explain what is meant by the statement 'Only projects which payback within three years when all cash flows are discounted are given the go-ahead.'   **(4 marks)**

The *initial set-up costs* of the project and the *net cash flow for each year of the project* are two pieces of information that the IS manager must collect or calculate to undertake the cost benefit analysis required by the company.

(b) List further pieces of information the IS manager must collect or calculate to complete the cost-benefit analysis required by the company.   **(7 marks)**

(c) What are the disadvantages of the CAET-IT cost-benefit policy?

(4 marks)

(15 marks)

84   (Question 3 of examination)

The IS manager has drawn up a detailed Data Flow Diagram (Figure 2) of the procedures in the Dispatch Department. Identify six errors in the diagram and explain how each should be corrected.

(12 marks)

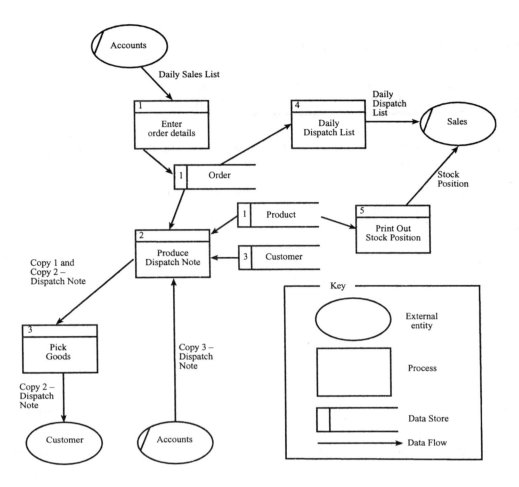

Figure 2: Dispatch Department Procedures

---

85   (Question 4 of examination)

Describe *three* potential responsibilities of the internal auditor in the integration project.

(12 marks)

Section B – THREE questions ONLY to be attempted

86 (Question 5 of examination)

The following activities, time estimates and precedences have been identified for the selection, purchase and implementation of a software package.

	Activity	Precedence	Estimate (days)
A	Define Project Initiation Document	–	5
B	Define requirements	A	8
C	Define training plan	B	3
D	Issue Invitation to Tender	B	3
E	Select Supplier	D	2
F	Install hardware and software	E	5
G	Training course	C, F	3
H	Enter master file data	G	5
I	Convert operational data	F	9
J	Parallel running	H, I	10

(a) (i) Construct a network chart for this project **(6 marks)**

Based on your network chart:-

(ii) What is the elapsed time of the project (in days)? **(2 marks)**

(iii) What are critical activities (the critical path) of the project? **(2 marks)**

(iv) How many days could activity H overrun without affecting the overall duration of the project? Assume that no other activities overrun. **(2 marks)**

(b) Briefly describe how project management software can assist in developing the initial project plan.

(3 marks)

(15 marks)

87 (Question 6 of examination)

ACCA Learning-aids Ltd. sells study and revision aids for the ACCA examinations. These aids include study texts, revision booklets, self-study packs, cassette tapes, CDs and instructional videos. They publish a catalogue listing the product code, product description and price of their goods. The catalogue also includes an Order Form. A completed Order Form is reprinted overleaf.

A new computer system is being developed for entering and storing order details. As part of this system it is essential that the information provided on the Order Form can be entered quickly and accurately into the system. It has also been stressed that the system should be easy to use.

Briefly describe *five* features that the system could include to assist the quick, accurate and easy entry of the order form details.

(15 marks)

ACCA learning-aids ltd.

ORDER FORM

Mr / Mrs / Miss/ Ms: _MR_

First Name: _STEPHEN_

Surname: _MOORE_

Address: _4121 MILLBANK_

HALIFAX

YORKSHIRE

Tel. no. _0197120_

Subject	Product Code	Product Description	Quantity	Price	Total price
Inf. Analysis	6121VO	Teach Yourself Video	1	17.99	17.99
Inf. Analysis	S211RC	Revision Study Kit	2	15.00	30.00
Audit Gwk	SS12RC	Revision Study Kit	1	15.00	15.00

Postage and Packing

UK	2.50
Europe	5.00
Rest of the World	7.50

Total _65.49_

---

88   (Question 7 of examination)

An Institute of Systems Analysts is currently computerising its membership details. The membership system will store personal details about each member. The Institute intends to offer an employment service to companies, providing career details of members who may be suitable for job vacancies.

The system will have to comply with the principles of a Data Protection Act passed by the National Government. The three most important principles of this Act are given below;

Personal data shall be accurate and, where necessary, kept up-to-date.

Personal data held for any purpose shall not be kept longer than is necessary for that purpose.

Appropriate security measures shall be taken against unauthorised access to, or alteration, or disclosure of, personal data and against accidental loss or destruction of personal data.

(a) Explain why each principle is important in the context of the membership system and describe how each principle might be enforced. **(12 marks)**

(b) The Institute is also worried about computer viruses. What is a computer virus? Briefly explain what measures might be taken to prevent a computer virus entering the membership computer system.

(3 marks)

(15 marks)

89   (Question 8 of examination)

(a) Describe the following two systems concepts. For each concept give an example of how it could be used in the design of a business information system;

  –   Filtering

  –   Coupling and Decoupling   **(10 marks)**

(b) Explain (using examples) the distinction between a *formal* and an *informal* information system.

(5 marks)

(15 marks)

90   (Question 9 of examination)

(a) The following two models may appear in a structured systems lifecycle

  –   Entity-relationship model (or Logical Data Structure)

  –   Entity Life History

  Briefly describe the purpose and notation of each of these models.   **(10 marks)**

(b) What benefits would there be if the two models above were created and maintained with a CASE tool?

(5 marks)

(15 marks)

ANSWERS TO JUNE 1998 EXAMINATION

Section A

82   (Answer 1 of examination)

Examiner's comments and marking guide

Question 1: This question asked candidates to briefly describe four potential benefits of integrating the application systems at the case study company, CAET-IT. Most candidates produced a good answer with excellent cross-references back to the case study scenario. However, some candidates are still ignoring instructions about how many points should be made (in this case, four) and produce lists of twelve or thirteen brief, unrelated points. Please follow the instructions in the question. Candidates must also be aware of duplication and ensure that they make enough distinct points to gain the marks on offer.

One mark for each valid point up to a maximum of four marks for each benefit. Four benefits required.

Step by step answer plan

Step 1   Read the question again and make sure you focus on precisely what is required.

Step 2   Note that you are asked for only four potential benefits. The examiner's answer gives you six to choose from but in the exam you are only required to provide four.

Step 3   Remember that you must cross reference your answer back to the scenario of the case study. You are not being invited to simply give general benefits.

Step 4   Benefits will include: information only held once; improve communication between departments; integrated hardware and software; better operational information; improved cashflow; better customer service.

Step 5   Now review your answer plan and ensure that it does precisely answer the question as set.

The examiner's answer

Six potential benefits are listed below. The first three benefits are obvious from the case study and should be described by most competent candidates. The last three benefits require a more careful consideration of the case study information and an understanding of order processing and accounts systems.

Information will only have to be held once. For example, information on products and customers is stored in both the Sales and Dispatch departments. There is evidence that the information between the two departments is inconsistent, hence the need for Dispatch to produce a regular print-out of the current stock position so that Sales can check and update its stock details. In the integrated system, all departments will share the same information. This should ensure that data will be consistent and unnecessary duplication will be eliminated.

Inter-communication between departments will be reduced. Many of the current inter-department data flows are caused by the need to provide information for the department to update its own records. For example, the Sales department receives the Daily Dispatch List from Dispatch in order to enter the dispatch data of the order in its own computer system. This would not be necessary in an integrated system where every department shares the same order file details. Thus many inter-department flows will be eliminated and data entry will be reduced, resulting in fewer transcription errors.

Integrated hardware and software environment. The company currently has three different operating environments. Sales has a UNIX-based minicomputer; Accounts a three user DOS network and Dispatch a single user Windows machine. Hence there are three different Operating Systems with different commands and interfaces. The software also comes from different sources and there is a mixture of a bespoke system (in Dispatch) and standard packages. The integration project provides the opportunity to standardise on hardware and software, providing an up-to-date, consistent operating environment.

Better operational information. The information necessary to make appropriate operational decisions is currently distributed between the departments. For example, in the current system the order confirmation is dispatched if the product is in stock *according to the information held in the Sales department*. It is possible that the order, once it is received in Dispatch, cannot be fulfilled because the actual stock figure is different and is insufficient to fulfil the order. It is also likely that, on some occasions, orders are not processed because the product appears to be out of stock (according to Sales department figures) when it is actually not.

Improved cash flow. In the current system, orders cannot be invoiced until they have been dispatched. This may be because there is some inconsistency between Sales and Dispatch stock figures and hence the invoice is only raised for actual dispatched goods. In the integrated system the Sales department will have access to the same (up-to-date) information as the Dispatch department and hence can reserve stock against the order. This should guarantee that the stock is available and so an invoice can be raised on receipt of order. This should lead to earlier payment and hence an improved cash flow.

Faster service to customers. In the current system Dispatch receives the Daily Sales List at the end of the day and so they cannot pick and dispatch the goods until the next working day. In the integrated system goods can be dispatched on the same day. This will provide faster customer service and may lead to increased orders from satisfied customers.

83   (Answer 2 of examination)

Examiner's comments and marking guide

Question 2: Question two continued the theme of cost-benefit analysis by focusing on the cost side of the cost-benefit analysis. Part (a) of this question asked candidates to explain the statement (made in the case study) that "only projects which payback within three years when all cash flows are discounted are given the go-ahead". Although this mixed two concepts, payback and discounted cash flow – which are often taught separately, candidates produced good answers. Good answers were also produced for part (c) of this question that asked candidates for disadvantages of the CAET-IT cost-benefit analysis.

However, part (b) did not often produce the answers the Examiner really wanted. This question asked for further pieces of information that the IS manager must collect or calculate to complete the cost-benefit analysis. Two example pieces of information, net cash flow for each year and initial set-up costs were given to provide candidates with a flavour of what was required. The answer the Examiner wanted was a simple list of other pieces of information (such as costs, benefits, discount factor etc.). However, many candidates described many types of costs (including initial, set-up costs!) and as a result only scored 2 or 3 marks for this part of the question. This was not disastrous in itself but the depth of these answers also seemed to affect later answers which may have been rushed due to spending too much time on this part of question two.

(a)   Up to two marks for each valid point up to a maximum of four marks.
(b)   Up to 1·5 marks for each piece of information up to a maximum of seven marks.
(c)   Up to two marks for each valid point up to a maximum of four marks.

Step by step answer plan

Step 1   Read the question again and make sure you focus on precisely what is required.

Step 2   Part (a) Note that you are required to combine payback with discounted cash flows.

Step 3   Part (b) The answer should include descriptions of particular costs of setup; benefits that would accrue each year; the discount factor to be used by the company; the cashflows to be discounted and the cumulative cashflow.

Step 4   Part (c) – the disadvantages include problems of valuation; the strict payback ignores cashflows after the payback period.

Step 5   Now review your answer plan and ensure that it does precisely answer the question as set.

The examiner's answer

(a) This statement refers to an approach to cost-benefit analysis called payback or Time to Payback. This approach calculates the length of time an investment takes to pay for itself. In this example all projects have to payback within three years. All cash flows have to be discounted by an appropriate discount factor to take into account the time value of money.

(b) To undertake the cost-benefit analysis required by the company the IS manager will have to determine;

The initial set-up costs of the project

The costs (such as maintenance and other operational costs) for each year of the project

The benefits (in financial terms) for each year of the project

The net cash flow for each year of the project

The discount factor used by the company and the discount rates for each year of the project

The discounted cash flows for each year of the project

The cumulative cash flow for each year of the project (as this will determine the payback period)

The following example shows a cost-benefit analysis using these principles. It is shown to help the reader. It was not required in the examination.

Example (with a discount rate of 10%)

				DCF	Cumulative	
Year 0 (initial set-up costs of the project)	£200,000			1·000	£200,000	–200,000
	Costs	Benefits	Net Cash flows			
Year 1	20,000	70,000	50,000	0.909	45,450	–154550
Year 2	20,000	90,000	70,000	0.826	57,820	–96730
Year 3	20,000	90,000	70,000	0.751	52,570	–44160
Year 4	10,000	90,000	80,000	0.683	54,640	+10480

In this example, the project pays back in Year 4 of the project. Hence, using the criteria used by CAET-IT, this project would not be sanctioned.

(c) Disadvantages include:

The problem of valuing benefits. Some of the benefits may be relatively easy to quantify (for example; time and paper savings). However, other benefits (particularly those arising from better management information and management control) may be more difficult to quantify accurately. For example, what is the value of orders **not** confirmed by Sales because they believed that goods were not in stock? Similarly, what is the cost of Dispatch having to apologise to Customers for the non-delivery of goods promised by Sales?

Does not take into account cash flows beyond the end of the payback period. The Time to Payback method does not consider cash flows after the payback period. Using the discounting principle in conjunction with the payback method, means that projects will be difficult to justify. Most costs will occur at the beginning of the project, while significant benefits will only accrue in later years and these may be heavily discounted (depending on the discount rate). This appears to be the case in the integration project where annual benefits and costs are fairly stable.

Did you answer the question?
Note how straightforward the answer was. In particular make sure you did not wander off the point in part (b) by either repeating what the examiner had said or failing to give any sort of detail which would earn you the marks.

84   (Answer 3 of examination)

Examiner's comments and marking guide

Question 3: This question asked the candidate to correct a Data Flow Diagram so that it reflected the business process described in the case study scenario. This was generally answered well and it is clear that this subject is now mastered by most of the candidates taking this examination. Some candidates included comments on all procedures, not just those in the Despatch Department.

Up to two marks for each valid error. Six errors required.

Step by step answer plan

Step 1   Read the question again and make sure you focus on precisely what is required.

Step 2   Simply go through each element of the diagram and in particular the processes and ensure that you think carefully about every aspect of the process; where the documentation comes from and what the process itself achieves and finally where the document is passed to.

Step 3   If you have not identified six errors, go back and make sure that you do write about six errors.

Step 4   Now review your answer plan and ensure that it does precisely answer the question as set.

The examiner's answer

Process 1

The Daily Sales List is received from Sales not Accounts. Change Accounts external entity to Sales.

Process 2

The Order and Product stores have the same identifier. Change one of the identifiers to 2.

The arrow on the Copy 3 data flow is going the wrong way. Show the arrowhead pointing to Accounts.

The Order store may have to be written to, confirming that an order has been dispatched.

Process 3

The Dispatch Note Copy 1 is stored. Create a data store 4: Dispatch Note written to by process 3.

Process 4

The process lacks an active verb. It should read Raise (or equivalent) Daily Dispatch List

Process 5

The Sales external entity is not currently repeated and hence does not need a diagonal line across the symbol. If the external entity serving process 1 is changed then the repetition symbol is now correct, but is not now required on the Accounts external entity. Amend repetition symbols as required.

Other

There is no process to update (i.e. insert, amend, delete) the Customer details. Establish a process called Update (or equivalent) Customer details.

There is no process to update (i.e. insert, amend, delete) the Product details. Establish a process called Update (or equivalent) Product details.

85   (Answer 4 of examination)

Question 4: Question four asked candidates to describe three potential responsibilities of the internal auditor in the integration project. Most candidates answered this question satisfactorily, sticking to three responsibilities and seeing the internal auditor as having an important and broad role through the systems development lifecycle. However, the best marks were reserved to candidates who applied their responsibilities to issues raised in the case study scenario of the case study. As in question one, some candidates did not produce enough material or detail to get the marks on offer.

One mark for each valid point to a maximum of four marks. Three roles required.

Step by step answer plan

Step 1   Read the question again and make sure you focus on precisely what is required.

Step 2   Note you are only required to provide three responsibilities.

Step 3   Possible areas are: reviewing the work of the IS manager; reviewing standards and products of solution provider; defining and benchmarking controls required; establishing internal standards for project development.

Step 4   Now review your answer plan and ensure that it does precisely answer the question as set.

The examiner's answer

Introduction (not required of the candidate)

Internal auditors are usually employees of the organisation they are asked to audit. The precise functions of *external* auditors are either laid down by statute and by a letter of engagement. In contrast the functions of the internal auditor are determined by the management of the organisation and hence will vary from company to company. Millichamp has defined internal audit as an 'independent appraisal activity within an organisation for the review of operations as a service to management: it is a managerial control which functions by measuring and evaluating the effectiveness of other controls'.

Internal audit is required to inspect, review, evaluate and make recommendations on the system of internal control in place in the organisation.

Internal control is defined as:

The whole system of controls, financial and otherwise, established in order to provide reasonable assurance of:

- effective and efficient operations
- compliance with laws and regulations
- internal financial control – to provide for the maintenance of proper accounting records and the reliability of financial information used within the business for decision making or for publication; and
- the safeguarding of assets against unauthorised use or disposition.

(Rutteman Report)

With regard to the work of the integration project, the internal audit department's potential responsibilities and interests are based upon the 'materiality' and risk associated with the project: but will consider;

Reviewing the work undertaken by the IS manager

The IS manager will have to follow standard project procedures for initiating, monitoring, reporting and terminating projects. The cost-benefit requirements described in question two suggest that there are formal procedures for initiating the project. It is likely that there are similar standards for other parts of the project lifecycle. A potential role of the internal auditor is to ensure that the internal project lifecycle has been followed by the IS manager (i.e. all stages have been completed) and that each stage has been properly and fairly completed. For example, the costs and benefits in the cost-benefit analysis are proper and realistic. There may be a, sometimes unconscious, tendency for IS managers to over-estimate benefits and underestimate costs!

Reviewing the standards and products of the bespoke solution provider

The company will be keen to ensure that the software developed for them will be of a high standard. High quality software is usually produced by following rigorous internal standards. The internal auditor may wish to evaluate the design methods of potential suppliers and to periodically review their work to ensure that they are adhering to their declared standards. Internal audit can also ensure that the products of the standard lifecycle (such as Data Flow Diagrams in the Functional Specification, programs in the systems design) are fulfilling the quality criteria required by the standards. Hence the internal auditor may be concerned with the method of production as well as the actual products themselves.

Defining the controls required by the business process

The integrated system will cover significant business processes. These processes must themselves have controls. For example; dispatch quantity cannot exceed ordered quantity, invoices can only be raised against confirmed orders, invoices cannot be revised after they have been sent to the customer etc. The internal auditor is a potential user of the system and so his or her requirements should be taken into account when producing the functional specification. Users generally only specify what they require – not how it will be controlled. This latter function is a potential role of the internal auditor. Furthermore, it may be the internal auditor who defines and agrees the contents of the software audit trail.

Establishing internal standards for project and development control

The first point (reviewing the project lifecycle followed by the IS manager) assumes that there is a lifecycle in place. One of the responsibilities of the internal auditor may be to establish this lifecycle in the first place: defining the stages of the project; the products that have to be produced at each stage; the quality criteria for accepting the products and the method used to determine whether the product meets the criteria. The internal auditor may also have to undertake training so that these internal project control procedures are understood. Similarly, the control procedures required of the external bespoke system provider may not have yet been determined. Procedures, documentation and review processes for this may have to be put in place.

86   (Answer 5 of examination)

(Examiner's comments and marking guide)

Question 5: Question five asked candidates to construct a network chart for a project. From this chart, candidates were asked to state the elapsed time of the project, the critical activities and the float or slack of one of the non-critical activities. Most candidates answering this question produced good answers, although the overrun of the non-critical activity was often wrongly answered. Part b of the question asked candidates to briefly describe how project management software can assist in developing the initial project plan. This was satisfactorily answered (most candidates scoring 2 or 3 marks) although there was a tendency to not focus sufficiently on the effect on the initial project plan.

Marks

(a) (i)   (i)   Correct notation – one mark

(ii) Correct network flow – three marks

(iii) Forward pass figures – one mark

(iv) Backward pass figures – one mark

Total 6

(ii) 42 days – two marks

(iii) A,B,D,E,F,I,J – two marks

(iv) 1 day – two marks

(b) One mark for each valid point up to a maximum of three marks.

(Step by step answer plan)

Step 1   Read the question again and make sure you focus on precisely what is required.

Step 2   It is a matter of great care to make sure that you do draw the chart carefully and in a logical sequence so that you can easily read and follow the activities that are taking place.

Step 3   Part (b) – project management software offers assistance by automating the process; allows introduction of constraints and availability of resources; a sort of what if analysis by assuming additional resources for various key parts of the process to see how that helps.

Step 4   Now review your answer plan and ensure that it does precisely answer the question as set.

The examiner's answer

(a) (i) See attached
     (ii) 42 days
     (iii) A,B,D,E,F,I,J
     (iv) 1 day.

(b) Project management software can assist in developing the initial project plan by;

Automating the construction of the project plan developed in the first part of this question. The planner only needs to enter the project activities, the precedences and the time estimates and the network plan will be constructed automatically and accurately. A Gantt Chart will also be produced.

The project plan developed in part (a) of this question assumes that there are no resource constraints. Project management software allows the planner to enter details of the resources available to the project. These resources can be allocated to the activities. This may introduce new constraints. For example, activities which can theoretically be undertaken in parallel may have to be undertaken in sequence because only one resource is available with the required skills. This will lead to a change in the elapsed time of the project. The elapsed time might also be affected by other resource constraints such as holidays and planned sick leave. Furthermore, the entry of resource costs (usually expressed in cost/day) produces an automatic costing of the initial project plan.

The project management software allows the planner to experiment with adding more resources or resource hours (such as overtime and weekend working). The planner may reduce the scope of the project (by removing activities) to meet any time constraints imposed by management. He or she may also experiment with different resource precedences or different activity breakdowns, to see their effect on the initial project plan.

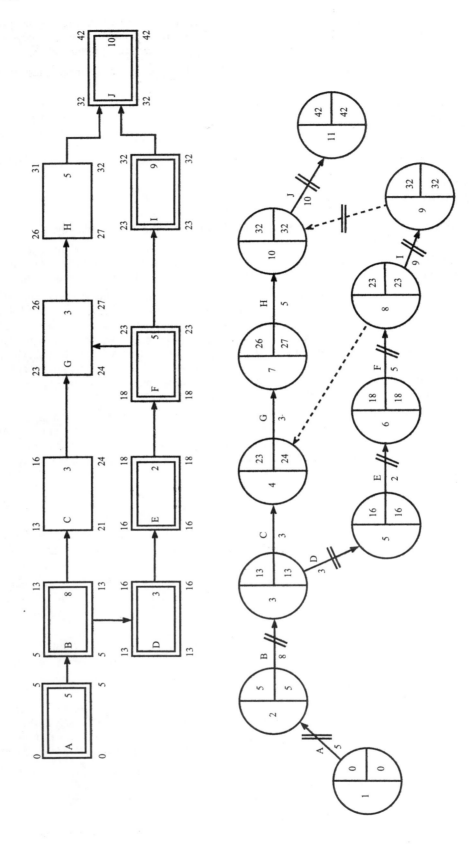

Question 5: Network Analysis

87   (Answer 6 of examination)

Examiner's comments and marking guide

Question 6: This question asked candidates to describe five features of a system to assist the quick, accurate and easy entry of order form details onto a new computer system. This was not a popular question, which surprised me. Most answers were satisfactory, although some were a little fanciful (such as Optical Mark Recognition). A large number of candidates were more concerned with re-designing the form rather than matching the computer system to the order form.

One mark for each valid point up to a maximum of three marks. Five methods required.

Step by step answer plan

Step 1   Read the question again and make sure you focus on precisely what is required.

Step 2   Features include: screen following order of order form; permanent data such as product titles to be stored in the computer; calculation of certain fields such as price; restricted access to certain lists; format checks; help facility.

Step 3   Now review your answer plan and ensure that it does precisely answer the question as set.

The examiner's answer

The sequence of data entry follows the physical order of data items on the form. It is quicker to enter information if the sequence of data fields on the screen matches their order on the physical form. The screen can also be made to look like the physical form so that the physical position of fields matches their manual equivalents.

Data already stored on the computer system is not re-entered. It is likely that the computer system will store information about the product code, product description and price of the study and revision aids offered by the company. Consequently, only the product code needs to be entered in order entry. The description and price can be retrieved from the system to confirm the entered product code.

Automatic calculation of certain fields. The total price field on each order line can be calculated automatically and checked with the calculation on the Order Form. The total price of the whole order can be calculated by adding up the prices of each order line and adding the appropriate postage and packing fee.

Selected values from a restricted list. At certain points in the data entry, the operator may be offered a restricted set of valid values from a pull-down list. For example, the subject must be a valid ACCA examination paper (a pull-down list of 14 papers), the products must be on the list provided in the catalogue and postage and packing must be one of three values.

Range and existence checks. Certain values on the form may be mandatory. For example, there will have to be one (and only one) postage and packing fee. Range checks may also be defined for fields such as quantity. It is unlikely that individual orders will exceed more than 10 for each item specified on the order form. Hence a range check (1 – 10) might be undertaken on this field to trap input errors.

Format checks. Format checks will assist the entry of fields such as product code (which appears to be 9999XX), unit price (£99.99) and (perhaps) telephone number. Values not adhering to the required format will be rejected. There may also be simple consistency checks between fields (for example; that the total price of each order line is not less than the unit price of the product ordered on that line.

Other. Context sensitive HELP facilities may help new users of the system. The HELP facility may also provide a tutorial showing how to enter order form details. Data entry should also be escapable so that the operator can rollback or abort data entry if they make a mistake. It should be possible to escape the input screen without changing stored data.

Did you answer the question?
Note that you are only asked for five features. It is quite easy to wander off the point of this question and, for example, redesign the form rather than make the computer fit the form; note that in practice if you took an off the shelf system, you might alter your own paperwork to suit the computer but you are not asked to do that in this case.

88   (Answer 7 of examination)

Examiner's comments and marking guide

Question 7: Part (b) of this question asked candidates to describe a computer virus and the measures that might be taken to prevent one entering a system. This was a very popular question with excellent answers! Many candidates scored three marks for this part of the question. Part a of the question looked at three principles of a Data Protection Act and asked candidates to explain why each is important in the context of the scenario described in the question and to describe how it might be enforced. This question was also answered satisfactorily. The best answers provided a good balance between the description of the principle in the case study and suggestions about how it might be enforced.

(a) One mark for each valid point up to a maximum of four marks for each principle. Three principles required.

(b) One mark for each valid point up to a maximum of three marks.

Step by step answer plan

Step 1   Read the question again and make sure you focus on precisely what is required.

Step 2   Note that you are not asked to write generally about the principles of data protection but rather explain them in the context of the particular system you have been given and you are also asked to describe how the principles might be enforced.

Step 3   Part (b) measures to prevent computer viruses will include anti-virus software; rigorous internal procedures; anti-hacking devices.

Step 4   Now review your answer plan and ensure that it does precisely answer the question as set.

The examiner's answer

(a) Personal data shall be accurate and, where necessary, kept up-to-date.

This principle means that all personal data (such as date of birth, sex, address and qualifications) must be *correct* and that data which might change (such as address and qualifications) are kept up-to-date. Perhaps the easiest way of ensuring that personal data is correct is to periodically print-out details from the system and send it to the member for confirmation. The accuracy of data may also be assisted by value range checks when numerical information (such as date of birth and salary) is entered. It may also be useful to record who provided the information. For example, the Institute could hardly be liable for mistakes caused by incorrect age and qualification information *supplied by the members themselves.*

Personal data held for any purpose shall not be kept longer than is necessary for that purpose.

This principle means that the purpose of collecting the information must be defined and, once that purpose has been served, the data must be deleted. For example, the member may supply information to the Institute about his or her current salary, qualifications and career history for the purpose of finding a new job. Once the member has a new job and tells the Institute that details should not be sent to any more prospective employers, then the current salary, qualifications and career history details should be automatically deleted by the system as they have now served their purpose. In some instances, time triggered programs might enforce this principle. For example, deleting all members who have not paid their membership fees within six months of receiving a payment reminder.

Appropriate security measures shall be taken against unauthorised access to, or alteration, or disclosure of, personal data and against accidental loss or destruction of personal data.

This principle means that the Institute must take measures to prevent unauthorised personnel gaining access to data. Unauthorised access to the system may be prevented by;

–   physical security measures such as door locks.

–   software measures such as passwords and log-in procedures.

The requirement to guard against accidental loss and destruction places responsibility on the Institute to provide back-up routines and restore routines and procedures. They may also have to consider off-site back-ups and disaster recovery strategy.

(b) A computer virus is a program written to mischievously damage the system. Once introduced into the system it spreads itself, causing disruption to programs and files. The replication of the virus makes it almost impossible to find its original source.

Measures to counter viruses include;

Purchasing anti-virus software and regularly updating it with new releases. This software detects known viruses and destroys them. However, it must be recognised that such software only protects against known viruses.

Implementing rigorous internal procedures, making sure that unauthorised disks are not introduced to the system. Games and public domain software may be prohibited and failure to comply with such regulations may lead to disciplinary action or dismissal.

Implementing anti-hacking procedures (such as physical security and password updates) to guard against new viruses.

89   (Answer 8 of examination)

Examiner's comments and marking guide

Question 8: Question eight asked candidates to describe two systems concepts (filtering and coupling/decoupling) and to give an example of how they might be used in the design of a business information system. Most candidates structured their answers correctly to provide a description and an application. Some candidates were not sure what filtering was and indeed omitted this altogether.

The final part asked candidates to explain the distinction between a formal and an informal information system. Candidates who knew the answer to this produced good answers, many scoring five marks.

(a) One mark for each valid point up to a maximum of five marks. Two concepts required.

(b) One mark for each valid point up to a maximum of five marks.

Step by step answer plan

Step 1   Read the question again and make sure you focus on precisely what is required.

Step 2   Note that you are asked to both describe and give an example of each concept. Make sure you do both those things.

Step 3   Part (b). Note you are asked to explain and also give examples. Make sure you do both of those things.

Step 4   Now review your answer plan and ensure that it does precisely answer the question as set.

The examiner's answer

(a) Filtering is concerned with selecting relevant or appropriate information. In many circumstances there is too much information and there are too many stimuli. The receiver cannot assimilate all the information and so has to choose which information to accept and which stimuli to react to. In doing so the receiver is filtering out information. Clearly the filter has to be effective. If the wrong information is selected then an incorrect action may result or an inappropriate decision made.

The principle of filtering is used in the definition of exception reports. The exception criteria are the filter. Normal, usual or expected data is filtered out to leave information which needs to be investigated or acted upon. For example, all product stocks that have fallen below a re-order level or all debts over 90 days. Many managers also use their secretaries or personal assistants as filters to prevent unnecessary or unwelcome telephone calls being put through to them.

Coupling is concerned with the link between sub-systems. Highly coupled sub-systems are closely linked, so that problems or delays in one sub-system will lead to difficulties with the next. For example, a failure to deliver raw materials of a product will lead to production disruption. Decoupling is concerned with relaxing the link between the two sub-systems so that they can work independently.

The principle of coupling and decoupling can be used in the design of a production system. One of the sub-systems may be concerned with the production of components which are subsequently used by another sub-system in the assembly of a final product. If the system is highly coupled then assembly can be disrupted by problems in production. The sub-systems can be decoupled by the production system producing *stock* which is subsequently used by the assembly sub-system. Stock or Inventory control is essentially a mechanism for decoupling processes.

(b) A formal information system is one based upon explicit messages, usually written down in standard forms and documents. The organisation usually defines explicit procedures and policies for dealing with these formal flows. For example; an invoice is a typical flow in a formal information system. There will be an agreed procedure for raising an invoice and for ensuring that it is paid.

An informal information system usually operates through direct personal contacts. The information is often subjective, open to interpretation and not written down. Examples include; informal undocumented meetings, social contacts, observation, rumour and the 'grapevine'. There will be no agreed format or procedures for conducting informal information flows.

90 (Answer 9 of examination)

Examiner's comments and marking guide

Question 9: The final question asked candidates to describe the purpose and notation of two models that appear in the structured systems lifecycle — the entity-relationship model and the entity life history. Answers to this part of the question were much clearer about the notation rather than the purpose. Indeed, many candidates ignored the purpose completely and so only scored a maximum of 5 or 6 marks in this part of the question. It is very helpful if answers to such questions include an example of the model. One marker commented that "the most amazing point about the answers to this question was that many did not include a diagram!"

Part (b) asked what benefits would there be if the two models were created and maintained with a CASE tool. This was satisfactorily answered.

(a) One mark for each valid point up to a maximum of five marks. Two models required

(b) One mark for each valid point up to a maximum of five marks.

Step by step answer plan

Step 1 Read the question again and make sure you focus on precisely what is required.

Step 2 Note that you really do have to draw a diagram in order to be able to describe your answer to this question.

Step 3 Note that you are asked to describe both the purpose and the notation. Make sure that you describe both of those elements.

Step 4 Part (b). The benefits of a CASE tool would be; easy to draw models; central data dictionary; easy to update; automatic file/program framework; automatic cross-referencing.

Step 5 Now review your answer plan and ensure that it does precisely answer the question as set.

The examiner's answer

(a) The entity-relationship model consists of entities and the relationships between them. Entities (or more properly entity types) are objects or 'things' that the organisation wants to store information about. Entities are usually shown as rectangles or soft boxes on the diagram and named with a singular noun (see Figure 9.1).

Entities can be;

Physical (e.g. candidate, examination centre)

Active (e.g. lecture, course)

Conceptual (e.g. region, examination level)

There are usually many *entity occurrences* of each entity. For example, there are many individual candidates for an examination. Each individual candidate is identified by a unique identifier – candidate (or student) number.

Relationships define a business relationship between two entities. This is usually shown as a line on the entity-relationship model. Relationships may be 1: many (1:m), for example each region covers many candidates and each candidate belongs to one region; 1:1; or many to many (m:n), for example each candidate takes many examinations, each examination is taken by many candidates. The 1:m and m:n relationships are shown in Figure 9.1. The many end of a relationship is usually represented with a 'crow's foot'.

The entity-relationship model is used to show users the business relationships between significant business objects. Users will be asked to confirm that these relationships exist and are correct as these represent the objects and relationships that will be supported by the eventual computer system. Hence it is an important way of modelling the business system and communicating with the user. The entity-relationship model may also form the basis of subsequent data and file design. The entities become physical files or database tables.

The entity life history (ELH) shows the system events that create, modify and delete each entity. The root of the ELH is the entity itself (from the entity-relationship model). The boxes below and to the left of the root show the events that create the entity. The boxes below and to the right show the events that delete each entity occurrence. Both entity creation and deletion may result from either one event OR another. For example, Figure 9.2 shows that an entity occurrence of candidate can be deleted by the event *Resignation received or Candidate died*. This optionality is shown by drawing small circles in the top right hand corner of the event boxes.

The boxes in the middle part of the ELH show the events that modify the entity. For example, the event *Change of address notification* could be received many times in the life of a particular entity occurrence. Consequently this modification is iterative and is shown by a small asterisk in the top right hand corner of the event box. The ELH shown in Figure 9.2 shows the following information;

A Candidate entity occurrence is created by *Receipt of application form*. It is modified by *Change of address notification*. This modification is iterative to take into account that the candidate may move several times. Finally, the entity occurrence can be deleted by either the event *Resignation received* or the event *Candidate died*.

An Entity Life History allows the system designer to consider the event perspective of the system, ensuring that events have been identified that create and (usually) modify the entity. It also focuses attention on the events that delete the entity and prompt a discussion about whether such events should exist (for example, some organisations never delete customer data) and what rules they should obey (for example, customers cannot be deleted if they have outstanding orders). It is unlikely that such delete events will have been identified by either the process (Data Flow Diagram) or data (entity-relationship) perspectives. The ELH may also provide a basis for subsequent design, particularly if the design is to be implemented in an object-oriented programming language where the events are defined within the context of the object.

(b) A CASE tool may provide the following benefits;

Easy to draw models. It will be easier to create each model and to produce a well balanced and professional looking diagram.

A central Data Dictionary. The Data Dictionary underlying the CASE tool will hold the data items within each entity. The format, value range, default values etc. of each data item can also be held within the Data Dictionary. This means that all the information held about the system is in one place and it is easy to maintain and update.

Easy to update models. It is very difficult to update hand-drawn models. Models held in a CASE tool can easily be edited, updated and re-printed.

Automatic file / program framework. Some CASE tools can automatically produce physical file and data structures from the entities defined in the entity-relationship model. Similarly, object-oriented program frameworks may be automatically produced by a CASE tool from the Entity Life History.

Automatic cross-referencing between the entities of the entity-relationship diagram and the Entity Life History defined for each entity. In most CASE tools the ELH is the 'child' model of the parent entity defined in the entity-relationship model.

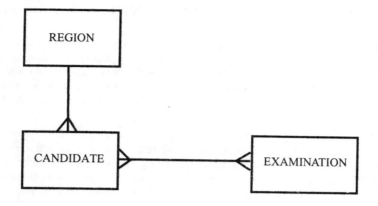

Figure 9·1

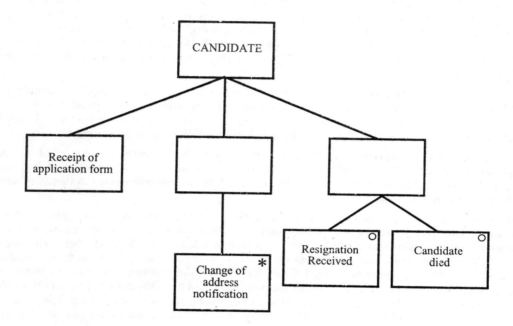

Figure 9·2

QUESTIONS TO DECEMBER 1998 EXAMINATION

Case Study

Caet Textiles is a large multinational clothing company. It is organised into six business units. These units are supported by an internal information systems (IS) department currently employing 30 staff.

There has been increasing internal criticism of the performance of the IS department. One of the business unit managers believes that the company should concentrate on its core business (clothing) and outsource the information systems function. 'We are not a software house. We just need a limited number of staff to commission, purchase and support the systems. We should outsource the rest to a specialist computer company to take responsibility for operating, managing and controlling the information systems function.'

A management consultancy has been appointed to examine the IS function. Its report has identified *four* shortcomings. These are described below.

Extract from management consultancy report:

Four shortcomings have been identified in the information systems function.

1 *Problems of operational understanding*
Some applications have been difficult to use. Such problems were particularly severe in the order processing system implemented one year ago.

The business unit manager commented that: 'The problem was that the system just did not reflect the way we worked. It looked all right on paper – but when we tried to use the system it was just unusable. The sequence of data entry did not match the manual order form, the menu structures were inappropriate and the error messages incomprehensible. Order entry was slow and error-prone so the operators soon had little confidence in the system.'

The IS project manager for this system reacted angrily when we put these points to him. 'The problem was that the users had not read the documentation. We showed them the sequence of the order entry with a simple flowchart. They just could not be bothered to read it. Then, when they got the system, they complained.'

2 *Fulfilling user requirements*
The functional correctness of some software projects has been an issue. A recent software project for the manufacturing business unit is a good example.

The business unit manager commented that: 'The manufacturing project was yet another example where the IS department, after continual delay and requests for more time, still failed to deliver a system that fulfilled the business requirements.'

In contrast the project manager responsible for the project asserted that: 'The users did not know what they wanted. Every time we thought we had got it right they changed their minds again. The only thing they never changed their minds about was the project deadline date!'

3 *Lack of user ownership*
User departments are reluctant to sign-off project deliverables, particularly those in the earlier stages of the project. There is a tendency to hope that it will come right in the end.

One of the business units responded to this criticism by commenting that: 'There appears to be very little visible progress in the earlier stages of the project (except for lots of meetings). There is nothing tangible to assess and sign-off.'

The IS staff agreed with this observation. One felt that users were quick to criticise but were less prepared to commit to requirements. 'There appears to be a climate of fear. They worry that if they sign-off requirements which are later shown to be wrong or incomplete then they will be reprimanded by their manager.'

4 *Little control over the costs of development*
The costs of the Information Systems department are currently divided equally between the six business units. There is no attempt to apportion the cost of IS resources to their use in each business unit.

The business units believe that: 'We have to pay the salaries of information systems staff whether they are working or not. So they might as well get on with something useful.'

In contrast the IS department felt that: 'The business units do not understand the costs of responding to their requirements. There is no accountability; no attempt to justify the costs of systems development against the benefits that the system will bring to the organisation.'

Section A – ALL FOUR questions are compulsory and MUST be attempted

91 (Question 1 of examination)

One of the business unit managers has suggested that the information systems function should be outsourced to external suppliers.

Required:
Describe three advantages to Caet Textiles of outsourcing the information systems function.

(15 marks)

92 (Question 2 of examination)

The IS department at Caet Textiles does not currently use structured software development techniques. The IS manager believes that the shortcomings identified by the management consultancy would be resolved by introducing a combination of structured techniques supported by CASE (Computer Aided Software Engineering) tools and prototyping with Fourth Generation Languages.

Required:
Briefly explain what is meant by

(a) Structured techniques supported by CASE tools;   **(7 marks)**

(b) Prototyping with Fourth Generation Languages.   **(8 marks)**
(15 marks)

93 (Question 3 of examination)

Required:
Explain how the combination of structured techniques and prototyping would address the specific shortcomings of:

(a) Problems of operational understanding   **(5 marks)**

(b) Fulfilling user requirements   **(5 marks)**

(c) Lack of user ownership   **(5 marks)**

identified in the management consultancy's report.

(15 marks)

94 (Question 4 of examination)

Required:
Describe solutions to tackle the other shortcoming, *little control over the costs of development,* identified in the management consultancy's report. Comment on any issues your solutions would raise.

(10 marks)

Section B – THREE questions ONLY to be attempted

95 (Question 5 of examination)

Investigating and documenting the current business system is one of the stages of the systems development life cycle.

Required:
(a) Briefly explain *two* reasons why it is important that the analyst should investigate and document the current business system.
(6 marks)

(b) Briefly describe *three* methods or models used in investigating and documenting the current business system. **(9 marks)**

(15 marks)

---

96 (Question 6 of examination)

Three typical office tasks are listed below. These tasks are undertaken in both computerised and non-computerised offices.

– Writing, amending and distributing business correspondence. For example, writing a sales letter and sending it to many potential customers.

– Undertaking mathematical calculations and exploring the implications of different values and assumptions. For example, producing a cash flow forecast based on a variety of interest rates, inflation rates and sales volumes.

– Communicating an order for goods or services to a supplier. For example, raising a purchase order, sending it to a supplier, confirming delivery and processing payment.

Required:
For each of these office tasks;
Describe how each has been affected by computerisation and what benefits such automation brings to the organisation.

(15 marks)

---

97 (Question 7 of examination)

The information systems (IS) department of a country's Department of Tax Collection is currently located in several cities. The government now wishes to centralise the computer systems at one location and is looking for a suitable site.

The committee organising the re-location of the department has identified the following two problems concerning the location of the installation. These will have to be taken into consideration when selecting the site. The problems are:

– Preventing and recovering from physical attack by groups opposed to tax collection.

– Guaranteeing the continuity of the supply and maintenance of essential services to the site.

Required:
Briefly describe what measures might be taken to address each of these problems.

(15 marks)

---

98 (Question 8 of examination)

(a) Two stages of computer software testing are:

– Systems testing;

– User acceptance testing.

Required:
Briefly describe each of these two stages. **(10 marks)**

(b) Certain deliverables in the development life cycle cannot be easily tested because they are in the form of written documentation. This is particularly true of deliverables in the analysis stage, such as data flow diagrams and entity-relationship models (logical data structures).

Required:
Explain how the correctness and quality of these deliverables can be checked. **(5 marks)**

(15 marks)

99   (Question 9 of examination)

A systems analyst has noted the following points in an interview with a user.

Orders are received from customers.

Orders may be received by post from trade customers or through e-mails from appointed agents. Each agent is responsible for many domestic customer accounts.
For example:
Agent *Cullum* is responsible for forty domestic accounts including *J. Haq*.

Each individual order is received from only one customer. For example order no: *107* was received from customer: *J. Haq*.

Customers place many orders in the year. For example *J. Haq* placed four orders in 1997 – order nos: *53, 107, 125 and 567*.

Orders are usually for multiple products. For example order no: *107* requested 14 copies of product no: *1435*, 23 copies of product no: *5342* and 1 copy of product no: *8474*.

Orders may be modified until the invoice is raised. Order modifications are usually due to changes in order quantities.

At the end of the week an invoice is raised. This lists the orders placed in that week and produces a detailed price breakdown and invoice total for all the orders placed in the week. The invoice is sent to the customer.

Customer payments are recorded in a spreadsheet. Some customers send cheques that cover many invoices. On some occasions a customer part-pays the invoice because there is a dispute over some of the products billed in the invoice.

Orders are deleted after seven years or if the customer goes into liquidation.

Required:
(a) Construct an entity-relationship diagram (logical data structure) from the information recorded in the interview. Clearly state any assumptions you have made.   **(10 marks)**

(b) The following information recorded in the interview cannot be easily represented on an entity-relationship model.

   –   Orders may be received by post from trade customers or through e-mails from appointed agents.

   –   Orders may be modified until the invoice is raised. Order modifications are usually due to changes in order quantities.

   –   Orders are deleted after seven years, or if the customer goes into liquidation.

Briefly describe an alternative model for documenting and analysing such information and explain why it is more appropriate than the entity-relationship model (logical data structure) for modelling this information.   **(5 marks)**

(15 marks)

End of Question Paper

ANSWERS TO DECEMBER 1998 EXAMINATION

91   (Answer 1 of examination)

Outsourcing might bring the following advantages. Three advantages are required.

Concentration on core business
One of the business unit managers has already commented on the need for Caet Textiles to concentrate on its core business. This means that all management effort can be focused on running a profitable and effective clothing company rather than being diluted by the management claims of departments which are not perceived as central to the delivery of the company's product. Caet Textiles currently has thirty information systems (IS) staff. It is unlikely that the company can offer a career structure for IS staff within this department and so fulfil the technical and financial aspirations of all staff. It is suggested that these are better satisfied in a company whose core business is the production of software – in the words of the business manager a 'specialist computer company'. Outsourcing the information systems department would allow managers to concentrate on developing and motivating their key operational employees.

Formalisation of the relationships between business users and suppliers
The consultancy's report suggests that there is a relatively informal relationship between business units and the IS department. It is reported that users are reluctant to sign-off or commit to project deliverables. It is unlikely that this informality could continue with an external supplier. The supplier would need to clearly establish the system requirements and provide a fixed price for providing software that fulfilled those requirements. They would expect these requirements to be formally agreed and signed-off by the user and may make this a condition of progressing to the next stage of development. Changes in requirements would be costed and the project plan (and hence delivery date) changed to reflect those requirements. The formal relationship between the business unit and the supplier forces users to formally define, sign-off and control their system requirements. The relationship between supplier and customer is much clearer in an outsourcing arrangement.

More visible control over costs
The contractual relationship between the business unit and the supplier would also directly link the development of systems to the actual cost of that development. IS costs are currently distributed between departments irrespective of use and demand. With an outsourced supplier it is likely that each development will be separately costed and the business unit will have to formally cost-justify that development, identifying whether the cost of the system is justified by the benefits it will deliver. Consequently the company will only develop systems that can be justified in a formal cost-benefit analysis. A similar discipline can be achieved by retaining an internal IS department and cross-charging between departments but this is usually not as effective as 'real money' does not change hands. The financial arrangement between the supplier and the customer again reinforces the formal customer–supplier relationship of the outsourcing agreement.

Variable resources to meet demands
The company currently has 30 staff in the IS department. However it is likely that the demand for staff will fluctuate with the system requirements of business units in the company. Consequently there will be times when the IS department is not large enough to fulfil all the demands placed upon it. Users will experience intolerable delay and this may lead to missed business opportunities or uncompetitiveness. At other times there will be insufficient projects to keep the IS department busy and so the organisation will be bearing overhead costs that may again make its product uncompetitive in the market-place. This problem is hinted at in one of the comments of the business units – 'they might as well get on with something'. In the outsourced arrangement the organisation can tailor its IS requirements to demand. The problem of dealing with fluctuating demand is passed on to the supplier.

92   (Answer 2 of examination)

(a)   Structured techniques are models designed to represent system procedures and requirements. The techniques are usually defined within a methodology such as SSADM (structured systems analysis and design method).

Structured techniques usually define models for use at various stages in the life cycle. For example, some models (such as the data flow diagrams) will be constructed to show how the organisation currently organises its business activity. Other models (such as an update process model) will be used much later in the development life cycle, in program design. Different models may be used to represent different system perspectives. Structured techniques often have a process view (data flow diagram), a data view (logical data model) and an event perspective (entity life history) designed to model the system from complementary viewpoints.

Most of these models are graphical or pictorial and hence their production and maintenance is enhanced by a CASE tool. A CASE tool is a software package designed to allow the rapid production and maintenance of high quality logical models. It is usually supported by an integrated data dictionary. Some CASE tools also include file and program generators that allow the logical design to progress into its physical equivalent.

(b) Prototyping is an approach to systems development where the requirements of the users are reflected in a series of *prototypes*. These prototypes are incomplete computer systems designed to show the user certain aspects of their system or requirements. The user comments on the prototype and these comments are then integrated into the next version of the prototype software. Hence prototyping reflects an incremental approach to systems development.

The prototyping literature usually distinguishes between developmental and throw away prototyping. In the first approach the prototype evolves into the final delivered software. In the latter method the prototype is developed to the point where it accurately reflects users' requirements. It is then abandoned and the operational software is developed from scratch, perhaps using some of the formal models discussed in part (a).

Prototypes have to be produced quickly. They must also be easy to modify in the light of user comments. It is difficult to produce such systems with conventional high level Third Generation Languages (3GLs) such as COBOL and FORTRAN. Consequently a number of products are marketed which contain features (such as screen and report generators) which facilitated faster systems production and maintenance. These products are marketed under the generic term of Fourth Generation Languages (4 GLs) to distinguish them from their predecessors. These languages often have little in common except to provide an environment where systems can be produced and amended quickly and effectively.

93   (Answer 3 of examination)

Problems of operational understanding

The consultant's report particularly identified the problem of representing an interface (order entry) with a model (in this case a flowchart). In this circumstance it is unlikely that formal structured techniques would have proved any better, although some methodologies may offer more appropriate models of the interface than the flowchart. The model would also have to be formally signed-off, so addressing the problem identified by the IS project manager ('they just could not be bothered to read it').

However, in this instance prototyping would directly address the problem. The comments of the business unit manager demonstrate that a key operational procedure was not implemented correctly in the delivered software. Prototypes for key operational interfaces enable users to gain experience with the 'look and feel' of the system before the software is delivered. A prototype would have at least identified the problems of the sequence of data entry and the inappropriate menu structures. It may have also included elements of error handling and reporting and so identified the 'incomprehensible' error messages mentioned by the business unit manager.

Fulfilling user requirements

The consultant's report identifies the problems of expressing the business requirements and controlling changes subsequently made to those requirements. These can be addressed through:

Structured techniques contain models which formally define the business systems and business rules prior to computer systems development. Hence users are forced to formally define what they want early in the project. These requirements are used as a basis for estimating deliverables which are then linked in the project plan. Changes in these requirements are easy to identify because they represent alterations to the business model. The effect of these changes can be estimated and their effect on the project plan demonstrated. This may, of course, lead to changes in the project deadline date. Structured techniques should ensure that requirements are unambiguously expressed and that changes to those requirements are clear to both developers and users.

Prototyping. Users may find it difficult to express their requirements using structured analysis models. In this instance the IS department may develop prototypes to allow users to more fully understand and explore their requirements. In such instances the prototype is assisting the user in 'knowing what they wanted'. Once this has been agreed it can be translated into a formal requirements specification using structured techniques.

Lack of user ownership

The consultant's report identified two particular problems under this heading – a reluctance to sign-off deliverables and a lack of visible progress. These could be addressed through:

Structured techniques. Adherence to structured techniques will mean that the user will be presented with a series of models that demonstrate progress through the life cycle. These deliverables will require formal acceptance. It can also be agreed (between the user and the developer) that progress to the next stage of development is not possible until the deliverable of the preceding stage is formally signed-off by the user. This will ensure formal user involvement in development to maintain the momentum of the project.

Prototyping. One of the problems with the formal models of the structured life cycle is that they are a representation of the system, not the system itself. This representation problem can be addressed by producing prototypes at key stages of the life cycle. This will again encourage user ownership, as users will be required to define and comment on the contents of the prototype, as well as showing tangible project progress.

94   (Answer 4 of examination)

The problem identified in the consultancy report concerned accounting for the cost of information systems development.

It is clear from the comments of the IS department that the business does not have to *formally construct a business case* where benefits produced by the system are compared with costs in a cost-benefit analysis. Such an approach would demand a change of policy at Caet Textiles so that the costs of the IS department are accounted for by actual use rather than as an evenly distributed overhead. Thus the IS department could be *established as a cost centre* and an internal daily charge agreed which would be used as a basis for costing each project. All projects would be subjected to formal cost-benefit analysis. The *decision to proceed with the project and indeed the internal priority of the project would be determined by the results of the business case.* This provides a standard way of evaluating and prioritising projects and should ensure that the company only develops systems that are worth while.

The competitiveness of the internal IS department could be tested by allowing external software suppliers to bid for internal projects. This *competitive tendering* will help the internal department stay competitive and hence set a daily rate that is compatible with outside suppliers. The problem of periods of low demand will have to be addressed. This problem is currently expressed in the business unit's assertion that: 'We have to pay the salaries of information systems staff whether they are working or not.' This may be addressed by allowing the IS department to *bid for external work,* so that they can compensate for periods of low internal demand.

95   (Answer 5 of examination)

(a) Reasons for investigating and documenting the current business system might include:

Many of the processes and functions of the current system will be required in any successor. It is important that proposed computer systems do not exactly mimic the operations of the current system. However, it is likely that fundamental processes performed in the current system (such as raise invoice and record payment) will be required in the future system. Consequently these functions must be understood and documented so that they can eventually be implemented successfully in the new system.

To gain the confidence of users. Users need to have confidence in the analysts developing the required computer system. One way of building this confidence is for analysts to competently investigate, document and model the current system. This allows them to show their competence in part of the life cycle which the user is very familiar with. In general, users value analysts who understand their business systems. Investigating and documenting the current system gives the analyst the opportunity to demonstrate understanding.

Understanding the system problems is essential for solving them. In some instances the investigation of the system identifies problems and difficulties that can be resolved without recourse to further system specification and development. There may be unnecessary bottlenecks in the process, duplicated clerical procedures and unnecessary checks and balances. Resolving these problems may lead to improved system performance irrespective of whether the system is eventually computerised.

(b) Methods or models include:

Interviewing

Interviews are formal meetings between the analyst and the user. These meetings are used to establish how the current system works, to discuss any problems in the current process and to identify and discuss screens (where appropriate), forms and reports used in the current system. Subsequent meetings will focus on the requirements for the new system. These interviews should be formally documented and their contents agreed with the interviewee. Interviews provide the opportunity for the analyst and user to establish a rapport and to investigate certain points in detail. However, they are time-consuming to organise, conduct and document.

Questionnaires

In some instances it is not practicable or economic to interview all the users of a system. In such instances the user may be sent a questionnaire listing questions about the current system (for example; what percentage of customers pay by cheque?) and the requirements of the successor (for example; do you want the system to support banded value added tax). Questionnaires (unlike interviews) can be tested prior to their distribution and each user is asked exactly the same questions. However, there is no opportunity to build rapport between the analyst and the user or to probe certain answers in more detail.

Data flow diagrams

Data flow diagrams are simple models which can be used to graphically document the operation of the current system. The processes of the current system described in user interviews (see above) may be modelled with a standard set of symbols. The diagramming notation usually includes symbols for a process, a data store, a data flow and an external entity (store or sink). There are also rules that govern the connections between these symbols (for example; a store cannot be directly linked to another store) so that the models are presented in a consistent way and can be subjected to standard checks in a walkthrough. These diagrams are presented to the user who may be asked to sign them off as a true representation of the current business process.

Decision tables

In some circumstances the user may have explained processes in an interview which lead to a variety of outcomes depending upon the conditions that apply. For example, the discount rate of the order may depend upon the size of the order, the customer type and the credit record of the customer. This explanation can be effectively modelled using a decision table, where actions and conditions are linked through a comprehensive set of combinations. In the limited entry decision table there is a simple formula for calculating how many combinations of conditions are possible. If the analyst identifies outcomes for each of these conditions then they can be fairly confident that they have fully analysed and documented the problem.

Other appropriate models and methods (such as entity-relationship models and flowcharts) will be given due credit.

96   (Answer 6 of examination)

Writing, amending and distributing business correspondence

The task of writing and amending business correspondence has been greatly affected by the development of word processing software which has allowed relatively unskilled users to type and print their own documents. The document is also saved as a file that can be retrieved for future amendment, extension and re-printing. In contrast amendments to typewritten documents could only be incorporated by re-typing the whole document. Word processing software has meant that users can produce their own high quality documents without the delay and cost caused by giving hand-written drafts to professional typists. This means that documents can be produced quickly, professionally and cheaply and to standards rarely attained by professional typists using conventional typewriters. The overhead costs of employing specialised secretaries and typists is reduced (or eliminated altogether).

The distribution of business correspondence has traditionally taken place through memos (in the internal post) and letters (through external mail services). Computerisation has brought along e-mail and electronic faxes which allow documents to be quickly distributed to many recipients. This speed of distribution brings commercial advantages as well as eliminating expensive paper. Both e-mail and electronic faxes also feature automatic proof of receipt and opening, a facility rarely available in conventional internal mail systems and only partially possible (proof of receipt) at an extra cost in a conventional external mail system.

Undertaking mathematical calculations and exploring the implications of different values and assumptions
Undertaking mathematical calculations and exploring different values and assumptions was possible, but time-consuming, with the electronic calculator. The ready accessibility of spreadsheet software has meant that relatively inexperienced users can construct complex models that can be used to explore different scenarios. More complex models can be constructed using decision support software. In both cases there are four significant advantages to the organisation;

(i) The time taken to explore the effect of different values is greatly reduced.

(ii) A larger number of scenarios can be explored to help understand the structure of the problem before the organisation commits itself to any business action. Thus action is taken on a better understanding of the implications of different values and this should help reduce and understand business risk.

(iii) It is possible to make mistakes using an electronic calculator and so calculations have to be checked and re-checked for accuracy. The spreadsheet (as long as the formulae are correct) guarantees accuracy for all combinations of values. Accuracy is important for decision-making as well as bringing time savings because there is no need to re-check the figures.

(iv) Models can be developed, implemented and shared with other employees in the organisation. This reduces costs and imposes common procedures and standards.

Communicating an order for goods or services to a supplier.
Conventional purchase orders are raised with a typewriter and sent to a supplier by post. A number of changes are possible in a computerised office. For example;

(i) Raising a purchase order as a word processing document using a standard purchase order template. This order can then be faxed or sent by e-mail to the supplier. This means that the order is sent instantaneously to the supplier and there is no use of expensive paper. A copy of the order is stored on a database for future reference.

(ii) Many suppliers have an Internet site which includes an on-line order entry facility. Ordered items are entered by the customer and prices are automatically displayed and totalled. These prices are retrieved from the latest catalogue. Shortages and discontinued items are also displayed. Payment details are also entered by the customer and a copy of the order is printed out on completion. In this approach the customer has up-to-date price information at the point of purchase and can also be sure that the product is available.

(iii) The link between supplier and customer can be formally established though electronic data interchange where orders from the customer are produced in an appropriate computer file that can be imported directly into the supplier's order processing system. This close link between the supplier's and customer's computer systems saves time and money. It is also used to send amendments to orders which are automatically recorded into the supplier's order processing system.

97   (Answer 7 of examination)

Physical attack from groups and organisations opposed to tax collection
The risks caused by this problem may be reduced by physical security measures such as high fences, security guards and controlled access to the site through barriers. Closed-circuit television can be used to monitor the perimeter fence and access points. These external site measures can be supported by preventing easy access to the computer installation itself through swipe-card controlled doors, passwords and identification badges. Many installations also insist that external visitors must be accompanied at all times. It might also be advantageous if the site is easy to defend (on a hill or on a plain with uninterrupted views rather than in an urban area) so that any possible terrorist attack has a greater chance of being spotted. It also helps if the site is not on commercial air routes so that unusual air activity is immediately obvious. Shatter-proof glass will also reduce the problems caused by an explosion.

The organisation must accept that there is a chance that an attack might succeed and so it must have comprehensive disaster recovery plans. In this instance it is suggested that there is a 'shadow' site located some distance from the main site (so that it cannot be threatened in the same attack or destroyed by the same accident). This site may be used as a back-up site with periodic dumps of data and programs or it may duplicate every transaction performed on the main site so that it can be switched into use as soon as the main site goes out of action.

The risk of fire may be countered by ensuring that the installation has fire doors and appropriate working fire extinguishers. Staff must be briefed in regular drills. Sprinkler systems must be installed, maintained and tested.

Problems of ensuring the supply and maintenance of essential services to the site
The disaster recovery procedures described above can also help the organisation recover from the failure of essential services to the site. However, there are also certain pragmatic measures the organisation can take to reduce the chance of such problems.

These include;

Un-interruptable power devices can be used to smooth the power supply so that problems are not caused by power surges and drops. This prevents power fluctuations that can damage computer media, hardware and software.

Duplication of essential services. For example, providing duplicate power supplies from different sources so that a failure of one power generator can be compensated for by switching supply to power provided by an alternative source. Many companies use back-up generators that produce power from other sources.

Established back-up procedures. Back-up procedures need to be established for programs and data and these procedures need to be tested and regularly reviewed. These procedures may include the off-site storage of back-up data and programs and media storage in water-proof and fire-proof safes.

Regular checks of essential services. Regular maintenance and checks of essential services can reduce the risk of problems. This includes inspection of wiring, pipes (a gas leak once caused a major computer fire) and roofs and windows (for leakage).

Location. The risks associated with the loss of essential services can be reduced if the computer installation is sited at a location where the provision and maintenance of such services is relatively easy. This means avoiding sites that are likely to be regularly threatened by fire (forest areas), floods (river valleys) and extreme weather such as high winds, torrential rain and thunderstorms.

98 (Answer 8 of examination)

(a) *Systems testing*
Individual programs are usually tested by the programmers who wrote them and by their team leader who has certain testing responsibilities. Once a program has passed 'program' or 'unit' testing it is passed on for systems testing. Systems testing is usually undertaken by a systems analyst or project leader.

Systems testing considers whether the individual units or programs fit together properly. In doing such tests the analysts will wish to verify that the programs interact successfully (passing data from one to the other) and correctly.

Systems testing will also usually consider the error trapping and reporting facilities of the system. Consequently the tester will enter values that will cause the system to fail or undertake procedures that will lead to sudden or unpredictable failure – such as switching off the machine in mid-process. The systems tester will also need to ensure that the error reporting messages are correct and that appropriate messages are displayed.

The systems tester may also take responsibility for ensuring that the interface is consistent (for example, the same function key is always used to quit the system) and, where appropriate, it conforms with agreed industry conventions and standards.

Finally, systems testing ensures that the system fulfils its functional requirements (as defined in the systems specification). It is the last chance to do this prior to the release of the system out of the department to its user.

User acceptance testing
After the completion of systems testing the system is passed on for 'user-acceptance' testing. In this stage, users, or their representatives, are asked to formally consider whether the system fulfils their requirements. In theory users should evaluate the system against the formal specification (defined in

entity-relationship models, data flow diagrams etc.) they approved earlier in the project. In practice, it is the time when deviations between the system's operations and user's actual requirements come to light.

User acceptance testing will consider the functional characteristics of the system but it is unlikely to replicate the detailed range and format checks undertaken in systems testing. By this stage users should expect error-trapping to work successfully. In contrast, user acceptance testing will focus on the usability of the system, checking that the natural flow of the business process is reflected in the way that the software works.

User acceptance testing may also be concerned with

- testing and agreeing cyclical activities (such as end of month and end of year routines)
- testing and accepting generalised house-keeping functions (such as back-up and restore)
- testing and accepting documentation.

(b) Systems and user acceptance testing is usually undertaken for physical working deliverables – programs or systems whose behaviour can be executed and documented. For example, a program to calculate the average price of timber can be tested to see if it performs (by not failing during operation) and that it performs the calculation accurately. This procedure is not always possible for deliverables early in the systems development life cycle – such as dataflow diagrams and logical data structures. Consequently these are usually reviewed in *structured walkthroughs*. A structured walkthrough is a formal meeting where a product is presented and checked for its:

Functional accuracy. This is usually undertaken by the user representative at the walkthrough. Their role is to confirm that a business process has been properly understood.

Technical accuracy and adherence to standards. A standards or audit representative is present to ensure that the product meets the quality standards defined in the methodology.

The walkthrough may also be attended by the presenter or author of the product, a chairperson and a scribe. The product will be formally accepted at the meeting or referred back for further work.

Walkthroughs are also appropriate for testing working deliverables such as programs and systems and so they are appropriate in all stages of the systems development life cycle. However, many analysis deliverables can *only* be checked by walkthrough – execution testing is just not possible.

99 (Answer 9 of examination)

(a)

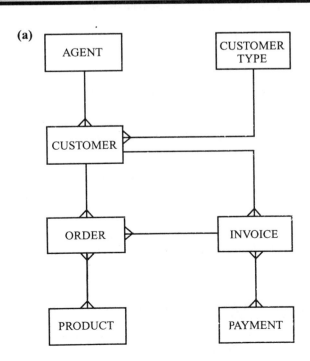

(b) This information concerns the events that create an order (by post or e-mail), the events that modify an order and the events that cause its eventual deletion. A number of models may be more appropriate for modelling this information. Credit will be given for appropriate models as well as for the one described here – the entity life history. The entity life history (ELH) explicitly focuses on the events that affect the object or entity and so is particularly relevant to this situation. An example of an entity life history is given below.

The left-hand side of the ELH represents the create events. The small circles in the event boxes show that an occurrence of order can be created by the receipt of an e-mail *or* the receipt of an order in the post. The central part of the ELH shows that the order can be modified. The small asterisk in the corner of the modify event box suggests that a particular order can be changed many times. Finally, the right-hand side of the ELH represents the delete event.

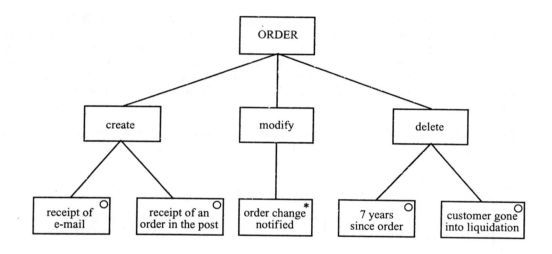

Certificate Examination – Paper 5
Information Analysis   **Marking Scheme**

1   One mark for each valid point up to a maximum of five marks for each advantage. Three advantages required.

2   Part (a): One mark for each valid point up to a maximum of seven marks.

     Part (b): One mark for each valid point up to a maximum of eight marks.

3   One mark for each valid point up to a maximum of five marks for each shortcoming. Three shortcomings required.

4   Up to two marks for each valid point. Maximum of 10 marks.

5   Part (a): Up to three marks for each reason. Two reasons required.

     Part (b): Up to three marks for each model or method. Three models/methods required.

6   Up to three marks for the effect of computerisation. Up to two marks for the benefits/advantages. Three tasks required giving 15 marks.

7   Up to five marks for each measure up to a maximum of 15 marks.

8   Part (a): Up to five marks for the description of each stage of testing. Two stages required giving 10 marks.

     Part (b): Up to five marks for the correctness and quality checking.

9   Part (a): See diagram. Maximum of 10 marks.

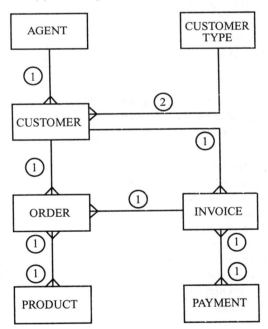

Part (b): Up to three marks for the description of the model. Up to two marks for showing why it is more appropriate.

ACCA

AT FOULKS LYNCH

HOTLINES
Telephone: 0181 844 0667
Enquiries: 0181 831 9990
Fax: 0181 831 9991

AT FOULKS LYNCH LTD
Number 4, The Griffin Centre
Staines Road, Feltham
Middlesex TW14 0HS

Examination Date:
☐ June 99
☐ December 99

	Textbooks	Revision Series	Lynchpins	Distance Learning (Include helpline & marking)	Open Learning (Include helpline & marking)
Module A – Foundation Stage					
1 Accounting Framework	£17.95 [UK] [IAS]	£10.95 [UK] [IAS]	£5.95 ☐	£85 ☐	£89 ☐
2 Legal Framework	£17.95 ☐	£10.95 ☐	£5.95 ☐	£85 ☐	£89 ☐
Module B					
3 Management Information	£17.95 ☐	£10.95 ☐	£5.95 ☐	£85 ☐	£89 ☐
4 Organisational Framework	£17.95 ☐	£10.95 ☐	£5.95 ☐	£85 ☐	£89 ☐
Module C – Certificate Stage					
5 Information Analysis	£17.95 ☐	£10.95 ☐	£5.95 ☐	£85 ☐	£89 ☐
6 Audit Framework	£17.95 [UK] [IAS]	£10.95 [UK] [IAS]	£5.95 ☐	£85 ☐	£89 ☐
Module D					
7 Tax Framework FA98	£17.95 ☐	£10.95 ☐	£5.95 ☐	£85 ☐	£89 ☐
8 Managerial Finance	£17.95 ☐	£10.95 ☐	£5.95 ☐	£85 ☐	£89 ☐
Module E – Professional Stage					
9 ICDM	£18.95 ☐	£10.95 ☐	£5.95 ☐	£85 ☐	£89 ☐
10 Accounting & Audit Practice	£22.95 [UK] [IAS]	£10.95 [UK] [IAS]	£5.95 ☐	£85 ☐	£89 ☐
11 Tax Planning FA98	£18.95 ☐	£10.95 ☐	£5.95 ☐	£85 ☐	£89 ☐
Module F					
12 Management & Strategy	£18.95 ☐	£10.95 ☐	£5.95 ☐	£85 ☐	£89 ☐
13 Financial Rep Environment	£20.95 [IAS]	£10.95 [IAS]	£5.95 ☐	£85 ☐	£89 ☐
14 Financial Strategy	£19.95 ☐	£10.95 ☐	£5.95 ☐	£85 ☐	£89 ☐
P & P + Delivery UK Mainland	£2.00/book	£1.00/book	£1.00/book	£5.00/subject	£5.00/subject
NI, ROI & EU Countries	£5.00/book	£3.00/book	£3.00/book	£15.00/subject	£15.00/subject
Rest of world standard air service	£10.00/book	£8.00/book	£8.00/book	£25.00/subject	£25.00/subject
Rest of world courier service†	£22.00/book	£20.00/book	£14.00/book	£47.00/subject	£47.00/subject

SINGLE ITEM SUPPLEMENT: If you only order 1 item, INCREASE postage costs by £2.50 for UK, NI & EU Countries or by £10.00 for Rest of World Services

TOTAL
Sub Total £
Post & Packing £
Total £

†*Telephone number essential for this service*   *Payments in Sterling in London*   Order Total £

DELIVERY DETAILS
☐ Mr ☐ Miss ☐ Mrs ☐ Ms   Other
Initials   Surname
Address

Postcode
Telephone   Deliver to home ☐
Company name
Address

Postcode
Telephone   Fax
Monthly report to go to employer ☐   Deliver to work ☐

PAYMENT
1 I enclose Cheque/PO/Bankers Draft for £_____
   Please make cheques payable to AT Foulks Lynch Ltd.

2 Charge Mastercard/Visa/Switch A/C No:

   Valid from: ⌊_⌋_⌋_⌋   Expiry Date: ⌊_⌋_⌋_⌋
   Issue No: (Switch only) ⌊_⌋_⌋

Signature   Date

DECLARATION
I agree to pay as indicated on this form and understand that AT Foulks Lynch Terms and Conditions apply (available on request). I understand that AT Foulks Lynch Ltd are not liable for non-delivery if the rest of world standard air service is used.

Signature   Date

Please Allow:
UK mainland	- 5-10 w/days
NI, ROI & EU Countries	- 1-3 weeks
Rest of world standard air service	- 6 weeks
Rest of world courier service	- 10 w/days

Notes: All delivery times subject to stock availability. Signature required on receipt (except rest of world standard air service). Please give both addresses for Distance Learning students where possible.

Form effective at Jan 99   *All details correct at time of printing.*   **Source: ACRSF9**